THE

ROCK
QUIZ, FACT & TRIVIA BOOK

THE

ROCK

QUIZ, FACT & TRIVIA BOOK

THOUSANDS OF FASCINATING FACTS AND
QUESTIONS FOR EVERY ROCK FAN

**COMPILED BY
KAREN INGHAM**

This is a Parragon Book
First published in 2000

Parragon
Queen Street House
4 Queen Street
Bath BA1 1HE
UK

Printed and bound in the UK
Cover Photos: Rex Features Ltd

© Dilemma Puzzles

ISBN 0-75253-204-9

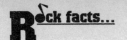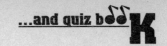
Hi Rock Fans!

How many times have you picked up a rock quiz book hoping to find page after page dedicated to your favourite music - and then being disappointed when you discover that Kylie Minogue has been given half a dozen pages? Well not this one. I have gathered together thousands of questions dedicated to rock musicians from all over the world from the past few decades.

I have also listed the album and single chart placings for each of the featured artists.

Enjoy the book and remember, Keep on Rocking!

Karen

•10 YEARS AFTER•

1 What was the name of the guitarist, who formed the band in 1966?

2 And in which English Midlands city did the group come from?

3 What was the title of the band's 1968 live album, which became their first UK chart success?

4 And in which club venue was the album recorded?

5 What was the title of the band's 1969 studio album, featuring the songs *Three Blind Mice* and *Speed kills*, which reached No. 6 in the UK charts?

6 Which US festival did the band play at, in August 1969?

7 And which song were the band playing when their performance at the festival was included in the documentary film about the event?

8 Which album, released in 1969, featured the tracks *Bad Scene* and *Stoned Woman*?

9 And which former member of Manchester band The Hollies photographed the cover for the album?

10 What was the title of the band's 1970 album, which reached No. 4 in the UK charts?

11 And which song, taken from the album, became the band's most successful single, when it reached No. 10 in the charts in 1970?

12 Which album was the first to be recorded on the band's new record label, Chrysalis, and featured synthesisers for the first time on a 10 Years After record?

13 What was the title of the solo album, released by Alvin Lee in 1974?

14 And which member of the band released the solo album *You And Me*, in the same year?

15 What was the title of the band's farewell album, featuring the tracks *Nowhere To Run* and *Stone Me*?

The Road To Freedom, 15 *Positive Vibrations*.
On *Cricklewood Green*, 11 *Love Like A Man*, 12 *A Space In Time*, 13 On
6 Woodstock, 7 *I'm Going Home*, 8 *Sssh*, 9 Graham Nash, 10
1 **Alvin Lee**, 2 Nottingham, 3 *Undead*, 4 Klook's Kleek, 5 *Stonedhenge*,

•AC/DC•

1 **Which brothers formed the band in Australia, in 1973?**

2 What were the titles of the band's first two albums, only released in their native Australia?

3 **Which 1977 album, featuring the songs *Dog Eat Dog* and *Whole Lotta Rosie*, was the first to enter the UK Top Twenty?**

4 In which British city was the band's 1978 live album, *If You Want Blood, You've Got It*, recorded?

5 **What was the title of the band's 1979 album, which reached No. 8 in the UK charts?**

6 And which famous rock producer was bought in to assist in the recording of the album?

7 **Which band did AC/DC support at Wembley Stadium, in August 1979?**

8 What was the name of the band's lead singer, who died from alcohol poisoning in 1980?

9 **And which singer was recruited to take his place?**

10 Which album was the first to be recorded with the new vocalist, and was also the band's first No. 1 album?

11 **And which single, taken from this album, reached No. 15 in the UK charts?**

12 Which album, released in 1981, featured the tracks *Let's Get It Up* and *Inject The Venom*?

13 **Which Stephen King film featured several original AC/DC songs, which later appeared on the album *Who Made Who*?**

14 Which album, recorded in 1985, featured the songs *Sink The Pink* and *Hell Or High Water*?

15 **Which single, taken from the 1987 album *Blow Up Your Video*, reached No. 12 in the UK charts?**

1 Angus and Malcolm Young, 2 *High Voltage* and *TNT*, **3 *Let There Be Rock*,** 4 Glasgow, **5 *Highway To Hell*,** 6 Mutt Lange, **7 The Who,** 8 Bon Scott, **9 Brian Johnson,** 10 *Back In Black*, **11 *Rock'n'Roll Ain't Noise Pollution*,** 12 *For Those About To Rock (We Salute You)*, **13 *Maximum Overdrive*,** 14 *Fly On The Wall*, **15 *Heatseeker*.**

• AEROSMITH •

1 What is the name of the band's drummer, who suggested the title "Aerosmith"?

2 What was the title of the band's first single release, taken from their eponymous debut album, in 1973?

3 Which album, produced in 1973 by Bob Ezrin and Jack Douglas, featured the songs *Lord Of The Thighs* and *Spaced*?

4 What was the title of the song taken from the band's 1975 album *Toys In The Attic*, which took 18 months before reaching No. 10 in the US charts?

5 And a phrase from which Mel Brooks film was said to have inspired the song?

6 Which 1976 album featured the songs *Last Child* and *Sick As A Dog*?

7 What was the title of the 1978 album, whose cover was illustrated by cartoonist Al Hirshfeld?

8 By what nickname did Steven Tyler and Joe Perry become known during the 1970's, due to their vast intake of illegal drugs?

9 Which Beatles song did the band cover, for their part in the film version of *Sgt Pepper's Lonely Hearts Club Band*?

10 Which member of the group announced he was quitting in 1979, due to musical and personal differences?

11 And, following the reformation of the group in 1986, what was the title of their new studio album, produced by Ted Templeton?

12 Which album from 1987 featured the hit singles *Rag Doll* and *Dude (Looks Like A Lady)*?

13 Which rap band helped revive Aerosmith's post-drug career, with a cover version of the song *Walk This Way*?

14 Which film comedy from 1994 featured Aerosmith performing *Shut Up And Dance* at an open air festival?

15 In what hi-tech way did the band distribute their 1994 song *Head First*?

1 Joey Kramer, 2 *Dream On*, 3 *Get Your Wings*, 4 *Walk This Way*, 5 *Young Frankenstein*, 6 *Rocks*, 7 *Draw The Line*, 8 The Toxic Twins, 9 *Come Together*, 10 Joe Perry, 11 *Done With Mirrors*, 12 *Permanent Vacation*, **13 Run DMC**, 14 *Wayne's World II*, 15 It was only available to download from the internet.

R ck facts... ...and quiz b k

• ALANIS MORISSETTE •

1 **Alanis recorded her first single at what age?**

2 In 1984 Alanis was given an acting part in which cable show?

3 **In 1995 Alanis made her debut on the UK chart with which single?**

4 What was Alanis' first UK Top Ten hit?

5 **Which two members of the Red Hot Chilli Peppers featured on *You Oughta Know*?**

6 In 1995 Alanis became the first Canadian female artist to achieve what?

7 **In 1995 who did Alanis open for at The Greatest Music Party In The World concert?**

8 Which Alanis Morissette track featured on the soundtrack of *City Of Angels*?

9 **In 1998 who did Alanis duet with on *Drift Away*?**

10 With whom does Alanis write all her music?

11 **How many Grammys did Alanis win for the album *Jagged Little Pill*?**

12 Which record label did Alanis sign with in 1995?

13 **And whose label is it?**

14 What was the title of Alanis' 1998 UK Top Ten hit?

15 **Which sport did Alanis compete in 1997?**

Rock facts... ...and quiz book

• ALICE COOPER •

1 **How, according to rock legend, did the band get their name?**

2 And, known personally as Alice Cooper himself, what is the lead singer's real name?

3 **And what does the singer's father do for a living?**

4 What was the name of the band's first album for Warner Bros, released in 1971, and featuring the single *Eighteen*?

5 **With which themed album, released in 1972, did the band have a No. 2 single with the title song?**

6 And sections from which Broadway musical were used on several of the tracks on the album?

7 **Which album from 1973 featured the hit single *No More Mr Nice Guy*?**

8 And which British folk singer provided the guest vocals for the title track?

9 **The intro to which Jimi Hendrix song was borrowed for the intro to the hit single *Elected*?**

10 What was the title of the first album, released by singer Alice Cooper, following his split from the rest of the band?

11 **And which actor provided a narrated section for the album, celebrating the Black Widow spider?**

12 Which ballad from this album was later a British hit single for singer Julie Covington?

13 **What caused the death of Alice Cooper's pet boa constrictor, which often appeared with him on stage?**

14 What caused Alice Cooper to be admitted to a psychiatric hospital, for several weeks in 1978?

15 **In which musical film, starring the Bee Gees, did he make a cameo appearance?**

1 It was the name of a Salem witch the band contacted during a ouija board session, 2 Vincent Furnier, **3 A Church Preacher,** 4 *Love It To Death*, **5 *School's Out*,** 6 *West Side Story*, **7 *Billion Dollar Babies*,** 8 Donovan, **9 *Dolly Dagger*,** 10 *Welcome To My Nightmare*, **11 Vincent Price,** 12 *Only Women Bleed*, **13 It was fatally bitten by the live rat it was being fed for breakfast,** 14 Chronic alcoholism, **15 *Sergeant Pepper's Lonely Hearts Club Band*.**

• BAD COMPANY •

1 Three ex-members of which two bands came together to form Bad Company in August 1973?

2 Where did the band take their name from?

3 Bad Company's debut album released in 1974 made the UK Top Ten, and US No.1 what was it's title?

4 What was the title of Bad Company's debut single?

5 In 1974 where did the band support The Who in concert?

6 In 1976 the band released a cover version of a Coasters' hit, what was it?

7 Which member left Bad Company in 1982?

8 And which band did he go on to form with Jimmy Page?

9 In 1983 who did Mick Ralphs tour with before releasing his solo album in 1985?

10 And what was the title of his solo album?

11 Who joined the band as vocalist in 1986?

12 On which various artists tribute album did Paul Rogers perform all lead vocals in 1993?

13 Who did Bad Company headline with on their 1995 US tour?

14 Which band was Raymond 'Boz' Burrell a member of before joining Bad Company?

15 What was the title of the band's 1982 album released after a three year break?

1 **Free and Mott The Hoople**, 2 The title of 1972 film starring Jeff Bridges, 3 *Bad Company*, 4 *Can't Get Enough*, 5 **Charlton Athletic Football Club**, 6 *Young Blood*, 7 **Paul Rogers**, 8 **The Firm**, 9 **Pink Floyd's Dave Gilmour** , 10 *Take This*, 11 **Brian Howe**, 12 *Tribute To Muddy Waters*, 13 **Ted Nugent**, 14 King Crimson, 15 *Rough Diamonds*.

•BILLY BRAGG•

1 In 1977 Billy Bragg formed a punk/R&B band, what was it called?

2 On whose show did Billy Bragg make his UK radio debut?

3 **Kirsty McColl reached the UK Top Ten in 1985 with a Billy Bragg song, what was it?**

4 In the same year Billy Bragg made his own chart debut with which song?

5 **What was the name of the politically active group of musicians Billy Bragg formed in 1985?**

6 Who sang the duet *She's Leaving Home* in aid of Childline with Billy Bragg?

7 **And who recorded the original version of the song?**

8 Who backed Billy Bragg on one of his songs on his *Tom's Album*?

9 **In 1991 Billy Bragg took part in BBC TV's *Great Journeys* travelling to Bolivia and Chile. Who went with him?**

10 What division in the army did Billy serve with before buying himself out after only 90 days?

11 **Which instrument does Billy play?**

12 What was on the B-side of the charity single *She's Leaving Home*?

13 **What nickname was Billy Bragg known as?**

14 Which new British label did Billy Bragg sign with in 1983?

15 **Who featured on the single *You Woke Up My Neighbourhood*?**

1 Riff Raff, 2 John Peel, 3 A New England, 4 Between The Wars, 5 Red Wedge, 6 Cara Tivey, 7 The Beatles, 8 R.E.M, 9 Andy Kershaw, 10 Tank division, 11 Guitar, 12 Wet Wet Wet's With A Little Help From My Friends, 13 The Bard Of Barking, 14 Go! Discs, 15 R.E.M's Michael Stipe and Peter Buck.

• BLACK SABBATH •

1 **What name did the band play under, until they changed to Black Sabbath in 1969?**

2 And which member of the band originated the name, due to his interest in horror novelist Dennis Wheatley?

3 **What do the initials N.I.B stand for, from a song off their eponymous debut album?**

4 What was the title of Black Sabbath's second studio album, featuring the songs *War Pigs* and *Iron Man*?

5 **And what position did the title track from the album reach in the UK singles chart in 1970?**

6 Which British keyboard player guested on the band's fifth album, *Sabbath Bloody Sabbath*?

7 **Which 1975 album featured the tracks *Hole In The Sky* and *Megalomania*?**

8 What was the title of the band's 1976 compilation double album?

9 **Which member of the band quit in 1977, only to rejoin in 1978?**

10 Which single, released in 1978, became the band's first UK chart hit since 1970?

11 **Which band did singer Ozzy Osbourne go on to form, when he quit Black Sabbath in 1979?**

12 And which vocalist was asked to join the band, to replace Ozzy Osbourne?

13 **What was the title of the first album produced by this new line up, released in 1980?**

14 Which singer joined the band in 1983, along with ELO drummer Bev Bevan, to play a series of headlining shows in the UK?

15 **For which event in 1985 did the original line up reform, for one night only?**

1 **Earth (also, before that, Polka Tulk),** 2 Bass player Geezer Butler, 3 **Naticity In Black,** 4 *Paranoid,* 5 **No. 4,** 6 Rick Wakeman, 7 **Sabotage,** 8 *We Sold Our Souls For Rock'n'Roll,* 9 **Ozzy Osbourne,** 10 *Never Say Die,* 11 **Blizzard Of Oz,** 12 Ronnie James Dio, 13 *Heaven And Hell,* 14 Ian Gillan, 15 **The Live Aid concert in Philadelphia.**

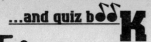

• BLONDIE •

1 What was the title of the band's debut single, released in 1976?

2 Which record label did the band move to in 1977, for the release of their second album?

3 **And what was the title of this second album?**

4 Which remake of a 1963 hit for Randy And The Rainbows became the band's first UK chart hit, reaching No. 2 in 1978?

5 **Which song, written by bass player Gary Valentine before quitting the band, reached No. 10 in the UK charts, and opens with the line "Was it destiny, I don't know yet"?**

6 Which producer, famous for his co-writing of many British glam rock singles in the early 1970's, did the band team up with for the 1978 album *Parallel Lines*?

7 **And which single, taken from the album, reached No. 1 in the US and UK chart in 1979?**

8 Which No. 1 album, released in 1979, featured the singles *Dreaming* and *Union City Blue*?

9 **Which single, which hit UK No. 1 in 1980, was used in the film American Gigolo?**

10 Which film, released in 1980, co-starred Meat Loaf, Debbie Harry and Alice Cooper?

11 **Which reggae song, previously recorded by The Paragons, was No. 1 in the UK for 2 weeks in 1980?**

12 And which album was the single taken from?

13 **Which song, which reached No. 1 in the US in 1981, was the first hit single to feature a white artist rapping?**

14 What was the title of Debbie Harry's 1981 solo album, featuring cover artwork by Alien creator H.R. Giger?

15 **What was the title of the final album to be released under the group name Blondie, before the group split up in 1982?**

1 *X-Offender*, 2 Chrysalis, 3 *Plastic Letters*, 4 *Denis*, 5 (*I'm Always Touched By Your) Presence Dear*, 6 Mike Chapman, 7 *Heart Of Glass*, 8 *Eat To The Beat*, 9 *Call Me*, 10 *Roadie*, 11 *The Tide Is High*, 12 *Autoamerican*, 13 *Rapture*, 14 *Koo Koo*, 15 *The Hunter*.

• BLUR •

1 Damon Albarn won a regional heat of which competition when he was 15?

2 By what name were Blur originally known?

3 In 1990 Blur released their debut single, what was it?

4 Which rival group supported Blur at a concert at the Town & Country Club in London in 1992?

5 Where did Blur get the title for their 1993 album *Modern Life Is Rubbish*?

6 Blur's 1994 album entered the UK chart at No.1, what was it called?

7 Which duo recorded a remix of *Girls And Boys* on the CD version of the Blur single *To The End*?

8 In 1994 Blur presented an edition of which TV show?

9 In 1995 Blur won a record amount of BRIT awards, how many?

10 In 1995 Damon Albarn played keyboards for which group on *Top Of The Pops* and what name did he call himself?

11 With whom did Damon Albarn perform *Waterloo Sunset* for C4's *The White Room*?

12 Which Blur single entered the UK chart at No.1 in 1995 keeping rival's Oasis at the No.2 spot?

13 Which 1996 film featured a solo track by Damon Albarn?

14 What was the title of Blur's 1999 album?

15 Who did Blur share an Ivor Novello songwriting award with?

• BOB DYLAN •

1 **Born in May 1941, what name was Bob Dylan given?**

2 At which New York venue did he play his first live gig, in April 1961?

3 **What was the title of Bob Dylan's 1963 album, which featured the song *Blowin' In The Wind*?**

4 Which band had a US and UK hit with the title song from Bob Dylan's 1964 album *The Times They Are A-Changin'*?

5 **Which album, also from 1964, featured the songs *All I Really Want To Do* and *It Ain't Me Babe*, which both became hit singles for other artists?**

6 What was the title of the film made during Bob Dylan's 1965 UK tour?

7 **Which album opened with the song *Subterranean Homesick Blues*, which became Bob Dylan's first US hit single?**

8 And which song from the album, featured on the soundtrack to the 1969 film *Easy Rider*, starts with the lines "Darkness at the break of noon, shadows even the silver spoon"?

9 **Why were Bob Dylan and his band almost booed off stage, at the Newport Folk Festival in the US?**

10 Which 1965 album featured the 6 minute long hit single, *Like A Rolling Stone*?

11 **And where, according to the title of the album's closing track, were they selling postcards of the hanging, and painting the mailbox brown?**

12 Which 1966 album featured the UK hit single *One Of Us Must Know*?

13 **And what was the full title of the album's opening song, which featured the repeated phrase "Everybody Must Get Stoned"?**

14 And which lengthy track takes up the whole fourth side of the album?

15 **What accident caused Bob Dylan to withdraw from public life in 1966, until his next public appearance in January 1968?**

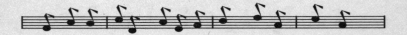

1 Robert Allen Zimmerman, **2** Gerde's Folk City, **3** *The Freewheelin' Bob Dylan*, **4** Peter, Paul and Mary, **5** *Another Side Of Bob Dylan*, **6** *Don't Look Back*, **7** *Bringing It All Back Home*, **8** *It's Alright Ma (I'm Only Bleeding)*, **9** The folk purists at the festival disapproved of his electric based backing group, **10** *Highway 61 Revisited*, **11** *Desolation Row*, **12** *Blonde On Blonde*, **13** *Rainy Day Women Nos. 12 & 35*, **14** *Sad Eyed Lady Of The Lowlands*, **15** He broke his neck when he crashed his Triumph 55 motorcycle.

• BOB DYLAN II •

1 **What was the title of the bootleg album, which featured recordings made by Bob Dylan, while he recuperated after an accident in 1966?**

2 And which band had a hit record with the song *The Mighty Quinn*, taken from these sessions?

3 **Whose memorial concert at Carnegie Hall marked Bob Dylan's return to public life?**

4 What was the title of Bob Dylan's first studio album to be recorded, following his accident?

5 **And which song, taken from this album, became a hit single for Jimi Hendrix?**

6 On which 1969 album did Bob Dylan duet with country singer Johnny Cash on the song *Girl From The North Country*?

7 **What was the title of Bob Dylan's surreal novel, released in November 1970?**

8 Which charity event became the only major live appearance made by Bob Dylan in 1971?

9 **What was the title of the soundtrack album recorded by Bob Dylan in 1973?**

10 And which song from this album became a hit single for Bob Dylan, and was later covered by Eric Clapton and Guns N' Roses?

11 **Which album, released in 1975, was influenced by the break up of Bob Dylan's marriage?**

12 Which "unofficial" album did Bob Dylan agree to release, in July 1975?

13 **Which country singer contributed vocals to the 1976 platinum selling album, *Desire*?**

14 What was the title of the farewell concert, given by Dylan's backing musicians, The Band, in San Francisco's Winterland Ballroom, in 1976?

15 **Who co-produced Bob Dylan's 1983 album, *Infidels*, recorded after he visited the Middle East?**

1 *Great White Wonder*, 2 Manfred Mann, 3 Woody Guthrie, who had died in September 1967, 4 *John Wesley Harding*, 5 *All Along The Watchtower*, 6 *Nashville Skyline*, 7 *Tarantula*, 8 George Harrison's Concert For Bangladesh, 9 *Pat Garrett And Billy The Kid*, 10 *Knockin' On Heaven's Door*, 11 *Blood On The Tracks*, 12 *The Basement Tapes* - the bootleg recordings from sessions held in 1967, 13 Emmylou Harris, 14 *The Last Waltz*, 15 Mark Knopfler.

• BREAD •

1 Which member of the band had recorded a solo album *Summer Holiday*, before forming the band in 1968?

2 Why did the band choose the name Bread in 1969?

3 What was the title of the band's second single, which reached No. 1 in the US charts in 1970?

4 And what was the title of the album from which the single came?

5 And which song, reissued from their unsuccessful debut album, reached No. 10 in the US following the success of their No. 1?

6 Which Oscar winning song, taken from the film *Lovers And Other Strangers*, had lyrics written by James Griffin and Robb Royer?

7 What was the title of the band's 1971 US No. 4 single, taken from the album *Manna*?

8 Which founder member of the band quit in 1971, to be replaced by Larry Knechtel?

9 What was the name of the 1972 album which, along with the title track, made No. 3 in the US charts?

10 Which song, which reached No. 5 in the US charts in 1972 for Bread, was also successful when covered by Ken Boothe in 1974 and Boy George in 1987?

11 What was the title of the band's 1972 album, featuring the singles *Sweet Surrender* and *Aubrey*?

12 What was the title of David Gates' 1973 solo album?

13 Which song, originally written and recorded by Bread, reached No. 1 in the UK when recorded by Telly Savalas?

14 What was the title of the band's 1977 album, recorded after the band reformed?

15 For which 1977 film, starring Richard Dreyfuss, did David Gates record the title track?

1 James Griffin, 2 They were stuck behind a bread delivery truck in a traffic jam, **3 Make It With You,** 4 On The Waters, **5 It Don't Matter To Me,** 6 For All We Know, **7 If,** 8 Robb Royer, **9 Baby, I'm-A Want You,** 10 Everything I Own, **11 Guitar Man,** 12 First, **13 If,** 14 Lost Without Your Love, **15 The Goodbye Girl.**

1 **What was the name of Bruce Springsteen's backing band formed in 1973?**

2 Who had a hit with a cover version of Bruce Springsteen's *Blinded By The Light* in 1977?

3 **Who was Bruce Springsteen's *Born To Run* credited as a tribute to?**

4 In 1976 Bruce Springsteen was apprehended by a security guard after climbing over who's wall?

5 **What was the title of Bruce Springsteen's 1980 album which spent over a year on both the UK and US charts?**

6 Bruce Springsteen had his first UK Top Ten hit in 1985, what was it?

7 **What was the title of Bruce Springsteen's 1985 double A-side?**

8 In 1985 which charity single did Bruce Springsteen contribute lead vocals to?

9 **What was the title of Bruce Springsteen's 1985 Christmas hit?**

10 In 1988 Natalie Cole had a hit with a Bruce Springsteen song, what was it?

11 **For which 1994 film did Bruce Springsteen record the theme song?**

12 Which BRIT award did Bruce Springsteen win in 1986?

13 **What is Bruce Springsteen's nick name?**

14 In 1986 who did Bruce Springsteen appear on stage with at a concert in Philadelphia?

15 **In 1986 Bruce Springsteen had a hit with *War* who made the original version?**

• BRYAN ADAMS •

1 **In which Canadian rock group did Bryan Adams replace Nick Gilder as lead singer?**

2 In 1976 Bryan Adams formed a songwriting partnership with which drummer?

3 **In 1998 Bryan Adams recorded a song with a member of the Spice Girls, name the song and singer?**

4 In 1985 Bryan Adams had his first UK hit what was it?

5 **Who did Bryan Adams support on his second UK tour in 1985?**

6 Where did Bryan Adams and his songwriting partner write the song *It's Only Love*?

7 **In 1987 Bryan Adams recorded a song for the charity album 'A Very Special Christmas', what was it called?**

8 In 1991 Bryan Adams had a hit with *(Everything I Do) I Do It For You* how long was it a UK No. 1?

9 **And for which film was it the theme song?**

10 In 1991 Bryan Adams released an album which entered the UK charts at No.1, what was it called?

11 **In 1991 why did Bryan Adams stop his concert halfway through a song?**

12 In 1994 Bryan Adams played a concert in Vietnam, the first major western pop star to do so since 1971 when which artist played there?

13 **Bryan Adams recorded *All For Love* the theme to the film *The Three Musketeers* with which two other artists?**

14 Which film features the Bryan Adams single *Have You Ever Really Loved A Woman*?

15 **In 1997 who did Bryan Adams sing the duet *I Finally Found Someone* with?**

• BRYAN FERRY •
• and ROXY MUSIC •

1 In which year were Roxy Music formed?

2 Bryan Ferry's first solo single was a cover version of a Bob Dylan song, what was it called?

3 **In 1971 which band did Bryan Ferry audition for but was unsuccessful?**

4 Who did Roxy Music support at the Empire Pool Wembley in 1972?

5 **Who left Roxy Music in 1973 and has since had a highly successful production career?**

6 What was the title of Bryan Ferry's first solo album?

7 **In 1972 Roxy Music had their first UK Top Ten hit, what was it?**

8 In 1979 Roxy Music released a single with the same title as an Abba single which charted at the same time, what was it?

9 **Roxy Music's first UK No.1 was a tribute to John Lennon, what was it?**

10 From which album was Roxy Music's hit single *Dance Away* taken?

11 **In 1974 Bryan Ferry had a hit with an old Platters song, what was it?**

12 Which Bryan Ferry single featured in the film *Legend*?

13 **What was the title of Bryan Ferry's 1985 UK No.1 album?**

14 Who featured on the sleeve of Roxy Music's album *Siren*?

15 **Which member of the Smiths featured on Bryan Ferry's album *Bete Noire* and co-wrote the single *The Right Stuff*?**

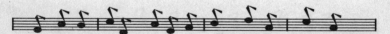

1 1971, 2 A Hard Rain's Gonna Fall, 3 King Crimson, 4 Alice Cooper,
5 Brian Eno, 6 These Foolish Things, 7 Virginia Plain, 8 Angel Eyes,
9 Jealous Guy, 10 Manifesto, 11 Smoke Gets In Your Eyes, 12 Is Your
Love Strong Enough, 13 Boys And Girls, 14 Jerry Hall, 15 Johnny Marr.

• BUDDY HOLLY •

1 What was the title of the first single released by Buddy Holly in April, 1956?

2 Under what name was the July 1956 single, *That'll Be The Day*, released?

3 And which John Wayne film was the song's title taken from?

4 Which single, recorded in 1957, was named after the girlfriend of drummer Jerry Allison?

5 Which song did Buddy Holly and The Crickets perform for their second appearance on *The Ed Sullivan Show*, in 1958?

6 When the song *Listen To Me* reached UK No. 16, in March 1959, how many UK top 20 hits did the group have in the charts simultaneously?

7 For what reason did Buddy Holly fail an initial army medical, allowing him to avoid military service?

8 In which US city did Buddy Holly record his first solo sessions, without The Crickets?

9 And what was the name of the woman he met in New York, who he was to marry in August 1958?

10 What was the title of the first single, released by Buddy Holly as a solo artist?

11 What was the name of the 1959 tour, which would be the last Buddy Holly would do?

12 Which other two pop stars joined Buddy Holly on the plane journey that was to prove fatal?

13 And what was the probable cause of the plane crash that killed the three passengers and the pilot?

14 Which Buddy Holly single became US No. 1 a few weeks after his death?

15 And what was the title of the song released by The Crickets in February 1959, the first not to feature Buddy Holly?

1 **Blue Days, Black Nights**, 2 Buddy Holly And The Three Tunes, 3 **The Searchers**, 4 *Peggy Sue*, 5 **Oh Boy!**, 6 4, 7 He had a stomach ulcer, 8 New York, 9 **Maria Elena Santiago**, 10 *Heartbeat*, 11 **The Winter Dance Party**, 12 Richie Valens and Big Bopper, 13 **Bad weather**, 14 *It Doesn't Matter Anymore*, 15 *Love's Made A Fool Of You.*

•CARL PERKINS•

1 **Which Elvis single inspired Carl Perkins to get a recording contract?**

2 With which record company did Carl Perkins make his first recordings?

3 **Which singer did Carl Perkins support in a tour of the southern states, in February 1955?**

4 Which song, written by Carl Perkins, reached No. 3 in the US charts in 1956?

5 **What tragedy struck Carl Perkins and his brother in 1956?**

6 Which song, later covered by The Beatles, did Carl Perkins record in 1956, with piano played by Jerry Lee Lewis?

7 **And which performer joined them, after the recording session, for a studio jam session, which was recorded and released years later, as *The Million Dollar Quartet*?**

8 In which 1957 musical film did Carl Perkins appear, performing *Glad All Over*?

9 **What was the title of Carl Perkins 1958 album, the first to be recorded for Columbia Records?**

10 Which single, released in 1959, became Carl Perkins' last chart entry, reaching No. 92 in the US charts?

11 **Which Carl Perkins number was recorded by the Beatles on the album *Beatles For Sale*, sung by George Harrison?**

12 Which performer's weekly TV shows did Carl Perkins appear on, throughout 1967?

13 **And what did the pair decide they had to give up, before going on to become born again Christians?**

14 Which 1970 film, starring Robert Redford, did Carl Perkins write songs for?

15 **What was the name of Carl Perkins' own production company and record label, formed in 1976?**

1 *Blue Moon Of Kentucky*, 2 Sun Records, 3 Elvis Presley, 4 *Blue Suede Shoes*, 5 **They were hospitalised after being involved in a car crash, making them miss out on publicity for the single *Blue Suede Shoes*. Jay Perkins died two years later, as a result of his injuries.** 6 *Matchbox*, 7 Elvis Presley, 8 *Jamboree*, 9 *Whole Lotta Shakin'*, 10 *Pointed Toe Shoes*, 11 *Everybody's trying To Be My Baby*, 12 Johnny Cash, 13 Alcohol and pills, 14 *Little Fauss And Big Halsy*, 15 Suede Records.

• CAT STEVENS •

1 **Cat Stevens released his debut single in 1966, what was it?**

2 What was his first UK Top Ten single?

3 **The Tremeloes' first hit without Brian Poole was a cover version of a Cat Stevens song, what was it?**

4 Which ex-Yardbird member produced Cat Stevens' 1970 album *Mona Bone Jakon*?

5 **Cat Stevens produced a short animated film to go with his 1971 album, what was it called?**

6 Who played piano on Cat Stevens' hit *Morning Has Broken*?

7 **And which 1972 cult movie featured the song?**

8 In 1974 Cat Stevens had a hit with a cover version of a Sam Cooke song, what was it?

9 **Which Cat Stevens' song did Rod Stewart have a hit with in 1977?**

10 Who did Cat Stevens duet with on his single *(Remember The Days Of The) Old School Yard*?

11 **What did Cat Stevens change his name to in 1977?**

12 What did he have removed from the sleeve artwork of his *Greatest Hits* album in 1981?

13 **Who had a hit with a cover version of Cat Stevens' *Wild World* in 1988?**

14 Which Boyzone hit single was a cover version of a Cat Stevens song?

15 **How did Cat Stevens cause outrage in 1989?**

1 **I Love My Dog**, 2 *Matthew And Son*, 3 **Here Comes My Baby**, 4 Paul Samwell-Smith, 5 *Teaser And The Firecat*, 6 Rick Wakeman, 7 *Harold And Maude*, 8 **Another Saturday Night**, 9 *First Cut Is The Deepest*, 10 Elkie Brooks, 11 **Yusef Islam**, 12 The Greek flag, 13 **Maxi Priest**, 14 *Father And Son*, 15 He endorsed the call for the execution of **Salman Rushdie.**

• CHER •

1 **In 1965 Cher recorded a cover version of a Bob Dylan song, what was it?**

2 In which year did Sonny & Cher have a UK No.1 with *I Got You Babe*?

3 **For which producer did Cher originally work as backing vocalist?**

4 In 1975 who made his American TV debut on Cher's show?

5 **In 1982 Cher featured as uncredited vocalist on which Meatloaf song?**

6 In 1984 Cher was nominated for an Oscar for best supporting actress in which film?

7 **In which 1987 film did Cher co-star with Jack Nicholson?**

8 Which singer produced Cher's 1987 hit *I Found Someone*?

9 **In 1988 Cher won an Academy Award for Best Actress in which film?**

10 Which group was Cher's single *Heart Of Stone* originally written for?

11 **In 1991 Cher had her first solo UK No.1 what was it?**

12 And in which film staring Cher did the song feature?

13 **With whom did Cher record a version of *I Got You Babe* in 1994?**

14 With whom did Cher record the charity single *Love Can Build A Bridge* in 1995?

15 **In 1991 Cher had her first UK No.1 album what was it?**

14 Chrissie Hynde and Neneh Cherry with Eric Clapton, 15 *Love Hurts.*
Song (*It's In His Kiss*), 12 *Mermaids*, 13 Beavis and Butt-Head,
8 Michael Bolton, 9 *Moonstruck*, 10 Bucks Fizz, 11 *The Shoop Shoop*
5 *Dead Ringer For Love*, 6 *Silkwood*, 7 *The Witches Of Eastwick*,
1 *All I Really Want To Do*, 2 1965, 3 **Phil Spector**, 4 David Bowie.

•CHRIS REA•

1 What was the name of the band Chris Rea joined in 1973?

2 And which singer had just left it to join Deep Purple?

3 In 1978 Chris Rea made his debut on the UK chart with which song?

4 And who recorded a cover version of it in 1982?

5 In 1989 Chris Rea had his first UK Top Ten hit, what was it?

6 And what was it written about?

7 What was the title of Chris Rea's 1988 Christmas single?

8 On which charity single did Chris Rea feature in 1989?

9 What was the title of Chris Rea's 1991 album which entered the UK chart at No.1?

10 In 1992 Chris Rea made a guest appearance on whose TV show?

11 Chris Rea composed the score for which 1993 movie?

12 Which song did Chris Rea contribute to Elton John's *Duets* album?

13 With which record label did Chris Rea originally sign?

14 From which album was the Chris Rea single *Stainsby Girls* taken?

15 With whom did Chris Rea record the single *Disco' La Passione* in 1996?

1 Magdalene, 2 David Coverdale, **3 Fool (If You Think It's Over),** 4 Elkie Brooks, **5 Road To Hell (Part 2),** 6 The M25 motorway, **7 Driving Home For Christmas,** 8 Band Aid II's Do They Know It's Christmas, **9 Auberge,** 10 Des O'Connor, **11 Soft Top, Hard Shoulder,** 12 If You Were Me, **13 Magnet,** 14 Shamrock Diaries, **15 Shirley Bassey.**

•CHUCK BERRY•

1 **Born in 1926, what profession did Chuck Berry formally train for, obtaining a degree from the Poro School?**

2 Which blues singer saw Chuck Berry in East St Louis' Cosmopolitan Club, recommending he contact Chess Records for a contract?

3 **What was the title of the first record released by Chuck Berry, based on the traditional country tune *Ida Red*?**

4 Which single from 1956 features the line "You know my temperature's rising, Need a shot of rhythm and blues"?

5 **In which film did Chuck Berry sing the song *You Can't Catch Me*?**

6 Which single, released in 1957, became Chick Berry's first UK chart hit?

7 **And in which single, also from 1957, did he sing "I got no kick against modern jazz, unless they try to play it too darned fast. They lose the beauty of the melody, until it sounds just like a symphony"?**

8 Which 1958 Chuck Berry single was adapted by The Beach Boys for their hit single *Surfin' USA*?

9 **For what crime did Chuck Berry serve two years in jail, from 1962 to 1964?**

10 Which Chuck Berry song was included on The Beatles second album, *Meet The Beatles*?

11 **Which 1964 single starts with the line "Riding along in my automobile, my baby beside me at the wheel"?**

12 What was the name of the theme park owned by Chuck Berry, situated just outside St. Louis?

13 **Members from which British band provided the backing for his album *The London Chuck Berry Sessions*?**

14 Which single reached No. 1 in the US, to become Chuck Berry's most successful single ever?

15 **For what reason was Chuck Berry sentenced to five months in jail in 1979?**

1 **Hairdressing and Cosmetology,** 2 **Muddy Waters,** 3 **Maybellene,** 4 *Roll Over Beethoven,* 5 *Rock Rock Rock,* 6 *School Day,* 7 *Rock And Roll Music,* 8 *Sweet Little Sixteen,* 9 Transporting a minor across a state line, for immoral purposes, 10 *Roll Over Beethoven,* 11 *No Particular Place To Go,* 12 Berryland Amusement Park, 13 **The Faces,** 14 *My Ding A Ling,* 15 Tax evasion.

• CLIFF RICHARD I •

1 Born on October 14th in 1940, what is Cliff Richard's real name?

2 What was the name of the five-piece vocal group, formed by Cliff Richard at Cheshunt Secondary Modern School, at the age of 14?

3 What were the first two songs recorded and released by Cliff Richard and The Drifters in 1958?

4 Which lead and rhythm guitarists joined the band in September 1958?

5 Which 1959 film, starring Anthony Quayle, featured Cliff Richard as a teenage delinquent?

6 And which song, taken from this film, stayed at No. 1 in the UK for 5 weeks in 1959?

7 And what was the title of the follow up single, which also made No. 1 for 5 weeks?

8 Which 1959 film, based on a play by Wolf Mankowitz, starred Cliff Richard as a manipulated teenage rock star?

9 What did Cliff Richard's backing band change their name to in 1959?

10 Which single, released in 1960, knocked Cliff Richard's *Please Don't Tease* off the No. 1 spot in the UK?

11 Which Cliff Richard single replaced Elvis Presley's 8 week run at No. 1 with *It's Now Or Never* in December 1960?

12 Which title song to Cliff Richard's 1961 film stayed at No. 1 in the UK for 6 weeks?

13 Which single, released in 1962 and reaching No. 1 in the UK, saw Cliff Richard's first co-writing credit?

14 And which film was the song taken from?

15 Which single, released in 1964, reached No. 25 in the US and No. 2 in the UK?

14 *Summer Holiday*, 15 *It's All In The Game.*
by the Shadows, 11 *I Love You*, 12 *The Young Ones*, 13 *Bachelor Boy*,
Doll, 7 *Travellin' Light*, 8 *Expresso Bongo*, 9 **The Shadows**, 10 *Apache*,
Crush, 4 Hank Marvin and Bruce Welch, 5 **Serious Charge**, 6 *Living*
1 **Harry Rodger Webb**, 2 The Quintones, 3 **Move It and Schoolboy**

•CLIFF RICHARD II•

1 **Which film was Cliff Richard's 1964 UK No. 7 hit *On The Beach* taken from?**

2 Which 1964 London Palladium pantomime starred Cliff Richard, and spawned a hit single and album?

3 **Which single, released in 1965, was held off the No. 1 spot by The Beatles' double a-side *We Can Work It Out/Day Tripper*?**

4 Which song, written by Mick Jagger and Keith Richards, reached No. 15 in the UK charts for Cliff Richard?

5 **Which evangelist did Cliff Richard join onstage at Earls Court in 1966, professing his Christian faith?**

6 Who wrote the music for the 1966 stage pantomime *Cinderella*, starring Cliff Richard?

7 **Which 1966 film featured puppets of Cliff Richard and The Shadows, singing the song *Shooting Star*?**

8 Which song did Cliff Richard sing at the 1968 Eurovision Song Contest, coming second?

9 **Which children's TV show did Cliff Richard appear on, in 1969?**

10 Which duet between Hank Marvin and Cliff Richard reached No. 25 in the UK charts, and was used as the title theme to a TV series?

11 **Which UK No. 6 single, released in 1970, became the 50th single of Cliff Richard's career?**

12 What was the title of the religious album, released by Cliff Richard in 1970?

13 **Which Australian singer was a regular guest on Cliff Richard's 1972 BBC TV series?**

14 Which song, performed by Cliff Richard, came third in the 1973 Eurovision Song Contest?

15 **Which film from 1974 co-starred Cliff Richard, Debbie Watling and George Cole?**

1 **Wonderful Life,** 2 Aladdin And His Wonderful Lamp, 3 **Wind Me Up** (**Let Me Go**), 4 Blue Turns To Grey, 5 **Billy Graham,** 6 The Shadows, 7 **Thunderbirds Are Go!,** 8 Congratulations, 9 **Sooty,** 10 The Joy Of Living, 11 **Goodbye Sam, Hello Samantha,** 12 About That Man, 13 **Olivia Newton John,** 14 Power To All Our Friends, 15 **Take Me High.**

• CLIFF RICHARD III •

1 Which 1975 BBC TV series arranged for Cliff Richard fan Helen Moon to meet her idol?

2 Which single, released in 1976, gave Cliff Richard his first US Top Ten hit?

3 What was the title of Cliff Richard's biography, written by Bill Latham, published in 1977?

4 Which song, released in 1979, reached No. 1 in the UK, and became Cliff Richard's biggest selling single worldwide?

5 Which British singer did Cliff Richard appear with in 1979 at the Royal Albert Hall, as part of its 75th birthday appeal?

6 What honour was awarded to Cliff Richard in 1980?

7 Which film, released in 1980, featured the duet *Suddenly*, sung by Cliff Richard and Olivia Newton-John?

8 Which title track, taken from a 1981 album, reached No. 4 in the UK charts?

9 Which US singer did Cliff Richard duet with on the 1983 UK No. 9 single *She Means Nothing To Me*?

10 Which 1986 West End musical, written by Dave Clarke, starred Cliff Richard in the lead role?

11 And which single, taken from the soundtrack to the musical and produced by Stevie Wonder, reached No. 17 in the UK charts?

12 Which spoof re-recording of a 1960 Cliff Richard hit reached No. 1 in the UK charts, when released as part of the Comic Relief charity effort?

13 Which single, a duet between Cliff Richard and Sarah Brightman and taken from the musical *Phantom Of The Opera*, reached No. 3 in the UK charts in 1986?

14 Which British singer duetted with Cliff Richard on the 1986 single *Slow Rivers*?

15 What was the title of Cliff Richard's 1987 album, which went on to become his greatest seller?

1 *Jim'll Fix It*, 2 *Devil Woman*, 3 *Which One's Cliff?*, 4 *We Don't Talk Anymore*, 5 Kate Bush, 6 The OBE, 7 *Xanadu*, 8 *Wired For Sound*, 9 Phil Everly, 10 *Time*, 11 *She's So Beautiful*, 12 *Living Doll*, 13 *All I Ask Of You*, 14 Elton John, 15 *Always Guaranteed*.

• CREAM •

1 Which three musicians made up the band?

2 What was the title of the band's debut album, released in 1967?

3 And what was the title of the first single taken from the album, which reached No. 11 in the UK charts?

4 Which album, also released in 1967, featured a psychedelic day-glo cover, by artist Martin Sharp?

5 And which single, taken from the album, became their first US chart hit?

6 And what do the initials *S.W.L.A.B.R* stand for, from the title of the B-side to this single?

7 Which single, released in 1968, was used as the theme tune to the film *The Savage Seven*?

8 What was the title of the double album set, released by the band in August 1968?

9 And at which venue was the live set from the album recorded?

10 What was the title of the last single to be released by the band, before announcing their break up in 1968?

11 At which London venue did the band play their last two farewell concerts?

12 Which band did Eric Clapton and Ginger Baker go on to form, with Ric Grech and Stevie Winwood?

13 What was the title of the last studio album to be released by Cream, in 1969?

14 And which Beatle co-wrote their last single, *Badge*, with Eric Clapton?

15 What was the title of Jack Bruce's debut solo album, released in 1969?

• CREEDENCE CLEARWATER REVIVAL •

1 **What were the names of the two brothers, who formed the band in 1959 with friends Stu Cook and Doug Clifford?**

2 Under what name was the band's first single released?

3 **And what was the title of the debut single?**

4 Which two members of the band were drafted into National Service in 1966, temporarily halting the band's career?

5 **And, deciding they needed a change, where did the band get their new name from?**

6 Which Dale Hawkins song became the first single to be released under the band's new name?

7 **Which song, released in 1969, became the band's first million seller, reaching No. 2 in the US charts?**

8 And what was the title of the band's second album, from which this single was taken?

9 **Which single, released in June 1969, also reached No. 2 in the US charts, behind the *Love Theme From Romeo And Juliet*?**

10 Which song prevented the band's September 1969 single, *Green River*, from reaching No. 1 in the US charts again?

11 **Which album, released in 1970, was named after the band's regular rehearsal venue?**

12 And which single, taken from the album, reached No. 2 in the US charts in October 1970?

13 **Which album, released in 1971, was the last to feature Tom Fogerty, before he announced he was to quit?**

14 And which single, taken from this album, reached No. 8 in the US charts?

15 **Which of the group's songs was the subject of a plagiarism suit, when it was accused of sounding like Little Richard's *Good Golly Miss Molly*?**

1 **John and Tom Fogerty,** 2 The Golliwogs, 3 ***Don't Tell Me No Lies,*** 4 John Fogerty and Doug Clifford, 5 **Creedence was a friend of the band, and Clearwater was the name of a beer,** 6 Suzie Q, 7 ***Proud Mary,*** 8 Bayou Country, 9 ***Bad Moon Rising,*** 10 Sugar Sugar by The Archies, 11 **Cosmo's Factory,** 12 Lookin' Out My Back Door, 13 **Pendulum,** 14 *Have You Ever Seen The Rain,* 15 *Travelin' Band.*

• CROSBY STILLS AND NASH •

1 **Which three bands did David Crosby, Stephen Stills and Graham Nash leave before forming their own group in 1968?**

2 At which 1969 rock festival did the group play their second live gig together?

3 **Which Stephen Stills song, written about his current girlfriend, opened their debut album?**

4 And which song from the album was later covered by Jefferson Airplane on the album *Volunteers*?

5 **Which Graham Nash song, from the group's debut album, reached No. 17 in the UK charts in 1969?**

6 Which musician was added to the group's lineup, joining in June 1969?

7 **What was the title of the group's second album, released in May 1970?**

8 And who originally wrote the song *Woodstock*, which featured on the album and was used for the soundtrack to the documentary film about the festival?

9 **And who was the only member of the group not to have been romantically linked with this songwriter?**

10 Which song opened Steven Stills 1970 solo album, and reached No. 14 in the US singles chart?

11 **And which famous guitarist played on the track *Old Times, Good Times*, taken from this solo album?**

12 What was the name of David Crosby's solo album, released in 1971, and featuring sessions work by Jerry Garcia and Joni Mitchell?

13 **What was the name of Neil Young's band, with which he had a 1971 hit album with *After The Gold Rush*?**

14 What was the title of Crosby, Stills, Nash and Young's 1971 double live album, which reached No. 1 in the US charts?

15 **Which members of the group toured together as a duo throughout the summer of 1972?**

1 David Crosby left The Byrds, Stephen Stills had been in Buffalo Springfield and Graham Nash had just left The Hollies, 2 Woodstock, 3 *Suite: Judy Blue Eyes*, 4 *Wooden Ships*, 5 *Marrakesh Express*, 6 Neil Young, 7 *Déjà vu*, 8 Joni Mitchell, 9 Stephen Stills (Crosby), Nash and Young all had affairs with Joni Mitchell), 10 *Love The One You're With*, 11 Jimi Hendrix, 12 *If Only I Could Remember My Name*, 13 Crazy Horse, 14 *4-Way Street*, 15 David Crosby and Graham Nash.

• CROWDED HOUSE •

1 Which group did the Finn brothers play in, before Neil Finn left to form Crowded House?

2 And which country were the brothers born in?

3 Which song, taken from the group's eponymous debut album, reached No. 2 in the US charts in 1987?

4 And which British solo artist sung this song for Nelson Mandela at his 70th Birthday Tribute concert at Wembley in 1988?

5 What was the title of the band's second album, which featured the single *Better Be Home Soon*?

6 Which guitarist joined the band onstage in Los Angeles in 1989, with the resulting tracks released on an EP as *Byrdhouse*?

7 Who joined the band briefly in 1991, to record the album *Woodface*, before leaving at the end of the year?

8 And which song, taken from this album, reached No. 17 in the UK charts?

9 And which other song from the album reached No. 7 in the UK charts when it was used by Chiltern Radio to accompany their weather forecasts?

10 Which honour did the Finn brothers receive in June 1993?

11 What was the name of the keyboard player, who joined the group in 1993?

12 What was the title of the band's 1993 album, which entered the UK charts at No. 4?

13 And which single, taken from the album, reached No. 19 in the UK charts?

14 Which member of the group quit in 1994, to be replaced by Peter Jones?

15 Which song, released in 1994, became the last single to be released under the band's name, before announcing they had split up?

Hester, 15 *Pineapple Head*.
Zealand, 11 Mark Hart, 12 *Together Alone*, 13 *Distant Sun*, 14 Paul
Feet, 9 *Weather With You*, 10 The O.B.E. for services to their native New
5 *Temple Of Low Men*, 6 Roger McGuinn, 7 Tim Finn, 8 *Fall At Your*
1 Split Enz, 2 New Zealand, 3 *Don't Dream It's Over*, 4 Paul Young,

•DAVID BOWIE I•

1 Which notable facial feature of the singer was a result of a fight he had while at school?

2 What was David Bowie's real name, and why did he have to change it?

3 Which 1967 novelty single featured poor joke references to The Rolling Stones and The London School Of Economics?

4 Which 1969 single was released to coincide with the Apollo moon landing?

5 Who became the regular producer for David Bowie in the late 1960's and early 1970's?

6 What was the name of the woman David Bowie married in 1970?

7 What was controversial about the cover to David Bowie's 1970 album *The Man Who Sold The World*?

8 With what name was their son christened?

9 And which track from the forthcoming *Hunky Dory* album was dedicated to his son?

10 On the album *Hunky Dory*, which American artist did David Bowie write a satirical song about?

11 And which fellow pop star was David Bowie referring to in his song *Queen Bitch*?

12 Which seminal album from 1972 featured the singles *Starman* and *Suffragette City*?

13 Which song did David Bowie offer to UK band Mott The Hoople in 1972, to revive their flagging career?

14 Which member of Bowie's backing band joined him in producing Lou Reed's debut solo single *Walk On The Wild Side*?

15 And what was the title of the album which featured this single?

1 He was punched in the face, leaving one of his eyes with a permanently dilated pupil, and a different colour from the other, 2 David Jones, but he changed it to Bowie after David Jones of the Monkees became famous, 3 *The Laughing Gnome*, 4 *Space Oddity*, 5 Tony Visconti, 6 Angela Barnet, 7 He was photographed wearing a full length dress - the cover was later withdraw, and replaced with a black and white photo, 8 Duncan Zowie Bowie, 9 **Kooks**, 10 Andy Warhol, 11 **Lou Reed**, 12 *The Rise And Fall Of Ziggy Stardust And The Spiders From Mars*, 13 *All The Young Dudes*, 14 Guitarist Mick Ronson, 15 *Transformer*.

•DAVID BOWIE II•

1 **What was the title of David Bowie's 1973 album, which developed his alter-ego character from the Ziggy Stardust album?**

2 And which song from the album reached No. 3 in the UK charts?

3 **What shock announcement did David Bowie make onstage at the Hammersmith Odeon, at the end of his current UK tour?**

4 Which song, originally from the 1971 album *Hunky Dory*, reached No. 3 in the UK in July 1973, when it was released as a single?

5 **And which British musician had played piano on the song?**

6 Which model posed with David Bowie on the cover of his 1973 cover versions album, *Pin-Ups*?

7 **And which song from the album, originally recorded by The Merseys, reached No. 3 when it was released as a single?**

8 Which artist had a UK No. 3 hit in 1974 with David Bowie's 1970 album track *The Man Who Sold The World*?

9 **What was the name of David Bowie's 1974 album, based on the George Orwell book *1984*?**

10 And why did the artwork on the album cover have to be changed?

11 **And which single from the album reached No. 5 in the UK charts?**

12 What was the title of the 1975 BBC documentary, made about David Bowie?

13 **Which album, released in 1975, featured John Lennon playing on two of the tracks?**

14 And which single, co-written with John Lennon, made No. 1 in the US for two weeks in 1975?

15 **Which album, released in 1976, introduced David Bowie's on-stage persona of The Thin White Duke?**

1 *Aladdin Sane*, **2** *Drive-In Saturday*, **3** He said it would be the last show they would ever do - although he only meant the last show in which he would appear as Ziggy Stardust, **4** *Life On Mars*, **5** Rick Wakeman, **6** Twiggy, **7** *Sorrow*, **8** Lulu, **9** Diamond Dogs, **10** It featured David Bowie, painted as a dog, with it's male genitalia prominently displayed - they had to be painted out, **11** *Rebel Rebel*, **12** *Cracked Actor*, **13** *Young Americans*, **14** *Fame*, **15** *Station To Station*.

•DAVID BOWIE III•

1 **Which film, released in 1976, starred David Bowie in the leading role?**

2 And which actor had the director, Nicholas Roeg, originally cast in this role?

3 **What was David Bowie found to be carrying in his luggage after a trip to Moscow, which Russian custom officials took exception to, detaining him for several hours?**

4 Which country did David Bowie move to in 1976, and stay for the next 3 years?

5 **Which album, released in 1977, was the first of three collaborations with Brian Eno?**

6 And which song from the album reached No. 3 in the UK charts in March?

7 **Which TV show did David Bowie appear on in 1977, duetting with the show's host on the song *Standing Next To You*?**

8 Which album, released in 1977, featured guitarwork by British guitarist Robert Fripp?

9 **Which film, directed by David Hemmings, starred David Bowie as a Prussian war veteran, Paul?**

10 Which classical children's piece by Prokofiev did David Bowie provide the narration for in a new recording, released in 1978?

11 **What was the title of the album, released in 1979, and recorded at the Mountain Studios in Montreux?**

12 Which play, which opened in 1980 in Denver, did David Bowie play the title role, to very favourable reviews?

13 **Which single, released in 1980, included several references to David Bowie's earlier character of Major Tom, and became his second UK No. 1?**

14 What was the title of the album, released in 1980, and featuring the singles *Fashion* and *Up The Hill Backwards*?

15 **Which song, co-written and performed with Queen, reached No. 1 in the UK charts in 1981?**

1 *The Man Who Fell To Earth*, 2 Peter O'Toole, 3 **Nazi memorabilia,** 4 West Berlin in Germany, 5 *Low*, 6 *Sound And Vision*, 7 **Marc Bolan's show,** *Marc*, 8 *Heroes*, 9 *Just A Gigolo*, 10 *Peter And The Wolf*, 11 *Lodger*, 12 *The Elephant Man*, 13 *Ashes To Ashes*, 14 *Scary Monsters (And Super Creeps)*, 15 *Under Pressure*.

•DAVID BOWIE IV•

1 Which film, released in 1983, co-starred David Bowie, Catherine Deneuve and Susan Sarandon?

2 Which duet with Bing Crosby, recorded in 1977, reached No. 3 in the UK charts when it was released in 1982?

3 Which song, taken from the album of the same name, reached No. 1 in the UK in 1983?

4 And what was the title of his world tour, which opened at Wembley Arena in June 1983?

5 Which single, co-written with Iggy Pop, reached No. 2 in the UK, despite the video being banned by the BBC?

6 Which single, taken from the 1984 album *Tonight*, made UK No. 6?

7 And which US artist duetted with David Bowie on the title track to the album?

8 Which song did David Bowie record with Mick Jagger, for the Live Aid charity fund?

9 Which film, directed by Julian Temple, did David Bowie have a No. 2 hit with the title track, in 1986?

10 And which children's film, released in 1986, did he star as The Goblin King?

11 What was the title of the world tour, undertaken in 1987 to promote David Bowie's album *Never Let Me Down*?

12 Which role did David Bowie play in the controversial 1988 film *The Last Temptation Of Christ*?

13 What was the name of the band, formed by David Bowie in 1989 with Reeves Gabrels and Tony and Hunt Sales?

14 And which single, released by the band in July 1989, only reached No. 52 in the UK charts?

15 What was the title of David Bowie's 1990 world tour, which was to be a greatest hits retrospective?

1 The Hunger, 2 *Peace On Earth/Little Drummer Boy*, **3 *Let's Dance*,**
4 The Serious Moonlight Tour, **5 *China Girl*,** 6 *Blue Jean*, **7 Tina Turner,**
8 *Dancing In The Street*, **9 *Absolute Beginners*,** 10 *Labyrinth*, **11 Glass**
***Spider*,** 12 Pontius Pilate, **13 Tin Machine,** 14 *Under The God*, **15 The**
Sound And Vision World Tour.

• DEEP PURPLE •

1 **How did the group come to be called Deep Purple?**

2 Name the singer and bassist who joined the group in 1969, to complete what fans regard as the classic line up?

3 **What was the name of the band's keyboard player, who composed the ambitious *Concerto For Group And Orchestra*, first performed in 1969?**

4 Which role in a Tim Rice and Andrew Lloyd Webber musical did Ian Gillan play, in a special production staged in New York?

5 **Which classic Deep Purple song was inspired by the burning down of the Swiss recording studios where the band were working?**

6 And what was the title of the album which featured this song?

7 **Which live album from 1973 features the debut performance of the song *Child In Time*?**

8 Which singer took up vocals with the band, after Ian Gillan announced he was leaving?

9 **And what was the title of the first album released with the new line up?**

10 What was the name of the band which guitarist Ritchie Blackmore formed, after leaving Deep Purple in 1975?

11 **What was the name of the children's musical, written by the band's former bassist, Roger Glover?**

12 Which band did David Coverdale go on to form, after leaving Deep Purple in 1976?

13 **In which year did the classic band line up reform, to record the album *Perfect Strangers*?**

14 And for how long did this line up stay together, before Ian Gillan and Roger Glover both quit the group again?

15 **What prevented the band from performing a planned concert in Tel Aviv, Israel, early in 1991?**

1 Named after guitarist Ritchie Blackmore's favourite song, 2 Ian Gillan and Roger Glover, **3 Jon Lord,** 4 Jesus, in *Jesus Christ Superstar*, **5 *Smoke On The Water*,** 6 *Burn*, **7 *Made In Japan*,** 8 David Coverdale, **9 *Burn*,** 10 Rainbow, **11 *The Butterfly Ball*,** 12 Whitesnake, **13 1984,** 14 4 years, until 1989, **15 Tel Aviv came under missile fire from Iraq.**

•DEF LEPPARD•

1 In which British city were the group formed?

2 What was the title of the band's first recording, a three-track EP?

3 **Why were the band forced to leave the stage, when they appeared at the 1980 Reading Festival?**

4 What was the name of the first album, recorded and released by the band in 1980?

5 **Which record producer did they start a long term working relation ship with in 1981?**

6 And what was the name of the first album he produced with the band?

7 **What was the name of the guitarist who replaced Pete Willis in 1982?**

8 Which US album kept Def Leppard's 1983 album, *Pyromania*, from the No. 1 slot?

9 **What disaster struck the band on a stretch of the A57 near Sheffield in 1984?**

10 Which album, released in 1987, had taken three years to record?

11 **And how many singles in total did they release from the album?**

12 How did guitarist Steve Clarke die in 1991?

13 **Which Hollywood movie featured the band's 1993 hit *Two Steps Behind*?**

14 Which band originally wrote the song *Action*, covered by Def Leppard on their 1993 album *Retro-Active*?

15 **Which member of the band was arrested and charged in 1995 with abusing his wife, Stacy?**

1 **Sheffield,** 2 *Getcha Rocks Off,* 3 **The British audience threw so many missiles at the stage, because it was felt that the group had sold out to American,** 4 *On Through The Night,* 5 **Mutt Lange,** 6 *High'n'Dry,* 7 **Phil Collen,** 8 *Thriller* by Michael Jackson, 9 **Drummer Rick Allen lost his left arm when he crashed his Corvette Stingray,** 10 *Hysteria,* 11 6 singles, 12 An overdose of prescribed drugs and alcohol, 13 *Last Action Hero,* 14 The Sweet, 15 **Rick Allen.**

•DION AND THE BELMONTS•

1 **Where did The Belmonts take their name from?**

2 In 1959 Dion took part in the tour which Buddy Holly died in a plane crash halfway through, what was the tour called?

3 **In 1959 Dion & The Belmonts made their debut on the UK chart with which single?**

4 In which year did Dion & The Belmonts split?

5 **What was the title of Dion's first solo UK chart entry?**

6 In which 1962 film did Dion appear?

7 **In 1962 Dion had his only UK Top Ten hit, what was it?**

8 And who had a hit with a cover version of the song in 1984?

9 **Which UK TV show did Dion walk out in the middle of when he became irritated by the audience dancing around him?**

10 In 1963 Dion released a cover version of a Drifters' hit what was it?

11 **Dion appeared on the cover of the Beatles' *Sgt. Pepper's Lonely Hearts Club Band* album as one of only two singers, who was the other one?**

12 In which year did Dion & The Belmonts release their reunion album *Together Again*?

13 **In 1969 Dion released a cover version of a Jimi Hendrix song, what was it?**

14 Which was the only Dion & the Belmonts album to chart in the UK?

15 **Which track did Dion contribute to the benefit album of Elvis Presley covers *The Last Temptation Of Elvis*?**

1 A street in the Bronx, 2 Winter Dance Party, **3 A Teenager In Love,** 4 1960, **5 Lonely Teenager,** 6 *Teenage Millionaire,* **7 *The Wanderer,*** 8 Status Quo, **9 *Ready Steady Go,*** 10 Ruby Baby, **11 Bob Dylan,** 12 1967, **13 *Purple Haze,*** 14 20 *Golden Greats,* **15 Mean Woman Blues.**

~ 42 ~

•DIRE STRAITS•

1 **Before joining Dire Straits Mark Knopfler was a journalist, for which newspaper did he work?**

2 Dire Straits' first European tour was as support act for which group?

3 **Dire Straits released their debut single in 1978. What was it called?**

4 After attending a concert in Los Angeles in 1979 who invited Mark Knopfler and Pick Withers to play on his next album?

5 **On whose album track, *Solo In Soho* was Mark Knopfler featured?**

6 In 1982 producer David Puttnam invited Mark Knopfler to compose and perform the soundtrack score to which film?

7 **How long was the Dire Straits single *Private Investigations*?**

8 In 1982 Pick Withers left the band, who replaced him?

9 **In 1983 Mark Knopfler released his first solo single, what was it?**

10 Tina Turner had a hit with a song written by Mark Knopfler which was a leftover from material written for Dire Straits *Love Over Gold* album, what was It?

11 **Who co-wrote and performed on the Dire Straits single *Money For Nothing*?**

12 A Dire Straits single was the first-ever commercially issued CD-single in the UK. What was it called?

13 **Which cable TV station's catchphrase is from the lyrics of a Dire Straits hit?**

14 In 1986 how did Mark Knopfler break his collarbone?

15 **In 1989 which Ivor Novello award did the band win?**

1 Yorkshire Evening Times, 2 Talking Heads, 3 *Sultans Of Swing*, 4 Bob Dylan, 5 Phil Lynott, 6 *Local Hero*, 7 **Seven minutes**, 8 Terry Williams, 9 *Going Home (theme from Local Hero)*, 10 *Private Dancer*, 11 **Sting**, 12 *Brothers In Arms*, 13 **MTV**, 14 In a celebrity car race before the Australian Grand Prix, 15 **Outstanding Contribution To British Music**

• DONOVAN •

1 **On which British TV show did Donovan perform for three consecutive weeks, during February 1965?**

2 And what was the title of Donovan's debut single, which reached No. 4 in the UK charts?

3 **Which US folk singer was Donovan often compared to during the mid 1960's, due to his denim cap and racked harmonica?**

4 Which single, released in 1966, reached No. 1 in the US singles chart?

5 **And which record producer had worked with Donovan on this single, and the same titled album?**

6 Which 1966 single reached No. 2 in the US charts, despite being banned in several states, for a variety of reasons?

7 **And which member of The Beatles provided backing vocals for the song?**

8 What was the title of the 1968 double album, which featured one disc of children's songs?

9 **Which hit single from 1968 did Donovan write while attending a Transcendental Meditation course in India with The Beatles?**

10 And which song, which reached No. 4 in the UK charts, was written in India with the help of George Harrison, although he went uncredited on the single?

11 **Which single from 1968 opens with a mythical monologue, and closes with a repeated chorus, reminiscent of The Beatles' song *Hey Jude*?**

12 Which single did Donovan record with the Jeff Beck Group in 1969?

13 **Which 1972 Franco Zefferelli film did Donovan provide the soundtrack for?**

14 Which album from 1973 became the last Donovan album to make the UK charts?

15 **Which 1973 Alice Cooper track did Donovan provide the instantly recognisable vocals for?**

1 **Ready Steady Go,** 2 *Catch The Wind,* 3 **Bob Dylan,** 4 *Sunshine Superman,* 5 **Mickie Most,** 6 *Mellow Yellow,* 7 **Paul McCartney,** 8 *A Gift From A Flower To A Garden,* 9 **Jennifer Juniper,** 10 *Hurdy Gurdy Man,* 11 **Atlantis,** 12 *Barabajagal (Love Is Hot),* 13 **Brother Sun, Sister Moon,** 14 *Cosmic Wheels,* 15 *Billion Dollar babies.*

~ 44 ~

•EDDIE COCHRAN•

1 Who did Eddie Cochran first play with, in a duo known as the Cochran Brothers?

2 In which 1956 film, starring Jayne Mansfield, did Eddie Cochran appear, singing *Twenty Flight Rock*?

3 What was the title of his debut single, released in 1957, and reaching No. 18 in the US charts?

4 Which country did Eddie Cochran tour in 1957, along with Gene Vincent and Little Richard?

5 Which song, released in 1958, became Eddie Cochran's first big chart hit, reaching No. 8 in the US charts?

6 In which film, released in 1959, did Eddie Cochran appear, along with Chuck Berry and Jackie Wilson?

7 And which song is he featured in the film singing?

8 Why did Eddie Cochran record the song *Three Stars* in February 1959?

9 Which song, released in 1959, reached No. 6 in the UK charts to become his biggest hit during his lifetime?

10 What was the title of Eddie Cochran's 1959 UK No. 22 hit, written about a good looking car?

11 And who had actually written the song?

12 Who did Eddie Cochran tour the UK with in 1960, co-headlining the shows with him?

13 On which UK rock show did Eddie Cochran make his TV debut?

14 What accident on the 17th April 1960 caused the death of Eddie Cochran?

15 What was the title of the song, already recorded by Eddie Cochran, which reached No. 1 in the UK when it was released after his death?

thrown through the windscreen, **15** *Three Steps To Heaven.*
was he and ,tsop pmal a otni dehsarc saw eh gnillevart saw rac ehT **41**
former girlfriend of Phil Everly, 12 Gene Vincent, **13** *Boy Meets Girls,*
10 *Somethin' Else,* **11 Sharon Sheeley,** Eddie Cochran's fiancé and
The Big Bopper, who died in a plane crash **9** *C'mon Everybody,*
7 *Teenage Heaven,* **8** As a tribute to Buddy Holly, Ritchie Valens and
Balcony, 4 Australia, **5** *Summertime Blues,* **6** *Go, Johnny, Go!,*
1 Schoolfriend, Hank Cochran, 2 *The Girl Can't Help It,* **3** *Sittin' In The*

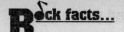

•E.L.O.•

1 **From which successful Birmingham band did the Electric Light Orchestra evolve?**

2 And which three members formed the original line up of the band?

3 **At which Croydon pub did the band make their debut performance?**

4 What was the title of the debut single written by Jeff Lynne?

5 **Which Chuck Berry standard was featured on the band's second album, following Roy Wood's resignation?**

6 What was the title of the band's fourth album, which was the first to feature a full orchestra score?

7 **And a still from which famous Hollywood film was used for the cover to the album?**

8 Which 1975 album featured the singles *Evil Woman* and *Strange Magic*?

9 **Where did Jeff Lynne get the inspiration for the band's new logo, which first appeared on the cover to their 1976 album *A New World Record*?**

10 And which single, taken from this album, starts with the line "Hello, how are you? Have you been alright through all those lonely, lonely, lonely, lonely nights?"?

11 **What was the title of the band's 1977 double album, featuring the songs *Turn To Stone* and *Sweet Talkin' Woman*?**

12 And what was the title of the four-song sub-section from the album, which closed with the single *Mr. Blue Sky*?

13 **Which 1979 album featured the singles *The Diary Of Horace Wimp* and *Confusion*?**

14 Which poorly received film project from 1980 did Jeff Lynne write an award winning title song for?

15 **Which 1983 album featured a spoken introduction, and several link pieces, recorded backwards?**

•ELTON JOHN•

1. **Born on March 25th 1947, what is Elton John's real name?**

2. Which lyricist did Elton John start working with in 1967?

3. **And how many songs had they completed via postal correspondence, before finally meeting each other in person?**

4. What was the title of Elton John's first fully fledged solo single, released in March 1968?

5. **For which band did Elton John play session piano in 1969, appearing on the singles *I Can't Tell The Bottom From The Top* and *He Ain't Heavy, He's My Brother*?**

6. Which 1971 album featured backing vocals by Dusty Springfield?

7. **What middle name did Elton John choose when he formally changed his name by deed poll to Elton John?**

8. For which glam rock single from July 1971 did Elton John appear on *Top of the Pops* providing backing piano?

9. **Which 1972 album featured the hit singles *Crocodile Rock* and *Daniel*?**

10. What was the first hit single to be taken from Elton John's 1973 album *Goodbye Yellow Brick Road*?

11. **Two members of which American vocal band provided backing vocals for Elton John's 1974 single *Don't Let The Sun Go Down On Me*?**

12. Which John Lennon single, from his *Walls And Bridges* album, did Elton John sing backing vocals on?

13. **Which tennis player was the 1975 song *Philadelphia Freedom* written in support for?**

14. What was the title of the largely autobiographical album, released in 1975, which became the first album to enter the US charts at No. 1?

15. **What did Elton John admit to being his real ambition in life, during an interview with Playboy magazine in 1976?**

1 Reginald Kenneth Dwight, 2 Bernie Taupin, **3 Over 20 songs,** 4 *I've Been Loving You Too Long*, **5 The Hollies,** 6 *Tumbleweed Connection*, **7 Hercules,** 8 *Get It On* by T.Rex, **9 *Don't Shoot Me, I'm Only The Piano Player*,** 10 *Saturday Night's Alright For Fighting*, **11 The Beach Boys,** 12 *Whatever Gets You Thru The Night*, **13 Billie Jean King,** 14 *Captain Fantastic And The Brown Dirt Cowboy*, **15 To retire and become chairman of Watford Football Club.**

•ELVIS COSTELLO•

1 Elvis Costello formed his first band in 1973 what were they called?

2 Who produced Elvis Costello's first album?

3 And what was it called?

4 In which year did Elvis Costello first play with his backing band The Attractions?

5 Elvis Costello had his first UK chart entry with which single?

6 Elvis Costello had his biggest hit to date in 1979, what was it?

7 In 1979 Elvis Costello produced which bands first album?

8 In 1980 Elvis Costello had a hit with *I Can't Stand Up For Falling Down*, who recorded the original version?

9 In 1985 Elvis Costello appeared in which Alan Bleasdale TV drama?

10 And what was the name of the theme tune he wrote for it?

11 Which song originally recorded by George Jones did Elvis Costello have a hit with a cover version of?

12 Which John Lennon song did Elvis Costello sing at the 1985 Live Aid concert?

13 Which Animals song did Elvis Costello record a cover version of in 1986?

14 For whose album *Flowers In The Dirt* did Elvis Costello co-write a number of songs?

15 Which member of Squeeze featured on Elvis Costello's album *Trust*?

•ELVIS PRESLEY I•

1 **What was Elvis' middle name, which was mis-spelled on his birth certificate?**

2 How old was he when he was entered into the Mississippi-Alabama fair and dairy show, and came second for singing the song *Old Shep*?

3 **Which town did the Presley family move to in September 1948?**

4 What was Elvis' first job, after graduating high school?

5 **How much did Elvis pay to the Memphis Recording Service to make a private recording for himself, including the songs *My Happiness* and *That's When Your Heartaches Begin* in July 1953?**

6 Who was the owner of the Sun Records label, who showed an interest in Elvis' early recordings?

7 **Which guitarist joined bass player Bill Black to record the first Elvis Presley single?**

8 And what was the title of the first Elvis single to be released?

9 **When the trio performed their first live gig together, under what name did they appear?**

10 In which year did Elvis sign a contract with entrepreneur Col. Tom Parker?

11 **What was the title of the A and B sides of the last single recorded and released on the Sun Records label?**

12 What was the title of the song which became Elvis' first US No. 1?

13 **On which show did Elvis make his US network TV debut?**

14 And on which TV show did Elvis' hip-gyrating performance lead to many letters of complaint?

15 **Which song from 1956 became Elvis' second million selling single, when it reached No. 3 in the US charts?**

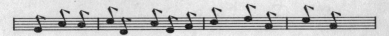

1 **Aaron**, 2 Ten years old, 3 **Memphis**, 4 A truck driver for Crown Electric Company, 5 $4, 6 Sam Phillips, 7 **Scotty Moore**, 8 *That's All Right*, 9 **Blue Moon Boys**, 10 1955, 11 *Mystery Train* and *I Forgot To Remember To Forget*, 12 *Heartbreak Hotel*, 13 *Stage Show*, 14 *The Milton Berle Show*, 15 *I Want You, I Need You, I Love You*.

•ELVIS PRESLEY II•

1 **Which song, taken from Elvis' first feature film, was based on the 19th century folk ballad *Aura Lee*?**

2 On which 1956 TV show were Elvis' appearances watched by over 80% of the US viewing public?

3 **And why was the usual host of the show unable to appear on Elvis' first night?**

4 What was the title of Elvis' second film, originally titled *The Lonesome Cowboy*?

5 **What was the name of the mansion, situated in the Memphis suburb of Whitehaven, bought by Elvis for $102,500 in 1957?**

6 Which Elvis song hit the top of the US charts in 1957, and became the biggest selling single of that year?

7 **What was the title of Elvis' third film, in which he plays the character Vince Everett?**

8 And which famous songwriting team came up with the title track from the film?

9 **When *Loving You* reached No. 24 in the UK charts, how many other singles did he have in the charts at the same time, setting a record?**

10 What important notice was served on Elvis on December 19th 1957?

11 **And which film was he currently making when he received the notice?**

12 Which single from 1958 entered the UK chart at No. 1, becoming the first record in UK history to do this?

13 **What personal tragedy struck Elvis on August 14th, 1958?**

14 Which Frank Sinatra album prevented Elvis' soundtrack album to *King Creole* from reaching No. 1 in the US album charts?

15 **What was the name of the step-daughter of a US Airforce captain, who Elvis first met at the Eagle's Club in Wiesbaden?**

1 **Love Me Tender**, 2 *The Ed Sullivan Show*, 3 He had had a car accident. The show was hosted by Charles Laughton, 4 **Loving You**, 5 **Gracelands**, 6 *All Shook Up*, 7 **Jailhouse Rock**, 8 Jerry Leiber and Mike Stoller, 9 **Six other singles**, 10 A US army draught notice, 11 *King Creole*, 12 **Jailhouse Rock**, 13 His mother died from a heart attack, after a bout of hepatitis, 14 . 15 **Priscilla Beaulieu.**

• ELVIS PRESLEY III •

1 **What rank did Elvis achieve in the army, before being demobbed in 1960?**

2 And at which UK airport did Elvis' plane stop for refuelling, making it the one and only time he was to set foot on UK soil in his lifetime?

3 **Which US singer officially greeted Elvis as he stepped off the plane at the US air base in New Jersey in 1960?**

4 And who hosted the TV special *Welcome Home Elvis*, shown across America in March 1960?

5 **Which single, released with over 1.25 million advanced orders, became the first Elvis single released in stereo?**

6 In which film, co-starring Juliet Prowse, was Elvis cast as US soldier Tulsa McLean?

7 **What did Elvis have removed in a Memphis hospital in June 1960?**

8 In which film from 1960 did Elvis play the part of Pacer Burton, a role turned down by Marlon Brando?

9 **Which US No. One single was based on a 19th century Italian song *O Sole Mio*?**

10 And how many weeks did the single stay at No. 1 in the UK charts?

11 **Which 1960 US No. 1 single for Elvis was originally recorded by Al Jolson?**

12 What was the title of Elvis' 1961 religious album, containing gospel material, which reached No. 13 in the US charts?

13 **And which album, also from 1961, featured one side of ballads and one side of rock and roll numbers?**

14 Which film and huge box office success co-starred Elvis Presley, Joan Blackman and Angela Lansbury?

15 **And which song from the film opens with the line "Wise men say ..."?**

•ELVIS PRESLEY IV•

1 **Which 1962 film featured the songs *Return To Sender* and *Where Do You Come From*?**

2 Which actress co-starred with Elvis in his 1964 film *Viva Las Vegas*?

3 **In which 1964 film does Elvis play dual roles as a US air force officer and his blonder haired relative?**

4 On celebrating their first 10 years together, how much money did Elvis and his manager, Col. Parker, say they had made from his first 17 films?

5 **What was the original US title of the 1965 film, known in the UK as *Harem Holiday*?**

6 Which romantic comedy from 1965, based on a 19th century song, starred Elvis Presley and Donna Douglas?

7 **At which Las Vegas hotel did Elvis marry Priscilla Beaulieu, in May 1967?**

8 In which 1968 film does Elvis play the part of an American Indian?

9 **Which song, taken from the musical *Carousel*, was released by Elvis in 1968 as an Easter special?**

10 Which song, written for the event, provided the finale for Elvis' 1968 TV special?

11 **In 1969, in which city did Elvis perform his first live concert in over 8 years?**

12 Which Elvis single reached No. 1 in the US charts in November 1969 to become his first US No. 1 in over 7 years, and also his last?

13 **Which song became UK No. 1 in August 1970, staying at the top of the charts for 6 weeks?**

14 For what reason was Elvis hospitalised in October 1973 at the Baptist Memorial Hospital in Memphis?

15 **When Elvis was found dead on the floor of his bathroom in 1977, what book had he apparently been reading?**

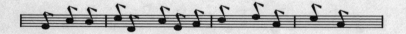

1 *Girls! Girls! Girls!*, 2 Ann-Margret, 3 *Kissin' Cousins*, 4 $135 million, 5 *Harum Scarum*, 6 *Frankie And Johnny*, 7 The Aladdin Hotel, 8 *Stay Away Joe*, 9 *You'll Never Walk Alone*, 10 *If I Can Dream*, 11 Las Vegas, 12 *Suspicious Minds*, 13 *The Wonder Of You*, 14 He had pneumonia, 15 The Scientific Search For The Face Of Jesus.

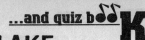
•EMERSON LAKE
AND PALMER•

1 Which member of the trio played the bass, as well as producing all the band's albums?

2 Which band had keyboard player Keith Emerson played with during the late 1960's, having had a UK hit with the song *America*?

3 At which venue did the band make their debut live performance?

4 And which British festival did the band appear at, just 4 days after their debut?

5 Which piano suite, written by Russian composer Moussorgsky, did the band arrange and perform live, releasing the recordings as a budget album in 1971?

6 Which US band had the original hit with the song *Nut Rocker*, released by the band as a single in 1972?

7 What was the title of the band's 1971 concept album, which reached No. 1 in the UK charts?

8 In what unusual way was Keith Emerson injured during the band's 1973 US tour?

9 What was the title of the band's fourth album, which featured the single *From The Beginning*?

10 What was the name of the record label, formed by the group in 1973?

11 What was the title of the band's 1973 album, which featured a cover design by Alien creator H.R.Giger?

12 Which member of the group had a solo hit in 1975 with the seasonal song *I Believe In Father Christmas*?

13 Which 1977 Emerson, Lake and Palmer double album consisted of three sides of solo material, with only the fourth side featuring the whole group?

14 And which arrangement of an Aaron Copland composition, taken from the album, reached No. 2 in the UK charts?

15 Which album, released in 1978, became the last studio album the band would record?

1 Greg Lake, 2 The Nice, **3 The Plymouth Guildhall in Devon, 4 The** Isle Of Wight Festival, **5 *Pictures At An Exhibition*, 6** B.Bumble And The Stingers, **7 *Tarkus*, 8** His piano was rigged to explode as part of a pyrotechnical stunt, but it was set off at the wrong time, **9 *Trilogy*, 10** Manticore, **11 *Brain Salad Surgery*, 12** Greg Lake, **13 *Works*, 14** Fanfare For The Common Man, **15** Love Beach.

•ERIC CLAPTON•

1 In 1963 Eric Clapton became lead guitarist with which group?

2 Which group did Eric Clapton form in 1966?

3 In 1969 which group did Eric Clapton form with Steve Winwood?

4 Who was the song *Layla* written about?

5 Who was Eric Clapton joined on stage by during a concert in Atlanta USA?

6 Eric Clapton was given his nickname in 1963 by Georgio Gomelsky, what is it?

7 In 1974 Eric Clapton had a hit with a cover version of a Bob Marley song, what was it?

8 Who produced Eric Clapton's 1986 album *August*?

9 In which 1986 film did Eric Clapton make a cameo appearance?

10 Which BRIT award did Eric Clapton receive in 1987?

11 Which single did Eric Clapton record with Elton John in 1992?

12 Who did Eric Clapton join on stage at Nelson Mandela's 70th Birthday Tribute Concert at Wembley in 1988?

13 In 1987 Eric Clapton teamed up with Michael Kamen to write the score for which Mel Gibson film?

14 Who co-wrote Eric Clapton's single *Lay Down Sally*?

15 The ballad inspired by Eric Clapton's son *Tears In Heaven* was originally written for which movie?

1 **The Yardbirds** , 2 Cream, 3 **Blind Faith**, 4 George Harrison's wife Patti,
5 **Pete Townshend and Keith Moon**, 6 Slowhand, 7 *I Shot The Sheriff*,
8 Phil Collins, 9 *Water*, 10 Outstanding Contribution To British Music,
11 *Runaway Train*, 12 Dire Straits, 13 *Lethal Weapon* , 14 Marcella
Detroit, 15 *Rush*.

• EURYTHMICS •

1 What was the name of the band Annie Lennox and Dave Stewart were members of before forming Eurythmics?

2 And what was the title of their 1979 UK Top Ten hit?

3 The Eurythmics made their debut on the UK chart in 1981 with which single?

4 What was the title of the Eurythmics only UK No.1?

5 Who did Annie Lennox record the duet *Sisters Are Doin' It For Themselves* with?

6 In 1988 Dave Stewart launched his own record label, what was it called?

7 Which film featured Annie Lennox and Al Green's duet *Put A Little Love In Your Heart*?

8 What was the name of the band Dave Stewart formed in 1990?

9 For which 1990 UK Top Ten hit did Dave Stewart team up with saxophonist Candy Dulfer?

10 Which group did Dave Stewart form with ex-Specials vocalist Terry Hall in 1992?

11 What was Annie Lennox's first UK Top Ten solo hit called?

12 Annie Lennox's 1992 album entered the UK chart at No.1 what was it?

13 Which track did Annie Lennox contribute to the AIDS charity album of Cole Porter songs *Red Hot & Blue*?

14 With whom did Annie Lennox record the duet *Something So Right*?

15 Which instrument did Annie Lennox play on the single *There Must Be An Angel (Playing With My Heart)*?

1 The Tourists, 2 I Only Want To Be With You, **3 Never Gonna Cry Again,** 4 There Must Be An Angel (Playing With My Heart), **5 Aretha Franklin,** 6 Anxious, **7 Scrooged,** 8 The Spiritual Cowboys, 9 Lily Was Here, **10 Vegas,** 11 Why, 12 Diva, **13 Ev'ry Time we Say Goodbye,** 14 Paul Simon, **15 Harmonica.**

• EXTREME •

1   **Formed in 1988, which US city did the band come from?**

2   In which country was the group's guitarist, Nuno Bettencourt, born?

3   **Which song, taken from the group's eponymous debut album, was featured in the 1989 film *Bill And Ted's Exellent Adventure*?**

4   What was the title of the group's second album, released in 1991?

5   **Which single, taken from the group's second album, reached No. 1 in the US charts in March 1991?**

6   And which record prevented the single from getting to No. 1 in the UK, where it stayed at No. 2 for several weeks?

7   **Which tribute concert did the band appear at, in 1992?**

8   What was the name of the band's 1992 album, which featured three distinct sections of music?

9   **And what was the title to the third section of the album, which consisted of a progressive rock style suite of songs?**

10   Which single, taken from the album, reached No. 15 in the UK charts in 1993?

11   **What was the title of the Kiss tribute album, for which the band contributed the old Kiss song *Strutter*?**

12   Which record label was formed in 1994 by the band's guitarist, Nuno Bettencourt?

13   **Which member of the band announced he was to leave, in April 1994?**

14   What was the title of the band's 1995 album, which was to be the last before the group dis-banded?

15   **Which band did Gary Cherone go on to sing for in 1996, after the group split up?**

1 Boston, 2 Portugal, 3 *Play With Me*, 4 *Pornograffitti*, 5 *More Than Words*, 6 Bryan Adams' (*Everything I Do*) *I Do It For You*, 7 The Concert For Life tribute to Freddie Mercury at Wembley Stadium, 8 *III Sides To The Story*, 9 *Everything Under The Sun*, 10 *Tragic Comic*, 11 *Kiss My Ass*, 12 Colorblind Records, 13 The drummer, Paul Geary, 14 *Waiting For The Punchline*, 15 Van Halen.

• FATS DOMINO •

1 **How was Fats Domino's career almost halted, when he was 14?**

2 Which song did Fats Domino record as his debut for Imperial Records?

3 **Which song, released in 1951, reached No. 9 in the US R&B charts?**

4 Which 1952 single became Fats Domino's second million selling record?

5 **Which single gave Fats Domino his first crossover hit, when it reached No. 10 in the regular US chart in 1955?**

6 And which white artist had a No. 2 hit in the US with the same song?

7 **Which Rock and Roll standard was a No. 3 US hit when recorded by Fats Domino in 1956?**

8 And which song, released in 1957, replaced this single at No. 1 in the US R&B charts?

9 **In which 1956 musical film did Fats Domino appear, performing the songs *I'm In Love Again* and *Honey Chile*?**

10 And in which 1957 film does Fats Domino appear, playing the song *Wait And See*?

11 **Which 1958 single, taken from the film of the same name, reached US No. 26?**

12 Which double A-side reached No. 50 in the US charts for Fats Domino in 1959?

13 **What was the title of the flip side of his 1960 single *Walking To New Orleans*, which became Fats Domino's last million seller, reaching No. 21 in the US charts?**

14 Which re-recording of a 1952 hit for Hank Williams reached No. 30 in the US charts for Fats Domino in 1962?

15 **Which Beatles single did Fats Domino record in 1968, only reaching No. 100 in the US charts?**

1 His fingers were almost chopped off in an accident at the bed factory where he worked, 2 *The Fat Man*, 3 *Rockin' Chair*, 4 *Goin' Home*, 5 *Ain't That A Shame*, 6 Pat Boone, 7 *Blueberry Hill*, 8 *Blue Monday*, 9 *Shake, Rattle and Rock*, 10 *Jamboree*, 11 *The Big Beat*, 12 *Telling Lies/When The Saints Go Marching In*, 13 *Don't Come Knocking*, 14 *Jambalaya (On The Bayou)*, 15 *Lady Madonna*.

• FLEETWOOD MAC •

1 Who were the original drummer and bassist who gave their names to the group?

2 And what was the name of the original blues guitarist who was part of the original line up?

3 Which American band covered one of the group's early singles, *Black Magic Woman*?

4 Following line up changes, what was the title of the group's 1970 album, named after the country location where the album was written?

5 What was the name of John McVie's wife, who joined the band for their next album, *Future Games*?

6 Which American couple joined the band in 1975, contributing the songs *Monday Morning* and *Rhiannon*?

7 Which album from 1977 became one of the biggest selling albums in the world?

8 And which sport is introduced on television with the track *The Chain* from this album?

9 Which single, taken from the group's 1979 album with the same name, featured the sound of the USC Trojan Marching Band?

10 Which member of the group produced all the band's records from this period?

11 And what was the title of the 1982 album, after which the band agreed to continue with solo projects?

12 What was the title of Stevie Nicks' solo album, released in 1983?

13 Which member of the band filed for bankruptcy in 1984?

14 What was the title of the 1987 Fleetwood Mac album, the first to be released for 5 years?

15 And what was the name of the first song to be released as a single from the album?

•FOREIGNER•

1 **Why did the band choose the name Foreigner?**

2 What was the title of the band's debut single, which reached No. 4 in the US charts in 1977?

3 **And which single, also released from the band's debut album, reached No. 6 in the US, as well as hitting the Top 30 in the UK?**

4 Which album, released by Foreigner in 1978, reached No. 3 in the US charts, and went on to sell over 5 million copies in the US?

5 **Which bassist, formerly with Roxy Music and The Small Faces, joined the band in 1979?**

6 Which album was the band's 1979 US No. 12 hit *Dirty White Boy* taken from?

7 **Which two members of the group left in 1980, with the group resuming as a 4-piece?**

8 What was the title of their 1981 album, produced by Mutt Lange, which stayed at No. 1 in the US for 10 weeks?

9 **Which single, released in 1981, reached No. 2 in the US charts, and stayed there for 10 weeks?**

10 And which single prevented it from reaching No. 1?

11 **Which Gospel orientated single reached No. 1 in the UK and US in 1985?**

12 And which No. 1 album had the song been taken from?

13 **Which member of the group released the solo album *Ready Or Not* in 1987?**

14 And which single, taken from the album, reached No. 5 in the US charts?

15 **Which vocalist joined the band in 1991 for the album *Unusual Heat*?**

• FRANK ZAPPA •

1 With which future solo artist did Frank Zappa form the band The Black-Outs in 1956?

2 What was the name of Frank Zappa's band, which recorded the debut album *Freak Out!* In 1965?

3 Which album, released in 1968, featured a cover design which parodied the Beatles' *Sgt. Pepper* album?

4 What was the title of Frank Zappa's 1969 solo album, released after breaking up his touring band?

5 And what reason did he give for breaking up the band?

6 Which British concert venue banned Frank Zappa from performing a proposed show in 1971, due to the obscene nature of some of the lyrics?

7 And which 1970 album, containing the obscene lyrics which were objected to, was the show intended to promote?

8 Which ex-Beatle joined Frank Zappa on stage at the Fillmore East venue in New York in 1971?

9 How was Frank Zappa injured during a concert at the Rainbow in London, resulting in him spending 9 months in a wheelchair?

10 What was the title of Frank Zappa's 1974 solo album, featuring bass work from ex-Cream member, Jack Bruce?

11 Which album, released in 1975, contained material by Frank Zappa, The Mothers Of Invention and Captain Beefheart?

12 Which 1979 album had a title which parodied the title of a No. 1 single by KC And The Sunshine Band?

13 What was the title of Frank Zappa's 1979 album, which was followed up by a double album, released in 1980?

14 And which technical guitarist featured on this 1980 double album?

15 Which album, released in 1982, featured vocals by Frank Zappa's daughter, Moon Unit?

1 Captain Beefheart (Don Van Vliet), 2 The Mothers Of Invention,
3 *We're Only in It For The Money*, 4 *Hot Rats*, 5 He said he was tired
of playing for people who clap for all the wrong reasons, 6 The Albert
Hall, 7 *200 Motels*, 8 John Lennon, 9 A fan pushed him off stage, and
into the orchestra pit, 10 *Apostrophe*, 11 *Bongo Fury*, 12 *Sheik
Yerbouti* (The single being *Shake Your Bootie*), 13 *Joe's Garage, Act I*
(*Joe's Garage Acts II and III* was released the following year),
14 Steve Vai, 15 *Ship Arriving Too Late To Save A Drowning Witch.*

• FREE •

1 **Who joined Free in 1968 after being fired from John Mayall's Bluesbreakers?**

2 Who named the group after his own 60's band 'Free At Last'?

3 **What was the title of Free's debut chart single released in 1970?**

4 And from which album was it taken?

5 **In 1969 Free toured the USA as support act to which group?**

6 When Free temporarily split in 1971 which band did Paul Rodgers form?

7 **And who did they tour the UK with in the same year?**

8 In which year did Free re-form?

9 **Who left the group in 1972 to form Sharks?**

10 Why was the band's tour cancelled for eight days in 1972?

11 **What was the name of the band Paul Kossoff formed in 1974?**

12 Before forming bad company which band did Paul Rodgers turn down an offer to join?

13 **Which member of the band died of heart failure on a flight from Los Angeles in 1976?**

14 Which member of the band had a minor hit in 1982 with *Do You Love Me*?

15 **In 1991 the band's *Alright Now* was re-released to coincide with it's use in a TV commercial, what was it advertising?**

1 **Andy Fraser**, 2 Alexis Corner, 3 *All Right Now*, 4 *Fire And Water*, 5 **Blind Faith**, 6 Peace, 7 **Mott The Hoople**, 8 1971, 9 Andy Fraser, 10 Paul Kossoff was knocked out on stage during rehearsals, 11 **Back Street Crawler**, 12 Deep Purple, 13 **Paul Kossoff**, 14 Andy Fraser, 15 **Wrigleys Chewing Gum.**

•GARY NUMAN•

1 **What was the name of the group Gary Numan formed in 1977 before changing the name to Tubeway Army?**

2 Tubeway Army's debut single reached UK No.1, what was it called?

3 **Gary Numan's first solo single also reached UK No. 1 what was it?**

4 What was the title of Gary Numan's first solo album?

5 **In 1980 Gary Numan featured on whose album *Clues*?**

6 What was the name of Gary Numan's own record label?

7 **Which Gary Numan album featured Queen's Roger Taylor?**

8 Which ex-Kajagoogoo member joined Gary Numan's touring troupe in 1991?

9 **Gary Numan was featured singing on a TV commercial in 1977 what was it for?**

10 Who did Gary Numan support on their 1993 tour?

11 **What was Gary Numan famous for wearing on stage?**

12 On whose TV show did the Gary Numan song *I Die : You Die* premiere?

13 **In which year did Gary Numan announce he was to retire from live work?**

14 What did Gary Numan attempt in 1981?

15 **What is Gary Numan's real name?**

•GENESIS•

1 **Two groups joined together to form Genesis. What were they called?**

2 Genesis were named and originally produced by who?

3 **In 1969 the band temporarily used which name so as not to be confused with the American group Genesis which later split up?**

4 In which year did Phil Collins join Genesis after auditioning with 14 others through a *Melody Makers* advert?

5 **In 1977 which member of the Royal family attended the London film premiere of *Genesis In Concert*?**

6 In 1978 Genesis had their first UK Top Ten hit, what was it?

7 **Which group featured on *Paperlate*, which was part of Genesis' *3x3* EP?**

8 In the 80's Mike Rutherford formed a successful side-band, what were they called?

9 **In 1984 Genesis had a hit with *In Too Deep* in which film was it featured?**

10 Genesis filmed a documentary for the BBC, what was it called?

11 **Who replaced Phil Collins when he left Genesis in 1996?**

12 On which Genesis album was *Turn It On Again*?

13 **In which year did Peter Gabriel leave Genesis?**

14 Which other band did Phil Collins belong to alongside Genesis?

15 **In 1983 all members of Genesis won which Ivor Novello award?**

•GEORGE HARRISON•

1 **What was the title of George Harrison's experimental album, released in 1969, featuring the new Moog synthesiser?**

2 Who produced George Harrison's 1971 triple album box set, *All Things Must Pass*?

3 **And what was the title given to the third LP in the set, which consisted of an all-star impromptu jamming session?**

4 Which US No. 1 single for George Harrison was judged to have been plagiarised from a 1963 song, *He's So Fine*?

5 **For which Beatles song was George Harrison awarded an Ivor Novello award in 1971?**

6 Who persuaded George Harrison to organise a benefit concert in aid of the victims of the famine and war in Bangladesh?

7 **What was the title of his 1973 album, which featured the hit single *Give Me Love (Give Me Peace On Earth)*?**

8 What was the name of George Harrison's own record label, which he set up in 1974?

9 **And who became the first artist to sign with the new label?**

10 Which record company sued George Harrison in 1976, for non delivery of a new album?

11 **What was the title of the 1978 Beatle spoof, written by Eric Idle and Neil Innes, in which George Harrison appears, in a cameo role, as a reporter?**

12 Which film company was set up in 1979 by George Harrison and US businessman, Denis O'Brien?

13 **What was the title of George Harrison's autobiography, published in 1979?**

14 Which single, released in 1981, was recorded as a tribute to John Lennon?

15 **Which British musician collaborated with George Harrison on his 1987 album *Cloud 9*?**

1 *Electronic Sounds*, **2** Phil Spector, **3** *Apple Jam*, **4** *My Sweet Lord*, **5** *Something*, **6** Ravi Shankar, **7** *Living In The Material World*, **8** Dark Horse, **9** Ravi Shankar, **10** A&M Records, **11** *The Rutles - All You Need Is Cash*, **12** Handmade Films, **13** *I, Me, Mine*, **14** *All Those Years Ago*, **15** Jeff Lynne.

• GUNS 'N' ROSES 1 •

1. **Where did lead singer Axl Rose get his first name from?**

2. When Axl Rose met up with old friend Izzy Stradlin in Los Angeles, what medical experiment did they partake in, to earn enough to live on?

3. **Which guitarist did the pair join up with, to form the band known firstly as Rose, then Hollywood Rose and finally L.A. Guns?**

4. At which Los Angeles club did guitarist Slash first see Axl Rose's group, before being asked to join?

5. **And what role did Slash's father play in the music business?**

6. What was the title of the band's four track EP, released in 1986?

7. **Which British band's 1987 US tour did Guns 'N' Roses open for?**

8. And why did the group pull out of the tour half way through?

9. **What was the title of the band's debut album, released in August 1987?**

10. And how many weeks did the album stay on the chart, before finally reaching No. 1 in the US?

11. **During a 5 day tour of the UK in 1987, which member of the band broke his hand in a bar brawl?**

12. Which US rock band did Guns'N'Roses support during a stadium tour in 1988?

13. **And what activities had to be confined to the band's own dressing room, according to a clause in their tour contract?**

14. At which UK venue were two fans killed during Guns 'N' Roses set?

15. **Which of the band's songs was used in the 1988 Clint Eastwood film *Dead Pool*?**

15 Welcome To The Jungle.
Aerosmith, **14** The Monsters Of Rock Festival at Castle Donnington,
drug use, so as not to tempt the recently 'cleaned up' members of
10 **57 weeks, 11 Steven Adler, the drummer, 12** Aerosmith, **13** Any
7 **Iron Maiden, 8** Axl Rose lost his voice, 9 ***Appetite For Destruction,***
4 Gazzarri's, **5 He designed album covers, 6** *Live ?!*@ *Like A Suicide,*
for 8$ per hour, as part of an experiment for UCLA, **3 Tracii Guns,**
1 **A local Indiana band he once played with, 2** They smoked cigarettes

•GUNS 'N' ROSES II•

1 **Which song, taken from *Appetite For Destruction*, reached No. 6 in the UK charts in a four-minute long edited version?**

2 Which member of the band was arrested and charged with making a public disturbance, after urinating in the aisle of an aeroplane in 1989?

3 **And which two members of the group caused controversy at the 1990 American Music Awards, after their drunken swearing was broadcast live?**

4 Who married Axl Rose in Las Vegas, in April 1990?

5 **And how long did the marriage last, before Axl Rose filed for divorce, claiming irreconcilable differences?**

6 Which Bob Dylan song, covered by the band, was featured in the Tom Cruise film *Days Of Thunder*?

7 **Which member of the group was sacked in 1990 by the other members for a combination of poor playing technique and drug dependence?**

8 And which former member of British band The Cult replaced him?

9 **Which 1991 film featured the Guns 'N' Roses song *You Could Be Mine*?**

10 And which film theme tune did the band cover in 1991, reaching No. 5 in the UK singles chart?

11 **What were the titles of the band's two studio double albums, which set a record when they were released simultaneously in September 1991?**

12 Which Michael Jackson single from the album *Dangerous* featured guitar work by Slash?

13 **Which member of the band announced he was to leave in 1992, because he was tired of touring and making videos?**

14 What was the title of the band's 1993 album, containing cover versions of punk songs?

15 **Which Rolling Stones cover version did the band record for the 1995 film *Interview With The Vampire*?**

1 *Sweet Child 'O Mine*, 2 Izzy Stradlin, 3 Slash and bass player Duff McKagan, 4 Erin Invicta Everly, daughter of singer Don Everly, 5 26 days, 6 Knockin' On Heaven's Door, 7 **Drummer Steven Adler**, 8 Matt Sorum, 9 *Terminator 2*, 10 Live And Let Die, 11 *Use Your Illusion I and II*, 12 Black And White, 13 Izzy Stradlin, 14 The Spaghetti Incident, 15 *Sympathy For The Devil*.

~ 66 ~

• HEART •

1 **By what name were Heart originally known?**

2 In 1975 Heart released their debut album what was it called?

3 **On which BBC show did Heart make their UK TV debut?**

4 In 1984 Ann Wilson recorded the duet *Almost Paradise* with Mike Reno, which was the love theme to which film?

5 **In 1981 Heart recorded a cover version of an Aaron Neville hit , what was it?**

6 In 1982 who joined the group as a replacement for Steve Fossen?

7 **In 1982 with which group did Heart tour UK with as support act?**

8 Heart made their debut on the UK chart in 1986 with which single?

9 **And who had rejected the song?**

10 What was Heart's first UK Top Ten single?

11 **Who supported Heart on their 1988 US tour?**

12 Which Ann Wilson solo song featured in the Eddie Murphy film *Golden Child*?

13 **Which track did Ann and Nancy Wilson contribute to the Disney album *For Our Children*?**

14 Which Heart UK Top Ten single was originally offered to Don Henley?

15 **Which extra-curricular group did Nancy and Ann form in 1992?**

1 The Army, 2 *Dreamboat Annie,* **3 *The Old Grey Whistle Test,*** 4 *Footloose,* **5 *Tell It Like It Is,*** 6 *Mark Andes,* **7 *Queen,*** 8 *These Dreams,* **9 *Stevie Nicks,*** 10 *Alone,* **11 *Michael Bolton,*** 12 *The Best Man In The World,* **13 *Autumn To May,*** 14 *All I Wanna Do Is Make Love To You,* **15 The Lovemongers.**

• HOT CHOCOLATE •

1 **Formed in London in 1969, which John Lennon song, recorded in a reggae style, became their first single?**

2 What are the names of the vocalist and bass player with the band who, together, wrote most of the band's material?

3 **Which famous record producer signed the band in 1970, and worked with them for much of their career?**

4 Which song, released in 1970, became the band's first hit, reaching No. 6 in the UK charts?

5 **Which song, released in 1974, reached No. 3 in the UK singles chart?**

6 And which album had the song been taken from?

7 **Which single, taken from the band's 1975 eponymous album, reached No. 3 in the US and No. 2 in the UK?**

8 Which single became the band's first No. 1, hitting the top of the UK charts in July 1977?

9 **Which title track from the band's 1978 album reached No. 12 in the UK charts?**

10 Which single became the band's tenth Top Ten UK record, when it reached No. 7 in May 1982?

11 **Which single, released in 1984, was the last new recording to be released by the band, before announcing their split in 1987?**

12 And how many UK chart singles had the group managed to record in their 14 year history?

13 **What was the title of Errol Brown's 1987 debut solo single?**

14 What was the title of Errol Brown's 1990 Christmas single, which failed to chart?

15 **And who had produced this single for Errol Brown?**

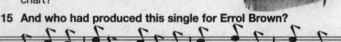

1 **Give Peace A Chance**, 2 Errol Brown and Tony Wilson, 3 **Mickie Most**, 4 Love Is Life, 5 **Emma**, 6 Cicero Park, 7 You Sexy Thing, 8 So You Win Again, 9 **Every 1's A Winner**, 10 Girl Crazy, 11 I Gave You My Heart (Didn't I), 12 30 chart singles, 13 Personal Touch, 14 Send A Prayer, 15 **Stock, Aitken and Waterman.**

•IGGY POP•

1 **What is Iggy Pop's real name?**

2 Which band was Iggy Pop a member of in the late 60's early 70's?

3 **In 1977 Iggy Pop released his first solo album, what was it?**

4 In 1977 who supported Iggy Pop and David Bowie on tour in 1977?

5 **What was the Iggy Pop song *The Passenger* inspired by?**

6 In which 1987 film did Iggy Pop make a cameo appearance?

7 **In 1986 Iggy Pop had his first UK Top Ten hit, what was it called?**

8 And who recorded the original version of the song?

9 **With whom did Iggy Pop record the duet *Well Did You Evah!* in 1991?**

10 In 1991 Iggy Pop played the part of Vincent Bugliosi in which opera?

11 **Which song did Iggy Pop perform at the 1994 Elvis Tribute concert?**

12 Which David Bowie Hit Single first appeared on Iggy Pop's first album?

13 **Which Iggy Pop single featured in the film *Trainspotting*?**

14 Who was Iggy Pop's only visitor while he was in a mental home in 1975?

15 **Who recorded a version of Iggy Pop's *The Passenger* in 1998?**

1 James Osterberg, 2 The Stooges, 3 *The Idiot*, 4 Blondie, 5 A Jim
Morrison poem, 6 *The Color Of Money*, 7 *Real Wild Child (Wild One)*,
8 Johnny O'Keefe, 9 Deborah Harry, 10 *The Manson Family*, 11 *Rip It
Up*, 12 *China Girl*, 13 *Lust For Life*, 14 David Bowie, 15 REM.

• INXS •

1 **By what name were INXS originally known?**

2 In 1983 INXS toured North America as guests of which two groups?

3 **Michael Hutchence made his acting debut in 1986, in which film?**

4 And what was the name of his solo Australian hit from the film?

5 **In 1986 who did INXS support at Wembley Stadium?**

6 In 1988 INXS had their first UK Top Ten hit, what was it?

7 **In 1989 Michael Hutchence formed a duo alongside INXS what was it called?**

8 Which part did Michael Hutchence play in the film *Frankenstein Unbound*?

9 **Which harmonica player featured on the INXS album *X*?**

10 Which BRIT award did INXS win in 1991?

11 **In 1991 an INXS album entered the UK charts at No.1. What was it?**

12 Which INXS song featured on the 1992 summer olympics collection *Barcelona Gold*?

13 **Who featured as uncredited artist on the single *Please (You Got That ---)*?**

14 Which 1995 film soundtrack featured a solo track by Michael Hutchence?

15 **In 1988 INXS released a video compilation, What was it called?**

•IRON MAIDEN•

1 What is the name of the group's bass player, who founded the group after meeting guitarist Dave Murray in 1976?

2 Which song was released as the band's first single, in 1980?

3 And how did the band's performance of the song on BBC's *Top Of The Pops* break with the current tradition of the programme?

4 What was the name of the band's graphic designer, who was responsible for the album cover artwork on all the band's releases?

5 And what was the name of the band's psychotic, skeletal mascot?

6 What was the title of Iron Maiden's second single, whose cover featured Margaret Thatcher being attacked by the band mascot?

7 Which guitarist joined the band in 1980, following the sacking of Dennis Stratton?

8 What was the title of the band's second album, featuring the songs *Wrathchild* and *Murders In The Rue Morgue*?

9 Which singer joined the band in 1981, replacing the original vocalist Paul Di'anno?

10 What was the name of the first album to be recorded by this new line up?

11 And which cult 1960's TV series inspired a song on the album?

12 Which album was the band's 1983 single *Flight Of Icarus* taken from?

13 Which 1984 album, and accompanying world tour, featured Egyptian influenced artwork?

14 And what was the title of the double album live set, recorded in 1985, during the band's year long promotional tour?

15 Which song, from the group's 1986 album *Somewhere In Time*, was inspired by a book by Alan Sillitoe?

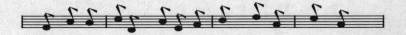

1 Steve Harris, 2 *Running Free*, **3 They insisted on playing the song live – the first time since The Who did the same in 1973**, 4 Derek Riggs, **5 Eddie**, 6 *Sanctuary* (The artwork prompted legal action, and subsequent prints had to have Margaret Thatcher's identity obscured), **7 Adrian Smith**, 8 *Killers*, **9 Bruce Dickinson**, 10 *The Number Of The Beast*, **11 The Prisoner**, 12 *Piece Of Mind*, 13 **Powerslave**, 14 *Live After Death*, 15 *The Loneliness Of The Long Distance Runner*.

• JAMES BROWN •

1 Abandoned by his mother at 4 years old and raised by his aunt, what sort of establishment did James Brown grow up in?

2 What was the name of James Brown's backing band, with which he recorded his first acetate, *Please, Please, Please*?

3 Recorded in 1958, which song became James Brown's first national chart success?

4 Which song, released in 1960, became James Brown's third million selling single?

5 At which New York venue was James Brown's 1962 live act recorded for release as an album?

6 Which song, formerly a hit for Perry Como and Billy Eckstine, reached No. 18 in the US charts for James Brown in 1963?

7 What was the title of the instrumental album, released in 1965, featuring the tracks *Mister Hip* and *Who's Afraid Of Virginia Woolf*?

8 Which single, released in 1965, became James Brown's first UK chart hit, reaching No. 25?

9 And which single, which reached No. 3 in the US charts in 1965, was originally titled *I Found You*?

10 Which British TV music show devoted a whole program to James Brown in March 1966?

11 Which soulful single, released in 1966, reached No. 8 in the US and No. 13 in the UK?

12 What was the title of the song recorded by James Brown, as part of the US Government's Stay In School campaign?

13 What was the first single to be released, following the replacement of The Famous Flames bandleader by Alfred Ellis?

14 For what reason did James Brown make a television appeal for calm and restraint, in April 1968?

15 And what was the title of the 1968 single which featured a patriotic spoken narration by James Brown?

1 A **bordello, run by his aunt,** 2 The Famous Flames , 3 *Try Me* **(I Need You)**, 4 *Think*, 5 **The Apollo Theatre in Harlem,** 6 *Prisoner Of Love,* 7 **Grits And Soul,** 8 *Papa's Got A Brand New Bag,* 9 *I Got You* **(I Feel Good)**, 10 *Ready Steady Go,* 11 *It's A Man's Man's World*, 12 *Don't Be A Drop Out,* 13 **Cold Sweat,** 14 The rioting in many US cities following the assassination of Martin Luther King, 15 *America Is My Home*.

• JAMES •

1 **What did Tim Booth originally join the group as?**

2 In 1985 James declined an offer to appear on the front cover of which magazine as the year's brightest prospect?

3 **James released their debut album in 1986 what was it called?**

4 What was the title of the album James recorded with Brian Eno?

5 **In 1985 who did James accept a support slot with on their UK tour?**

6 Dave Baynton-Power joined the group in 1990 who did he replace?

7 **James had their first UK Top Ten hit in 1991, what was it?**

8 Who did James replace at the 1992 Glastonbury Festival?

9 **Who did Tim Booth team up with for the one-off Booth And The Bad Angel?**

10 In 1997 James had a UK Top Ten hit, their first since 1991, what was it?

11 **What was the title of James' 1992 EP?**

12 Who wrote the James track *Sunday Morning*?

13 **Which re-mixed single did James release in 1999?**

14 In which year were James formed?

15 **Which instrument does Jim Glennie play?**

• JANET JACKSON •

1 **In which US TV show did Janet Jackson play the role of Penny Gordon Woods?**

2 In which year did she release her debut album?

3 **Which song, taken from her 1984 album *Dream Street*, was sung as a duet with Cliff Richard?**

4 Which album, released in 1986, featured the singles *What Have You Done For Me Lately*? and *Nasty*?

5 **Who directed the video to Janet Jackson's US No. 1 *When I Think Of You*?**

6 And which future US solo artist choreographed the dance pieces featured in several Janet Jackson videos?

7 **Which single, released in 1989, reached No. 1 in the US charts?**

8 And which album was this single taken from?

9 **What was the value of the record deal, signed by Janet Jackson with Virgin Records, in 1991?**

10 Which duet with Luther Vandross reached No. 2 in the UK in 1992?

11 **And which film was the song taken from?**

12 Which single, released in 1993, stayed at No. 1 in the US charts for 8 weeks?

13 **In which 1993 film, directed by John Singleton, did Janet Jackson make her film debut?**

14 Which 1995 song, reaching No. 5 in the US charts, was a duet between Janet and her brother Michael Jackson?

15 **What was the title of Janet Jackson's 1995 compilation album, including a new single, *Runaway*?**

1 Good Times, 2 1982, **3 Two To The Power, 4** Control, **5** Julien Temple, **6** Paula Abdul, **7 Miss You Much, 8** Rhythm Nation 1814, **9** $50 million, **10** The Best Things In Life Are Free, **11 Mo' Money, 12** That's The Way Love Goes, **13 Poetic Justice, 14** Scream, **15 Design Of A Decade 1986/1996.**

~ 74 ~

• JANIS JOPLIN •

1 **Which US state was Janis Joplin born in?**

2 And which famous psychedelic band, from the same state, did she almost join in 1965, before moving to San Francisco?

3 **While at college, what did fellow students cruelly vote her, in an end of year poll, due to her plain looks?**

4 What was the name of the band she joined shortly after moving to San Francisco?

5 **And which famous San Francisco nightclub were they the house band for?**

6 At which international pop festival did Janis Joplin with Big Brother And The Holding Company give a famous show-stopping performance?

7 **And which US pop singer can be seen, in the film to the festival, looking stunned at Janis Joplin's performance, and simply mouthing "Wow"?**

8 What was the original title to the 1968 album, shortened on the insistence of the record company, to *Cheap Thrills*?

9 **Who became Janis Joplin's new backing band in 1969?**

10 And, after an unsuccessful tour with this band, what was the name of the backing band she formed and toured with in 1970?

11 **How did Janis Joplin pay tribute to dead blues singer Bessie Smith, who she cited as the major influence on her singing?**

12 At which Hollywood hotel was Janis Joplin found dead in October 1970?

13 **And what was found to be the cause of her death?**

14 Which single, released after her death, made No. 1 in the US?

15 **And by what nickname was she often known, which was used as the title of the album, released after her death?**

1 Texas, 2 The 13th Floor Elevators, **3 The ugliest man on campus,** 4 Big Brother And The Holding Company, **5 The Avalon Ballroom,** 6 Monterey International Pop Festival, **7 Mama Cass Elliot,** of the **Mamas and Papas,** 8 *Dope, Sex and Cheap Thrills*, **9 The Kozmic Blues Band,** 10 The Full Tilt Boogie Band, **11 She bought a headstone for the grave of the singer,** 12 The Landmark Hotel, **13 An accidental overdose of heroin,** 14 *Me And Bobby McGee*, **15 Pearl.**

• JEFFERSON AIRPLANE •

1 What was the title of the band's first single, released in 1966?

2 Who became the group's new lead singer in 1966, when original singer, Signe Anderson, left to have a baby?

3 And what was the name of the band she had just left?

4 Along with *Somebody To Love*, which other song did she bring with her from her old band?

5 **And, according to this song, what do "the pills that mother gives you" do?**

6 What was the title of the group's 1967 album, featuring the songs *My Best Friend* and *Plastic Fantastic Lover*?

7 **On their 1968 album, *Crown Of Creation*, which ex-member of The Byrds wrote the song *Triad*, a song about a ménage à trois?**

8 What was the title of the group's 1969 live album, recorded at the famous Fillmore East and Fillmore West venues?

9 **What did singer Grace Slick and guitarist Paul Kantner initially name their daughter, born in 1971?**

10 And what name did they finally decide on giving to her?

11 **And what was the title of the 1972 album, featuring their daughter on the cover?**

12 After much personal wrangling, in which year did the group re-form, under the name Jefferson Starship?

13 **And what was the title of the first album the band released under this name?**

14 What was the first single to be released by a new incarnation of Starship, fronted by Grace Slick, after more line up changes?

15 **And what was the title of the album which featured the song?**

1 *It's No Secret*, 2 Grace Slick, 3 The Great Society, 4 *White Rabbit*,
5 *They don't do anything at all*, 6 *Surrealistic Pillow*, 7 David Crosby,
8 *Bless Its Pointed Little Head*, 9 *God*, 10 China, 11 *Sunfighter*, 12 1974,
13 *Dragonfly*, 14 *We Built This City*, 15 *Knee Deep In The Hoopla*.

~ 76 ~

•JERRY LEE LEWIS•

1 Which religious school in Texas was Jerry Lee Lewis expelled
   from, in 1949?

2 In what way did Jerry Lee Lewis break the law, in 1952?

3 **What was the title of the first single recorded by Jerry Lee Lewis,
   and released on the Sun Records label?**

4 Which performers did Jerry Lee Lewis join in an impromptu session at
   Sun Studios in 1956, the recordings of which later became known as
   the Million Dollar Quartet?

5 **On which show did Jerry Lee Lewis make his US TV debut,
   in 1957?**

6 Which 1957 musical film did Jerry Lee Lewis appear in, along with Carl
   Perkins, Fats Domino and Frankie Avalon?

7 **How did Jerry Lee Lewis break the law again, in 1958, leading to
   the cancellation of many of his UK shows?**

8 And which single, just recorded by Jerry Lee Lewis, did his record
   company refuse to distribute, fearing a widespread scandal?

9 **What tragedy struck Jerry Lee Lewis in 1962?**

10 Which Chuck Berry song did Jerry Lee Lewis cover in 1962, reaching
   No. 38 in the UK charts?

11 **What was the title of the album, recorded by Jerry Lee Lewis in
   December 1964?**

12 Which 1965 film, starring David Hemmings, did Jerry Lee Lewis
   appear in?

13 **What was the title of Jerry Lee Lewis' 1965 album, featuring the
   Chuck Berry covers of *Roll Over Beethoven* and *Johnny
   B.Goode*?**

14 Which cover version of a Kris Kristofferson song became Jerry Lee
   Lewis' biggest chart hit since his early days, when released in 1972?

15 **By what nickname was Jerry Lee Lewis commonly known by?**

1 **Assembly Of God Institute Bible School,** 2 He married Jane Mitcham
at a shotgun wedding in 1953, while still married to Dorothy Barton,
3 ***Whole Lotta Shakin' Goin' On,*** 4 Carl Perkins and Elvis Presley, 5 *The
Steve Allen Show,* 6 *Jamboree,* 7 He secretly married his 13 year old
second cousin, **Myra Gale,** while still married to his second wife,
8 *High School Confidential,* 9 His son, **Steve,** drowned in the swimming pool at his home, 10 *Sweet Little Sixteen,* 11 *The Greatest Live
Show On Earth,* 12 *Be My Guest,* 13 *The Return Of Rock,* 14 *Me And
Bobby McGee,* 15 *The Killer.*

• JETHRO TULL •

1 Which instrument does founder member, Ian Anderson, play standing on one leg?

2 Where did the group get the name Jethro Tull from?

3 At which London club did the group play regularly, from June 1968?

4 What was the title of the group's first album, released in November 1968?

5 Which band did guitarist Mick Abrahams form, following his departure from Jethro Tull?

6 Which band's TV spectacular, *Rock'n'Roll Circus*, did the group perform on?

7 What was unusual about the structure of the group's 1969 single *Living in The Past*?

8 What gimmick was used for the gatefold sleeve of the band's 1969 album, *Stand Up*?

9 What was the title of Jethro Tull's 1971 concept album?

10 Which album and title track were the first to be produced from the band's mobile recording studio?

11 Which member of the band left in 1976, to concentrate on his artwork?

12 What was the title of Jethro Tull's 1976 album, containing material originally intended for a stage play?

13 For which folk band did Ian Anderson produce the 1974 album *Now We Are Six*?

14 And what was the name of the folk-influenced album, released by Jethro Tull in 1977?

15 Which commercial association, based in Scotland, did Ian Anderson become a founding member of?

1 **The flute**, 2 An 18th century agriculturist, 3 **The Marquee Club**, 4 *This Was*, 5 **Blodwyn Pig**, 6 The Rolling Stones, 7 It was written with a 5/4 time signature, 8 Pop up figures of the band in the centre, 9 *Aqualung*, 10 *Minstrel in The Gallery*, 11 **Jeffrey Hammond-Hammond**, 12 *Too Old To Rock'n'Roll, Too Young To Die*, 13 **Steeleye Span**, 14 *Songs From The Wood*, 15 **The Environmental Committee of the Scottish Salmon Growers' Association.**

•JIMI HENDRIX•

1 **Which part of the US armed forces did he join, in 1961?**

2 And why was he honourably discharged in 1962?

3 **What was the name of the first group formed and fronted by Jimi Hendrix himself, in 1966?**

4 Which member of British band The Animals advised Jimi to move to England, and later became his producer?

5 **Which drummer and bass player were recruited in England, to form the Jimi Hendrix Experience?**

6 What was the title of the first single released by the band, in December 1966?

7 **What was the name of the band's second single, which reached No. 3 in the UK charts?**

8 Which classic album kept the Experience's debut album, *Are You Experienced?*, off the No. 1 spot in the UK charts?

9 **At which pop festival of 1967 did The Jimi Hendrix Experience make their US live debut?**

10 And with what famous stunt, which had become a regular feature of his live act, did he end the show?

11 **Which inappropriate pop act toured the US with Jimi Hendrix in July 1967?**

12 What was the title of the B-side to The Experience's 1967 single *The Burning Of The Midnight Lamp*, which contained the initials of two psychedelic drugs?

13 **What was the title of The Experience's second album, released in November 1967?**

14 Which Bob Dylan song, recorded and released by the band in 1968, reached No. 5 in the UK charts?

15 **And which double album set was the single taken from?**

1 The Paratroopers, 2 He broke his ankle on landing his 26th parachute jump, **3 Jimmy James And The Blue Flames, 4** Chas Chandler, **5** Mitch Mitchell and Noel Redding, **6** Hey Joe, **7 Purple Haze, 8** The Beatles' *Sgt. Pepper's Lonely Hearts Club Band*, **9 The Monterey International Pop Festival, 10** He set light to, and smashed up his guitar, **11 The Monkees, 12** *The Stars That Play With Laughing Sam's Dice* (the drugs being STP and LSD), **13** *Axis: Bold As Love*, **14** All Along The Watchtower, **15** *Electric Ladyland.*

Rock facts... ...and quiz book
• JOAN ARMATRADING •

1 **Which instrument did Joan teach herself to play at an early age?**

2 Before going solo who was she in partnership with?

3 **Which group did Joan support on tour in 1975?**

4 In 1976 her debut single reached No.10 on the UK chart, what was it?

5 **For which 1978 film did Joan write and perform the theme?**

6 Who produced Joan's 1981 album *Walk Under Ladders*?

7 **What was the title of Joan's 1983 greatest hits collection?**

8 Who featured as guest keyboard player on the album *Secret Secrets*?

9 **At which tribute concert did Joan perform in 1988?**

10 On which BBC radio show did Joan appear in 1989?

11 **Which 70's musical did Joan tour with?**

12 Which record label did Joan sign with in 1975?

13 **What was the title of her 1980 self-produced hit?**

14 Joan had her last top twenty hit to date in 1983 what was it?

15 **Where does Joan originally come from?**

1 **Piano**, 2 Pam Nestor, 3 **Supertramp**, 4 *Love And Affection*, 5 *The Wild Geese*, 6 Steve Lillywhite, 7 *Track Record*, 8 Joe Jackson, 9 Nelson Mandela's 70th birthday, 10 *Desert Island Discs*, 11 *Hair*, 12 A&M, 13 *Me, Myself, I*, 14 *Drop the Pilot*, 15 St Kitts, West Indies.

~ 80 ~

•JOE COCKER•

1 In 1960 Joe Cocker played in his brother Victor's band, what were they called?

2 In 1968 Joe Cocker's second chart single made UK No.1 what was it?

3 And who sent him a congratulatory telegram and placed music press ads praising the record?

4 What was the name of Joe Cocker's band which split in 1969 after he cancelled a US tour?

5 In 1970 Joe Cocker had a hit with a cover version of *The Letter* who had a hit with the original version?

6 Who duetted with him singing *Feelin' Alright* on *Saturday Night Live* doing his famous Cocker impersonation?

7 On which Crusaders' single did Joe Cocker sing guest lead vocals in 1981?

8 With whom did Joe Cocker sing the Top Ten hit *Up Where We Belong*?

9 And which film soundtrack was it from?

10 For which film did Joe Cocker record the song *You Can Leave Your Hat On*?

11 Where did Joe Cocker perform a free concert in 1989?

12 Which song did Joe Cocker contribute to the album *Two Rooms: Celebrating The Songs Of Elton John And Bernie Taupin*?

13 Who supported Joe Cocker on his 1992 North American tour?

14 Which 1992 film featured Joe Cocker's duet with Sass Jordan *Trust In Me*?

15 Joe Cocker had his first UK Top Ten album in 1992. What was it called?

•JOHN LENNON•

1 **What was the title of the first solo album to be released by John Lennon, in 1968?**

2 And what was featured on the cover of the album, which caused it to be withdrawn, and later issued in a brown paper bag?

3 **Which protest song was recorded in 1969, during John and Yoko's Bed-In in Canada?**

4 What was the title of John Lennon's 1969 solo single, written about drug withdrawal?

5 **Why were a series of lithographs, produced by John Lennon, seized by police while on exhibition in London?**

6 Which single, produced by Phil Spector and featuring George Harrison on guitar, reached No. 5 in the UK charts in 1970?

7 **What form of new age therapy did John and Yoko partake in during much of 1970?**

8 And which album, released in 1971, mostly contained material inspired by this course of therapy?

9 **What was the title of John Lennon's 1971 solo album, featuring the songs *Jealous Guy* and *Crippled Inside*?**

10 And which song from the album directly insulted John Lennon's former songwriting partner, Paul McCartney?

11 **Which Christmas single reached No. 4 in the UK charts in 1972?**

12 Why were John and Yoko served with deportation papers when John's US visa expired in 1972?

13 **What was the name of John Lennon's personal assistant, with whom he started a relationship in 1974, following a temporary separation from Yoko?**

14 Who duetted with John Lennon on the 1974 single *Whatever Gets You Thru' The Night*, which reached No. 1 in the US charts?

15 **And which album had the single been taken from?**

1 *Unfinished Music No. 1 - Two Virgins*, 2 A naked picture of John and Yoko, 3 *Give Peace A Chance*, 4 *Cold Turkey*, 5 **They were thought to be obscene**, 6 *Instant Karma*, 7 **Primal Scream therapy**, 8 John Lennon and The Plastic Ono Band, 9 *Imagine*, 10 *How Do You Sleep?*, 11 *Happy Xmas (War Is Over)*, 12 The US authorities would not renew the visa, due to John and Yoko's conviction for possession of cannabis in 1968, 13 **May Pang**, 14 Elton John, 15 *Walls And Bridges*.

•KATE BUSH I•

1 Which musician brought Kate Bush to the attention of record company EMI in 1975?

2 For how many weeks was her debut single, *Wuthering Heights*, at No. 1 in the UK?

3 And what is the link between *Wuthering Heights* author Emily Bronte and Kate Bush?

4 What was the title of her debut album, released in 1978?

5 And which guitarist guested on the album, and played the guitar solo on *Wuthering Heights*?

6 What was the title of her 1979 album, featuring the single *Hammer Horror*?

7 And which track from the album reached No. 14 in the UK charts in April 1979?

8 What tragedy struck Kate and her band, during her one and only tour to date, in 1979?

9 Which 1980 hit single for Peter Gabriel features vocals by Kate Bush?

10 Which single, accompanied by an artistic but raunchy video, reached No. 5 in the UK charts in 1980?

11 And what was the name of the album from which the single was taken?

12 What was the title of Kate Bush's 1980 Christmas single, which reached No. 29 in the UK charts?

13 Which single, released in 1981, featured a video with many of the performers on roller skates?

14 Which entertainer provided didgeridoo work on the title track to Kate Bush's 1982 album *The Dreaming*?

15 And which song, taken from the album, became the first single not to chart in the UK?

1 **Dave Gilmour** of Pink Floyd, 2 **4 weeks**, 3 **They share the same birthday (30th July)**, 4 *The Kick Inside*, 5 **Dave Gilmour**, 6 *Lionheart*, 7 *Wow*, 8 Their lighting director, Billy Duffield, was killed in an accident, 9 *Games Without Frontiers*, 10 *Babooshka*, 11 *Never For Ever*, 12 **December**, 13 *Sat In Your Lap*, 14 Rolf Harris, 15 *There Goes A Tenner*.

•KATE BUSH II•

1 **After a two-year break from public life, which single reached No. 3 in the UK in 1985 to become Kate Bush's biggest seller since *Wuthering Heights*?**

2 And what was the title of the song changed from, in order to prevent it being banned from radio play?

3 **What was the name of the 1985 album, whose title track reached No. 18 in the UK charts?**

4 And what was the sub-title to the second side of the album, which was presented as a concept piece?

5 **Which single, taken from the album, was accompanied by a video, featuring Hollywood actor Donald Sutherland?**

6 What was the title of Kate Bush's 1987 Greatest Hits package, which reached No. 1 in the UK album and video charts?

7 **What was the title of the Kate Bush and Peter Gabriel duet, which reached No. 9 in the UK charts in 1986?**

8 Which British violinist played on Kate Bush's 1986 single, *Experiment IV*?

9 **Which 1988 film featured the Kate Bush song *This Woman's Work*?**

10 Which Bulgarian vocal group contributed to Kate Bush's 1989 album *The Sensual World*?

11 **What was the title of the boxed set, released by EMI in 1990, which consisted of all the artist's recorded work to date?**

12 Which song did Kate Bush record for the Elton John/Bernie Taupin tribute album *Two Rooms*, released in 1991?

13 **What was the title of the first single to be released from Kate Bush's 1993 album *The Red Shoes*, which reached No. 12 in the UK charts?**

14 Which pop artist co-produced and performed on the track *Why Should I Love You?*, taken from the album?

15 **And which British comedian provided backing vocals on this song?**

~ 84 ~

• KISS •

1 What was bass player Gene Simmons' profession, before forming Kiss with friend Paul Stanley?

2 And what unusual physical attribute is Gene Simmons fond of showing off, especially during live shows?

3 Along with leather outfits and platform boots, what other visual gimmick were the band best known for?

4 What was the name of the group's 1976 album, which opens with a dramatisation of a fatal teenage road accident?

5 Which famous groupies did the band write about on their 1977 album *Love Gun*?

6 What gimmick did the group use in 1978, prompting rumours that they were to split up?

7 Which cartoon makers made a live action film, featuring the band?

8 And what was the title of the film?

9 Which band member left the group in 1979, releasing the solo album *Out Of Control*?

10 What did the band allow for the first time, after the release of the 1980 album *Kiss Unmasked*?

11 What caused guitarist Ace Frehley to quit the group in 1982?

12 What caused former drummer Eric Carr's death in 1991?

13 And which song, originally recorded by British band Argent, did the band record in tribute to Eric Carr?

14 And which 1992 Hollywood film was the song featured in?

15 For what type of sessions did the original line up reform in 1996?

1 A teacher, 2 His tongue, which is reputedly one foot long, **3 Their make-up, 4** *Destroyer*, **5 The Plaster Casters, 6** Each member released their own solo album on the same day, **7 William Hanna and Joseph Barbera, 8** *Kiss Meets The Phantom Of The Park*, **9 Peter Criss, 10** To be photographed without their make-up, **11** He had a serious car accident, as well as habitual drug problems, **12** Cancer, **13 God Gave Rock And Roll To You, 14** *Bill And Ted's Bogus Journey*, **15** MTV's Unplugged series.

•LED ZEPPELIN•

1 Which two well known sessions musicians formed the basis of the band?

2 And which two members, both from the Birmingham area, completed the line up for the group?

3 How did Keith Moon, drummer with The Who, inadvertently name the band?

4 Which decision by the band's manager ensured that they would sell more albums than any other artist on the Atlantic label?

5 Which famous track opened Led Zeppelin's second album, released in 1969?

6 Why did critics dismiss Led Zeppelin's third album as sounding like Crosby, Stills and Nash?

7 And in which country did the group write much of the material for this, and subsequent albums?

8 Who was the infamous former owner of Boleskine Lodge, the Scottish mansion bought by guitarist Jimmy Page in the early 1970's?

9 How was Led Zeppelin's fourth and officially untitled album generally known by fans?

10 And which 8 minute song from the album became the most requested track on American radio?

11 What gimmick did the band use in the packaging to their 1973 album *Houses Of The Holy*, which many people thought would adversely affect the album's sales?

12 What was the name of Led Zeppelin's own record label, set up in 1974?

13 Which member of the band was badly injured, with his wife, in a car accident in 1975?

14 Which epic 10 minute song opens Led Zeppelin's 1976 album *Presence*?

15 And what was the title of the double live album set, also released in 1976?

1 Jimmy Page and John Paul Jones, 2 Robert Plant and John Bonham, 3 He commented that the band, whose material was based on only **heavy rock, would go down like a lead balloon,** 4 They wouldn't release any singles in the UK, 5 ***Whole Lotta Love,*** 6 The second side of the record was filled with acoustic-driven songs, 7 Wales, **in a cottage called Bron-Y-Aur,** 8 Aleister Crowley, 9 **Runes, or Four Symbols, after the artwork on the sleeve,** 10 *Stairway To Heaven*, 11 **The album title and band's name doesn't appear anywhere on the sleeve,** 12 Swan Song, 13 **Robert Plant,** 14 *Achilles Last Stand*, 15 **The Song Remains The Same.**

•LIONEL RICHIE•

1 Which US soul band did Lionel Richie play with until 1982?

2 Which song, written by Lionel Richie for his wife, reached No. 1 in the US in 1978?

3 Which song, written by Lionel Richie and sung by Kenny Rogers, stayed at No. 1 in the US charts for 6 weeks?

4 And what was the title of the album he wrote and produced for Kenny Rogers in 1981?

5 What was the title of the final studio album, released by The Commodores in 1981?

6 And which single, taken from the album, reached No. 4 in the US charts?

7 Which ballad did Lionel Richie write in 1981 for a Franco Zeffirelli film?

8 And which US singer duetted with Lionel Richie on the song, which stayed at No. 1 in the US charts for 9 weeks?

9 What was the title of the first solo single, released by Lionel Richie in 1982?

10 Which dance track, released in 1983, stayed at No. 1 in the US for 4 weeks, and spent over 4 months in the chart?

11 And what was the title of the album from which the single was taken?

12 What was the value of the sponsorship deal, made between Lionel Richie and Pepsi-Cola In 1984?

13 Which single, released in 1984, became Lionel Richie's first solo UK No. 1?

14 Which charity single, released in 1985, was co-written by Lionel Richie and Michael Jackson?

15 Which song, released in 1985, became the US Christmas No. 1?

1 The Commodores, 2 *Three Times A Lady,* **3 Lady,** 4 *Share Your Love,*
5 *In The Pocket,* 6 *Oh No,* 7 *Endless Love,* 8 Diana Ross, **9 Truly,**
10 *All Night Long (All Night),* **11 *Can't Slow Down,*** 12 $8.5 million,
13 *Hello,* 14 *We Are The World,* **15 *Say You Say Me.***

~ 87 ~

•LITTLE RICHARD•

1 **Born in Georgia in 1932, what religion did he and his family follow?**

2 Which record company was he signed to in 1956?

3 **And what was the name of the first single he recorded and released for this company, which reached No. 17 in the US charts?**

4 And which singer recorded a cover version of this song, reaching No. 12 in the charts?

5 **Which single, released in 1956, was originally titled *The Thing*?**

6 What was then name of Little Richard's backing band, who toured Los Angeles with him in 1957?

7 **What was the name of the Jayne Mansfield film which featured a title song written and performed by Little Richard?**

8 What was the title of the album, released in 1957, which became the only charting album Little Richard recorded in the 1950's?

9 **Which film was Little Richard's 1957 song, *Keep A Knockin'*, taken from?**

10 During a tour of which country did Little Richard renounce his rock and roll life, and plan to enter theological college?

11 **Which Top Ten single, released in 1958, was accompanied by the B-side *Hey Hey Hey Hey*?**

12 And which British band recorded a cover version of the B-side *Hey Hey Hey Hey* in a medley, along with Little Richard's 1959 single *Kansas City*?

13 **Which famous record producer worked with Little Richard during 1960, on a set of gospel songs for Mercury Records?**

14 At which Hamburg club did Little Richard play a 14 day contract, sharing the bill with The Beatles?

15 **And which member of The Beatles was most impressed by the vocal style of Little Richard, and always sung the lead vocal when the band covered one of his songs?**

1 Seventh Day Adventist, 2 Speciality Records, **3 *Tutti Frutti*,** 4 Pat Boone, **5 *Long Tall Sally*,** 6 The Upsetters, **7 *The Girl Can't Help It*,** 8 *Lucille*, **9 *Mr Rock'n'Roll*,** 10 Australia, **11 *Good Golly Miss Molly*,** 12 The Beatles, **13 Quincy Jones,** 14 The Star Club, **15 Paul McCartney.**

• LULU •

1 **Born on November 3rd 1948, what is Lulu's real name?**

2 What was the name of Lulu's band, formed in 1963?

3 **On which British show did the group make their TV debut?**

4 Which single, a re-recording of an Isley Brothers song, reached No. 7 in the UK chart when released as the group's debut single?

5 **Which song, originally a runner-up at the Brighton Song Festival, reached No. 8 in the UK charts in 1964?**

6 What first did Lulu achieve during her 1966 tour with The Hollies?

7 **For which 1967 film, starring Sidney Poitier, did Lulu make a 5 week run at No. 1 in the US charts with the title song?**

8 Which single, released in 1968, reached No. 9 in the UK charts?

9 **Which act caused controversy when they appeared on Lulu's 1968 TV show, by playing an impromptu tribute to recently disbanded group Cream?**

10 Which song was performed by Lulu in the 1969 Eurovision Song Contest, drawing for first place with the entries from France, Spain and Holland?

11 **Which pop star did Lulu marry, on the 18th April, 1969?**

12 Which song, originally written and recorded by David Bowie, reached No. 3 in the UK charts in 1974?

13 **Having divorced in 1973, which hairdresser did Lulu marry in 1976?**

14 What was the name of Lulu's 1993 comeback album, which featured a No. 11 hit with its title track?

15 **Which British boy band reached No. 1 in the UK charts in 1993 with a duet, sung with Lulu?**

1 **Marie McDonald McLaughlin Lawrie,** 2 Lulu and The Luvvers, 3 **Thank Your Lucky Stars,** 4 *Shout,* 5 *Leave A Little Love,* 6 The first British female singer to perform behind the Iron Curtain, during a tour of Poland, 7 *To Sir With Love,* 8 *Me The Peaceful Heart,* 9 The Jimi Hendrix Experience, 10 *Boom-Bang-A-Bang,* 11 Maurice Gibb of the Bee Gees, 12 *The Man Who Sold The World,* 13 John Frieda, 14 *Independence,* 15 Take That.

• MADNESS •

1 Formed in 1977 by three school friends, under what name did the band play, until changing their name to Madness in 1979?

2 What was the title of the band's debut single, which reached No. 16 in the UK charts in 1979?

3 What was the name of the band's debut album, which gave them a No. 7 UK hit with the title track?

4 Which 1980 No. 3 single for Madness was later covered by British comedienne Tracy Ullman?

5 What was the title of the band's second 1980 No. 3 single, taken from the album *Absolutely*?

6 Which album, released in 1981, was recorded entirely in the Bahamas?

7 Who had the original hit with the band's 1982 No. 4 single *It Must Be Love*?

8 Which single, released in 1982, stayed at No. 1 in the UK charts for 2 weeks?

9 Which song became the group's biggest US hit, when it reached No. 7 in the charts in 1983?

10 Which single, released in 1983, was held off the No. 1 spot in the UK charts by *Red Red Wine* by UB40?

11 Which No. 11 single, released in 1984, featured a brief voice over by the actor featured in the song?

12 What was the name of the record label, formed by the band in 1984?

13 And which artist had the first hit single on the label, with the song *Listen To Your Father*?

14 Which No. 18 single, released in 1986, was intended as the group's farewell song?

15 At which London open-air venue in 1992 did the band reform to play their Madstock! live shows?

1 The Invaders, 2 The Prince, 3 One Step Beyond, 4 My Girl, 5 Baggy *Trousers*, 6 *Seven*, 7 Labi Siffre, 8 House Of Fun, 9 *Our House*, 10 *Wings Of A Dove*, 11 *Michael Caine*, 12 Zarjazz, 13 Feargal Sharkey, 14 Waiting For The Ghost Train, 15 Finsbury Park.

• MADONNA •

1 **What was the name of the band Madonna formed with her boyfriend Dan Gilroy in 1979?**

2 What was Madonna's first UK Top Ten single?

3 **Madonna had her first major role in which film?**

4 Which of Madonna's boyfriends' wrote the hit *Holiday*?

5 **Who were Madonna's support act on her 1985 *The Virgin Tour*?**

6 At the 1985 *Live Aid* concert, who said "Madonna is a woman who pulled herself up by her bra-straps"?

7 **In 1985 Madonna became the only woman to have three singles in the UK Top 15 since who 30 years earlier?**

8 Who sang duet with Madonna on her album track *Love Song*?

9 **In 1990 Madonna starred in Warren Beatty's film *Bugsy*, what part did she play?**

10 What is the title of Madonna's greatest hits album released in 1990?

11 **In 1990 why was Madonna sued by her next door neighbour?**

12 From which film was the Madonna single *I'll Remember* taken?

13 **What did Madonna dress as for the American promotion of her book *Sex*?**

14 In 1993 Madonna released a cover version of *Fever* who made the original version?

15 **What did Madonna refuse to do for the film *Evita*?**

1 The Breakfast Club, 2 *Holiday*, 3 *Desperately Seeking Susan*, 4 John 'Jellybean' Benitez, 5 The Beastie Boys, 6 Bette Midler, 7 Ruby Murray, 8 Prince, 9 Breathless Mahoney, 10 *The Immaculate Collection*, 11 For having a fence which blocked his view, 12 *With Honors*, 13 Little Bo Peep, 14 Little Willie John, 15 A screen test.

~ 91 ~

• MANIC STREET PREACHERS •

1 By what name were the band originally known?

2 In 1989 the band released a self-financed single, what was it called?

3 What was the Manic Street Preachers' debut UK chart single called?

4 What did Richey Edwards do when asked during an interview with Steve Lamacq if the band were sincere?

5 What was the title of the Manics' debut album?

6 What had the band planned to do after releasing their debut album?

7 Who did Nicky Wire say he "hoped would go the same way as Freddie Mercury pretty soon"?

8 Which rock group did the Manics support in 1993?

9 How did Nicky Wire injure a security guard in 1992?

10 In which year did Richey Edwards disappear on the eve of a US tour?

11 What was the title of the Manics' first single without Richey?

12 Which track did the Manics contribute to the charity album *Help*?

13 In 1992 the Manics recorded a cover version of a Guns 'N' Roses song, what was it?

14 Which coveted award did the band win in 1997 for *Everything Must Go*?

15 In 1998 the Manics had their first UK No.1. What was it?

• MARILLION •

1 **In which English town was the group formed?**

2 And where did the band get their name from?

3 **What is the real name of the band's singer, known as Fish?**

4 And how had he come by his nickname?

5 **At which London venue in 1982 did the band play their first headlining gig?**

6 What was the title of the band's debut single, which reached No. 60 in the UK charts?

7 **And what was the subject of the band's follow up single, *He Knows, You Know*?**

8 Who replaced the original bass player, Diz Minnitt, in March 1982?

9 **What was the title of the band's debut album, featuring the songs *The Web* and *Chelsea Monday*?**

10 And which song, taken from the album, did the group perform on their first appearance on BBC's *Top of the Pops*?

11 **What was the title of the band's second album, which featured the singles *Punch And Judy* and *Assassing*?**

12 Which song, taken from the group's 1985 album *Misplaced Childhood*, reached No. 2 in the UK singles chart?

13 **Which album was the band's 1987 single *Incommunicado* taken from?**

14 What was the title of the band's 1988 compilation album, consisting of material not available on any studio album?

15 **Who became the new vocalist with the band, following Fish's resignation to pursue a solo career?**

1 Aylesbury, 2 A shortening of their original name, Silmarillion, taken from the J.R.R. Tolkein book of the same name. **3 Derek Dick, 4** Because he liked to take long baths, **5 The Marquee Club, 6** *Market Square Heroes*, **7** Drug use, **8** Peter Trewavas, **9** *Script For A Jester's Tear*, **10** *Garden Party*, **11** Fugazi, **12** Kayleigh, **13** *Clutching At Straws*, **14** *B-Sides Themselves*, **15 Steve Hogarth.**

• MEATLOAF •

1 In 1966 Meatloaf formed a band which opened for acts such as The Who and Iggy Pop, what was it called?

2 In 1969 Meatloaf applied for a job at the Aquarius Theatre in Los Angeles, doing what?

3 Meatloaf appeared in the musical *Hair* in 1970, which part did he play?

4 Which female sang vocals on Meatloaf's *Paradise By The Dashboard Light*?

5 In 1978 how did Meatloaf tear ligaments in his leg, leaving him in a wheelchair for a month?

6 Which female singer starred with Meatloaf in the film *Roadie* in 1979?

7 On which Meatloaf album featured Roger Daltry?

8 In 1986 Meatloaf recorded a duet with John Parr, what was it called?

9 How long did Meatloaf's *I'd Do Anything For Love (But I Won't Do That)* stay at UK No. 1?

10 In which musical and film did Meatloaf play the part of Eddie?

11 What was the name of the album intended for Meatloaf which Jim Steinman released as a solo?

12 A Meatloaf album was the first ever to enter the British charts at No. 1 which one was it?

13 How many years in total did Meatloaf's *Bat Out Of Hell* album spend on the UK chart?

14 Meatloaf's first UK Top Ten hit *Dead Ringer For Love* featured which female singer?

15 In 1994 what did *Rolling Stone Magazine* name Meatloaf as?

1 **Popcorn Blizzard,** 2 Parking lot attendant, 3 Ulysses **S.Grant,** 4 Ellen Foley, 5 He fell off stage at a concert in **Toronto,** 6 Debbie Harry, 7 *Bad Attitude,* 8 *Rock 'n' Roll Mercenaries,* 9 7 weeks, 10 *The Rocky Horror Picture Show,* 11 *Bad For Good,* 12 *Dead Ringer,* 13 8, 14 Cher, 15 Most Unwelcome Comeback.

• METALLICA •

1 **Which New Wave heavy metal group did Lars Ulrich tour the UK with in 1981?**

2 Who replaced Ron McGovney on bass in 1982?

3 **Which band did Dave Mustaine go on to form after being fired from Metallica?**

4 What was the title of Metallica's debut UK chart album?

5 **In which year did Metallica have their first UK No.1 album?**

6 Who did Metallica tour the US with as guest band?

7 **Which member of the band was killed in 1986 when their tour bus crashed?**

8 Metallica had their first UK Top Ten hit in 1991 what was it?

9 **How was James Hetfield injured while on stage in 1992?**

10 What was the title of Metallica's 1987 EP?

11 **Which festival did Metallica play at in 1985?**

12 Which song did James Hetfield sing at the 1992 Freddie Mercury tribute concert?

13 **In 1986 a Metallica album made the US Top Thirty without the help of radio play or a hit single, what was it?**

14 What was the hit single *One* written about?

15 **Who sang backing vocals on Metallica's 1997 single *The Memory Remains*?**

soldier kept alive on a life support machine, 15 **Marianne Faithull.**
Of Rock Festival, 12 *Stone Cold Crazy,* 13 *Master Of Puppets,* 14 A
prop exploded , 10 The $5.98 EP-Garage Days Revisited, 11 **Monsters**
5 **1991,** 6 Ozzy Osbourne, 7 **Cliff Burton,** 8 *Enter Sandman,* 9 **A stage**
1 **Diamond Head,** 2 Cliff Burton, 3 **Megadeth,** 4 *Ride The Lightning,*

• MICHAEL JACKSON I •

1 **In 1972 Michael Jackson had a hit with his first solo release, what was it?**

2 In 1972 Michael Jackson reached UK No. 3 with *Rockin' Robin*, who recorded the original version?

3 **Michael Jackson's father Joe was an ex-guitarist with which group?**

4 What was Michael Jackson's first UK No. 1?

5 **Which record label did Michael Jackson move to after leaving Motown in 1975?**

6 Which part did Michael Jackson play in the movie version of *The Wiz*?

7 **In 1980 Michael Jackson released the first of many songs written by ex-Heatwave member Rod Temperton, what was it?**

8 In 1980 what did Michael Jackson become the first solo artist to do?

9 **Who wrote Michael Jackson's hit *Girlfriend*?**

10 In 1980 Michael Jackson rejoined the Jacksons to promote their new album what was it called?

11 **In 1982 Diana Ross had a hit with a single written for her by Michael Jackson, what was it called?**

12 What was the title of the duet Michael Jackson wrote and performed with Paul McCartney in 1982?

13 **Who produced Michael Jackson's record breaking album *Thriller*?**

14 Who played lead guitar on Michael Jackson's *Beat It*?

15 **Who recorded the ghostly rap on Michael Jackson's *Thriller* single?**

• MICHAEL JACKSON II •

1 In 1984 who released a novelty version of Michael Jackson's *Beat It* and what was it called?

2 Who did Michael Jackson record the duet *State Of Shock* with in 1984?

3 **With who did Michael Jackson write the USA For Africa single *We Are The World*?**

4 Why were relations between Michael Jackson and Paul McCartney damaged in 1985?

5 **In 1987 which two female singers turned down the offer of the duet *I Just Can't Stop Loving You* with Michael Jackson?**

6 In 1988 Michael Jackson released his autobiography. What was the title?

7 **Which member of Guns 'N' Roses featured on Michael Jackson's *Black Or White* single?**

8 Which model featured on Michael Jackson's *In The Closet* video?

9 **In 1993 Michael Jackson had his first TV interview for 14 years on a special edition of whose show?**

10 For which film did Michael Jackson record the song *Will You Be There*?

11 **What is the name of Michael Jackson's own record label?**

12 What was the title of Michael Jackson's hit single recorded with his sister Janet?

13 **In 1982 Michael Jackson accepted the largest individual sponsorship deal in history from which company?**

14 Which Michael Jackson single was the first black record to receive airplay on the MTV video station?

15 **What was the title of the 1996 single Michael Jackson recorded with his nephews 3T?**

1 *Eat It* by Weird Al Yankovic, 2 Mick Jagger, **3 Lionel Richie, 4** Michael outbid Paul McCartney to buy the rights to more than 250 Lennon/McCartney songs, **5 Whitney Houston and Barbra Streisand,** 6 *Moonwalk*, **7 Slash,** 8 Naomi Campbell, **9 Oprah Winfrey, 10** *Free Willy*, **11 MJJ,** 12 *Scream*, **13 Pepsi-Cola,** 14 *Beat It*, **15 Why.**

• MORRISSEY AND THE SMITHS •

1 In which year were the Smiths formed?

2 What was the title of the book Morrissey had published in the early 1980's?

3 In 1983 the Smiths made their UK chart debut with which single?

4 Who did the Smiths back on her single *Hand In Glove* in 1984?

5 In 1984 the Smiths had their first UK Top Ten hit, what was it?

6 Which member of the Smiths was injured in a car crash in 1986 ?

7 Who did Johnny Marr team up with to form *Electronic* in 1990?

8 In which year did the Smiths split?

9 Whose fan club was Morrissey UK president of in the early 1980's?

10 Morrissey's debut solo album entered the UK chart at No.1. What was it?

11 What was the title of Morrissey's first solo UK Top Ten hit?

12 Which actress featured on the promotional video for Morrissey's single *Ouija Board Ouija Board*?

13 Whose reunion concert did Morrissey appear at in 1992?

14 Guitarist Mark Nevin co-wrote Morrissey's album *Kill Uncle* which group was he an ex-member of?

15 Which member of the Smiths successfully sued Morrissey and Marr for 25% share of the groups earnings?

• MOTORHEAD •

1 What is the real name of the band's front man, Lemmy?

2 Which psychedelic heavy rock band did bass player Lemmy join in 1971?

3 And why was he sacked from the band in 1975?

4 What was the nickname of the band's drummer, Phil Taylor, who joined in 1975?

5 Which guitarist joined in 1976, completing the classic trio line up?

6 What was the title of the band's first single, recorded in 1976 but never released?

7 What was the name of the group's 1979 album, whose title track became their first Top 40 hit?

8 And which album, also released in 1979, featured the tracks *Dead Men Tell No Tales* and *Lawman*?

9 What was the title of the 1976 album, rejected at the time, released in 1979?

10 Which single, released in 1980, became the band's most successful single, reaching No. 15 in the UK charts?

11 Which band did Motorhead join with in 1981, to record the EP *St. Valentine's Day Massacre*?

12 Which live album, recorded in London in 1980, reached No. 1 in the UK charts in 1981?

13 With which famous 19 year old model did Lemmy record a single in 1985, although legal action by his former record company prevented its release?

14 Which 1986 album was named after a gadget featured in the Woody Allen film, *Sleeper*?

15 Which Comic Strip comedy did Lemmy appear in, in 1987?

1 Ian Kilmister, 2 Hawkwind, 3 He was arrested and jailed for 5 days in Canada, on drugs charges, 4 Philthy Animal, 5 Eddie Clarke, 6 *White Line Fever*, 7 *Overkill*, 8 *Bomber*, 9 *On Parole*, 10 *Ace Of Spades*, 11 *Girlschool*, 12 *No Sleep Till Hammersmith*, 13 Samantha Fox, 14 *Orgasmatron*, 15 *Eat The Rich*.

•NEIL YOUNG•

1 Where in the world was Neil Young born, on November 12th 1945?

2 Which band did he join in 1965, after moving to Los Angeles?

3 What was the name of Neil Young's backing band, formed in 1969?

4 And what was the name of the first album, released in 1969, to feature this backing band?

5 Which trio did Neil Young perform with for the first time, at the Fillmore East venue in New York in 1969?

6 And what was the title of the first album, recorded by this quartet in 1970?

7 For which 1970 film, starring Beau Bridges, did Neil Young write several songs?

8 Which album, released by Neil Young in 1970, reached No. 8 in the US charts?

9 Which political event inspired Neil Young to write the song *Ohio*?

10 What was the title of Neil Young's fourth solo album, which reached No. 1 in the US and UK charts in 1972?

11 And which US No. 1 single, taken from the album, featured Linda Ronstadt and James Taylor on backing vocals?

12 What was the name of the autobiographical documentary film, made by Neil Young in 1973?

13 Which Neil Young album, released in 1974, was described by *Rolling Stone magazine* as one of the most despairing albums of the decade?

14 Which long time partner did Neil Young join with, to record the 1976 album *Long May You Run*?

15 Which 1979 live album was accompanied by a film, directed by Neil Young, featuring concert footage from his latest tour?

1 Toronto, Canada, 2 Buffalo Springfield, 3 Crazy Horse, 4 *Everybody Knows This is Nowhere*, 5 Crosby, Stills and Nash, 6 *Deja Vu*, 7 *Landlord*, 8 *After The Goldrush*, 9 The killing of protesting students during riots at Kent State University, 10 *Harvest*, 11 *Heart Of Gold*, 12 *Journey Through The Past*, 13 *On The Beach*, 14 Stephen Stills, 15 *Rust Never Sleeps*.

• NICK CAVE •

1   What was the name of the first band Nick Cave formed?

2   Changing their name to Birthday Party the band earned a deal with 4AD records after appearing on whose radio show in 1980?

3   What did the band finally change their name to in 1982?

4   What was the title of Nick Cave's first book, published in 1988?

5   Name the duet Nick Cave recorded with Shane McGowan?

6   What was the song *The Mercy Seat* written about?

7   In which 1987 Wim Wenders film did Nick Cave feature?

8   With whom did Nick Cave record the hit *Where The Wild Roses Grow*?

9   In 1991 who did Nick Cave star in the film *Johnny Suede* with?

10   In 1996 Nick cave released his best-selling album to date, what was it?

11   Nick Cave's original bassist, Barry Adamson, was a former member of which group?

12   Which song did Nick Cave contribute to Wim Wender's 1991 film *Until The End Of The World*?

13   In 1986 Nick Cave released an album of cover versions, what was it called?

14   What was the title of Nick Cave's novel published in 1989?

15   What nationality is Nick Cave?

1 Boys Next Door, 2 John Peel's, **3 Nick Cave & the Bad Seeds,** 4 King Ink, **5 What A Wonderful World,** 6 The final minutes of a prisoner waiting for the electric chair, 7 *Wings Of Desire*, 8 Kylie Minogue, **9 Brad Pitt,** 10 Murder Ballads, **11 Magazine,** 12 (I'll Love You) *Till The End Of Time*, **13 Kicking Against The Pricks,** 14 *And The Ass Saw The Angel*, **15 Australian.**

• NIRVANA •

1 **Nirvana's debut on the UK chart made the Top Ten. What was it?**

2 And what was it named after?

3 **In 1991 who did Nirvana support on tour in Europe?**

4 Which track appears after ten minutes of silence at the end of the CD of the album *Nevermind*?

5 **Who did Kurt Cobain marry in 1992?**

6 How was Chris Novoselic knocked unconscious at the 1992 MTV Video Music Awards?

7 **Nirvana had their first UK No.1 album in 1993, what was it?**

8 To which 1993 album did Nirvana contribute *I Hate Myself And Want To Die*?

9 **Where did Nirvana play their final show?**

10 In which year did Kurt Cobain commit suicide?

11 **Which band did Dave Grohl join in 1995?**

12 Which BRIT award did Nirvana win in 1993?

13 **Which record label did Nirvana sign with in 1992?**

14 What was Nirvana's last UK Top Ten hit?

15 **In 1991 Nirvana released a cover version of a Velvet Underground song, what was it?**

1 *Smells Like Teen Spirit*, 2 A Deodorant, 3 Sonic Youth, 4 *Endless, Nameless*, 5 Courtney Love, 6 He threw his guitar in the air and it hit him on the head, 7 *In Utero*, 8 *The Beavis And Butt-Head Experience*, 9 **Munich, Germany**, 10 1994, 11 **The Foo Fighters**, 12 Best International Newcomer, 13 **Geffen Records**, 14 *Heart-Shaped Box*, 15 *Here She Comes Now*.

• OASIS •

1   **For which group did Noel Gallagher fail an audition to become lead singer, but worked for them as a guitar technician and roadie?**

2   By which name were Oasis originally known?

3   **In 1993 who did Oasis open for at the Krazy House, Liverpool?**

4   In 1994 the band's live debut outside the UK in Holland was cancelled, why?

5   **In 1994 Oasis released a cover version of a Beatles song, what was it?**

6   Oasis' debut album entered the UK charts at No. 1 what was it called?

7   **In 1995 Liam walked off stage during a concert in America because the audience were throwing what at him?**

8   On whose No. 1 album *Stanley Road* did Noel appear as guest?

9   **In 1996 why did Noel Gallagher turn down the Ivor Novello Songwriter Of The Year award?**

10 Who did Alan White replace as drummer with Oasis?

11 **In 1995 who did Noel record *Come Together* with for the Bosnian benefit album *Help*?**

12 And what did they call themselves?

13 **Who recorded a spoof cover version of Oasis' *Wonderwall*?**

14 In 1995 what did Alan McGee founder of their record label present Noel with at a Christmas party?

15 **What was Oasis' first UK No.1 single?**

1 Inspiral Carpets, 2 Rain, 3 The Verve, 4 They caused a drunken rampage on the ferry and were deported, 5 I Am The Walrus, 6 Definitely Maybe, 7 Wire-rimmed prescription glasses, 8 Paul Weller, 9 Because it was being shared with Blur, 10 Tony McCarroll, 11 Paul Weller and Paul McCartney, 12 The Smokin' Mojo Filters, 13 Mike Flowers Pops, 14 A chocolate Rolls Royce, 15 Some Might Say.

• PAUL McCARTNEY I •

1 What was the title of the first solo single released by Paul McCartney in 1971?

2 Which album, released in 1971, features the songs *Uncle Albert/Admiral Halsey* and *The Back Seat Of My Car*?

3 Which guitarist joined Paul and Linda McCartney in 1971 to form the band Wings?

4 And which Midlands band had he been a member of?

5 What was the title of the first Wings album, released in November 1971?

6 Which political single from 1972 was widely banned on the radio?

7 And which single from later in the year was also banned by the BBC, because of it's apparent drug references?

8 Why was Paul McCartney fined £100 in March 1973?

9 What was the title of Wings' 1973 album, which featured the songs *My Love* and *One More Kiss*?

10 And what form of writing appeared on the back cover of the album?

11 Which Bond theme, written by Paul McCartney and produced by ex-Beatle producer George Martin, reached No. 9 in the UK singles chart in 1973?

12 Which 1973 single, with a pun title, was inspired by Paul McCartney's Landrover Jeep?

13 Which album, released in 1974, features several famous people on the cover, including Michael Parkinson, Clement Freud, John Conteh and Christopher Lee?

14 And which single, taken from the album, was inspired by Paul McCartney's pet Labrador puppy?

15 What prevented Paul McCartney and Wings from touring in America until the middle of 1974?

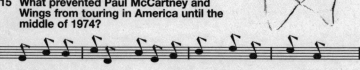

• PAUL McCARTNEY II •

1. **Which album, released in 1975, included the single *Listen To What The Man Said*?**

2. And which British TV soap theme appeared as the last track on the album?

3. **Which single, released in 1976 and reaching No. 1 in the US, was Paul McCartney inspired to write, following criticism over his lightweight and sentimental material?**

4. And which single, also taken from the 1976 album *Wings At The Speed Of Sound*, contains a sly reference to the Everly Brothers?

5. **Which rock and roll artist's publishing rights did Paul McCartney buy in 1976?**

6. What was the title of the triple album set, documenting Wings' 1976 tour of the US?

7. **Which single, co-written by Paul McCartney and Denny Laine, became the biggest selling UK single of all time, staying at No. 1 for 9 weeks?**

8. Which album from 1978 was largely recorded on a yacht in the Virgin Islands, and featured the single *With A Little Luck*?

9. **And which song from the album was later covered by Michael Jackson on his 1979 album, *Off The Wall*?**

10. For which rock star's wedding did Paul McCartney, George Harrison and Ringo Starr play together for the first time in 9 years?

11. **What was the title of the last album, released in 1979, to be credited to Wings?**

12. What was the title of the 1980 song which was Paul McCartney's first solo single to be released since 1971?

13. **In which country was Paul McCartney arrested, jailed then extradited, after being found in possession of nearly 8 oz of cannabis?**

14. What was the title of Paul McCartney's second solo album, released in 1980, and featuring the singles *Coming Up* and *Waterfalls*?

15. **With which artist did Paul McCartney record the 1982 song *Ebony And Ivory*?**

1 *Venus And Mars* **2** *Crossroads* **3** *Silly Love Songs* **4** *Let 'Em In*
5 **Buddy Holly** **6** *Wings Over America* **7** *Mull Of Kintyre* **8** *London Town*
9 *Girlfriend* **10** Eric Clapton - who was marrying Patti Harrison, George's
ex-wife **11** *Back To The Egg* **12** *Wonderful Christmas Time* **13** Japan
14 *McCartney II* **15** Stevie Wonder

• PAUL McCARTNEY III •

1 Which album, recorded in 1982, included the song *Here Today* as a tribute to John Lennon, who was shot dead in 1980?

2 Which song, taken from the album *Thriller*, did Paul McCartney and Michael Jackson duet on?

3 And which Paul McCartney/Michael Jackson duet, taken from the album *Pipes Of Peace*, stayed at No. 1 in the US singles chart for 6 weeks?

4 What was the title of Paul McCartney's first feature film, described as a musical fantasy drama?

5 Which daily newspaper cartoon strip did Paul McCartney buy the rights to in 1984?

6 And what was the title of the song, released in November 1984, which featured the cartoon strip in its video?

7 Which song, performed by Paul McCartney, closed the Wembley Live Aid concert in 1985?

8 For which 1986 film, starring Dan Aykroyd and Chevy Chase, did Paul McCartney write the theme tune?

9 What was the title of Paul McCartney's 1986 album, featuring the singles *Press* and *Only Love Remains*?

10 For what reason did Paul McCartney not attend the Beatles' induction ceremony into the Rock And Roll Hall Of Fame in New York?

11 What was the title of the album Paul McCartney was asked to record for exclusive release in Russia in 1988?

12 Which British songwriter did Paul McCartney collaborate with in 1989?

13 And which Paul McCartney album, released in June 1989, featured the results of this collaboration?

14 Which cover version of an Elvis Presley song did Paul McCartney record for the 1990 tribute album *The Last Temptation Of Elvis*?

15 What was the title of the double album live set, recorded during Paul McCartney's 1990 world tour?

1 *Tug Of War*, 2 *The Girl Is Mine*, 3 *Say, Say, Say*, 4 *Give My Regards To Broad Street*, 5 *Rupert The Bear*, 6 *We All Stand Together*, 7 *Let It Be*, 8 *Spies Like Us*, 9 *Press To Play*, 10 He claimed he still had business differences with the other two surviving members of the group, 11 *Back In The USSR*, 12 Elvis Costello, 13 *Flowers In The Dirt*, 14 *It's Now Or Never*, 15 *Tripping The Live Fantastic*.

• PAUL WELLER AND THE JAM •

1 **The Jam released their debut single in 1977 what was it?**

2 In 1978 the Jam had a hit with a cover version of a Kinks' track, what was it?

3 **In 1980 what did the Jam's single *Going Underground/Dreams Of Children* become the first to do?**

4 In 1982 the Jam had their first UK No.1 album what was it?

5 **In 1982 the Jam became the first band since The Beatles to do what?**

6 Which member of the Belle Stars sang duet with Paul Weller on the Jam single *The Bitterest Pill (I Ever Had To Swallow)*?

7 **In which year did the Jam split?**

8 Which group did Paul Weller go on to form after the Jam?

9 **In 1995 Paul Weller had his first solo UK Top Ten hit, what was it?**

10 What was the title of the documentary video about Paul Weller's career released in 1994?

11 **Which BRIT award did Paul weller win in 1995?**

12 In 1995 Paul Weller released an album which featured Noel Gallagher and Steve Winwood, what was it called?

13 **And what was it named after?**

14 The Style Council appeared on the very first broadcast of which UK TV show with their debut hit *Speak Like A Child* what was the show?

15 **What was the Style Council's hit *Soul Deep* inspired by?**

•PEARL JAM•

1 **Where did Pearl Jam take their name from?**

2 Who did Pearl Jam open for on tour in 1991?

3 **Which member of the band left in 1991?**

4 In 1992 Pearl Jam released their first single, what was it?

5 **What was the title of the tribute album recorded by members of Pearl Jam and Soundgarden for Mother Love Bone's dead lead singer Andrew Wood?**

6 Pearl Jam were featured in the film *Singles* which part did they play?

7 **Pearl Jam had their first UK No.1 single in 1994, what was it called?**

8 Who was Eddie Vedder compared to in 1993?

9 **What was the name of Stone Gossard's side band?**

10 With whom did Pearl Jam perform *Keep On Rockin' In The Free World* at the 1993 MTV Video Music Awards?

11 **Pearl Jam had their first UK Top Ten album in 1993, what was it?**

12 Which ex-member of the Red Hot Chilli Peppers joined the band in 1995?

13 **Who had Eddie Vedder been swimming with when he had to be rescued after a rip tide swept him out to sea in New Zealand?**

14 Who stood in for Eddie Vedder when he fell ill during a concert in San Francisco in 1995?

15 **Who did Eddie Vedder play drums for in a wig and dark glasses at a concert in philadelphia in 1995?**

1 Eddie Vedder's great grandmother's fruit jam, 2 Alice In Chains, 3 **Dave Krusen,** 4 *Alive,* 5 *Temple of The Dog,* 6 Matt Dillon's backing band Citizen Dick, 7 *Spin The Black Circle,* 8 Jim Morrison, 9 *'Shame'* later changed to Brad, 10 Neil Young, 11 *VS,* 12 Jack Irons, 13 Tim Finn of Crowded House, 14 Neil Young, 15 His wife Beth Leibling's band Hovercraft.

• PINK FLOYD •

1 Which three founder members of the group first met while studying architecture at Regent Street Polytechnic in London?

2 When the fourth member of the group, Syd Barrett, was asked to join, where was he studying?

3 Which London underground club did the group start regular Sunday afternoon appearances?

4 What was the name of the band's first single, released in 1967?

5 Which British DJ described the group as a "con" on the TV show Juke Box Jury?

6 What was the title of the group's first album, featuring the songs *Interstellar Overdrive* and *Lucifer Sam*?

7 Which member of the band, and major songwriter, suffered a drug induced nervous breakdown in 1968 and quit?

8 And which guitarist was asked to join the band after this?

9 Pink Floyd joined Jethro Tull, Tyrannosaurus Rex and Roy Harper to play the first free open air concert at which London location?

10 What was the title of the debut solo album, released by the band's former guitarist and front man?

11 What was the title of the album, recorded by the band as a soundtrack to the film *The Valley*?

12 Which album, released in 1973, went on to sell over 20 million copies worldwide?

13 Which song, taken from the groups 1975 album *Wish You Were Here*, was written as a tribute to Syd Barrett?

14 Which album sleeve featured a photograph of a 40 foot inflatable pig, floating over Battersea Power Station?

15 In 1978, which artist's debut single did Dave Gilmour record a guitar solo for?

• PRINCE •

1 **What was the name of the band, formed in Minneapolis by Prince in 1973, featuring Alexander O'Neal, Terry Lewis and Jellybean Johnson in the line up?**

2 And how was the particular sound and style created by the group referred to in their home town?

3 **What was the title of Prince's debut album, released in 1978, and taking over 5 months in the studio to record?**

4 And what was the risqué title to the first single, taken from the album?

5 **What was the title of Prince's second album, completed in only 5 weeks, and containing the tracks *Why You Wanna Treat Me So Bad*? And *I Wanna Be Your Lover*?**

6 And which song, taken from the album, became a No. 1 UK hit for Chaka Khan in 1984?

7 **Which album, released in 1981, made No. 21 in the US charts, with the title track reaching No. 70 in the singles chart?**

8 What was the name of the girl group, formed by Prince, which opened for him during the promotional tour for the album 1999?

9 **Which single, taken from *1999*, reached No. 6 in the US charts?**

10 What was the name of the film, and accompanying album, released by Prince in 1984?

11 **And what were the names of Prince's backing singers, featured on the album?**

12 Which single, taken from the album, made No. 1 in the US and No. 4 in the UK?

13 **Which album, released in June 1985, was the first to be recorded at Prince's new Paisley Park studios in Minneapolis?**

14 And which single, taken from the album, reached No. 2 in the US charts?

15 **Under what pseudonym did Prince write the song *Manic Monday*, a No. 2 hit for US group The Bangles?**

1 **Flyte Tyme**, 2 Upbeat, 3 **For You**, 4 Soft And Wet, 5 **Prince**, 6 I Feel For You, 7 **Controversy**, 8 Vanity 6, 9 **Little Red Corvette**, 10 Purple Rain, 11 **Wendy and Lisa**, 12 When Doves Cry, 13 **Around The World In A Day**, 14 Raspberry Beret, 15 Christopher.

~ 110 ~

•PRODIGY•

1 **Where were Prodigy formed?**

2 Prodigy's debut single made the UK Top Ten, what was it?

3 **Which record label did the band sign with in 1991?**

4 Prodigy had their first UK No.1 album in 1994, what was it called?

5 **Who did Prodigy collaborate with on *Their Law* in 1993?**

6 What was Prodigy's first UK No.1 single?

7 **What did Keith Flint have done to his hair in 1996?**

8 Where was the video for *Firestarter* shot?

9 **Who guested on Prodigy's album track *Narayan*?**

10 And which band was he from?

11 **Which MTV Europe award did Prodigy win in 1998?**

12 And for which single did they win two MTV Video Music awards?

13 **Which two UK festivals did Prodigy headline at in 1998?**

14 What was the title of Liam Howlett's solo album released in 1998?

15 **In 1996 Prodigy released a single which entered the UK chart at No.1. What was it?**

1 **Braintree, Essex,** 2 *Charly,* **3 XL,** 4 *Music For The Jilted Generation,*
5 **Pop Will Eat Itself,** 6 *Firestarter,* 7 **He had a bright green mohican,**
8 The London Underground, 9 **Crispian Mills,** 10 Kula Shaker, 11 **Best
Dance Act,** 12 *Smack My Bitch Up,* **13 Reading and T in the Park,**
14 *The Dirtchamber Sessions; Vol 1,* **15 *Breathe.***

• PUBLIC IMAGE LTD •

1 What was the sleeve design on Public Image Ltd's. debut single?

2 On which BBC-TV show did John Lydon guest with Joan Collins in 1979?

3 In 1980 when the police raided John Lydon's house what did they find him waving at them?

4 What was the title of P.I.L.'s 1983 UK Top Ten single?

5 Who was left as P.I.L.'s only full-time member in 1983?

6 Which 1983 film did John Lydon appear in with Harvey Keitel?

7 In 1984 who did John Lydon team up with for the one-off single *World Destruction* under the name Time Zone?

8 Whose former house in Hollywood did John Lydon buy in 1992?

9 Who was the original bass player with Public Image Ltd.?

10 In which year were Public Image Ltd. formed?

11 With whom did John Lydon record the Top 20 single *Open Up*?

12 In 1997 John Lydon released his debut solo album, what was it?

13 With which band did John Lydon re-group with in 1996?

14 Which record label did Public Image Ltd. Sign in 1978?

15 P.I.L. released their last single in 1992 what was it?

1 A mock newspaper, 2 Juke Box Jury, 3 A ceremonial sword, 4 *This Is Not A Love Song*, 5 John Lydon, 6 *Cop Killer*, 7 Afrika Bambaataa, 8 Mae West, 9 Jah Wobble, 10 1978, 11 Leftfield, 12 *Psycho's Path*, 13 The Sex Pistols, 14 Virgin Records, 15 *Cruel.*

•PULP•

1 **What were Pulp originally called?**

2 Which BBC DJ invited the band to do a session on his radio show in 1981?

3 **How did Jarvis Cocker end up in a wheelchair for a year in 1986?**

4 Pulp released their debut album in 1982 though it failed to chart, what was it called?

5 **In 1993 Pulp made their debut on the UK singles chart with what?**

6 Pulp had their first UK Top Ten hit in 1995, what was it?.

7 **Who did Pulp replace at the 1995 Glastonbury Festival?**

8 How did Jarvis Cocker injure his foot in 1995?

9 **In 1995 Pulp released an album which entered the UK chart at No.1, what was it?**

10 Whose performance at the 1996 BRIT awards was disrupted by Jarvis Cocker walking on stage, causing a fracas?

11 **Whilst making their TV debut on BBC's *Top of the Pops* Jarvis Cocker flashed his T-shirt at the camera, what did it have written on it?**

12 Which member of the band left in 1996?

13 **Which track did Pulp contribute to the *Velvet Goldmine* soundtrack?**

14 In which UK city were Pulp formed?

15 **What was the title of Pulp's 1994 EP?**

1 Arabacus Pulp, 2 John Peel, 3 He jumped out of a window to impress a girlfriend, 4 It, 5 *Lip Gloss*, 6 *Common People*, 7 Stone **Roses, 8** He kicked his microphone across the stage after the band's equipment broke down?, 9 *Different Class*, 10 Michael Jackson, 11 I **Hate Wet Wet Wet**, 12 Russell Senior, 13 We Are The Boys, 14 Sheffield, 15 *The Sisters EP*.

•QUEEN I•

1. **What was the name of the group, initially formed by Guitarist Brian May and drummer Roger Taylor, before Queen was formed?**

2. What was singer Freddie Mercury's real name?

3. **Which 1974 single became the band's first UK hit single?**

4. Who was the band's flamboyant producer throughout most of the 1970's?

5. **What did Brian May build his own trademark guitar from?**

6. In what subject did John Deacon graduate from University?

7. **Which band did Queen support on their first UK tour in 1973?**

8. What forced the band to abandon their first US tour in 1974?

9. **Which album featured the singles *Now I'm Here* and *Killer Queen*?**

10. Which album, named after a Marx Brothers film, did the band record in 1975, using 6 different studios?

11. **And which single from the album became the first to be widely promoted by an accompanying video?**

12. And which DJ had forced the record companys to release the over long track, by repeatedly playing it on his Capital Radio show?

13. **Which member of the band wrote the second single taken from the album, *You're My Best Friend*?**

14. What was the title of the band's 1976 album, also named after a Marx Brothers film, which featured the single *Good Old Fashioned Lover Boy*?

15. **Which member of the group became the first to release a solo record, with *I Wanna Testify*?**

1 **Smile,** 2 Freddy Bulsara, 3 *Seven Seas Of Rhye,* 4 Roy Thomas-Baker, 5 **An old fireplace,** 6 Electronics, 7 **Mott The Hoople,** 8 Guitarist Brian May collapsed with hepatitis, and later developed an ulcer, 9 *Sheer Heart Attack,* 10 *A Night At The Opera,* 11 *Bohemian Rhapsody,* 12 Kenny Everett, 13 Bassist, John Deacon, 14 *A Day At The Races,* 15 **Drummer, Roger Taylor.**

•QUEEN II•

1 **Which artist's 1976 album, *All American Alien*, did Brian May, Freddie Mercury and Roger Taylor guest on?**

2 Which gospel flavoured single reached No. 13 in the US charts in 1977?

3 **Which double A-side, released in November 1977, reached No. 2 in the UK charts?**

4 And which album was the single taken from?

5 **Which skiffle artist's 1978 comeback album, *Puttin' On The Style*, featured guest guitarwork by Brian May?**

6 From 1978, in which Swiss town did the band start recording all their material?

7 **Which double A-side, released in 1978, reached No. 11 in the UK charts?**

8 And which album had the single come from?

9 **And why was the artwork on the gatefold sleeve of the album changed after it's initial release?**

10 What was the title of the band's 1979 live album double set?

11 **And which song, taken from the album, reached No. 3 in the UK singles chart?**

12 Which rockabilly style single, taken from the 1980 album *The Game*, reached No. 2 in the UK charts?

13 **And which single, also from *The Game* and written by bass player John Deacon, became the band's first No. 1 US single?**

14 Which 1980 science fiction film did Queen provide the soundtrack for?

15 **Under which category were Queen the first rock band to be listed in the 1980 *Guinness Book of Records*?**

1 Ian Hunter, 2 *Somebody To Love*, 3 *We Are The Champions/We Will Rock You*, 4 *News Of The World*, 5 Lonnie Donegan, 6 Montreux, 7 *Bicycle Race/Fat Bottomed Girls*, 8 *Jazz*, 9 It featured naked women riding bicycles, like the cover of the *Bicycle Race/Fat Bottomed Girls* single, and was changed to prevent retailers insisting on selling it in a brown paper bag, 10 *Live Killers*, 11 *Love Of My Life*, 12 *Crazy Little Thing Called Love*, 13 *Another One Bites The Dust*, 14 *Flash Gordon*, 15 In a list of Britain's highest paid executives.

• QUEEN III •

1. **What was the title of drummer Roger Taylor's 1981 solo album, featuring the single *Future Management*?**

2. Released in 1981, for how many weeks was *Queen's Greatest Hits* In the UK album charts?

3. **Which solo artist did Queen record the song *Under Pressure* with in 1981, which reached No. 1 in the UK singles chart?**

4. And, with the success of this single and their *Greatest Hits* album, what feat did Queen become the first band to achieve?

5. **What was the title of the band's danced-based album, released in 1982?**

6. Which single, written by Roger Taylor, reached No. 2 in the UK charts in 1984, and set a record for the band, with all 4 members now having written a Top Ten song?

7. **And which album featured this single, along with *I Want To Break Free* and *It's A Hard Life*?**

8. What was the title of Freddie Mercury's first solo single, released in 1984?

9. **And which album had the song been taken from?**

10. Which film soundtrack featured Queen's 1985 single *One Vision*?

11. **Which song, taken from the 1986 film *Highlander*, reached No. 3 in the UK chart?**

12. What was the name of the band formed by Roger Taylor in 1987, in which he played the guitar?

13. **With which opera singer did Freddie Mercury duet on the 1987 song *Barcelona*?**

14. Which album, released in 1989, featured the singles *I Want It All* and *The Invisible Man*?

15. **What was the title of the band's 1991 single, which became the third longest UK No. 1 single, at 6 minutes and 32 seconds?**

1 *Fun In Space*, 2 312 weeks, **3 David Bowie,** 4 They were the first band to be at the top of the UK singles, album and video charts simulta- neously, **5 *Hot Space*,** 6 *Radio Ga Ga*, **7 *The Works*,** 8 *Love Kills*, **9 *Mr. Bad Guy*,** 10 *Iron Eagle*, **11 *A Kind Of Magic*,** 12 The Cross, **13 Monserrat Caballe,** 14 *The Miracle*, **15 *Innuendo***

~ 116 ~

• RADIOHEAD •

1 How old was Thom Yorke when he formed his first band?

2 Where did Radiohead take their name from?

3 **Radiohead made their debut on the UK chart in 1993, with which single?**

4 In the same year they had their first UK Top Ten single, what was it?

5 **In 1996 who did Radiohead open for during a US tour?**

6 By what name were Radiohead originally known?

7 **What was the title of Radiohead's 1994 EP?**

8 Which charity album did Thom Yorke help instigate with Brian Eno?

9 **And which track did Radiohead record for the album?**

10 Who did Radiohead support on tour in 1995?

11 **What was the title of Radioheads first UK No.1 album?**

12 And which actress owned the eerie old mansion where they recorded it?

13 **Which Pink Floyd track did Radiohead with Sparklehorse record a cover version of for the tribute album *Come Again*?**

14 Which record label did Radiohead sign with in 1991?

15 **Name Radiohead's bass player**

1 10, 2 A Talking Heads' album track, 3 *Anyone Can Play Guitar,*
4 Creep, 5 Alanis Morissette, 6 On A Friday, 7 *My Iron Lung,* 8 War
Child charity album *'Help',* 9 *Lucky,* 10 REM, 11 *OK Computer,* 12 Jane
Seymour, 13 *Wish You Were Here,* 14 Parlophone, 15 Colin
Greenwood.

~ 117 ~

• RAINBOW •

1 Which band was Ritchie Blackmore a member of before forming Rainbow?

2 And with which American band did he record the single *Black Sheep Of The Family* in 1975?

3 Who joined the band as drummer in 1975?

4 Which was the first Rainbow album to reach the UK Top Ten?

5 Ronnie James Dio left Rainbow in 1978, which band did he later join?

6 Rainbow had their first UK Top Ten hit in 1979, what was it?

7 In 1981 the band had their biggest hit with *I Surrender*, from which album was it taken?

8 Who banned the showing of Rainbow's video for the single *Street Of Dreams* because it visually demonstrated hypnosis?

9 In which country did Rainbow play their last live show?

10 In which year did Rainbow split?

11 Which band did Ritchie Blackmore and Roger Glover re-join after Rainbow split?

12 In 1986 Rainbow released a greatest hits album what was it called?

13 Rainbow released a comeback album in 1995, what was it?

14 Under which name were Rainbow first formed?

15 Rainbow had their last UK chart single to date in 1983, what was it called?

1 Deep Purple, 2 ELF, **3 Cozy Powell,** 4 *On Stage,* **5 Black Sabbath,** 6 *Since You've Been Gone,* **7 *Difficult To Cure*,** 8 MTV, 9 Japan, 10 1984, **11 Deep Purple,** 12 *Finyl Vinyl,* **13 *Stranger In All Of Us*,** 14 Ritchie Blackmore's Rainbow, **15 *Can't Let You Go*.**

•RED HOT CHILI PEPPERS•

1 **By which name were the Red Hot Chili Peppers originally formed?**

2 Which member of the band died from a heroin overdose in 1988?

3 **The Red Hot Chili Peppers made their debut on the UK chart with a cover version of a Stevie Wonder song, what was it?**

4 Which member of the band left in 1988 and later joined Pearl Jam?

5 **The Red Hot Chili Peppers made their debut on the UK album chart with what?**

6 In 1991 Anthony Kiedis appeared in the movie *Point Blank* in which 1976 film did he make his acting debut?

7 **Which track did the band record for the soundtrack to *Wayne's World*?**

8 John Frusciante left the Red Hot Chili Peppers in 1992, what was the title of his solo album released in 1994?

9 **Which Hollywood actor fatally collapsed in Los Angeles whilst enjoying a night out on the town with Flea?**

10 Which two members of the band featured on Alanis Morissette's single *You Oughta Know*?

11 **Which track did the band contribute to the 1995 John Lennon tribute album *Working Class Hero*?**

12 The Red Hot Chili Peppers had their first UK Top Ten hit in 1994, what was it?

13 **In 1990 Flea and Chad Smith were found guilty of what?**

14 In 1993 Arik Marshall appeared in an episode of which cartoon series?

15 **Before joining the Red Hot Chili Peppers, Dave Navarro was a member of which band?**

1 *Los Faces,* 2 Hillel Slovak, 3 *Higher Ground,* 4 Jack Irons, 5 *Blood Sugar Sex Magik,* 6 *F.I.S.T.,* 7 *Sikamikanico,* 8 *To Clara,* 9 River Phoenix, 10 Flea and Dave Navarro, 11 *I Found Out,* 12 *Give It Away,* 13 Battery and sexual harassment, 14 *The Simpsons,* 15 Jane's Addiction.

• REM •

1 **Michael Stipe was a student at The University Of Georgia, what did he study?**

2 On which TV programme did REM make their European debut?

3 **In 1983 the group played seven stadium concerts opening for which British band?**

4 In 1987 REM released a collection of out-takes and B-side material as an album, what was it called?

5 **Which was the first REM single to reach the UK Top Ten?**

6 In 1988 Michael Stipe with 10,000 Manics singer Natalie Merchant and the Roaches performed a song for the Walt Disney album *Stay Awake*, which one was it?

7 **In 1989 Michael Stipe formed his own film and video company, what was it called?**

8 Michael Stipe co-wrote and featured on whose single *You Woke Up My Neighbourhood*?

9 **Which was REM's first album to enter the UK chart at No. 1?**

10 In 1995 which member of the band was rushed from the stage during a concert complaining of a severe headache which turned out to be an aneurysm?

11 **Which was the first year REM played the Glastonbury Festival?**

12 In which magazine were REM given the Lifetime Achievement award in 1998?

13 **In 1997 which member of REM was the first to release a solo album?**

14 From which REM album was the UK Top Ten single *Daysleeper* taken?

15 **Who featured on the REM single *Shiny Happy People*,**

1 **Painting and photography,** 2 The Tube, 3 **The Police,** 4 *Dead Letter Office,* 5 *Shiny Happy People,* 6 *Little April Shower,* 7 **C-00,** 8 Billy Bragg, 9 ***Out Of Time,*** 10 Bill Berry, 11 1999, 12 Q Magazine, 13 **Mike Mills,** 14 *Up,* 15 **Kate Pierson of the B-52's**

~ 120 ~

•ROBBIE WILLIAMS•

1 **Where in the UK was Robbie Williams born?**

2 In which year did he leave Take That, to follow a solo career?

3 **Who originally wrote and recorded Robbie Williams' debut single, *Freedom*, released in July 1996?**

4 Which US heavy metal band did Robbie Williams parody in the video to his 1998 single *Let Me Entertain You*?

5 **How many Brit Award nominations did Robbie Williams receive in 1998?**

6 And how many awards did he actually walk away with?

7 **Which film memorabillia is Robbie Williams known to collect?**

8 What was the title of Robbie Williams debut solo album, released in 1997?

9 **Which UK magazine named Robbie Williams their 1998 "Man of the year"?**

10 Who originally wrote the looping melodic string pattern, used by Robbie Williams in his 1998 single *Millennium*?

11 **Which member of pop group The Corrs has Robbie Williams been romantically linked to?**

12 Which artist did Robbie Williams perform a duet with, at the 1998 Brit Awards?

13 **Which 1999 British film featured the Robbie Williams song *Man Machine* in its soundtrack?**

14 Which two pop artists did Robbie Williams collaborate with on his 1998 single *No Regrets*?

15 **Which track did Robbie Williams record for the 1998 Noel Coward tribute album, *20th Century Blues*?**

The Divine Comedy, **15** *Bad Times Are Just Around The Corner.*
14 Neil Tennant, from the Pet Shop Boys, and Neil Hannon, from *Barrels*, **13** Tom Jones, **12** Tom Jones, **11 Andrea Corr,** *Stock and Two Smoking*
10 John Barry, from his 1967 Bond theme *You Only Live Twice*,
Millennium, **7** *Star Wars* **memorabillia,** 8 *Life Thru A Lens*, **9** *The Face*,
6 Three, Best Male Artist, Best Single for *Angels*, Best Video for
1 Newcastle-Under-Lyme, **2** 1985, **3 George Michael,** 4 Kiss, **5 Six,**

•ROBERT PLANT•

1 **With which band did Robert Plant make his recording debut?**

2 Which band did Robert Plant join as lead singer in 1968?

3 **Robert Plant's debut solo album made the UK Top Ten, what was it called?**

4 Robert Plant made his debut on BBC's *Top of the Pops* in 1983 with which song?

5 **What was the name of the group Robert Plant formed with Jimmy Page, Jeff Beck and Nile Rogers in 1984?**

6 Who played drums when Robert Plant performed with his original group at the Live Aid concert in Philadelphia?

7 **Which track did Robert Plant contribute to the charity album *The Last Temptation Of Elvis* in 1990?**

8 In 1992 which song did Robert Plant sing at the Freddie Mercury tribute concert at Wembley Stadium?

9 **What was the name of the duet Robert Plant recorded with Tori Amos in 1995?**

10 Who was once a roadie for the band Robert Plant made his recording debut with?

11 **Which Robert Plant song featured classical violinist Nigel Kennedy?**

12 Who did Robert Plant reunite with for the 1994 album *No Quarter*?

13 **How was Robert Plant injured in 1975?**

14 In 1993 Robert Plant recorded a cover version of a Tim Hardin song, what was it?

15 **Which course did Robert Plant drop out of to take up music?**

•ROBERT PALMER•

1 What was the name of the band Robert Palmer formed in 1971?

2 What was Robert Palmer's debut UK chart single?

3 In 1982 Robert Palmer had a hit with a cover version of *Some Guys Have All The Luck*. Who recorded the original version?

4 Which group did Robert Palmer join on a temporary basis in 1985?

5 And which members of Duran Duran were also in the group?

6 In 1986 Robert Palmer had his first UK Top Ten hit, what was it?

7 And who directed the award-winning video which accompanied it?

8 In 1985 Robert Palmer had his first UK Top Ten album, what was it?

9 Which 1990 film featured Robert Palmer's *Life In Detail*?

10 With which group did Robert Palmer record a cover version of Bob Dylan's *I'll Be Your Baby Tonight* in 1990?

11 In 1992 where did Robert Palmer perform while on the way to New York?

12 Who featured on Robert Palmer's single *Johnny And Mary*?

13 Robert Palmer recorded a cover version of a Todd Rundgren song on his album *Secrets*, what was it?

14 In 1986 Robert Palmer had a hit with *I Didn't Mean To Turn You On* who had a hit with the original version?

15 Which record label did Robert Palmer sign with in 1988?

1 Vinegar Joe, 2 *Every Kinda People*, 3 The Persuaders, 4 The Power Station, 5 John and Andy Taylor, 6 *Addicted To Love*, 7 Terence Donovan, 8 *Riptide*, 9 *Pretty Woman*, 10 UB40, 11 The QE2, 12 Gary Numan, 13 *Can We Still Be Friends*, 14 Cherrelle, 15 EMI.

•ROD STEWART I•

1 **In which city was Rod Stewart born?**

2 With which football club did Rod Stewart sign an apprenticeship in 1961?

3 **Whose band did he join in 1966?**

4 When Rod Stewart left to join the band The Faces, which guitarist did he bring with him?

5 **What was the title of Rod Stewart's 1970 solo album, featuring the tracks *It's All Over Now* and *My Way Of Giving*?**

6 Which song, originally released as the B-side to *Reason To Believe*, topped the charts in the US and UK in 1971?

7 **And which Radio 1 DJ appeared on BBC TV, playing mandolin on the song with the rest of the band?**

8 And which album, also a No. 1 in the US and UK, was the song taken from?

9 **Which 1972 album featured the cover versions *Angel* and *Twisting The Night Away*?**

10 And which No. 1 single, taken from the album, mentions Marilyn Monroe and Jackie Onassis?

11 **What was the title of the Scotland World Cup Football Squad's 1974 album, on which Rod Stewart contributed guest vocals?**

12 Which 1974 album featured the No. 7 single *Farewell*?

13 **And which song, taken from the album, was written by Paul McCartney?**

14 With which Swedish actress did Rod Stewart start a much publicised affair in 1975?

15 **What was the title of Rod Stewart's 1975 solo album, which contained the No. 1 single *Sailing*?**

•ROD STEWART II•

1 **Which single, a No. 5 hit in the UK, was widely banned, because of the sexual content of it's lyrics?**

2 Why was Rod Stewart's 1975 single *Sailing* re-released in 1976, when it reached No. 3 in the UK charts?

3 **Which cover version of a Cat Stevens song reached No. 1 in the UK charts for Rod Stewart in 1977?**

4 Which album, released in 1977, featured the UK No. 3 single *You're In My Heart*?

5 **Which Faces-style rock single reached No. 5 in the UK charts in 1978?**

6 What was the title of the disco orientated No. 1 single, released by Rod Stewart in 1978?

7 **And which album was the single taken from?**

8 Which album, released in 1980, featured the singles *Oh God, I Wish I Was Home Tonight* and *Passion*?

9 **Which 1982 film, starring Michael Keaton, featured Rod Stewart's recording of the song *That's What Friends Are For*?**

10 Which single, released in 1983, reached No. 1 in the UK charts?

11 **What was the title of Rod Stewart's 1984 album, featuring the songs *Infatuation* and *Some Guys Have All The Luck*?**

12 Which cover version of a song by Free reached No. 72 in the US charts, when released by Rod Stewart in 1985?

13 **Which album, released in 1986, did Rod Stewart have a No. 2 UK hit with the title track?**

14 And which single, taken from the album, was co-written by Bryan Adams?

15 **Which cover version, recorded by Rod Stewart in 1987, was used in the soundtrack to the film *Innerspace*?**

1 *Tonight's The Night (Gonna Be Alright)*, **2** It was used for the BBC documentary *Sailor*, **3** *First Cut is The Deepest*, **4** *Foot Loose And Fancy Free*, **5** *Hot Legs*, **6** *D'Ya Think I'm Sexy*, **7** *Blondes Have More Fun*, **8** *Foolish Behaviour*, **9** *Night Shift*, **10** *Baby Jane*, **11** *Camouflage*, **12** *All Right Now*, **13** *Every Beat Of My Heart*, **14** *Another Heartache*, **15** *Twistin' The Night Away*.

•ROY ORBISON•

1 **What was the title of the first single recorded by Roy Orbison, and released on the Sun Records label?**

2 What was the name of the backing band Roy Orbison recorded his early singles with?

3 **What was the title of the last single to be released by Roy Orbison and his band, before they split up in 1956?**

4 Which song, written by Roy Orbison, was recorded by the Everly Brothers, and was used as the B-side to their hit single *All I Have To Do Is Dream*?

5 **Which 1960 song, recorded by Roy Orbison, reached No. 2 in the US, and No. 1 in the UK?**

6 Which song, released in 1961 and a No. 2 US hit for Roy Orbison, reached No. 1 in the UK when recorded by Don McLean in 1980?

7 **Which British band made their BBC radio debut, singing the 1962 Roy Orbison hit *Dream Baby*?**

8 Which song, written by Roy Orbison himself, reached No. 7 in the US charts in 1963?

9 **Why did dark glasses become part of Roy Orbison's image, following a tour of the UK in 1963?**

10 Which single, released in 1964, reached No. 1 in the US and UK for three weeks?

11 **How did Roy Orbison injure himself during his 1966 UK tour, forcing him to appear on stage with crutches?**

12 What tragedy struck the singer in June 1966?

13 **Which film did Roy Orbison appear in in 1967, playing a part originally intended for Elvis Presley?**

14 What further personal tragedy struck Roy Orbison while on tour in Britain in 1968?

15 **What type of surgery did the singer undergo at St Thomas' Hospital, Nashville, in 1978?**

1 *Ooby Dooby*, 2 The Teen Kings, 3 *Devil Doll*, 4 *Claudette*, 5 *Only The Lonely*, 6 *Crying*, 7 The Beatles, 8 *In Dreams*, 9 He had left his regular glasses on a plane, and had to wear his shaded pair in order to see properly, 10 *Oh! Pretty Woman*, 11 He fell off a motorcycle in Hawkstone Park in Birmingham, 12 His wife, Claudette, was knocked off her motorcycle and killed, 13 *The Fastest Guitar Alive*, 14 A house fire at his home in Nashville killed two of his sons, 15 A coronary by-pass.

• SANTANA •

1 **At which San Francisco club did the band play their debut gig?**

2 What was the name of the band's phenomenal drummer, who replaced original drummer, Rod Harper, in 1968?

3 **Which song, played by the band at the Woodstock festival in 1969, featured in the documentary film of the event?**

4 Which song, taken from the band's eponymous debut album, reached No. 9 in the US charts in 1970?

5 **What was the title of Santana's second album, which stayed in the UK album charts for over a year?**

6 Who recorded the original version of the song *Black Magic Woman*, which became a No. 4 US hit for Santana in 1971?

7 **With which drummer did Carlos Santana record a live album in Hawaii in 1972?**

8 Which instrumental track, taken from their 1971 album, reached No. 27 in the UK charts when re-released in 1974?

9 **Which religious order did Carlos Santana become a devotee of in 1973?**

10 What was the title of the 1975 triple live album, recorded and originally released in Japan?

11 **Which guitarist did Carlos Santana duet with on the song *Black Queen*, at the *Night Of The Hurricane* benefit concert in 1976?**

12 What was the title of the band's 1976 album, featuring the single *Let It Shine*?

13 **At which venue did the band perform a concert, broadcast simultaneously on BBC TV and radio?**

14 Which band had the original hit with the song *She's Not There*, which reached No. 11 in the UK charts when released by Santana in 1977?

15 **What was the title of the band's 1979 album, featuring the single *One Chain (Don't Make A Prison)*?**

1 The Avalon Ballroom, 2 Michael Shrieve, 3 *Soul Sacrifice*, 4 *Evil Ways*, 5 *Abraxas*, 6 Fleetwood Mac, 7 Buddy Miles, 8 *Samba Pa Ti*, 9 Sri Chinmoy, 10 *Lotus*, 11 Stephen Stills, 12 *Amigos*, 13 The Royal Albert Hall, 14 The Zombies, 15 *Inner Secrets*.

•SEX PISTOLS•

1 In which year were the Sex Pistols formed?

2 In 1976 the Sex Pistols made their debut UK TV appearance on which show?

3 Where did the Sex Pistols sign their contract to A&M records in 1977?

4 And which label were the group originally signed to but dropped due to adverse publicity?

5 How long did the Sex Pistols remain with A&M?

6 Why did the picture on the sleeve of the Sex Pistols single *God Save The Queen* cause a furore in the press?

7 In 1977 the group made their *Top of the Pops* debut performing which single?

8 In 1977 who took the Sex Pistols place on NBC-TV *Saturday Night Live* show when the group were denied entry into the USA?

9 Which group did Johnny Rotten form using his real name in 1978?

10 And what is his real name?

11 Who was Sid Vicious accused of murdering in 1978?

12 In which year did Sid Vicious die?

13 And how did he die?

14 What was the title of the Sex Pistols' 1979 film and album?

15 Who featured on the Sex Pistols' single *No One Is Innocent*?

1 1975, **2** *So It Goes*, **3** **Outside Buckingham Palace**, **4** EMI, **5** **6 days**,
6 It featured the Queen with a safety pin through her mouth, **7** *Pretty*
Vacant, 8 Elvis Costello, **9** **Public Image Limited** , 10 John Lydon,
11 **His girlfriend Nancy Spungen**, 12 1979, **13** Heroin overdose,
14 *The Great Rock 'n' Roll Swindle*, **15** **Ronnie Biggs**.

•SIMON AND GARFUNKEL I•

1 **Under what name did the duo record their first single?**

2 And what was the title of the song?

3 **What did Art Garfunkel study at college?**

4 What was the title of the album, released in 1964, under the name Simon And Garfunkel?

5 **Which song from the duo's debut album became their first hit, when it was overdubbed with a heavier rhythm track without their knowledge?**

6 And which band had a UK No. 3 hit with a cover version of this song?

7 **Which song, written by Paul Simon for his girlfriend Kathy Chitty, reached No. 5 in the US charts?**

8 Which song, which reached No. 13 in the US charts in 1966, was later revived in 1987 by US group The Bangles?

9 **What was the title of the duo's 1966 album, featuring the track *Scarborough Fair*?**

10 Which band reached No. 13 in the US charts in 1967 with a cover version of Paul Simon's *59th Street Bridge Song*?

11 **Which 1968 film were the duo commissioned to write the sound track for?**

12 And which song, featured in the film, reached No. 1 in the US charts in 1968?

13 **Why did the duo walk out of the recording of the BBC's *Top Of The Pops* in 1968?**

14 Which album, released in 1968, featured the tracks *America* and *At The Zoo*?

15 **Which single, released in 1969, reached No. 6 in the UK charts?**

1 **Tom And Jerry,** 2 *Hey Schoolgirl,* 3 **Mathematics and architecture,** 4 *Wednesday Morning, 3 A.M.,* 5 *The Sound Of Silence,* 6 The Bachelors, 7 *Homeward Bound,* 8 *Hazy Shade Of Winter,* 9 *Parsley, Sage, Rosemary and Thyme,* 10 Harpers Bizarre, 11 *The Graduate,* 12 *Mrs. Robinson,* 13 They objected to the go-go girls dancing to their record, 14 *Bookends,* 15 *The Boxer.*

•SIMON AND GARFUNKEL II•

1 **Which single, released in 1970, stayed at No. 1 in the US charts for 6 weeks?**

2 And which Everly Brothers cover version did the duo record for their final album, released in 1970?

3 **Which political song, written by Paul Simon, caused arguments between the duo, when Art Garfunkel objected to recording it?**

4 Which song did Paul Simon write to signify the end of the duo's relationship, although Art Garfunkel missed the obvious references to him in the lyrics?

5 **Which film did Art Garfunkel go on to feature in, once the duo had split up, in 1970?**

6 Which song, released in 1970 and reaching No. 18 in the US charts, was based on a traditional Andes folk tune?

7 **Which actress made the charts in May 1970 with a cover version of *Keep The Customer Satisfied*?**

8 Which single, taken from the duo's last album, reached No. 4 in the US charts?

9 **For how many weeks was the duo's album *Bridge Over Troubled Water* at No. 1 in the UK charts?**

10 For which Presidential candidate did they reunite to play a benefit concert, in 1972?

11 **Which live track, taken from the duo's 1972 greatest hits package, reached No. 25 in the UK charts?**

12 Which film, co-starring Jack Nicholson and Ann-Margret, did Art Garfunkel appear in, playing the role of roommate, Sandy?

13 **Which Hollywood actress did Paul Simon marry in the 1970's?**

14 What was the title of Paul Simon's 1973 album, featuring the tracks *Tenderness* and *Loves Me Like A Rock*?

15 **Which song, written by Mike Batt, became a No. 1 single in the UK in 1979 for Art Garfunkel?**

•SIMPLE MINDS•

1 By what name were Simple Minds originally known?

2 In 1985 which film featured Simple Minds' *Don't You Forget About Me*?

3 In 1980 who invited Simple Minds to support him on his European tour?

4 In 1981 who quit the band and was replaced for a short time by Kenny Hyslop?

5 Who sang guest vocals on Simple Minds' *Speed Your Love To Me*?

6 In 1983 Steve Lillywhite began producing for Simple Minds, who introduced him to them?

7 Who did Jim Kerr marry in 1984?

8 Which two singers rejected the song *Don't You Forget About Me* before it was offered to Simple Minds?

9 At the *Live-Aid* concert in 1985 which song did Simple Minds dedicate to Amnesty International?

10 In 1989 which Simple Minds single, at over six minutes long became the second longest UK No.1 behind the Beatles' *Hey Jude*?

11 Where did Simple Minds take their name from?

12 Simple Minds' album *The Rain* included a cover version of a Lou Reed song, what was it?

13 In 1981 which record company did they sign with, renouncing rights and back royalties?

14 In 1982 a compilation album of the band's early tracks was released, what was it called?

15 Who did Simple Minds' support on tour in 1984?

1 Johnny & The Self Abusers, 2 *The Breakfast Club*, 3 Peter Gabriel, 4 Brian McGee, 5 Kirsty MacColl, 6 U2's Bono, 7 Chrissie Hynde, 8 Billy Idol and Bryan Ferry, 9 *Ghostdancing*, 10 *Belfast Child*, 11 A line in a David Bowie song, 12 *Street Hassle*, 13 Virgin, 14 *Celebration*, 15 The Pretenders.

• SLADE •

1 **What was the name of the Wolverhampton band which future Slade guitarist, Dave Hill, and drummer, Don Powell, played in during 1965?**

2 And, when the line up was completed by Noddy Holder and Jimmy Lea, under what name did they record their first single?

3 **Which musician became the band's manager and producer, after seeing them at Rasputin's club in London?**

4 Under what name did the band release their first Album, *Beginnings*?

5 **Which Bobby Marchan song became the band's first hit single, under the name Slade?**

6 Which single, released in 1971, stayed at No. 1 in the UK charts for four weeks?

7 **Which 1972 No. 1 hit single starts with the line "I don't want to drink my whiskey like you do"?**

8 And which album was the song taken from?

9 **Which Chuck Berry song kept the band's single, *Gudbuy T'Jane*, off the No. 1 spot in the UK?**

10 What was the title of the band's 1973 No. 1 single, later covered by 1990's band Oasis?

11 **Which member of the band suffered severe head injuries in a car crash in July 1973?**

12 Which single was recorded by the band during a US tour, and sold over 1/4 million on its first day of release?

13 **What was the title of the film which featured Slade as a fictitious mid 1960's band?**

14 Which 1981 single became the band's first Top Ten hit for six years?

15 **Which US heavy metal group had hit singles with cover versions of Slade's *Cum On Feel The Noize* and *Mama Weer All Crazee Now*?**

1 The Vendors, 2 The 'N Betweens, **3 Chas Chandler,** 4 Ambrose Slade, **5 Get Down And Get With It,** 6 Coz I Luv You, 7 **Mama Weer All Crazee Now,** 8 Slayed, 9 *My Ding-A-Ling,* 10 *Cum On Feel The Noize,* **11 Drummer Don Powell,** 12 *Merry Christmas Everybody,* 13 *Slade In Flame,* 14 *We'll Bring The House Down,* **15 Quiet Riot.**

• SMASHING PUMPKINS •

1 **Which two members of Smashing Pumpkins originally formed the band as a duo?**

2 In which American city were the band formed?

3 **In 1992 Smashing Pumpkins released their debut UK single, what was it called?**

4 And from which album was it taken?

5 **Who featured on piano on the album *Siamese Dream*?**

6 In 1994 Smashing Pumpkins were banned from appearing on BBC's *Top of the Pops* because of objection to the lyrics of which song?

7 **Which member of the band died from a heroin overdose in 1996?**

8 Which member of the band was sacked in 1996?

9 **What was the name of the band Billy Corgan was a member of before forming Smashing Pumpkins?**

10 What was the title of Smashing Pumpkins album of outtakes and B-sides, released in 1994?

11 **Which Smashing Pumkins' single featured in the film *Batman And Robin*?**

12 In 1998 which member of the band released a solo album?

13 **Which ex-member of Filter joined Smashing Pumpkins in 1996?**

14 In 1996 Smashing Pumpkins had their first UK Top Ten hit, what was it?

15 **In 1994 Smashing Pumpkins recorded a cover version of a Depeche Mode song, what was it?**

1 Billy Corgan and D'Arcy, 2 Chicago, 3 *I Am One*, 4 *Gish*, 5 REM's Mike Mills , 6 *Disarm*, 7 Jonathan Melvoin, 8 Jimmy Chamberlain, 9 The Marked, 10 *Pisces Iscariot*, 11 *The End Is The Beginning Is The End*, 12 James Iha, 13 Matt Walker, 14 *Tonight Tonight*, 15 *Never Let Me Down*.

• SONIC YOUTH •

1 In which year were Sonic Youth formed?

2 Name the drummer who joined the band in 1985

3 **With which album did Sonic Youth make their debut on the UK chart?**

4 And which independent label released it after being set up especially to release Sonic Youth material?

5 **Under what name did the band record *The Whitey Album*?**

6 Which label did the band sign with in 1986?

7 **Sonic Youth made their debut on the UK singles chart in 1992 with what?**

8 For whom did Sonic Youth open for on a US tour in 1991?

9 **For whose tribute album did Sonic Youth record a track for in 1994?**

10 And which track did they record?

11 **What was the title of Thurston Moore's debut solo album released in 1995?**

12 Which benefit concert arranged by the Beastie Boys did Sonic Youth perform at in 1996?

13 **Which UK TV show featured the band in an hour-long special documentary in 1989?**

14 In 1992 Sonic Youth had their first UK Top Ten album, what was it?

15 **What was the name of the side line group Kim Gordon formed in 1995?**

1 **1981,** 2 Steve Shelley, 3 *Daydream Nation*, 4 Blast Fast, 5 Ciccone **Youth,** 6 Geffen, 7 **100%,** 8 Neil Young & Crazy Horse, 9 **The Carpenters,** 10 *Yesterday Once More*, 11 *Psychic*, 12 Tibetan Freedom Concert, 13 *The South Bank Show*, 14 *Dirty*, 15 Free Kitten.

• SQUEEZE •

1 **Where did Squeeze take their name from?**

2 In 1979 Squeeze had their first UK Top Ten hit, what was it?

3 **Which band did Jools Holland make a TV documentary with in 1980?**

4 Which TV show did Jools Holland co-host from 1982 to 1987?

5 **Who replaced Jools Holland in Squeeze?**

6 In 1981 with whom did Glenn Tilbrook team up with for the one-off single *From A Whisper To A Scream*?

7 **What was the name of the musical released in 1983 based on Chris Difford and Glenn Tilbrook songs?**

8 Who did Squeeze support on a US tour in 1990?

9 **Which two members of Squeeze released a single in 1984?**

10 And what was it called?

11 **Squeeze split in 1982, in which year did they re-form?**

12 Before Squeeze, Gilson Lavis was tour manager and drummer with which American rock star?

13 **What was the title of Squeeze's debut single released in 1978?**

14 Who did Squeeze support on his UK tour in 1992?

15 **After leaving Squeeze Jools Holland fronted his own band, what were they called?**

1 A Velvet Underground Album, 2 Cool For Cats, 3 The Police, 4 The Tube, 5 Paul Carrack, 6 Elvis Costello, 7 Labelled with Love, 8 Fleetwood Mac, 9 Difford and Tilbrook, 10 Love's Crashing Waves, 11 1985, 12 Chuck Berry, 13 Take Me I'm Yours, 14 Bryan Adams, 15 The Millionaires.

• STATUS QUO •

1 In 1964 the group accept a four-month contract doing what?

2 Status Quo worked as whose backing band in 1968?

3 **In 1968 who co-wrote Status Quo's *Ice In The Sun*?**

4 Status Quo supported who on a UK tour in 1969?

5 **When Status Quo played *Rockin' All Over The World* on *Top Of The Pops* in 1977, what was Alan Lancaster substituted with?**

6 In 1991 which BRIT award did Status Quo win?

7 **At what event in 1995 did the group perform *Rockin' All Over The World*?**

8 In 1991 how did Status Quo gain their entry into *The Guinness Book of Records*?

9 **In 1995 Status Quo released *Fun Fun Fun* with The Beach Boys, why did BBC Radio 1 refuse to play it?**

10 In 1968 Status Quo had their first UK Top Ten hit, what was it called?

11 **What is Status Quo's only UK No.1 single to date?**

12 By which two names were Status Quo originally known?

13 **In 1976 who did Status Quo sign a pioneering sponsorship deal with?**

14 Who wrote *Rockin' All Over The World* and which group was he a member of?

15 **In 1994 which football team used the tune to *Burning Bridges* and made UK No.1?**

• STEREOPHONICS •

1 What nationality are the Stereophonics?

2 In which year was the band formed?

3 Which BRIT award did the band win in 1998?

4 What was the title of the Stereophonics' debut album?

5 In 1998 what event at Wembley Stadium did the band open for?

6 The Stereophonics were the first band to play where since Queen in the 1970's?

7 Which new record label did the band sign with in 1996?

8 What was the title of the Stereophonics' album released in 1999?

9 At which 1999 concert did the band co-headline with Blur?

10 Before the band took off Kelly Jones attended a course studying what?

11 With which rock group did the Stereophonics perform at Wembley in 1999?

12 The Stereophonics made their debut on the UK chart in 1997 with which single?

13 What was the Stereophonics' first UK Top Ten single?

14 By which name were the Stereohonics originally known?

15 What is the name of the Stereophonics' drummer?

1 Welsh, 2 1996 , 3 Best Newcomer, 4 Word Gets Around, 5 Wales-South African rugby match, 6 Cardiff Castle, 7 Richard Branson's V2 label, 8 Performance & Cocktails, 9 T In The Park, 10 Scriptwriting, 11 Aerosmith, 12 Local Boy In The Photograph, 13 The Bartender And The Thief, 14 The Tragic Love Company, 15 Richard Cable.

• SUEDE •

1. **Where did Suede take their name from?**

2. Suede were to release their debut single *Be My God* in 1990 but fell out with their record label. It featured Mike Joyce. With which band was he formerly a drummer?

3. **In 1992 Justine Frischman quit suede, which group did she go on to form?**

4. In 1992 Suede achieved which rare distinction before they even released any material?

5. **With which single did Suede make their debut on *Top Of The Pops*?**

6. In 1993 Suede had their first UK Top Ten hit, what was it?

7. **In 1993 Suede's debut album entered the UK chart at No.1 with the biggest one-week sales by a debut act since who?**

8. Richard Oakes joined Suede in 1994 who did he replace?

9. **With whom did Brett Anderson record *Les Yeux Fermes* for an Aids charity album?**

10. In 1992 Suede signed with which record label?

11. **In 1992 Suede recorded a cover version of a Pretenders' hit for the compilation album *Ruby Trax*, what was it?**

12. In 1994 where did Simon Gilbert appear as guest speaker at a meeting to lower the age of homosexual consent to 16?

13. **By which name were Suede known in the US due to there already being an act called Suede?**

14. Suede recorded a track for the 1995 charity album *Help* what was it?

15. **What did Neil Codling have named after him by a professor at the University of Durban?**

• SUPERGRASS •

1 Which BBC-TV show is Danny Goffey's father a presenter of?

2 What was Supergrass' debut UK chart single?

3 Who did Supergrass open for on tour in 1995?

4 In 1995 Supergrass had their first UK Top Ten hit, what was it?

5 In 1995 what did Supergrass appear on stage at Glastonbury wearing?

6 What was the title of Supergrass' UK No.1 debut album released in 1995?

7 What were Supergrass named as at the 1996 BRIT Awards?

8 For which single did Supergrass receive The Best Contemporary Song Trophy at the 1996 Ivor Novello Award ceremony?

9 Which name were Supergrass originally formed as?

10 Which record label did the band sign with in 1994?

11 In 1995 who did Gaz Coomes turn down an offer to model for?

12 The B-side of Supergrass' 1997 single was a cover version of a Smiths song. What was it?

13 Which UK festival did Supergrass play in 1999?

14 In which UK city were the band formed?

15 What did Steven Spielberg offer the band a chance to star in?

1 Top Gear, 2 Caught By The Fuzz, 3 The Bluetones, 4 Lenny, 5 Stone Roses Masks, 6 I Should Coco, 7 Best Newcomer, 8 Alright, 9 The Jennifers, 10 Parlophone Records, 11 Calvin Klein, 12 Some Girls Are Bigger Than Others, 13 V99, 14 Oxford, 15 A 90's remake of The Monkees.

• SUPERTRAMP •

1. **What important role was played by Stanley August Miesegaes, who met the group's vocalist and keyboard player, Richard Davies, in 1969 in Germany?**

2. Who wrote the book, *The Autobiography Of A Supertramp*, from which the band took its name?

3. **Which open air festival did the band perform at, in 1970?**

4. What was the title of the band's second album, which featured tattoos on its front cover?

5. **Which song opened the band's 1974 album *Crime Of The Century*?**

6. And where had the album been recorded?

7. **Which album, released in 1975, featured the songs *Another Man's Woman* and *Poor Boy*?**

8. Which single, taken from the 1977 album *Even In The Quietest Moments*, reached No. 15 in the US charts?

9. **And which other single from the album contains the lines "Diamonds are what I really need - Think I'll rob a store, escape the law and live in Italy"?**

10. Which 1979 album opened with the track *Gone Hollywood*, and spawned four hit singles?

11. **And which single from the album won the Best Song award at the 1980 Ivor Novello awards in London?**

12. Which album did the group release just before guitarist Roger Hodgson left for a solo career?

13. **And what was the title of Roger Hodgson's 1984 solo album?**

14. Which song, taken from the 1985 album *Brother Where You Bound*, became a hit single in the US?

15. **What was the title of the band's 1997 reunion album, their first recording since 1988?**

1 He was a Dutch millionaire, who agreed to fund the formation of the band, 2 W.H.Davies, 3 The Isle Of Wight Festival, 4 Indelibly Stamped, 5 *School*, 6 At a farmhouse in Southcombe, Somerset, 7 *Crisis? What Crisis?*, 8 *Give A Little Bit*, 9 *From Now On*, 10 *Breakfast In America*, 11 *The Logical Song*, 12 *Famous Last Words*, 13 *In The Eye Of The Storm*, 14 *Cannonball*, 15 *Some Things Never Change*.

• SWEET •

1 **What was the name of the band, formed by Brian Connolly, Steve Priest and Mick Tucker in 1968?**

2 And who was the fourth member of the band, who joined when they shortened their name to Sweet?

3 **On which British children's pop show did the band make their TV debut?**

4 Which famous glam rock writing duo provided much of Sweet's early material?

5 **What was the title of the band's UK debut single, released in 1971, and reaching No. 13?**

6 Which song prevented Sweet's second hit single, *Co-Co*, from reaching No. 1 in the UK?

7 **For which 1972 single did the band dress up as Red Indians when performing the song on TV?**

8 Which No. 1 hit from 1973 opens with the sound of a police siren?

9 **Which 1973 hit single for Sweet was also a hit for US vocalist Tia Carrere, when featured in the film *Wayne's World*?**

10 What was the title of the band's 1974 album, which only included material written by the band themselves?

11 **Which 1975 single became the first song written by the band to enter the UK singles chart, reaching No. 2?**

12 And which Bay City Rollers song prevented it from reaching No. 1?

13 **What was the title of the band's 1975 single, which opens with the line "So you think you can take another piece of me, to satisfy your intellectual needs"?**

14 Which film was the band's 1978 single *Love Is Like Oxygen* featured in?

15 **Which member of the band left to pursue a solo career in 1979?**

•T.REX I•

1. **Under what name did Marc Bolan make his 1965 TV debut, singing his song *The Wizard* on *Ready, Steady, Go!***

2. And what was the name of the band he played guitar for in 1967?

3. **What was the name of the percussionist and backing vocalist, who joined Marc Bolan in 1967 to form Tyrannosaurus Rex?**

4. Which Radio London DJ did a lot to promote the band, inviting them to play at his regular underground shows?

5. **Which young record producer did the group sign a contract with in 1968?**

6. Which gimmick did the group use to double the length of their first single, *Debora*?

7. **Who became the group's new percussionist, following Steve Took's disappearance during a US tour?**

8. And what was the title of the first single to be released by the new line up?

9. **Which instrument does Marc Bolan play on the 1970 album *A Beard Of Stars*, for the first time on a Tyrannosaurus Rex record?**

10. Which UK No. 2 single was the first to be released under the shortened name T.Rex?

11. **How many weeks did the band's 1971 single *Hot Love* stay at UK No. 1?**

12. Which 1971 worldwide hit was based around the riff to Chuck Berry's song *Little Queenie*?

13. **And what was the title of the album which featured this single?**

14. In the group's 1972 No. 1 single *Telegram Sam*, which rock legend is referred to by the lines "Bobby's alright. He's a natural born poet, he's just out of sight"?

15. **Which single, also from 1972, became their fourth to get to No. 1?**

1 Toby Tyler, 2 John's Children, **3 Steve Took,** 4 John Peel, **5 Tony Visconti,** 6 The second half of the single is merely a repeat of the first half, but played backwards, **7 Mickey Finn, 8** *By The Light Of A Magical Moon,* **9 An electric guitar,** 10 *Ride A White Swan,* **11 Six weeks,** 12 *Get It On,* **13** *Electric Warrior,* 14 Bob Dylan, **15** *Metal Guru.*

•T. REX II•

1 **Which single, which reached No. 2 in the UK charts in 1973, features the line "I drive a Rolls Royce, because it's good for my voice"?**

2 What was the title of the film documentary, featuring a mix of fantasy sequences and the band's performances at the Wembley Empire Pool, released in December 1972?

3 **And who had directed the film?**

4 Whose BBC TV show did Marc appear on in 1973, duetting on the song *Life's A Gas*?

5 **Which song, released in 1973, became the band's tenth and final UK Top 5 hit?**

6 Which backing singer, who co-wrote the song *Tainted Love*, joined the band in 1973, and became Marc Bolan's girlfriend?

7 **What was the unusual double title of the group's 1974 album, which featured the tracks *Venus Loon*, *Teenage Dream* and *Painless Persuasion And The Meathawk Immaculate*?**

8 What was the name of Marc Bolan and Gloria Jones' son, born in September 1975?

9 **Which single, taken from the 1976 album *Futuristic Dragon*, reached No. 15 in the UK charts?**

10 Which Phil Spector song did Marc Bolan and Gloria Jones release as a duet in 1977?

11 **What was the title of the last studio album to be recorded and released in Marc's lifetime?**

12 Which publication did Marc start writing a weekly music column for in 1977?

13 **What was the title of Marc Bolan's own music show, which he hosted in 1977, and featured performances by David Bowie, The Boomtown Rats and The Jam?**

14 What colour was the Mini car, driven by Gloria Jones, which killed Marc Bolan when it crashed into a tree near Barnes Common in London?

15 **And how old would Marc Bolan have been just two weeks after the accident happened?**

• TALKING HEADS •

1 Who did Talking Heads support in their first gig in 1975?

2 Who joined the band in 1976?

3 In 1978 on which programme did Talking Heads make their British TV debut?

4 In 1978 who supported Talking Heads on their UK tour?

5 Talking Heads single *Psycho Killer* was originally performed by which two members of the band as part of the group Artistics?

6 In 1981 Chris Frantz and Tina Weymouth formed a spin-off funk group, what was it called?

7 What was the name of the 1981 ballet which featured David Byrne's music?

8 In 1982 whose album *Mesopotamia* did David Byrne produce?

9 In 1985 Talking Heads had their first UK Top Ten hit, what was it called?

10 Which Talking Heads' single featured in the film *Down And Out In Beverly Hills*?

11 Which rock star's cousin produced Talking Heads' first releases?

12 In 1988 who did David Byrne appear live with in London?

13 In 1977 who saw Talking Heads headlining at London's Rock Garden and later formed a lasting professional relationship with the band?

14 In 1986 Talking Heads recorded which film soundtrack?

15 Who is the only non-American member of the band?

Eno, **14** *True Stories*.**15** David Byrne
11 Jon Bon Jovi's cousin Tony Bongiovi, **12** David Bowie, **13** Brian
Catherine Wheel, **8** B52's, **9** *Road To Nowhere*, **10** *Once In a Lifetime*,
Straits, **5** David Byrne and Chris Frantz, **6** The Tom Tom Club, **7** The
1 The Ramones, **2** Jerry Harrison, **3** *The Old Grey Whistle Test*, **4** Dire

~ 144 ~

• TEXAS •

1 In which year were Texas formed?

2 Texas' debut single made the UK Top Ten, what was it?

3 **In 1992 Texas had a hit with a cover version of *Tired Of Being Alone*, Who sang the original?**

4 What was the title of Texas' 1997 UK No.1 album?

5 **Who is the lead singer of Texas?**

6 In 1998 Texas released a reworked version of their hit *Say What You Want*. Who else featured on it?

7 **Texas released their debut album in 1989, what was it called?**

8 In 1997 Texas had a UK No.5 hit with which song?

9 **What was the title of Texas' 1999 album?**

10 What nationality are Texas?

11 **In 1992 Texas recorded a cover version of a Guns 'N' Roses hit, what was it?**

12 Which instrument does John McElhone play?

13 **And which two other bands did he play with before Texas?**

14 Which two original members left the group?

15 **What are Texas named after?**

•THE ANIMALS•

1 **Which keyboard player formed the band in 1962, with Eric Burdon and Chas Chandler?**

2 Which British city did the band come from?

3 **Which record producer did the band sign a contract with in 1964?**

4 What was the title of the band's debut single, which reached No. 21 in the UK charts in 1964?

5 **Why did the band's record company, EMI, almost refuse to release the band's UK and US No. 1 hit *House Of The Rising Sun*?**

6 Which single, released in October 1964, became the band's second hit, reaching No. 8 in the UK charts?

7 **Why was the intended 1965 Animals concert at the Apollo Theatre in Harlem cancelled at the last minute?**

8 Which cover version of a Nina Simone hit reached No. 3 in the UK charts for the band?

9 **Which film, about the growing pop culture in Britain, did the band appear in in 1965?**

10 Which member of the band announced he was leaving, and was replaced by Dave Rowberry?

11 **And what was the name of the band he went on to front, having 11 chart hits?**

12 Who had the original hit with the song *Bring It On Home To Me*, which reached No. 7 in the UK charts for The Animals in 1965?

13 **Which album, released by the band in 1965, reached No. 6 in the UK charts?**

14 Which single, written by songwriting team Barry Mann and Cynthia Weil, reached No. 2 in the UK charts for The Animals?

15 **Which member of the band quit in 1966, to become a business man in Newcastle?**

1 **Alan Price,** 2 Newcastle Upon Tyne, 3 **Mickie Most,** 4 *Baby Let Me Take You Home,* 5 At 4 1/2 minutes, it was considered too long, 6 *I'm Crying,* 7 The US immigration department ruled that there were problems with work permits, and stopped the show from going ahead, 8 *Don't Let Me Be Misunderstood,* 9 *Pop Gear,* 10 Alan Price, 11 **The Alan Price Set,** 12 Sam Cooke, 13 *Animal Tracks,* 14 *We've Gotta Get Out Of This Place,* 15 **John Steel.**

•THE BEACH BOYS I•

1 Name the three Wilson brothers who, along with their cousin Mike Love and friend Al Jardine, formed the original line up of the band?

2 By what name were the band first known, inspired by the candy-stripe shirts they wore on stage?

3 What was the title of the first single, recorded and released by the band in 1961?

4 Which member of the group left temporarily, to study dentistry, and was replaced by David Marks?

5 Which instrument did head Beach Boy Brian Wilson play on stage?

6 Which Chuck Berry song was used, uncredited, with new surf orientated lyrics, for the band's first Top Ten US single *Surfin' USA*?

7 Which song, written by Brian Wilson, reached US No. 1 for surf duo Jan and Dean?

8 What was the title of the band's first hot-rod single, which reached No. 15 in the US?

9 And which friend of the band co-wrote most of the hot-rod songs from this period with Brian Wilson?

10 In which country did the group make their first overseas tour, in January 1964?

11 Which US No. 5 single starts with the line "Well, she got her daddy's car and she cruised to the hamburger stand, now"?

12 Who originally managed the band, until he was sacked after a fight in the studio with Brian Wilson?

13 Which record producer's unique sound did Brian Wilson try to emulate with his own band's recordings?

14 Which single from July 1964, featuring the B-side *Don't Worry Baby*, became The Beach Boys first No. 1 hit?

15 And who had Brian Wilson originally written the song *Don't Worry Baby* for?

1 **Brian, Dennis and Carl Wilson**, 2 The Pendletones, 3 *Surfin'*, 4 Al Jardine, 5 **The bass**, 6 *Sweet Little Sixteen*, 7 *Surf City*, 8 *Little Deuce Coupe*, 9 **Gary Usher**, 10 Australia, 11 *Fun, Fun, Fun*, 12 The boys' father, Murray Wilson, 13 Phil Spector and his Wall Of Sound, 14 *I Get Around*, 15 Phil Spector's band The Ronettes, but he rejected it.

1 Which US No. 9 hit single, from October 1964, closes with the repeated lines "Won't last forever, It's kind'a sad"?

2 Which 1964 album became the band's first US No. 1?

3 **And what first did the album achieve?**

4 What illness was Brian Wilson struck down with while on tour in December 1964?

5 **And what long-running health problem contributed to his decision to stop touring with the band?**

6 Which future solo star temporarily took Brian Wilson's place during the band's live shows, playing bass?

7 **And who became Brian's permanent replacement, when he joined the band in April 1965?**

8 Which song, originally recorded for the album *The Beach Boys Today!*, reached No. 1 in the US charts when it was revamped and re-recorded in May 1965?

9 **Which song, taken from the album *Summer Days (And Summer Nights)* reached No. 3 in the US singles chart in 1965, and was later recorded by rock singer David Lee Roth?**

10 Why were DJ's unhappy about playing The Beach Boys 1965 release *The Little Girl I Once Knew*, which lead to it's disappointing position in the charts?

11 **Which singer provided the lead vocal on The Beach Boys cover version of *Barbara Ann*, released in 1966?**

12 And which album, released in 1966, featured this, and several other impromptu-sounding songs?

13 **Which Beatle album, released in the US in 1965, gave Brian Wilson the inspiration record The Beach Boys' 1966 album *Pet Sounds*?**

14 What was the title of the first single to be released as a Brian Wilson solo record, in April 1966?

15 **Which song, released in May 1966 and reaching No. 2 in the UK, was an adaptation of a traditional Caribbean tune?**

1 *When I Grow Up To Be A Man*, 2 *The Beach Boys Concert*, 3 **The first live performance disk to reach No. 1 in the album charts**, 4 A nervous breakdown, 5 He was deaf in one ear, and was worried that on-stage amplification would damage the hearing in his one good ear, 6 Glen Campbell, 7 **Bruce Johnston**, 8 *Help Me Rhonda*, 9 *California Girls*, 10 They were worried that the song's unusual 4-beat silences would cause listeners to turn it off, as it sounded like dead air, 11 **Dean Torrence (he was uncredited, because he was contracted to another record company)**, 12 *The Beach Boys Party*, 13 *Rubber Soul*, 14 *Caroline, No*, 15 *Sloop John B.*

•THE BEACH BOYS III•

1 **Which album prevented The Beach Boys' *Pet Sounds* from reaching No. 1 in the UK charts?**

2 Which song from *Pet Sounds* was described by Paul McCartney as "The perfect pop song"?

3 **And why was the song widely banned on radio throughout the world?**

4 What was the name of the former advertising slogan writer who provided the lyrics for the songs on *Pet Sounds*?

5 **What were the names of Brian Wilson's two pet beagles, whose barking at a passing train was used to close the *Pet Sounds* album?**

6 Which single, released in October 1966, took over 6 months to record, in 4 different studios?

7 **What was the original name of the planned follow up album to *Pet Sounds*, which eventually became *Smile*?**

8 What was the full title to the instrumental segment from the *Smile* album, which was to represent the element of fire?

9 **Which lyricist worked with Brian Wilson on most of the material for the *Smile* album?**

10 And what was the name of the rolling Wild West influenced song from the album, which became the first single to be released on the band's own label, Brother Records?

11 **Which song did Brian Wilson perform solo, when he appeared on the 1967 TV special *Inside Pop - The Rock Revolution*, hosted by composer Leonard Bernstein?**

12 Why was Carl Wilson arrested and held for 5 days by the FBI in April 1967?

13 **Which pop festival were the band supposed to be headlining in 1967, when they pulled out unexpectedly?**

14 And which performer at the festival famously criticised the band for sounding like a "Psychedelic barber-shop quartet"?

15 **After Brian Wilson abandoned the *Smile* album in 1967, under what name was much of the album's material re-recorded and released?**

1 *Revolver* by The Beatles, 2 *God Only Knows*, 3 Because of the word God in the title, 4 Tony Asher, 5 Banana and Louie, 6 *Good Vibrations*, 7 *Dumb Angel*, 8 *Mrs O'Leary's Cow* (said to be the cause of the Great Fire Of Chicago, when it kicked over a lamp in it's stall), 9 Van Dyke Parks, 10 *Heroes And Villains*, 11 *Surf's Up*, 12 He refused to report for military service after receiving his US army draught notice, 13 The Monterey International Pop Festival, 14 Jimi Hendrix, 15 *Smiley Smile*.

•THE BEACH BOYS IV•

1 **What was the title of the band's 1968 back-to-their-roots album, which featured the single _Darlin'_?**

2 Which spiritual leader did the band tour with in 1968, although many of the dates were cancelled, due to poor ticket sales?

3 **Which cover version of a Ronettes hit, taken from The Beach Boys' album _20/20_, reached No. 10 in the UK chart?**

4 Who co-wrote the band's August 1969 hit, _Breakaway_, with Brian Wilson?

5 **Which elemental track, originally intended for the abandoned _Smile_ project, was revived for the Beach Boys' 1970 album _Sunflower_?**

6 What was the initial title to the band's 1971 ecological album, which became _Surf's Up_, after the inclusion of another track from the unreleased _Smile_?

7 **Which 1974 Elton John single, which reached No. 2 in the US charts, features backing vocals by Carl Wilson and Bruce Johnston?**

8 Which member of the band was featured on the US TV show _Saturday Night Live_, being arrested by the Surf Police, played by Dan Aykroyd and John Belushi, for not being able to surf?

9 **Which British musician played the saxophone on the band's 1976 hit _It's OK_?**

10 And which song, written by Bruce Johnston and recorded by Barry Manilow, won the 1977 Song Of The Year at the Grammy Awards?

11 **What did the initials in the title of the band's 1978 album _M.I.U_ stand for?**

12 What was the title of Dennis Wilson's 1977 solo album, which opened with the track _River Song_?

13 **Which song, originally from their 1968 album _Wild Honey_, was re-recorded in a disco style for their 1979 album _L.A.?_**

14 Which member of the group drowned while diving from his boat, moored at the Marina Del Rey in California?

15 **And what special dispensation, concerning his funeral, was granted to his family by US President Ronald Regan?**

normally reserved for members of the navy.
Night, 14 Dennis Wilson, 15 Allowing Dennis to be buried at sea -
album was recorded, 12 _Pacific Ocean Blue_, 13 _Here Comes The_
The Songs, 11 Maharishi International University, which is where the
Let The Sun Go Down On Me, 8 Brian Wilson, 9 Roy Wood, 10 _I Write_
4 Murray Wilson, his father, 5 _Cool Cool Water_, 6 _Landlocked_, 7 _Don't_
1 _Wild Honey_, 2 The Maharishi Mahesh Yogi, 3 _I Can Hear Music_,

•THE BEATLES I•

1 **What was the name of the band which first featured John Lennon, Paul McCartney and George Harrison in its line up?**

2 Which drummer joined the band in 1960, shortly before their first visit to Germany?

3 **And in which German city did the band regularly play at the Indra and Kaiserkeller clubs during 1960?**

4 Which Liverpool club did the band start making regular lunchtime appearances at, during 1961?

5 **What was the name of the Liverpool record shop owner, who became the band's manager in 1962?**

6 What was the name of the group's ex-bass player, who died of a brain haemorrhage in Germany?

7 **Who became the group's record producer, when they signed to EMI records in June 1962?**

8 When the group sacked their drummer Pete Best, which band did Ringo Starr leave to join The Beatles?

9 **Which member of the group got married, on August 23rd, at a Liverpool registry office?**

10 During the band's first full recording sessions for EMI, why did they reject the song *How Do You Do It*, despite knowing it would be a No. 1 single?

11 **Which song became the group's debut single?**

12 Which single, taken from the group's debut album, reached No. 1 in three out of the four British record charts?

13 **On which music show did the band make their BBC TV debut?**

14 Which single, the first to officially reach No. 1 in all British record charts, started the band's uninterrupted run of 11 consecutive No. 1 singles?

15 **Which song from September 1963 became Britain's top selling single, until 1977, when it was beaten by *Mull Of Kintyre* by Wings?**

1 **The Quarry Men,** 2 Pete Best, **3 Hamburg,** 4 The Cavern, **5 Brian Epstein,** 6 Stuart Sutcliffe, **7 George Martin,** 8 Rory Storm and The Hurricanes, **9 John Lennon - to Cynthia Powell,** 10 It had been written by Mitch Murray, and the band decided it would only record their own material for single releases, **11 Love Me Do,** 12 Please Please Me, **13 The 625 Show,** 14 *From Me To You,* **15 *She Loves You.***

•THE BEATLES II•

1 Which John Lennon quip, before The Beatles' performed their final song at the 1963 Royal Variety Performance, made the headlines the following day?

2 Which single, which became their third UK No. 1, was written specifically with an American sound, to try and break the band in the US?

3 At which US airport were the group met by thousands of rioting fans, at the start of their first tour of America?

4 The Beatles made their US TV debut, watched by an estimated 73 million people, on which show?

5 Which heavyweight boxer did the group meet, during a publicity photo session, while touring in Miami?

6 What was the title of John Lennon's book of nonsense verse, published in March 1964?

7 During April, 1964, how many singles did The Beatles have simultaneously in the US Top Five singles chart?

8 Which member of the band was rushed to hospital, suffering from severe tonsillitis, causing him to miss the opening leg of their first world tour?

9 Who directed The Beatles in their first feature film, *A Hard Day's Night*, released in the summer of 1964?

10 And, from the improvised sequence of the press reception in the film, what was John Lennon's answer to the question "How did you find America"?

11 What brought The Beatles performance to a halt twice, during a show at the Las Vegas Convention Centre?

12 Which US musician, and future influence on the band, met The Beatles backstage, after the final concert of their 1964 US tour?

13 And why did he mistakenly believe the band to be regular cannabis smokers?

14 What was the title of The Beatles' fourth album, which was to be the last one to feature cover versions of other people's material?

15 Which single from 1964 is introduced with the sound of bass guitar feedback?

14 *Beatles For Sale*, 15 I *Feel Fine*.

1 Speaking to the audience, he said " If those in the cheaper seats could clap their hands" then, looking up to the royal box, he added "And the rest of you, if you'd just rattle your jewellery", 2 I *Want To Hold Your Hand*, 3 The John F. Kennedy International Airport in New York, 4 The *Ed Sullivan Show*, 5 Cassius Clay, 6 *In His Own Write*, 7 5 singles in all 5 top places, 8 Ringo Starr, 9 Richard Lester, 10 "Turn left at Greenland", 11 The stage was pelted with jelly babies, after George Harrison had said they were his favourite sweets, 12 Bob Dylan, 13 He misheard the line "I Can't Hide" from *I Want To Hold Your Hand*, thinking they were singing "I Get High", Bob Dylan made sure that all members of the band tried the drug there and then,

~ 152 ~

• THE BEATLES III •

1 What was the original title to The Beatles' second feature film, *Help!*, which was made in 1965?

2 Which single was the first to feature Paul McCartney playing lead guitar?

3 What was the title of John Lennon's second book, released in June 1965?

4 Which song from The Beatles' album *Help!* was the first to feature Paul McCartney and backing musicians, without any other members of the band?

5 What award was bestowed on the members of the band, in a ceremony on the 26th October, 1965?

6 Which 1965 double A-side became The Beatles' third Christmas UK No. 1?

7 And which album, accompanying this single release, featured the first recording of a sitar on a Western pop record?

8 Which member of the group married Patti Boyd, at Esher registry office on 21st January 1966?

9 Which band had a UK No. 1 with a cover version of The Beatles' *Michelle*?

10 Which British newspaper published an interview with John Lennon, which contained the controversial remark "We're more popular than Jesus now"?

11 Which actress was romantically linked with Paul McCartney during the mid-sixties, whose brother provided the inspiration for the song *Paperback Writer*?

12 What was the title of the US compilation album, whose cover, featuring The Beatles in butcher's overalls, draped in cuts of meat and dismembered dolls, caused the album to be withdrawn and released in a less offensive cover?

13 Which country banned all Beatle records from its radio stations, following John Lennon's comments about Jesus?

14 What was the title of The Beatles' 1966 album, which featured a black and white op-art cover, designed by friend of the band, Klaus Voorman?

15 And which double A-side from the album was at No. 1 in the UK throughout August and September?

1 **Eight Arms To Hold You**, 2 *Ticket To Ride*, 3 *A Spaniard In The Works*, 4 *Yesterday*, 5 **The MBE**, 6 *Day Tripper/We Can Work It Out*, 7 *Rubber Soul*, 8 George Harrison, 9 **The Overlanders**, 10 The Evening Standard, 11 Jane Asher (her brother was in publishing), 12 *Yesterday And Today*, 13 **South Africa**, 14 *Revolver*, 15 *Yellow Submarine/Eleanor Rigby*

•THE BEATLES IV•

1 Which artist did John Lennon meet for the first time at the Indica Gallery in London, in 1966?

2 And which Richard Lester film had John Lennon just finished making?

3 **What was the title of the British film, released in December 1966, which featured a score written by Paul McCartney and producer George Martin?**

4 Which double A-side, released in February 1967, was the first Beatle single to break their run of 11 consecutive UK No. 1 singles?

5 **And which song prevented it from reaching No. 1 in the UK?**

6 On which day of 1967 was The Beatles' album *Sgt Pepper's Lonely Hearts Club Band* released in the UK?

7 **And which artist was responsible for designing the cover of the album?**

8 Which member of the band was the first to publicly admit to taking LSD?

9 **And which newspaper published a petition, signed by many leading British figures, including The Beatles, calling for the legalisation of Marijuana?**

10 What was the name of the Indian guru, who the band studied with on a weekend retreat in Bangor, in August 1967?

11 **How did the group's manager, Brian Epstein, die in 1967?**

12 Why was the promotional film, made by The Beatles to accompany their winter 1967 single *Hello Goodbye*, not shown on British television?

13 **Which British actress did Paul McCartney announce his engagement to on Christmas day, 1967?**

14 What was the name of The Beatles' film, shown on British TV on Boxing day, 1967?

15 **Which film score did George Harrison write during the early part of 1968?**

1 Yoko Ono, 2 How I Won The War, 3 The Family Way, 4 Penny Lane/Strawberry Fields Forever, 5 Release Me by Engelbert Humperdinck, 6 June 1st, 7 Peter Blake, 8 Paul McCartney, 9 The Times, 10 Maharishi Mahesh Yogi, 11 An accidental overdose of sleeping pills, 12 The Musicians Union had imposed a ban on miming, 13 Jane Asher, 14 Magical Mystery Tour, 15 Wonderwall.

•THE BEATLES V•

1 What was the name of the company set up by The Beatles in 1968, to provide funding for new talent, as well as selling Beatles merchandise?

2 And what feature of their Savile Row offices caused many complaints from neighbouring businesses?

3 Which singer starred in her own BBC TV series in 1968, featuring a theme tune written by Paul McCartney?

4 And what was the title of the theme tune?

5 What was the title of the first single to be released by the band on their own Apple label?

6 And which singer, who won her heat on TV's *Opportunity Knocks*, became the first artist to be signed to The Beatles' Apple label?

7 What was the name of the full length animated film, based on The Beatles' songs, released in June 1968?

8 Which song, written by Paul McCartney to console John Lennon's son, Julian, during his parent's break up, became the longest single to reach No. 1 in the UK charts?

9 Simply titled *The Beatles*, how did fans refer to the band's 1968 double studio album, because of the stark packaging?

10 What was the original title of the band's 'back to their roots' album, which they started to film at Twickenham Studios in 1969?

11 Where did the band perform their last live show together, which was stopped by the police after complaints about noise?

12 Who was appointed as the group's new manager, in 1969?

13 Which photographer married Paul McCartney at Marylebone registry office, on the 12th March 1969?

14 And in which British territory did John Lennon marry Yoko Ono a week later?

15 And where did John and Yoko perform their seven day Bed-In in May 1969, to promote world peace?

1 **Apple Corps,** 2 A psychedelic mural was painted on the building's exterior, which was too colourful for many people - they were made to paint it over, 3 **Cilla Black,** 4 *Step Inside Love,* 5 *Lady Madonna,* 6 Mary Hopkin, 7 *Yellow Submarine,* 8 *Hey Jude,* 9 *The White Album,* 10 *Get Back,* 11 On the roof of their Apple offices in Savile Row, 12 Allen Klein, 13 **Linda Eastman,** 14 Gibraltar, 15 The Amsterdam Hilton, Holland.

• THE BEATLES VI •

1 Which Beatles single, recorded by John Lennon and Paul McCartney alone, became the band's last UK No. 1 single?

2 Which album featured a sleeve with a photograph of the band on a zebra crossing, just outside their recording studios?

3 And which line officially ended the album, and the final studio recordings that the band made?

4 In 1969, which member of the band was rumoured to have been killed in 1966, and replaced by a look alike?

5 Which single, taken from the band's last studio album was the first to be written by George Harrison?

6 And which US singer called it "the greatest love song of the last 50 years"?

7 Which John Lennon song was used for the World Wildlife Fund's charity album *No One's Gonna Change Our World*?

8 Which famous US record producer was asked to work on the abandoned tapes to The Beatles' *Get Back* sessions?

9 And which member of the group claimed that some of the tracks off the album had been ruined by orchestral and choral overdubs?

10 Which song kept The Beatles' single *Let It Be* off the No. 1 spot in the UK singles chart in 1970?

11 In January 1970, why did police shut down an art exhibition, featuring lithographs made by John Lennon?

12 What was the title of the last studio album to be released by The Beatles, in 1970?

13 And which member of the band released his first solo album at the same time, taking most of the blame for their break up?

14 What was the name of John Lennon's new band, which had hits with *Give Peace A Chance* and *Cold Turkey*?

15 Which Beatle went on to record a triple album set in 1970, titled *All Things Must Pass*?

1 *The Ballad Of John And Yoko*, 2 *Abbey Road*, 3 "And in the end, the love you take is equal to the love you make", 4 Paul McCartney, 5 *Something*, 6 Frank Sinatra, 7 *Across The Universe*, 8 Phil Spector, 9 Paul McCartney, 10 *Wand'rin' Star* by Lee Marvin, 11 The lithographs were considered pornographic, 12 *Let It Be*, 13 Paul McCartney, 14 The Plastic Ono Band, 15 George Harrison.

• THE BLACK CROWES •

1 **By what name were the Black Crowes originally known?**

2 The Black Crowes made their debut on the UK chart with which song?

3 **And who had a hit with the original version?**

4 Who did the Black Crowes support on tour in 1990?

5 **In 1991 the Black Crowes were nominated for the Best New Artist award at the Grammys. Who beat them?**

6 Who replaced Jeff Cease when he left the band in 1991?

7 **In 1991 whose tour were the Black Crowes thrown off of for deploring corporate music finance?**

8 Why was Johnny Colt arrested in 1992?

9 **The Black Crowes released their first feature-length video in 1992, what was it called?**

10 Who produced the Black Crowes 1999 album *By Your Side*?

11 **And which band does he usually produce?**

12 Who did the Black Crowes support on 1995's *Voodoo Lounge* tour?

13 **In which American state was the band formed?**

14 In 1992 the Black Crowes had their first UK Top Ten album, what was it?

15 **And which ex-member of the Gregg Allman Band produced and guested on the album?**

1 **Mr. Crowes Garden,** 2 *Hard To Handle,* 3 **Otis Redding,** 4 Robert Plant, 5 **Mariah Carey,** 6 Marc Ford, 7 **Z.Z. Top,** 8 For obstruction of justice after helping a drunken fan, 9 *Who Killed That Bird Out On Your Window Sill - The Movie,* 10 Kevin Shirley, 11 **Aerosmith,** 12 The Rolling Stones, 13 **Georgia,** 14 *Southern Harmony And Musical Companion,* 15 **Chuck Leavell.**

•THE BOOMTOWN RATS•

1 **What was Bob Geldof's regular job before forming the band in 1975?**

2 Where did the band get their name from?

3 **What was the title of the first single, taken from their eponymous debut album, released by the band in 1977?**

4 Which famous rock producer worked with the band on their 1978 album *A Tonic For The Troops*?

5 **And which song, taken from the album, became the band's first Top Ten record, reaching No. 6 in the UK?**

6 Which single, released in October 1978, was at No. 1 in the UK charts for 2 weeks?

7 **And which single became the band's second No. 1 hit in the UK in July 1979?**

8 And where had Bob Geldof got the idea for the song?

9 **Which album, released in 1979, featured the singles *Diamond Smiles* and *Someone's Looking At You*?**

10 Which single, which made No. 3 in the UK, was the first to be released by the band on Mercury Records?

11 **Which album from 1981 was co-produced by the band and Tony Visconti?**

12 And which single, taken from this album, became the first not to reach the Top 30 in the UK?

13 **In which 1982 film did Bob Geldof play the lead role of Pink?**

14 Which song, released in 1984, became the last charting single the band would have?

15 **Who co-wrote the 1984 charity record *Do They Know It's Christmas* with Bob Geldof?**

• THE BYRDS •

1 **Name the three founder members of the group, who were originally known as The Jetset?**

2 Which film did the band see in 1964, prompting them to pursue a career in pop?

3 **Which Bob Dylan song did the band record as their first single?**

4 Which main songwriter from the group announced he was to leave in 1966, partly because of his fear of flying?

5 **Which single from 1966 was widely banned on radio, due to perceived drug references?**

6 The 1967 single *So You Want To Be A Rock And Roll Star* was said to have been inspired by the success of which American group?

7 **What much used musical descriptive phrase was first applied to The Byrds, to categorise their hard sound?**

8 Which member of the band quit, after the recording of his single *Lady Friend*?

9 **And which song of his did the group refuse to record, due to it's amoral lyrics, prompting him to quit?**

10 What was the title of the group's 1968 album, featuring the songs *Goin' Back* and *Draft Morning*?

11 **And how was their recently departed band member represented on the cover of the album?**

12 Which 1969 cult film featured several tracks recorded by The Byrds?

13 **Which band, formed from ex-members of The Byrds, did drummer Gene Parsons join, following his decision to leave the group in 1972?**

14 What was the title of the 1973 album, featuring early demos of Byrds material?

15 **In the late 1960's, what did guitarist Jim McGuinn change his name to, following his conversion to the Indonesian religion, Subud?**

1 **Jim McGuinn, Gene Clarke and David Crosby,** 2 The Beatles' *A Hard Days Night*, 3 *Mr Tambourine Man*, 4 Gene Clarke, 5 *Eight Miles High*, 6 The Monkees, 7 **Heavy Metal,** 8 David Crosby, 9 *Triad*, 10 *The Notorious Byrd Brothers*, 11 **Along with the three remaining members, the cover featured the head of a horse, said to represent David Crosby,** 12 *Easy Rider*, 13 The Flying Burrito Brothers, 14 *Preflyte*, 15 **Roger McGuinn.**

•THE CARS•

1 **With which British producer did the band record their debut album, in 1977?**

2 What was the title of the band's debut single, which reached No. 27 in the US charts?

3 **Which single reached No. 3 in the UK charts in 1978?**

4 And how was the single presented, making it the first of it's kind to be sold in the UK?

5 **What was the title of the band's second album, released in 1979?**

6 And which single, taken from the album, reached No. 14 in the US charts?

7 **Which album, released in 1980, contained the singles *Touch And Go* and *Don't Tell Me No*?**

8 Which title track to the band's 1982 album reached No. 4 in the US charts?

9 **Which member of the band released a solo album titled *Beatitude* in 1983?**

10 What was the title of the band's 1984 single, which was accompanied by an award winning computer generated video?

11 **Which single, released in September 1984, became the band's biggest selling single, reaching No. 5 in the UK and No. 3 in the US?**

12 And which charity were all royalties for the song donated to in 1985?

13 **What was the title of Elliot Easton's solo album, released in 1985?**

14 Which album, released by the group in 1987, featured the singles *You Are The Girl* and *Strap Me In*?

15 **Following their announcement in 1988 that the group would split up, which song became their final US charting single?**

1 Roy Thomas Baker, 2 Just What I Needed, 3 My Best Friend's Girl, 4 It was the first commercially available picture disc, 5 Candy-O, 6 Let's Go, 7 Panorama, 8 Shake It Up, 9 Ric Ocasek, 10 You Might Think, 11 Drive, 12 The Band Aid Trust, 13 Change No Change, 14 Door To Door, 15 Coming Up You.

•THE CLASH•

1 Who became the band's manager in 1976?

2 Which Clash album was voted Best Album of the 1980's by *Rolling Stone* magazine?

3 What was the title of the Clash's debut UK single?

4 In 1977 Joe Strummer and Nicky Headon were both fined £100 for failure to appear in court to answer a robbery charge, what were they accused of stealing?

5 Mickey Gallagher joined the Clash as temporary member for their US tour in 1979, which band did he normally play with?

6 What was the title of the fictionalized documentary film about a Clash roadie which was released in 1980?

7 What was the Clash's first UK Top Ten album called?

8 Which member of the band disappeared on the eve of a UK tour in 1982 causing it to be cancelled?

9 Who left the band in 1982?

10 What was Nicky Headon arrested and charged with in 1982?

11 Who did the Clash support on their farewell US tour in 1982?

12 After being sacked from the Clash in 1983 which group did Mick Jones go on to form?

13 What was the name of Joe Strummer's 1988 solo tour?

14 The Clash had their only UK No. 1 in 1991, what was it?

15 Which group did Joe Strummer join as lead singer in 1991?

1 Malcolm McLaren, 2 *London Calling,* **3** *White Riot,* 4 A pillowcase from a Holiday Inn, **5 Ian Dury & the Blockheads,** 6 *Rude Boy,* **7** *Give 'Em Enough Rope,* **8 Joe Strummer,** 9 **Nicky Headon,** 10 Stealing a bus stop in London, **11 The Who,** 12 Big Audio Dynamite, **13 Rock Against The Rich,** 14 *Should I Stay Or Should I Go,* **15 The Pogues.**

•THE DAVE CLARK FIVE•

1 **What job did group leader Dave Clark do before forming the band in 1958?**

2 And which instrument did Dave Clark play in the band?

3 **What was the title of the first single released by the band to make the UK charts?**

4 And which band reached UK No. 1 with the same song, released at the same time as the Dave Clark Five version?

5 **Which single, released in 1964, reached No. 1 in the UK, replacing The Beatles'** *I Want To Hold Your Hand* **at the top of the chart?**

6 Which UK No. 2 single for the band was banned by most concert venue managers, fearing that the foot stamping break in the record would damage the flooring?

7 **In which 1964 film did the band co-star with Nancy Sinatra and British band The Animals?**

8 And which song, featured in the film, reached No. 26 in the UK charts?

9 **Which Chuck Berry song did the band record in 1965, reaching No. 24 in the UK charts?**

10 What was the title of the 1965 film, featuring the band, which spawned a Top Ten single and soundtrack album?

11 **Which remake of a Bobby Day hit reached No. 1 in the US charts in 1965?**

12 When the group were featured on the Ed Sullivan Show in June 1966, how many appearances had they made on the show, setting a record?

13 **What was the title of the film company, set up by the band in 1967?**

14 Which album, released in 1967, became the band's last to chart in the US?

15 **Which revival of a Jackie DeShannon hit reached No. 31 in the UK charts in 1969?**

1 He was a film stuntman, 2 The drums, 3 *Do You Love Me*, 4 Brian Poole And The Tremeloes, 5 *Glad All Over*, 6 *Bits And Pieces*, 7 *Get Yourself A College Girl*, 8 *Thinking Of You Baby*, 9 *Reelin' And Rockin'*, 10 *Catch Us If You Can*, 11 *Over And Over*, 12 12 appearances, 13 *Big Five Films*, 14 *You Got What It Takes*, 15 *Put A little Love In Your Heart*.

•THE DOORS•

1 **On which California beach did Jim Morrison first meet keyboard player Ray Manzarek?**

2 Whose book gave Jim Morrison the inspiration to name the band The Doors?

3 **In which club on Sunset Boulevard did the band make their first public appearance?**

4 And at which famous Los Angeles night club did they become the house band?

5 **And why did they get fired from this job?**

6 Which song from their eponymous debut album was at No. 1 in the US charts for three weeks in the summer of 1967?

7 **And why was the group banned from further appearances on the** *Ed Sullivan Show* **after their live performance of this song?**

8 What was the title of the band's second album, released in the Autumn of 1967?

9 **How did Jim Morrison describe himself in the outro lyrics to the 1968 song** *Not To Touch The Earth*, **which became a suitable nick name for him, much used by the music press?**

10 Which British songwriter sued The Doors for plagiarism for their single *Hello, I Love You*, claiming it sounded much like one of his band's 1964 hits?

11 **In which American state was Jim Morrison charged with lewd and lascivious behaviour, after exposing himself on stage?**

12 What was the name of his long time girlfriend, who became his common law wife in Spring 1970?

13 **And what was the name of the journalist which he also married, in an occult witches ceremony?**

14 What was the name of the last album recorded by Jim Morrison and The Doors?

15 **In which European city was Jim Morrison found dead in the bath?**

1 **Venice Beach,** 2 Aldous Huxley's The Doors Of Perception, 3 **The London Fog Club,** 4 **Whisky A-Go-Go,** 5 The obscene lyrics and violence used during a performance of their song *The End*, 6 *Light My Fire*, 7 **They agreed to change the line in the song "Girl, we couldn't get much higher" to avoid accusations of drug usage, but Jim Morrison sung it anyway,** 8 *Strange Days*, 9 **The Lizard King,** 10 Ray Davies of The Kinks - the song is very similar to *All Day And All Of The Night*, 11 **Miami,** 12 Pamela Courson, 13 **Patricia Kennealy,** 14 *LA Woman*, 15 **Paris.**

• THE EAGLES •

1 Which artist did the group back, before striking out on their own?

2 Where in the world did the band record their 1972 debut album?

3 Which 1973 album featured the hit single *Tequila Sunrise*?

4 What was the name of the 1975 album, whose title track became the group's first chart single in the UK?

5 And which BBC radio series used the album track *Journey Of The Sorcerer* as its theme tune?

6 Which guitarist joined the band in 1976, following Bernie Leadon's announcement he was to leave?

7 And what was the title of the first album he recorded with the band?

8 And, according the title of the song from the album, who was *Johnny Come Lately*?

9 And which artists prevented the album from reaching No. 1 in the UK?

10 Which 1979 album, featuring the single *Heartache Tonight*, was to be the last studio album the group would record?

11 And, according to the album, what did the Greeks not want?

12 Whose 1982 single, *Leather And Lace*, did Don Henley play guest drums on?

13 And what was the name of Don Henley's 1983 solo album?

14 In 1985, which solo single by guitarist Glenn Frey was featured in the film *Beverly Hills Cop*?

15 What was the title of the band's album, released in 1994, after the group reformed?

THE EVERLY BROTHERS

1 **What was the title of the Everly Brothers first hit record, which reached No. 2 in the US charts in 1957?**

2 Which hit single, released in October 1957, was banned from Boston radio stations, because it was regarded as immoral?

3 **What was the title of their debut album, released in 1958?**

4 Which single, released in 1958, reached No. 1 in the US and UK charts?

5 **Which famous guitarist, and friend of the brothers' father, supervised many of their early recordings, and contributed sessions guitar work on several of their singles?**

6 Which song, written by the Everly Brothers themselves, stayed at the top of the UK singles chart for 8 weeks in 1960?

7 **Which 1961 No. 1 song was presented as a double A-side, with *Ebony Eyes*?**

8 What was the title of the Bing Crosby song that reached No. 1 in the UK in 1961 for The Everly Brothers?

9 **Which part of the armed forces were the brothers inducted into at the end of 1961?**

10 And which US TV show did the brothers appear on, in their full uniforms, while on weekend leave from the army?

11 **Which cover version of a Buddy Holly song reached No. 30 in the UK charts for the brothers, in 1965?**

12 What was the title of The Everly Brothers 1966 album, featuring the song *It's All Over*?

13 **And which British artist had a UK Top Ten hit with *It's All Over*, in 1967?**

14 What was the title of the album, recorded by the brothers in 1966 in London?

15 **And three members of which British group contributed 8 out of the 12 songs used on the album?**

1 **Bye Bye Love**, 2 Wake Up Little Susie, 3 **The Everly Brothers - They're Off And Running**, 4 All I Have To Do Is Dream, 5 Chet Atkins, 6 Cathy's Clown, 7 **Walk Right Back**, 8 Temptation, 9 **The Marines**, 10 The Ed Sullivan Show, 11 **That'll Be The Day**, 12 In Our Image, 13 Cliff Richard, 14 Two Yanks In England, 15 **The Hollies**.

1 **Which song, recorded in 1962, became the band's first hit, staying at No. 1 in the US singles chart for 5 weeks?**

2 And which follow up single, which also made No. 1, took its title from a comment made in a John Wayne film?

3 **Which song, released in March 1963, set a record for the band, by being the first to have three consecutive No. 1 singles?**

4 And which 1964 single broke this run of No. 1, when it was held at No. 3 by *I Want To Hold Your Hand* and *She Loves You*, by The Beatles?

5 **Which song, taken from the album *Born To Wander*, was later a No. 1 hit for British band The Tremeloes?**

6 Which song reached No. 12 in the US charts for The Four Seasons, but made No. 1 in the UK charts 10 years later, when recorded by The Bay City Rollers?

7 **Under what pseudonym did the band record the Bob Dylan song *Don't Think Twice, It's Alright* in 1965?**

8 Which song, a US chart hit for Frankie Valli in 1967, became a UK Top Ten hit a year later, when recorded by Andy Williams?

9 **What was the title of the group's 1969 concept album?**

10 For which artist did the band's keyboard player, Bob Gaudio, co-write the album *Watertown*, released in 1970?

11 **Which member of the band retired in 1971, due to hearing problems?**

12 Which Frankie Valli solo single reached No. 1 in the US charts in 1975?

13 **Which song, which failed to chart when originally released in 1972, made UK No. 7 when re-issued in 1975, due to the growing interest in the disco sound?**

14 Which song, originally written about prohibition in 30's America, stayed at No. 1 in the US for three weeks in 1976?

15 **Which song, written by Barry Gibb, was a Top Ten hit for Frankie Valli in 1978?**

1 **Sherry,** 2 Big Girls Don't Cry, 3 **Walk Like A Man,** 4 Dawn (Go Away), 5 **Silence Is Golden,** 6 Bye Bye Baby (Baby Goodbye), 7 **Wonder Who,** 8 Can't Take My Eyes Off You, 9 ***The Genuine Imitation Life Gazette,*** 10 Frank Sinatra, 11 **Guitar player Tommy DeVito,** 12 My Eyes Adored You, 13 ***The Night,*** 14 December '63 (Oh, What A Night), 15 *Grease*

1 **What did Grateful Dead frontman, Jerry Garcia, lose as a result of a childhood accident?**

2 After forming a stable line up in 1965, what name did the band initially play under?

3 **The opening night of which famous West-Coast venue saw one of the earliest performances of the band under their new name, The Grateful Dead?**

4 Which chemist and important figure in the US counter culture offered financial help to the band, as well as designing a state of the art PA system?

5 **Which famous area of San Francisco did the band move to in 1966?**

6 Which record company signed the band in 1967?

7 **What was the title of the band's second album, featuring the songs *Alligator* and *The Faster We Go, The Rounder We Get*?**

8 Whose ill-fated concert did the band play, at Livermere, California?

9 **And which track from The Grateful Dead's 1970 album, *Workingman's Dead*, was written about the violent events at the concert?**

10 Which 1969 album, with a palindromic title, contained the songs *Mountains Of The Moon* and *China Cat Sunflower*?

11 **What was the name of the spin off band, formed by Jerry Garcia in 1970, which featured on the Grateful Dead album *American Beauty*?**

12 What was the title of Jerry Garcia's debut solo album, released in 1971?

13 **What was the nickname given to the group's keyboard player Ron McKernan?**

14 What was the title of the Grateful Dead's first album release on their own record label?

15 **Which member of the band died in 1973 , from a stomach haemorrhage and liver failure brought about by alcohol?**

1 The third finger on his right hand, 2 The Warlocks, **3 The Fillmore West Auditorium in San Francisco,** 4 Owsley Stanley, **5 Haight-Ashbury,** 6 Warner Bros., **7 *Anthem Of The Sun*,** 8 The Rolling Stones Altamont Speedway concert, **9 *New Speedway Boogie*,** 10 *Aoxomoxoa*, **11 New Riders Of The Purple Sage,** 12 *Hooteroll!*, **13 Pigpen,** 14 *Wake Of The Flood*, **15 Ron "Pigpen" McKernan.**

•THE KINKS•

1 **Where in London were the brothers Ray and Dave Davies born?**

2 What was the title of the first single, a cover version, to be released by the band, in 1964?

3 **Which famous sessions guitarist played on the group's first No. 1 single, *You Really Got Me*?**

4 Where did Ray Davies write the group's second No. 1 single, *Tired Of Waiting For You*?

5 **Which single from 1965, written by Ray Davies, was accused of having homosexual overtones?**

6 Which footballer was the 1966 song *Dedicated Follower Of Fashion* reputedly written with in mind?

7 **And which summer single, also from 1966, knocked The Beatles' *Paperback Writer* off the No. 1 slot in the UK?**

8 Which song, featured on The Kinks 1967 album *Something Else*, was later covered by The Jam?

9 **According to the 1967 song, *Waterloo Sunset*, where do Terry and Julie meet every Friday night?**

10 Which word in the lyrics to the band's 1969 song *Plastic Man* caused it to be banned by the BBC?

11 **And which lyric from the song *Lola* did Ray Davies have to fly back to London from a US tour to re-record, after the BBC complained about advertising?**

12 Which 1972 album featured the songs *Holiday*, *20th Century Man* and *Have A Cuppa Tea*?

13 **Which Preservation Society did the group write about in 1968?**

14 Which singer was Ray Davies romantically linked to during the early eighties?

15 **What was the title to Ray Davies' autobiography, released in 1995?**

1 Muswell Hill, 2 *Long Tall Sally,* **3 Jimmy Page,** 4 On the Metropolitan line of the London Underground, **5 *See My Friends,*** 6 George Best, **7 *Sunny Afternoon,*** 8 *David Watts,* 9 **Waterloo station,** 10 Bum, **11 Coca-Cola had to be changed to Cherry Cola,** 12 *Muswell Hillbillies,* **13 *The Village Green Preservation Society,*** 14 Chrissie Hynde of The Pretenders, **15 *X-Ray.***

•THE MONKEES 1•

1 Who was the writer and director, who came up with the idea of The Monkees?

2 Which member of the band had already released a single, titled *What Are We Going To Do*?

3 Which member of the group most often played the bass guitar on stage?

4 Which songwriting team were responsible for *The Monkees Theme*, and several of their early hits?

5 What was the title of the band's debut single, which reached US No. 1 in November 1966?

6 Which song, written by Neil Diamond, became the band's second US No. 1, in December 1966?

7 What was the title of the band's second album, which was certified Gold on advanced sales alone?

8 Who was the band's musical director, who filed a $35 million law suit following his sacking from Screen Gems Music?

9 Why did fans of the group march in protest to the US embassy in London, in April 1967?

10 What was the title of the band's third album, which featured the tracks *Shades Of Grey* and *For Pete's Sake*?

11 And which song, taken from the album, had a title inspired by the BBC TV series *Till Death Us Do Part*?

12 What was the name of Davy Jones' boutique, which he opened in New York in 1967?

13 With which mis-matched rock act did the band start a tour with in 1967?

14 Which single, which reached No. 3 in the US charts in August 1967, features the lines "And Mr. Green, he's so serene, he's got a TV in every room"?

15 What was the title of the 1967 single, written by John Stewart, which became the band's third US No. 1?

1 Bob Rafelson, 2 Davy Jones, **3 Peter Tork,** 4 Tommy Boyce and Bobby Hart, **5 *Last Train To Clarksville*,** 6 *I'm A Believer*, **7** *More Of The Monkees*, 8 Don Kirshner, **9 Davy Jones had been called up for military service in the US,** 10 *Headquarters*, **11** *Randy Scouse Git*, 12 Zilch, **13 The Jimi Hendrix Experience,** 14 *Pleasant Valley Sunday*, **15** *Daydream Believer*.

•THE MONKEES II•

1 What was the title of the band's somewhat psychedelic album, released in 1967, and featuring the tracks *The Door Into Summer and Words*?

2 And which Mike Nesmith song, taken from the album, opens with the line "Just a loudmouth Yankee, I went down to Mexico"?

3 When the final episode of the band's TV series was broadcast in March 1968, how many shows had they made in total?

4 What was the title of the 1968 film, which The Monkees starred in?

5 And who had co-written the film, along with the TV show producer Bob Rafelson?

6 Which song, released as a single in 1968, opened and closed the film?

7 Which rock musician appeared in the film with a cow, and advised the band to work more on their music?

8 Which song, originally a hit for The Coasters, reached No. 17 in the UK charts in 1968?

9 Which member of the group quit in December 1968, buying out his contract for $160,000?

10 What was the title of the 1970 album, released under The Monkees name, but featuring only Davy Jones and Mickey Dolenz?

11 What was the title of Mike Nesmith's 1970 solo album, containing the hit single *Joanne*?

12 And which song became a UK hit for Mike Nesmith, in April 1977?

13 Which British children's TV series did Mickey Dolenz direct in 1979?

14 Which member of the group was left $47 million by his mother, who owned the patent for Liquid Paper?

15 What was the title of the band's comeback album, featuring all new songs, released in September 1987?

1 *Pisces, Aquarius, Capricorn and Jones Ltd.,* 2 *What Am I Doing Hanging 'Round,* 3 58 shows, 4 *Head,* 5 Jack Nicholson, 6 *The Porpoise Song,* 7 Frank Zappa, 8 *D.W. Washburn,* 9 Peter Tork, 10 *Changes,* 11 *Magnetic South,* 12 *Rio,* 13 *Metal Mickey,* 14 Mike Nesmith, 15 *Pool It.*

Rock facts... ...and quiz book

• THE MOODY BLUES •

1. What was the title of the band's 1964 debut single, which they perform on ITV's *Ready Steady Go*?

2. Which US R&B artist had the original hit with *Go Now*, which reached No. 1 in the UK charts when released by The Moody Blues?

3. Which band did The Moody Blues support during their first US live appearance in 1965?

4. Who was the lead singer and guitarist with the band, who left in 1966 to be replaced by Justin Hayward?

5. What was the title of the band's first hit single, released in 1968, featuring the new line up?

6. And which album, originally intended as a stereo sampler record for Decca, did the single come from?

7. Which album, also released in 1968, opens with the track *Ride My See Saw*?

8. And which counter culture figure was celebrated in the segment from the album, titled *House Of Four Doors*?

9. Which British rock festival, held in 1969, did the band play on the opening day?

10. Which album, released in 1970, featured the tracks *Higher And Higher* and *Watching And Waiting*?

11. Which song, taken from the album *A Question Of Balance*, reached No. 2 In the UK charts in 1970?

12. What is the origin of the band's 1971 album title *Every Good Boy Deserves Favour*?

13. When the band were awarded their 6th gold disc during a US visit, who did they tell the record company they wanted to present them with the award?

14. Which song, taken from the 1972 album *Seventh Sojourn*, reached No. 12 in the US charts?

15. What was the title of Justin Haywood's 1978 solo single, taken from Jeff Wayne's album *War Of The Worlds*?

14 I'm Just A Singer (In A Rock And Roll Band), 15 Forever Autumn.
Silverheels, who played Tonto in *The Lone Ranger TV* series,
musicians to name the notes on the treble stave in sheet music, 13 Jay
Children's Children, 11 *Question*, 12 The Aide Memoir used by
Lost Chord, 8 Timothy Leary, 9 The Isle Of Wight Festival, 10 To Our
5 *Nights in White Satin*, 6 *Days Of Future Passed*, 7 *In Search Of The*
1 Lose Your Money, 2 Bessie Banks, 3 The Kinks, 4 Denny Laine,

•THE MOVE•

1 Which founder member of the group left Mike Sheridan And The Nightriders to form The Move?

2 Which London club did the band play at regularly during 1966?

3 And who had they replaced as house band at the venue?

4 Which classical theme was borrowed for the main riff to The Move's debut single, *Night Of Fear*?

5 What was the title of the band's third single, which was the first record to be played on the brand new BBC Radio 1?

6 And why did British Prime Minister Harold Wilson sue the group over publicity for the record?

7 What was the title of the track, recorded by the band, about an inmate at a mental asylum?

8 What was the title of the band's 1968 live EP, featuring a cover version of The Byrds' *So You Want To Be A Rock 'n' Roll Star*?

9 Which single, released in 1969, became the first UK No. 1 for the band?

10 What was the name of the band's lead singer, who resigned from the band to start a solo career?

11 Who was the lead singer with the Birmingham band Idle Race, who joined The Move in 1970?

12 And what was the title of the first album recorded by the new line up, which featured the songs *Brontosaurus* and *When Alice Comes Back To The Farm*?

13 What was the name of the project, designed to run concurrently with The Move, which would expand upon the classical arrangements used by bands such as The Beatles?

14 And, following disagreements with Jeff Lynn, which band did Roy Wood form, quitting the new project?

15 What was the title of the last single released by The Move in May 1972?

15 *California man.*
12 *Looking On*, 13 The Electric Light Orchestra, 14 Wizzard,
8 *Something Else*, 9 *Blackberry Way*, 10 Carl Wayne, 11 Jeff Lynne,
Prime Minister having sex with his secratary, 7 *Cherry Blossom Clinic*,
cards printed to promote the single, which featured a cartoon of the
Tchaikovsky, 5 *Flowers In The Rain*, 6 The group's manager had post-
1 Roy Wood, 2 The Marquee, **3 The Who**, 4 *The 1812 Overture*, by

• THE POLICE 1 •

1 Which member of the group's father worked as a CIA agent?

2 And which progressive rock band, managed by his brother, did he play with before forming the band in 1977?

3 What is the real name of the band's vocalist, Sting?

4 And how did he come about his nickname?

5 Which guitarist joined the band in June, 1977, to complete the final line up?

6 What were the band asked to do when they appeared on a US chewing gum commercial in 1978?

7 What was the title of the group's second single, which was the first to make the UK chart in 1978?

8 And what was the title of the band's debut album, which reached No. 6 in the UK charts in 1979?

9 Which single, which was released as their debut in 1978, reached No. 12 in the UK charts when it was re-released in 1979?

10 In which film, starring Phil Daniels, did Sting appear as the character The Ace Face?

11 Which single, released in 1979, became the band's first UK No. 1?

12 What was the title of the band's second album, which included the tracks *Deathwish* and *Contact*?

13 And which single, taken from this album, became the band's second No. 1?

14 In 1980, The Police became the first western band to play a rock concert in which country?

15 Which single, which failed to chart when released in 1978, reached No. 6 in the UK when re-released in 1980?

1 Stewart Copeland, 2 Curved Air, 3 Gordon Matthew Sumner, 4 From a black and yellow striped jersey he frequently wore, 5 Andy Summers, 6 Asked to dye their hair blonde, 7 Can't Stand Losing You, 8 Outlandos D'Amour, 9 Roxanne, 10 Quadrophenia, 11 Message In A Bottle, 12 Reggatta De Blanc, 13 Walking On The Moon, 14 India, 15 So Lonely.

•THE POLICE II•

1 **What was the subject of the band's 1980 No. 1 single *Don't Stand So Close To Me*?**

2 And which album, also containing the single *De Do Do Do, De Da Da Da*, was the song taken from?

3 **What was the subject of the band's 1981 No. 2 single, *Invisible Sun*?**

4 Which album, released in 1981, contained the singles *Every Little Thing She Does Is Magic* and *Spirits In The Material World*?

5 **Which 1982 Francis Ford Coppola film featured a musical score written by Stewart Copeland?**

6 And what was the title of Sting's first solo single, also taken from a film soundtrack?

7 **Which single, released in 1983, stayed at No. 1 for 4 weeks in the UK and 8 weeks in the US?**

8 And which album, which stayed at No. 1 in the US charts for 17 weeks, was this single taken from?

9 **Which guitarist worked with Andy Summers on the solo albums *I Advance Masked* and *Bewitched*?**

10 What was the title of Sting's debut solo album, released in 1985?

11 **For which 1988 TV series did Stewart Copeland write the theme tune?**

12 What was the title of Sting's second studio solo album, released in 1987, and featuring the tracks *Fragile* and *We'll Be Together*?

13 **Who was the real life subject of Sting's 1988 single *An Englishman In New York*?**

14 And in which film, starring Daniel Day Lewis, did the song feature?

15 **Which foreign leader was Sting's solo song *They Dance Alone* written about?**

1 An illicit affair between a teacher and a pupil, 2 *Zenyatta Mondatta*, 3 The troubles in Northern Ireland, 4 *Ghost In The Machine*, 5 *Rumblefish*, 6 *Spread A Little Happiness*, 7 *Every Breath You Take*, 8 *Synchronicity*, 9 Robert Fripp, 10 *Dream Of The Blue Turtles*, 11 *The Equalizer*, 12 *Nothing Like The Sun*, 13 Quentin Crisp, 14 *Stars And Bars*, 15 General Pinochet.

• THE PRETENDERS •

1 Which music magazine did Chrissie Hynde write for before forming The Pretenders?

2 Who produced the Pretenders' debut single *Stop Your Sobbing*?

3 Where did The Pretenders take their name from?

4 The Pretenders had their first UK No.1 in 1979, what was it?

5 Who had a hit in 1980 with a cover version of Chrissie Hynde's *Private Life*?

6 Which member of The Pretenders died in 1982 as a result of cocaine and heroin addiction?

7 Who did Chrissie Hynde marry in 1984?

8 Who did Chrissy Hynde team up with for the UK No.1 single *I Got You Babe* in 1985?

9 Which film featured The Pretenders' cover version of 10cc's *I'm Not In Love*?

10 What was the title of the No.1 charity single Chrissy Hynde recorded with Cher, Eric Clapton and Neneh Cherry?

11 What was the name of the 1995 C4-TV documentary about The Pretenders ?

12 Which band was guitarist Robbie McIntosh a member of before joining the Pretenders?

13 Why were Chrissy Hynde and Ray Davis turned away from the registry office on their wedding day?

14 Which group did bassist Tony Butler later go on to join?

15 In 1989 what did Chrissy Hynde confess to doing to a McDonalds years earlier?

1 *New Musical Express*, 2 Nick Lowe, 3 The Platters' hit *The Great Pretender*, 4 *Brass In Pocket*, 5 Grace Jones, 6 James Honeyman-Scott, 7 Jim Kerr, 8 UB40, 9 *Indecent Proposal*, 10 *Love Can Build A Bridge*, 11 *The Pretenders: No Turn Left Unstoned*, 12 The Average White Band, 13 The registrar refused to marry them because they were arguing too much, 14 Big Country, 15 Firebombed it.

• THE RAMONES •

1 What did each of the four members of the group change, when the band formed in 1974?

2 And which country did their drummer, Tommy, come from?

3 What was the title of the band's debut single, released in 1976?

4 Which two punk bands replaced The Ramones, when they pulled out of a UK concert tour with The Sex Pistols?

5 Which album, released in 1977 and featuring the tracks *Glad To See You* and *Gimme Gimme Shock Treatment*, reached No. 45 in the UK charts?

6 Which single reached No. 22 in the UK charts in June 1977?

7 How did Joey come to suffer second degree burns in 1977, requiring hospital treatment?

8 Which member of the band quit in 1978, but stayed on to become their producer?

9 Which album, released in 1978 and featuring the single *Don't Come Close*, reached No. 32 in the UK charts?

10 In which 1979 film did the band appear, playing the title track?

11 Which famous record producer worked with the band on their 1980 album *End Of The Century*?

12 And which cover version of a 1964 Ronettes hit reached No. 8 in the UK charts for the group?

13 Which member of the group was rushed to hospital and under went brain surgery, following a fight over his girlfriend, in August 1983?

14 Which album was the band's 1985 single, *Somebody Put Something In My Drink*, taken from?

15 Which 1989 Stephen King film did the band contribute several tracks for?

1 **They changed their surnames to Ramone**, 2 Hungary, 3 **Blitzkrieg Bop**, 4 The Damned and The Clash, 5 **Leave Home**, 6 *Sheena Is A Punk Rocker*, 7 He dropped a full teapot, 8 Tommy Ramone (aka. Thomas Erdelyi), 9 **Road To Ruin**, 10 *Rock'n'Roll High School*, 11 **Phil Spector**, 12 Baby I Love You, 13 **Joey**, 14 *Animal Boy*, 15 **Pet Sematary.**

•THE ROLLING STONES I•

1 Where did Keith Richards and Mick Jagger first meet each other?

2 What was the name of the R&B group which Keith Richards and Mick Jagger joined in 1960?

3 Which other founder member joined Jagger and Richards to form The Rolling Stones in April 1962?

4 And where did the name Rolling Stones come from?

5 Which member of the group joined the band in 1963, replacing Tony Chapman, and completed the final line up?

6 What was the name of the 19 year old, who became the band's manager in 1963?

7 What was the title of the Chuck Berry song, released by the band as their debut single?

8 What was the title of the song, composed by John Lennon and Paul McCartney, which became the band's second single?

9 Who wrote and recorded the original version of the group's third single, *Not Fade Away*?

10 Which BBC panel game did the group make an appearance on, causing many letters of complaint, in 1964?

11 What was the name of Mick Jagger's girlfriend, who had a UK hit with the song *As Tears Go By*, written by Jagger and Richards?

12 What was the title of the first Jagger-Richards composition to reach No. 1 in the UK singles chart?

13 And which 1965 single became their first single to be the UK and US No. 1?

14 Which US TV show did the band make a second appearance on in May 1965, despite the host promising the group would not be back after it's first appearance, a year earlier?

15 What was the title of the band's 1966 album, featuring the No. 1 single *Get Off Of My Cloud*?

1 They both went to Maypole County Primary School in Wilmington, Kent, 2 Little Boy Blue And The Blue Boys, 3 Brian Jones, 4 A song by Muddy Waters, 5 Charlie Watts, 6 Andrew Oldham, 7 Come On, 8 I Wanna Be Your Man, 9 Buddy Holly, 10 Juke Box Jury, 11 Marianne Faithfull, 12 The Last Time, 13 (I Can't Get No) Satisfaction, 14 The Ed Sullivan Show, 15 December's Children (And Everybody's).

•THE ROLLING STONES II•

1. Which album from 1966 became the first to feature only Jagger-Richards compositions?

2. And which drug did the band criticise in the song *Mother's Little Helper*, taken from the album?

3. Which single from 1966, said to have been inspired by the death of Mick Jagger's mother, features Brian Jones playing a sitar?

4. Which late 1966 single did the band promote by dressing up in drag?

5. What were the Rolling Stones famously forced to do, during a performance of their 1967 single *Let's Spend The Night Together* on *The Ed Sullivan Show*?

6. Why was the Rolling Stones' first appearance on *Sunday Night At The London Palladium* also their last?

7. Which member of the band drew the cartoons, featured on the back of the band's 1967 album *Between The Buttons*?

8. What tragedy stuck the band, at Keith Richards home in Sussex?

9. And which other member of the band was arrested on drugs charges, in May 1967?

10. Following the strict jail sentences given to Mick Jagger and Keith Richards, which newspaper printed a sympathetic editorial, titled "Who breaks a butterfly on a wheel"?

11. And which single, released by the band to comment on their recent trouble with the authorities, was accompanied by a video, parodying the trials of Oscar Wilde?

12. And which fellow musicians provided the backing vocals for this single?

13. What was the name of the Rolling Stones' psychedelic album, released in December 1967?

14. And what gimmick was used for the front cover of the album?

15. And which single from the album featured string and piano arrangements by future Led Zeppelin founder John Paul Jones?

1 *Aftermath*, 2 Valium, 3 *Paint It Back*, 4 *Have You Seen Your Mother, Baby (Standing In The Shadows)*, 5 **Change the lyrics to *Let's Spend Some Time Together***, 6 They refused to join the rest of the performers, waving to the audience on the revolving stage at the end of the show, 7 **Charlie Watts**, 8 They were raided by the Drug Squad, with Keith Richards and Mick Jagger being charged with possession, 9 **Brian Jones**, 10 *The Times*, 11 *We Love You*, 12 John Lennon and Paul McCartney, 13 *Their Satanic Majesties Request*, 14 A lenticular 3D photograph of the band, 15 *She's A Rainbow*.

THE ROLLING STONES III

1 Which 1968 single indicated a return to R&B, after the group's brief psychedelic phase?

2 Which member of the group bought the former home of *Winnie The Pooh* author A.A.Milne, in November 1968?

3 Which album, released in 1968, featured the songs *Sympathy For The Devil* and *Street Fighting Man*?

4 And why did Decca withdraw the original album design, in favour of a plain white sleeve, made out like an invitation?

5 What was the title of the band's TV special, featuring The Who, John Lennon, Eric Clapton and others, which was filmed in 1968 but never released?

6 Which member of the band announced he was quitting the group, as he no longer agreed with the material they were releasing?

7 And which musician did the group announce would take his place?

8 When the Rolling Stones played a free concert in Hyde Park in July 1969, who did they dedicate their performance to?

9 Which film did Mick Jagger fly to Australia in the summer of 1969 to star in?

10 Which song, released in 1969, became the last UK No. 1 single the band would have to date?

11 Which member of the group had a child by girlfriend and *Barbarella* star Anita Pallenberg, in August 1969?

12 Which filmmaker was responsible for the film *Sympathy For The Devil*, which featured the band working in the studio, interspersed with surreal poetry readings?

13 Where in the US did the Rolling Stones give a disastrous free concert, during which a fan was stabbed to death by Hell's Angels?

14 And which song did the band refuse to perform live, following this concert?

15 Which album, released in December 1969, featured the songs *Gimme Shelter*, *Midnight Rambler* and *Monkey Man*?

1 *Jumping Jack Flash*, **2** Brian Jones, **3** *Beggars Banquet*, **4** The original cover, depicting a graffiti covered toilet, was thought to be in bad taste, **5** *The Rolling Stones' Rock And Roll Circus*, **6** Brian Jones, **7** Mick Taylor, **8** Brian Jones, who had drowned at his home two days earlier, **9** *Ned Kelly*, **10** *Honky Tonk Women*, **11** Keith Richards, **12** Jean-Luc Goddard, **13** Altamont Speedway at Livermore in California, **14** *Sympathy For The Devil*, because it was what they were playing when the stabbing took place, **15** *Let It Bleed*.

1 **What was the title of the film, released in 1970, which starred Mick Jagger and James Fox?**

2 And what was the title of the song taken from the film, which was released as a Mick Jagger solo record?

3 **What was the name of the group's manager, who they sacked in 1970?**

4 What was the title of the live album, recorded at Madison Square Garden in 1969, and released in September 1970?

5 **Which record label did the group leave in 1970, to form their own label, Rolling Stones Records?**

6 Which artist designed the cover to the Rolling Stones' 1971 album *Sticky Fingers*, which featured a fully working fly zip?

7 **Which single, taken from this album, attracted widespread criticism for its sexist and racist lyrics?**

8 What was the title of the band's 1971 double album, largely recorded in a mobile recording unit set up at a French Chateaux?

9 **And which single, taken from the album, was written by Mick Jagger while the rest of the band flew to Las Vegas for one of their regular gambling weekends?**

10 Which member of the band fell asleep and accidentally set fire to himself at the Londonderry House Hotel in Hyde Park?

11 **In which country was the Rolling Stones' 1973 album *Goats Head Soup* recorded?**

12 And which song from the album reached US No. 1 in October 1973?

13 **Which member of the group was the first to release a solo album, titled *Monkey Grip*?**

14 Under what nickname did Mick Jagger and Keith Richards produce the band's 1974 album *It's Only Rock 'n' Roll*?

15 **Which member of the group announced he was to leave in December 1974?**

1 *Performance*, 2 *Memo From Turner*, 3 Allen Klein, 4 *Get Yer Ya-Ya's Out*, 5 Decca, 6 Andy Warhol, 7 *Brown Sugar*, 8 *Exile On Main Street*, 9 *Tumbling Dice*, 10 Keith Richards, 11 Jamaica, 12 *Angie*, 13 Bill Wyman, 14 The Glimmer Twins, 15 Mick Taylor.

• THE ROLLING STONES V •

1 **Which former member of The Faces joined The Rolling Stones at the end of 1974?**

2 What was the title of the album released in 1975 by the band's old label, Decca, containing early 1960's recordings and demos?

3 **For what reason was Keith Richards arrested in Arizona, during the band's 1975 US tour?**

4 What was The Rolling Stones' 1976 film *Ladies And Gentlemen: The Rolling Stones* the first film to feature?

5 **Which album, released in 1976, contained the single Fool To Cry?**

6 What tragedy struck Keith Richards in June 1976?

7 **Which British rock festival did the band headline in August 1976?**

8 In which country were Keith Richards and his girlfriend Anita Pallinberg arrested for possession of heroin and cocaine, with intent to supply?

9 **Which 1978 album featured a controversial cover, depicting several famous people in a mock wig advert?**

10 And what was the title of the disco orientated track, taken from the album, which became the band's first 12" single?

11 **What conditions were imposed on Keith Richards on being found guilty of possession of heroin by a Canadian court in 1978?**

12 What was the title of Ron Wood's 1979 solo album?

13 **Which member of the group announced his intention to leave in 1982, on the group's 20th anniversary?**

14 Which member of the band was punched in the eye by hero Chuck Berry, after meeting in New York after a concert?

15 **What was the title of Bill Wyman's solo single, released in August 1981?**

1 Which single, taken from the band's 1981 album *Tattoo You*, reached No. 7 in the UK charts?

2 Which 27 year old model married Keith Richards in 1983?

3 Which 1983 album featured a title track about military oppression in South America?

4 Which singer recorded a cover version of The Rolling Stones' *Beast Of Burden*, which featured Mick Jagger in the video?

5 Which first did the band's 1984 compilation video, *Rewind*, achieve?

6 What was the title of Mick Jaggers debut solo album, featuring the single *Just Another Night*?

7 Which US singer joined Mick Jagger onstage during the Philadelphia Live Aid concert in 1985?

8 What was the name of the band's long serving keyboard player, who died of a heart attack in 1985?

9 And which album, released in 1986, was dedicated to his memory?

10 Which single, taken from this album, became the first to miss the UK charts in the band's career?

11 Which of the group's singles was voted the No. 1 song of all time by readers of US magazine *Rolling Stone*, in 1988?

12 What was the title of Keith Richards' debut solo album, released in 1988?

13 And what was the name of his backing band, who played with him during the US promotional tour for the album?

14 What was the name of the restaurant opened by Bill Wyman in London, in 1989?

15 And which 19 year old did he marry in secret in June 1989?

1 *Start Me Up*, 2 Patti Hansen, 3 *Undercover*, 4 Bette Midler, 5 The first music video to be certified as 18 in the UK, 6 *She's The Boss*, 7 Tina Turner, 8 Ian Stewart, 9 *Dirty Work*, 10 *One Hit (To The Body)*, 11 *(I Can't Get No) Satisfaction*, 12 *Talk Is Cheap*, 13 X-Pensive Winos, 14 *Sticky Fingers*, 15 Mandy Smith.

•THE SISTERS OF MERCY•

1 **In which UK city were Sisters Of Mercy formed?**

2 Which radio show did the band record a session for in 1982?

3 **What was the name of the band's drum machine?**

4 Who did Wayne Hussey replace in the band in 1983?

5 **What was the name of the group Wayne Hussey and Craig Adams formed in 1985?**

6 What was Sisters Of Mercy's first UK Top Ten album?

7 **Which female member joined the band in 1987?**

8 Which group was Tim Bricheno a former member of before joining the band in 1990?

9 **Who did the band support at a concert at Crystal Palace in 1993?**

10 Which record label did the band sign with in 1984?

11 **Who produced the band's single *Corrosion*?**

12 Which punk group was Tony James a former member of?

13 **With which band did Sisters Of Mercy make a joint tour with in 1991?**

14 Which Rolling Stones song did the band record for their 1992 album?

15 **And what was the title of the album?**

•THE SMALL FACES•

1 **Why did the band call themselves The Small Faces?**

2 What was the title of the band's debut single, released in 1965?

3 **What was the name of the keyboard player, who replaced original keyboard player Jimmy Winston in November 1965?**

4 What was the title of the first single written by the band themselves, which reached No. 10 in 1966?

5 **Which UK TV show were the group performing on, when lead singer and guitarist Steve Marriott collapsed from exhaustion?**

6 Which Beatles double A-side was knocked off the UK No. 1 slot by The Small Faces song *All Or Nothing*?

7 **Which No. 4 hit for the band borrowed its melody line from the hymn *Angels From The Realms Of Glory*?**

8 What was the suggested occupation of the main character in the band's 1967 single *Here Comes The Nice*?

9 **Which psychedelic single featured the lines "I feel inclined to blow my mind, get hung up, feed the ducks with a bun"?**

10 And what is the name of the special effect, now common in the recording industry, which this single was the first to feature?

11 **During a tour of which country were the band, along with The Who and singer Paul Jones, thrown off an airliner, for drunken behaviour?**

12 Which 1968 single starts with the lines "Wouldn't it be nice to get on with my neighbours, but they make it very clear, they've got no room for ravers"?

13 **What was the title of the band's 1968 album, released in a cover designed to look like a tin of tobacco?**

14 And which British comedian recorded several nonsense links between tracks on the album, including the intro "Are you sitting comfeybold, two square on your botty"?

15 **What was the name of the band Steve Marriott formed, after leaving The Small Faces in 1969?**

13 *Ogden's Nut Gone Flake*, 14 Stanley Unwin, 15 Humble Pie.
9 *Itchycoo Park*, 10 Flanging, or Phasing, 11 Australia, 12 Lazy Sunday,
Submarine/*Eleanor Rigby*, 7 *My Mind's Eye*, 8 Amphetamine dealer,
3 Ian McLagan, 4 *Hey Girl*, 5 *Ready, Steady, Go*, 6 *Yellow*
group were notably short in height, 2 *Whatcha Gonna Do About It*,
1 A "Face" was a mod term for a smart young person, and all the

•THE STONE ROSES•

1 On which TV adaptation was John Squire a set maker?

2 Which name did the band reject in 1984 before choosing The Stone Roses?

3 In 1987 what did Alan "Reni" Wren moonlight as?

4 Which member of New Order produced the single *Elephant Stone*?

5 In 1989 The Stone Roses were heard for only 45 seconds on BBC TV's *The Late Show*, why was this?

6 In 1990 how did the band cause £23,000 worth of damage to their record label FM Revolver's office during a dispute with them?

7 With which single did The Stone Roses make their UK chart debut in 1989?

8 The Stone Roses had their first UK Top Ten hit in 1989, what was it?

9 In 1992 which label did the band sign with after a lengthy dispute with their former label Silvertone?

10 Which magazine did The Stone Roses give their first interview in 5 years to in 1994?

11 Who replace Alan "Reni" Wren as drummer in 1995?

12 In which year did the band first tour the USA?

13 And how did John Squire break his collar bone and shoulder blade during the tour?

14 In 1995 how did Ian Brown almost cause a riot at the band's concert at Newport, Wales?

15 John Squire quit The Stone Roses in 1996 to form which band?

1 **Wind In The Willows,** 2 The Angry Young Teddy Bears, 3 A kisso-gram, 4 Peter Hook, 5 Their volume blew the studio fuses, 6 They staged a paint attack, 7 **She Bangs The Drums,** 8 *What The World Is Waiting For!* Fool's Gold, 9 **Geffen Records,** 10 *The Big Issue,* 11 **Robbie Maddix,** 12 1995, 13 In a mountain bike accident, 14 He went on stage wearing a Cardiff City football shirt, 15 The **Seahorses.**

~ 185 ~

• THE STRANGLERS •

1 Which subject did Hugh Cornwell teach before forming the Stranglers?

2 Who did the Stranglers support on tour in 1976?

3 In 1977 the A-side of a Stranglers' single was banned by the BBC what was it?

4 Which jazz singer featured as guest artist on *Old Codger* the B-side to *Walk on By*?

5 Why did Hugh Cornwell spend a month in jail in 1980?

6 Hugh Cornwell released his first solo single in 1985, what was it called?

7 In 1988 the Stranglers released a cover version of which Kinks song?

8 In which year did Hugh Cornwell quit the Stranglers?

9 Which group did the Stranglers support on tour in 1991?

10 In 1992 the Stranglers became the first group ever to play a rock concert, where?

11 In which year were the Stranglers formed?

12 The Stranglers made their debut on the UK album chart in 1977, with what?

13 What was the name of the Stranglers' original drummer?

14 Which record label did the Stranglers sign with in 1976?

15 Why were the Stranglers arrested in France in 1980?

1 Science, 2 Patti Smith, **3 Peaches, 4** George Melly, **5 Possession of drugs, 6** One In A Million, **7** All Day And All Of The Night, **8** 1990, **9 Simple Minds, 10** Dartmoor prison, **11** 1974, **12** Stranglers IV (Rattus Norvegicus), **13 Jet Black, 14** United Artists, **15 Inciting a riot.**

• THE VELVET UNDERGROUND •

1 Name the classically trained musician who, on meeting vocalist Lou Reed, decided to form a band?

2 Where had the group taken their name from?

3 Who became the group's manager, after seeing them perform at the Café Bizarre in Greenwich Village?

4 And which German singer did the new manager suggest should join the band?

5 What was the name of Andy Warhol's New York arts collective, where the band spent much of their time?

6 What was the full title of the band's debut album, released in 1967?

7 Which album, released by the band in 1968, was recorded in just 1 day, at the end of a tour?

8 Which member of the band was fired in March 1968, to be replaced by Doug Yule

9 Which album, released in 1969, features the songs *Pale Blue Eyes* and *Beginning To See The Light*?

10 And which song from the album opens with the line "I've been up, I've been down. I've been 'round from side to side"?

11 Who was the drummer in the band, who was temporarily replaced by Billy Yule in 1970 when she fell pregnant?

12 Which album, released in 1970, featured the tracks *Sweet Jane* and *Rock And Roll*?

13 Which member of the band quit in 1970, to become a clerical worker in his father's accountancy firm?

14 What was the title of the band's 1973 album, which contained the tracks *Little Jack* and *Crash*?

15 How did former band member Nico die, in 1988?

• THE VERVE •

1 In 1992 The Verve made their debut on the UK chart with which song?

2 In which year were The Verve formed?

3 Where did The Verve take the backing music for *Bitter Sweet Symphony* from?

4 Which Verve single entered the UK charts at No.1?

5 Who stood in for Nick McCabe for the 1998 American tour?

6 Who was The Verve's manager?

7 What is Richard Ashcroft's nickname?

8 Who was The Verve's drummer?

9 What was the title of The Verve's 1997 No.1 album?

10 The Verve split in 1999 in which UK city did they perform their farewell concert?

11 Which record label did The Verve sign with in 1991?

12 What was the title of The Verve's debut album?

13 What did Richard Ashcroft collapse from during their 1994 US tour?

14 Which member of Suede tried out as a guitarist with The Verve in 1995 when Nick McCabe left briefly?

15 Which was The Verve's last UK Top Ten single?

1 *She's A Superstar*, 2 1990, 3 The Rolling Stones track *The Last Time*, 4 *The Drugs Don't Work*, 5 B.J. Cole, 6 Jazz Summers, 7 Mad Richard, 8 Peter Salisbury, 9 *Urban Hymns*, 10 Wigan, 11 Virgin's Hut label, 12 *A Storm in Heaven*, 13 Severe dehydration, 14 Bernard Butler, 15 *Lucky Man*.

• THE WHO •

1 **Which grammar school did Pete Townsend, John Entwistle and Roger Daltrey all attend?**

2 Under what name did the group appear after their fourth and final member, Keith Moon, joined them in 1964?

3 **Which of their early singles was returned by the Decca engineers, when it was thought that the intentional, harsh feedback during the break must have been a recording fault?**

4 And which British TV show adopted the song for their theme tune?

5 **Which 1967 single, with its blatant references to self abuse, was inspired by a vaudeville poster owned by Pete Townsend's girl friend?**

6 Which psychedelic single from 1967, widely banned on radio because of it's perceived drug references, was described by Pete Townsend as simply "a song about a man with exceptionally good eye sight"?

7 **Which pirate radio station's jingles were used to link the tracks on The Who's 1968 album *The Who Sell Out*?**

8 What was the name of the Indian spiritual leader who influenced much of Pete Townsend's writing from the late 1960's?

9 **Why was their 1968 song *Magic Bus* banned on many US radio stations?**

10 Which single, taken from the seminal album *Tommy*, was described by Radio 1 DJ Tony Blackburn as "Sick"?

11 **How was Keith Moon's chauffeur, Neil Boland, killed in January 1970?**

12 Which new rock venue in Finsbury Park was opened by The Who, performing three headlining nights?

13 **What was the title of their greatest hits compilation album, released in winter 1971?**

14 Who directed the film version of the group's rock opera *Tommy*, released in 1975?

15 **And which actress co-starred with Roger Daltrey in the film, playing the part of Tommy's mother?**

14 Ken Russell, 15 Ann-Margret.

heads after a gig, 12 The Rainbow, 13 *Meaty Beaty Big And Bouncy,*
he panicked and took control of the car, trying to escape from skin-
11 Keith Moon, who couldn't drive, accidentally ran him over when
way," were thought to be suggestive of promiscuity, 10 *Pinball Wizard.*
including "I drive my baby every day, each time we go a different
See For Miles, 7 Radio London, 8 Meher Baba, 9 Many of the lines,
Anyhow, Anywhere, 4 *Ready Steady Go!*, 5 *Pictures Of Lily,* 6 *I Can*
1 Acton County Grammar School, 2 The High Numbers, 3 *Anyway,*

• THE YARDBIRDS •

1 **What was the name of the vocalist, who formed the band in 1963?**

2 And which US writer's book did the band get their name from?

3 **Who replaced the band's original guitarist, Tony Topham, in 1963?**

4 What was the title of the band's debut album, featuring their versions of the songs *Smokestack Lightning* and *Good Morning Little Schoolgirl*?

5 **And at which London venue was the album recorded live?**

6 Which single became the band's first chart hit, reaching No. 3 in the UK charts in 1965?

7 **Which band did Eric Clapton go on to join, following his departure from The Yardbirds?**

8 And which guitarist left the band The Tridents to replace Eric Clapton in The Yardbirds?

9 **What was the title of the band's 1966 single, recorded at Chess Studios in Chicago, which reached No. 3 in the UK charts?**

10 Which guitarist joined the band in 1966, replacing original bass player, Paul Samwell-Smith?

11 **Which song, taken from the band's eponymous studio album, reached No. 11 in the US charts?**

12 Which 1966 film, starring David Hemmings, featured The Yardbirds playing the song *Stroll On*?

13 **Which 1967 album, produced by Mickie Most, featured the tracks *White Summer* and *Smile On Me*?**

14 Which Manfred Man song did the group cover in 1967, reaching No. 45 in the US charts?

15 **Which song, recorded in 1968, became the last recording made by the band, before they split up in July?**

Clown, 15 *Goodnight Sweet Josephine.*
Sideways Down, 12 *Blow Up,* 13 *Little Games,* 14 *Ha Ha Said The*
8 Jeff Beck, 9 *Shapes Of Things,* 10 Jimmy Page, 11 *Over Under*
5 **The Marquee,** 6 *For Your Love,* 7 **John Mayall's Blues Breakers,**
1 **Keith Relf,** 2 Jack Kerouac, 3 **Eric Clapton,** 4 *Five Little Yardbirds,*

~ 190 ~

•THIN LIZZIE•

1 **Which adaptation of an Irish folk tune became the band's first Top Ten single?**

2 Which guitarist, who had played with Phil Lynott in the band Skid Row, joined the band in 1974, but only stayed for four months?

3 **And which two guitarists replaced him, joining the band full time in June 1974?**

4 What was the title of the band's first single release, featuring the new line up?

5 **And which album was this single taken from?**

6 What was the title of the book of poems, written by vocalist Phil Lynott, published in 1974?

7 **Which disease did Phil Lynott contract in 1975, due to his intravenous drug use?**

8 Which album from 1975, featuring the songs *Rosalie* and *Suicide*, became the band's first UK chart album?

9 **Which single, taken from the 1976 album *Jailbreak*, became the group's most successful single?**

10 At which London venue did the band perform a televised concert, shown in March 1978?

11 **What was the title of the band's double album live set, released in 1978, which stayed in the UK charts for 62 weeks?**

12 What was the title of guitarist Gary Moore's solo single, featuring Phil Lynott on vocals, which reached No. 8 in the UK charts in 1979?

13 **Which guitarist played with the band during their US and Japanese tours of 1979, before leaving to form Ultravox?**

14 Who did Phil Lynott marry, in February 1980?

15 **What was the title of Phil Lynott's debut solo single, released in 1980?**

1 *Whiskey In The Jar,* 2 Gary Moore, 3 Brian Robertson and Scott Gorham, 4 *Philomena,* 5 *Nightlife,* 6 *Songs For While I'm Away,* 7 *Hepatitis,* 8 *Fighting,* 9 *The Boys Are Back In Town,* 10 The Rainbow Theatre, 11 *Live And Dangerous,* 12 *Parisienne Walkways,* 13 Midge Ure, 14 Caroline Crowther, daughter of British TV presenter Leslie Crowther, 15 *Dear Miss Lonely Hearts.*

•TINA TURNER•

1 **Born on November 26th 1939, what is Tina Turner's real name?**

2 Which song became the first single to be released under the name Ike and Tina Turner, when the planned session singer failed to turn up, and the vocals were recorded by Tina?

3 **Which famous producer offered Ike $20,000 to sign Tina to a new management and production contract?**

4 And what was the title of the only single released under this contract, which reached No. 88 in the US charts?

5 **Which cover version of a Beatles song reached No. 57 in the US charts when it was released in 1970?**

6 Which title track from Ike and Tina Turner's 1973 album reached No. 4 in the UK charts?

7 **Which role did Tina Turner play in the 1975 Ken Russell film *Tommy*?**

8 In which year did Tina leave abusive husband Ike, to follow her own solo career?

9 **Which British band did Tina open for in 1981, during their 10th US tour?**

10 Which song, released in 1982, gave Tina Turner her first solo success, reaching No. 6 in the UK charts?

11 **Which single, taken from a forthcoming solo album, reached No. 1 in the US in 1984?**

12 And which No. 1 album, featuring a title track written by Mark Knopfler, was the single taken from?

13 **Which role was played by Tina Turner in the 1985 film *Mad Max: Beyond Thunderdome*?**

14 And which song, taken from the soundtrack to the album, reached No. 3 in the UK charts?

15 **Who duetted with Tina Turner on the 1985 single *It's Only Love*?**

1 **Annie Mae Bullock**, 2 *A Fool In Love*, 3 **Phil Spector**, 4 *River Deep, Mountain High*, 5 **Come Together**, 6 *Nutbush City Limits*, 7 The Acid Queen, 8 1976, 9 **The Rolling Stones**, 10 *Let's Stay Together*, 11 **What's Love Got To Do With It?**, 12 *Private Dancer*, 13 **Aunty Entity**, 14 *We Don't Need Another Hero*, 15 **Bryan Adams.**

•TORI AMOS•

1. Why was Tori thrown out of her scholarship at music school?

2. What instrument does she play?

3. Which Al Stewart album features backing vocals by Tori Amos?

4. Tori made her debut on the UK chart in 1991 with which single?

5. Which Led Zeppelin song did Tori record a cover version of in 1992?

6. To which film soundtrack album did Tori contribute *The Happy worker*?

7. Tori Amos had her first UK Top Ten hit in 1994, what was it?

8. Tori Amos' second album entered the UK chart at No.1, what was it?

9. With who did Tori sing the duet *I Wanna Get Back With You* on his 1994 album?

10. Which REM song did Tori record a cover version of for the film soundtrack *Higher Learning*?

11. Which band did Tori Amos front before going solo in 1988?

12. With whom did Tori sing the duet *Down By The Seaside* for the Led Zeppelin tribute album *Encomium*?

13. Tori Amos had her first UK No.1 with which single in 1997?

14. Which single released in 1991 told the true story of Tori's traumatic rape in 1985?

15. In 1996 Tori Amos featured on whose single *Blue Skies*?

1 For playing by ear, 2 Piano, 3 *Last Days Of The Century*, 4 *Silent All These Years*, 5 *Whole Lotta Love*, 6 *Toys*, 7 *Cornflake Girl*, 8 *Under The Pink*, 9 Tom Jones, 10 *Losing My Religion*, 11 Y Kant Tori Read, 12 Robert Plant, 13 *Professional Widow (It's Got To Be Big)* (re-mix), 14 *Me And My Gun*, 15 BT.

• TRAFFIC •

1 **Which group did vocalist and keyboard player Steve Winwood leave, prior to forming Traffic in 1967?**

2 What was the title of the band's debut single, which reached No. 5 in the UK charts in July 1967?

3 **Who recorded a 1985 cover version of the song *Hole In My Shoe*, which reached No. 2 in the UK charts for Traffic in 1967?**

4 For which 1967 British film, starring Barry Evans, did Traffic record the title song?

5 **Which member of the band quit at the end of 1967, only to rejoin 6 months later?**

6 What was the title of the band's 1968 album, featuring the tracks *Heaven Is In Your Mind* and *Berkshire Poppies*?

7 **And which song, taken from the album, became the last single the band would have in the UK charts?**

8 When the band split for the first time, in 1969, which supergroup did Steve Winwood form with Eric Clapton, Ginger Baker and Rick Grech?

9 **What was the title of the album released in 1969, as a farewell album before the group split?**

10 What was the title of Steve Winwood's solo album, released in 1970?

11 **For which album, featuring the single *Empty Pages*, did the band reform in 1970 to record?**

12 With which West Coast pop star did Dave Mason record a duet album, in 1971?

13 **Which live album was the band's 1971 single *Gimme Some Lovin'* taken from?**

14 And which band had had the original hit with this song?

15 **In which country did the band record their 1973 album *Shoot-Out At The Fantasy Factory*?**

•U2•

1 Who produced U2's first album *Boy* in 1980?

2 In 1983 U2 had a hit with a song inspired by the Polish Solidarity Movement, what was it?

3 In 1984 who did Bono sing a duet with at a concert at Slane Castle, Eire?

4 Who did U2 support on a UK tour in 1980?

5 In 1984 U2 formed their own record label, what was it called?

6 To whom was the U2 single *Pride (In The Name Of Love)* dedicated?

7 Bono featured on which Irish folk group's single *In A Lifetime* in 1986?

8 In 1986 The Edge recorded a soundtrack album with Sinead O'Connor, what was it called?

9 In 1986 who was Bono joined onstage by at a concert in Philadelphia?

10 In 1987 U2 released an album which became the fastest-selling album in UK chart history, what was it?

11 What was the name of U2's documentary movie made in 1988?

12 Who did U2 record the single *When Love Comes To Town* with?

13 What did Bono order 10,000 of during a concert in America in 1992?

14 Where did U2 get the title for the album *Achtung Baby* from?

15 In 1990 who recorded a cover version of U2's *I Still Haven't Found What I'm Looking For?*

•VAN HALEN•

1 **Which two brothers formed the group in 1973?**

2 What condition did lead singer David Lee Roth suffer from as a child?

3 **Under what name did the group play, before choosing the name Van Halen in 1975?**

4 While playing in several Los Angeles clubs, which fellow West Coast band, featuring guitarist Randy Rhoads, became deadly rivals with Van Halen?

5 **Which bass player offered to produce a demo tape for the band, after hearing them play at the Starwood club in Los Angeles?**

6 Who became the band's producer, following their signing to Warner Bros. Records?

7 **Which Kinks cover version became Van Halen's first chart single?**

8 And which instrumental track from the band's eponymous debut album popularised Eddie Van Halen's two-handed tapping guitar technique?

9 **When the group started their first tours, what seemingly petty contractual clause did the band use to check that the full agreements had been read by the venue's management?**

10 Which single, taken from Van Halen's second album, reached No. 15 in the US charts?

11 **Which album from 1980 opened with the song *And The Cradle Will Rock*?**

12 Which actress did Eddie Van Halen marry in April 1981?

13 **Who had the original hit with the song *(Oh) Pretty Woman*, released by Van Halen as a single in 1982?**

14 And what was the name of the album from which the single was taken?

15 **For which US No. 1 single did Eddie Van Halen record an improvised guitar solo as a favour to Michael Jackson?**

• WHITESNAKE •

1 **Which band did lead singer David Coverdale leave, prior to setting up Whitesnake?**

2 In which country did David Coverdale record his vocals for the first two Whitesnake albums?

3 **What was the title of the band's 1978 four-track EP?**

4 Which former Deep Purple member joined the band in August 1978?

5 **And which other former member of Deep Purple took over the drums from David Dowle in 1979?**

6 What was the title of the band's 1979 album, featuring a risque cover which was widely banned in the US?

7 **Which single became the band's first chart hit, reaching No.13 in the UK charts?**

8 Which album, released in 1980, featured the tracks *Sweet Talker* and *Blindman*?

9 **Which British rock festival did the band headline at in 1981?**

10 Which album, recorded in 1982 with a new Whitesnake line-up, featured the single *Here I Go Again*?

11 **What was the title of the album, co-written by David Coverdale and guitarist John Sykes, released in 1987?**

12 And which guitarist replaced John Sykes during the promotional tour for this album?

13 **And how did this guitarist injure himself, leading to his replacement by Steve Vai?**

14 What is the name of the actress, featured in several of the band's promotional videos, who married David Coverdale in 1989?

15 **Which 1990 film featured the Whitesnake song *Last Note Of Freedom*?**

1 Deep Purple, 2 West Germany, **3 *Snake Bite*,** 4 Jon Lord, **5 Ian Paice,** 6 Love Hunter, **7 *Fool For Your Loving*,** 8 Come An' Get It, **9 The Monsters Of Rock as Castle Donnington,** 10 *Saints 'n' Sinners*, **11 *Whitesnake 1987*,** 12 Adrian Vandenburg, **13 Tendonitis, brought about by extreme finger exercises on guitar and piano,** 14 Tawny Kitaen, **15 *Days Of Thunder*.**

• WIZZARD •

1 **Which band did Roy Wood leave, following disagreements with fellow musician Jeff Lynn, before forming Wizzard?**

2 At which venue did Wizzard make their debut performance, as part of the line up to the 1972 London Rock'n'Roll Festival?

3 **What was the title of Wizzard's debut single, which reached No. 6 in the UK charts?**

4 What sort of drink did the band sing about on their debut album, Wizzard Brew?

5 **What was the title of the band's first UK No. 1 single?**

6 And which American record producer's style did Roy Wood borrow for most of the band's output at this time?

7 **Which teen ballad reached No. 1 in the UK in September 1973?**

8 What was the title of the band's 1973 Christmas single?

9 **And what sound effect introduced the single?**

10 What style did Roy Wood use on the band's 1974 album *Introducing Eddy And The Falcons*?

11 **Which unusual pop instrument was used on Wizzard's 1975 single *Are You Ready To Rock*?**

12 What was the title of Roy Wood's second solo album, featuring the songs *Any Old Time Will Do* and *Look Thru' The Eyes Of A Fool*?

13 **Which Birmingham based late night TV show featured a title tune written and performed by Wizzard?**

14 Which band's 1986 cover version of *Waterloo* did Roy Wood provide a saxophone solo for?

15 **Which single, released in 1975, was the last to be credited to the band Wizzard?**

1 **The Electric Light Orchestra, itself a spin off from Roy Wood's earlier band, The Move,** 2 Wembley Stadium, 3 **Ball Park Incident,** 4 A Jolly Cup Of Tea, 5 **See My Baby Jive,** 6 Phil Spector and his Wall Of Sound, 7 *Angel Fingers,* 8 I Wish It Could Be Christmas Every Day, 9 The sound of a cash register, 10 1950's Rock'n'Roll, 11 **The Bagpipes,** 12 *Mustard,* 13 *O.T.T,* 14 Doctor And The Medics, 15 *Rattlesnake Roll.*

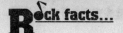
• XTC •

1 **What is the name of the main vocalist, who formed the band in 1977 with Colin Moulding and Terry Chambers?**

2 And from which West country town did the band come from?

3 **What was the title of the band's debut EP, released by Virgin Records in 1977?**

4 Which album, released in 1978, featured the singles *This Is Pop*? and *Statue Of Liberty*?

5 **Who was the original keyboard player with the band, who quit in 1979 to be replaced by Dave Gregory?**

6 What was the title of the band's second album, featuring the tracks *Beatown* and *Crowded Room*?

7 **Which 1980 film, starring Tim Curry, featured the XTC track *Take This Town*?**

8 Which single, taken from the 1980 album *Black Sea*, reached No. 16 in the UK charts?

9 **Which song, released in 1982, became the band's biggest success, reaching No. 10 in the UK charts?**

10 And which UK No. 5 album was the song taken from?

11 **What was the title of the band's compilation album, released in 1982 after an announcement that the band would never play live again?**

12 Under what name did the band record a psychedelically tinged mini-album, *25 O'clock*, released in 1985?

13 **Which album, released in 1989, became the band's biggest success, reaching No. 28 in the UK album charts?**

14 Which band released the single *Hands Across The Ocean*, written and produced by Andy Partridge in 1990?

15 **What was the title of the band's official biography, published in 1992?**

1 Andy Partridge, 2 Swindon, **3 3-D,** 4 White Music, **5 Barry Andrews,** 6 Go 2, **7 Times Square,** 8 Sgt. Rock (Is Going To Help Me), **9 Senses Working Overtime,** 10 English Settlement, **11 Waxworks,** 12 The Dukes Of Stratosphere, **13 Oranges And Lemons,** 14 The Mission, **15 Chalkhills And Children.**

•YES•

1 **Which band's farewell concert did the newly formed Yes open, at the Royal Albert Hall in 1968?**

2 What was the title of the band's first UK single release?

3 **Which Beatle song did the band cover on their 1969 eponymous debut album?**

4 Which virtuoso guitarist joined the band in 1970, replacing Peter Banks?

5 **And which classically trained keyboard player joined the band in 1971, completing the classic Yes line up?**

6 Which artist was responsible for designing the band's logo, and creating the futuristic artwork on many of their album sleeves?

7 **And which album, from 1971, was the first to feature his artwork?**

8 Which 1972 album featured the songs *And You And I* and *Siberian Khatru*?

9 **Which studio double album, released in 1973, was based on Shastric scriptures?**

10 What was the title of Rick Wakeman's solo album, released in 1974, shortly before he announced he was quitting the band?

11 **Which 20 minute track, taken from the band's 1974 album *Relayer*, was based on Tolstoy's book *War And Peace*?**

12 Which single, taken from the band's 1977 album *Going For The One*, reached No. 7 in the UK charts?

13 **Which Greek musician recorded the album *Short Stories* with Yes singer Jon Anderson, in 1980?**

14 Which two members of the band Buggles joined Yes in 1980, replacing Jon Anderson and Rick Wakeman?

15 **And what was the name of the first album to be recorded by this new line up?**

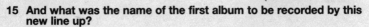

• ZZ TOP •

1 What is the name of the singer and guitarist, who formed the band in 1969?

2 What is the name of the band's bass player, who formed a band called The Warlocks with his brother in 1967?

3 What was the title of the band's first single, released in 1969?

4 Which album, released in 1972, contained the tracks *Francene* and *Just Got Paid*?

5 And which British group did they support, during their 1972 nationwide US tour?

6 Which album, released in 1973, became the band's first gold record?

7 Which single, taken from the band's 1975 album *Fandango!*, reached No. 20 in the US charts?

8 When the group returned to public life in 1979, after a two year break, which member of the group had not grown a long beard, which became the band's trademark?

9 Who provided the horn section, featured on the band's 1979 album *Deguello*?

10 What was the title of the band's 1983 album, named after their 1933 Ford Coupé?

11 And which single, taken from this album, reached No. 10 in the UK charts when released in 1984?

12 Which album, released in 1985, featured the songs *Velcro Fly* and *Delirious*?

13 Which film soundtrack was the band's 1990 hit *Doubleback* taken from?

14 Which Elvis Presley hit did Z.Z. Top cover in 1992, reaching No. 10 in the UK singles chart?

15 Which album, released in 1994, contained the singles *Pincushion* and *Breakaway*?

1 **Billy Gibbons**, 2 Dusty Hill, 3 *Salt Lick*, 4 *Rio Grande Mud*, 5 **The Rolling Stones**, 6 *Tres Hombres*, 7 *Tush*, 8 Frank Beard, the drummer, 9 **Billy Gibbons, Dusty Hill and Frank Beard themselves**, 10 *Eliminator*, 11 *Gimme All Your Lovin'*, 12 *Afterburner*, 13 *Back To The Future III*, 14 *Viva Las Vegas*, 15 *Antenna*.

UK
SINGLES
&
ALBUMS

•10 YEARS AFTER•

SINGLES

6 JUN 70	LOVE LIKE A MAN	10

ALBUMS

21 SEP 68	UNDEAD	26
22 FEB 69	STONEDHENGE	6
4 OCT 69	SSSSH	4
2 MAY 70	CRICLEWOOD GREEN	4
9 JAN 71	WATT	5
13 NOV 71	SPACE IN TIME	36
7 OCT 72	ROCK AND ROLL	27
28 JUL 73	RECORDED LIVE	36

•AC/DC•

SINGLES

10 JUN 78	ROCK 'N' ROLL DAMNATION	24
1 SEP 79	HIGHWAY TO HELL	56
2 FEB 80	TOUCH TOO MUCH	29
28 JUN 80	DIRTY DEEDS DONE DIRT CHEAP	47
28 JUN 80	HIGH VOLTAGE (LIVE VERSION)	48
28 JUN 80	IT'S A LONG WAY TO THE TOP (IF YOU WANNA ROCK 'N' ROLL)	55
28 JUN 80	WHOLE LOTTA ROSIE	36
13 SEP 80	YOU SHOOK ME ALL NIGHT LONG	38
29 NOV 80	ROCK 'N' ROLL AIN'T NOISE POLLUTION	15
6 FEB 82	LET'S GET IT UP	13
3 JUL 82	FOR THOSE ABOUT TO ROCK (WE SALUTE YOU)	15
29 OCT 83	GUNS FOR HIRE	37
4 AUG 84	NERVOUS SHAKEDOWN	35
6 JUL 85	DANGER	48
18 JAN 86	SHAKE YOUR FOUNDATIONS	24
24 MAY 86	WHO MADE WHO	16
30 AUG 86	YOU SHOOK ME ALL NIGHT LONG (RE-ISSUE)	46
16 JAN 88	HEATSEEKER	12
2 APR 88	THAT'S THE WAY I WANNA ROCK 'N' ROLL	22
22 SEP 90	THUNDERSTRUCK	13
24 NOV 90	MONEYTALKS	36
27 APR 91	ARE YOU READY	34
17 OCT 92	HIGHWAY TO HELL (LIVE)	14
6 MAR 93	DIRTY DEEDS DONE CHEAP (LIVE)	68
10 JUL 93	BIG GUN	23
30 SEP 95	HARD AS A ROCK	33
11 MAY 96	HAIL CAESAR	56

•AC/DC•

ALBUMS

5 NOV 77	LET THERE BE ROCK	17
20 MAY 78	POWERAGE	26
28 OCT 78	IF YOU WANT BLOOD YOU'VE GOT IT	13
18 AUG 79	HIGHWAY TO HELL	8
9 AUG 80	BACK IN BLACK	1
5 DEC 81	FOR THOSE ABOUT TO ROCK	3
3 SEP 83	FLICK OF THE SWITCH	4
13 JUL 85	FLY ON THE WALL	7
7 JUN 86	WHO MADE WHO	11
13 FEB 88	BLOW UP YOUR VIDEO	2
6 OCT 90	THE RAZOR'S EDGE	4
7 NOV 92	LIVE	5
7 OCT 95	BALLBREAKER	6

ADAM AND THE ANTS

SINGLES

2 AUG 80	KINGS OF THE WILD FRONTIER	48
11 OCT 80	DOG EAT DOG	4
6 DEC 80	ANTMUSIC	2
27 DEC 80	YOUNG PARISIANS	9
24 JAN 81	CARTROUBLE	33
24 JAN 81	ZEROX	45
21 FEB 81	KINGS OF THE WILD FRONTIER (RE-ENTRY)	2
9 MAY 81	STAND AND DELIVER	1
12 SEP 81	PRINCE CHARMING	1
12 DEC 81	ANT RAP	3
27 FEB 82	DEUTSCHER GIRLS	13
13 MAR 82	THE ANTMUSIC EP (THE B-SIDES)	46
22 MAY 82	GOODY TWO SHOES	1
18 SEP 82	FRIEND OR FOE	9
27 NOV 82	DESPERATE BUT NOT SERIOUS	33
29 OCT 83	PUSS 'N' BOOTS	5
10 DEC 83	STRIP	41
22 SEP 84	APOLLO 9	13
13 JUL 85	VIVE LE ROCK	50
17 FEB 90	ROOM AT THE TOP	13
28 APR 90	CAN'T SET RULES ABOUT LOVE	47
11 FEB 95	WONDERFUL	32
3 JUN 95	GOTTA BE A SIN	48

ALBUMS

15 NOV 80	KINGS OF THE WILD FRONTIER	1
17 JAN 81	DIRK WEARS WHITE SOX	16
14 NOV 81	PRINCE CHARMING	2
23 OCT 82	FRIEND OR FOE	5
19 NOV 83	STRIP	20
14 SEP 85	VIVE LE ROCK	42
24 MAR 90	MANNERS AND PHYSIQUE	19
15 APR 95	WONDERFUL	24

Rock facts... ...and quiz book

• AEROSMITH •

SINGLES

17 OCT 87	DUDE (LOOKS LIKE A LADY)	45
16 APR 88	ANGEL	69
9 SEP 89	LOVE IN AN ELEVATOR	13
24 FEB 90	DUDE (LOOKS LIKE A LADY) (RE-ISSUE)	20
14 APR 90	RAG DOLL	42
1 SEP 90	THE OTHER SIDE	46
10 APR 93	LIVIN' ON THE EDGE	19
3 JUL 93	EAT THE RICH	34
30 OCT 93	CRYIN'	17
18 DEC 93	AMAZING	57
2 JUL 94	SHUT UP AND DANCE	24
20 AUG 94	SWEET EMOTION	74
5 NOV 94	CRAZY / BLIND MAN	23
8 MAR 97	FALLING IN LOVE (IS HARD ON THE KNEES)	22
21 JUN 97	HOLE IN MY SOLE	29
27 DEC 97	PINK	38
12 SEP 98	I DON'T WANT TO MISS A THING	4

ALBUMS

5 SEP 87	PERMANENT VACATION	37
23 SEP 89	PUMP	3
1 MAY 93	GET A GRIP	2
12 NOV 94	BIG ONES	7

• ALANIS MORISSETTE •

SINGLES

5 AUG 95	YOU OUGHTA KNOW	22
28 OCT 95	HAND IN MY POCKET	26
24 FEB 96	YOU LEARN	24
20 APR 96	IRONIC	11
3 AUG 96	HEAD OVER FEET	7
7 DEC 96	ALL I REALLY WANT	59
31 OCT 98	THANK U	5

ALBUMS

26 AUG 95	JAGGED LITTLE PILL	12

• ALICE COOPER •

SINGLES

15 JUL 72	SCHOOL'S OUT	1
7 OCT 72	ELECTED	4
10 FEB 73	HELLO HURRAY	6
21 APR 73	NO MORE MR. NICE GUY	10
19 JAN 74	TEENAGE LAMENT '74	12
21 MAY 77	(NO MORE) LOVE AT YOUR CONVENIENCE	44
23 DEC 78	HOW YOU GONNA SEE ME NOW	61
6 MAR 82	SEVEN·AND SEVEN IS	62
8 MAY 82	FOR BRITAIN ONLY / UNDER MY WHEELS	66
18 OCT 86	HE'S BACK (THE MAN BEHIND THE MASK)	61
9 APR 88	FREEDOM	50
29 JUL 89	POISON	2
7 OCT 89	BED OF NAILS	38
2 DEC 89	HOUSE OF FIRE	65
22 JUN 91	HEY STOOPID	21
5 OCT 91	LOVE'S A LOADED GUN	38
6 JUN 92	FEED MY FRANKENSTEIN	27
28 MAY 94	LOST IN AMERICA	22
23 JUL 94	IT'S ME	34

•ALICE COOPER•

ALBUMS

5 FEB 72	KILLER	27
22 JUL 72	SCHOOL'S OUT	4
9 SEP 72	LOVE IT TO DEATH	28
24 MAR 73	BILLION DOLLAR BABIES	1
12 JAN 74	MUSCLE OF LOVE	34
15 MAR 75	WELCOME TO MY NIGHTMARE	19
24 JUL 76	ALICE COOPER GOES TO HELL	23
28 MAY 77	LACE AND WHISKY	33
23 DEC 78	FROM THE INSIDE	68
17 MAY 80	FLUSH THE FASHION	56
12 SEP 81	SPECIAL FORCES	96
12 NOV 83	DADA	93
1 NOV 86	CONSTRICTOR	41
7 NOV 87	RAISE YOUR FIST AND YELL	48
26 AUG 89	TRASH	2
13 JUL 91	HEY STOOPID	4
18 JUN 94	THE LAST TEMPTATION	6

•BAD COMPANY•

SINGLES

1 JUN 74	CAN'T GET ENOUGH	15
22 MAR 75	GOOD LOVIN' GONE BAD	31
30 AUG 75	FEEL LIKE MAKIN' LOVE	20

ALBUMS

15 JUN 74	BAD COMPANY	3
12 APR 75	STRAIGHT SHOOTER	3
21 FEB 76	RUN WITH THE PACK	4
19 MAR 77	BURNIN' SKY	17
17 MAR 79	DESOLATION ANGELS	10
28 AUG 82	ROUGH DIAMONDS	15

•BEE GEES•

SINGLES

27 APR 67	NEW YORK MINING DISASTER 1941	12
12 JUL 67	TO LOVE SOMEBODY	50
26 JUL 67	TO LOVE SOMEBODY (RE-ENTRY)	41
20 SEP 67	MASSACHUSETTS	1
22 NOV 67	WORLD	9
31 JAN 68	WORDS	8
27 MAR 68	JUMBO / THE SINGER SANG HIS SONG	25
7 AUG 68	I'VE GOTTA GET A MESSAGE TO YOU	1
19 FEB 69	FIRST OF MAY	6
4 JUN 69	TOMORROW TOMORROW	23
16 AUG 69	DON'T FORGET TO REMEMBER	2
28 MAR 70	I.O.I.O.	49
5 DEC 70	LONELY DAYS	33
29 JAN 72	MY WORLD	16
22 JUL 72	RUN TO ME	9
28 JUN 75	JIVE TALKIN'	5
31 JUL 76	YOU SHOULD BE DANCING	5
13 NOV 76	LOVE SO RIGHT	41
29 OCT 77	HOW DEEP IS YOUR LOVE	3
4 FEB 78	STAYIN' ALIVE	4
15 APR 78	NIGHT FEVER	1
13 MAY 78	STAYIN' ALIVE (RE-ENTRY)	63
25 NOV 78	TOO MUCH HEAVEN	3
17 FEB 79	TRAGEDY	1
14 APR 79	LOVE YOU INSIDE OUT	13
5 JAN 80	SPIRITS (HAVING FLOWN)	16
17 SEP 83	SOMEONE BELONGING TO SOMEONE	49
26 SEP 87	YOU WIN AGAIN	1
12 DEC 87	E.S.P.	51
15 APR 89	ORDINARY LIVES	54
24 JUN 89	ONE	71

• BEE GEES •

SINGLES CONT...

2 MAR 91	SECRET LOVE	5
21 AUG 93	PAYING THE PRICE OF LOVE	23
27 NOV 93	FOR WHOM THE BELL TOLLS	4
16 APR 94	HOW TO FALL IN LOVE PART 1	30
1 MAR 97	ALONE	5
21 JUN 97	I COULD NOT LOVE YOU MORE	14
8 NOV 97	STILL WATERS (RUN DEEP)	18
18 JUL 98	IMMORTALITY	5

ALBUMS

12 AUG 67	BEE GEES FIRST	8
24 FEB 68	HORIZONTAL	16
28 SEP 68	IDEA	4
5 APR 69	ODESSA	10
9 MAY 70	CUCUMBER CASTLE	57
17 FEB 79	SPIRITS HAVING FLOWN	1
7 NOV 81	LIVING EYES	73
3 OCT 87	E.S.P.	5
29 APR 89	ONE	29
6 APR 91	HIGH CIVILISATION	24
25 SEP 93	SIZE ISN'T EVERYTHING	23

• BILLY BRAGG •

SINGLES

16 MAR 85	BETWEEN THE WARS (EP)	15
28 DEC 85	DAYS LIKE THESE	43
28 JUN 86	LEVI STUBBS TEARS	29
15 NOV 86	GREETINGS TO THE NEW BRUNETTE	58
14 MAY 88	SHE'S LEAVING HOME	1
10 SEP 88	WAITING FOR THE GREAT LEAP FORWARDS	52
8 JUL 89	WON'T TALK ABOUT IT	29
6 JUL 91	SEXUALITY	27
7 SEP 91	YOU WOKE UP MY NEIGHBOURHOOD	54
29 FEB 92	ACCIDENT WAITING TO HAPPEN (EP)	33
31 AUG 96	UPFIELD	46
17 MAY 97	THE BOY DONE GOOD	55

ALBUMS

21 JAN 84	LIFE'S A RIOT WITH SPY VS SPY	30
20 OCT 84	BREWING UP WITH BILLY BRAGG	16
4 OCT 86	TALKING WITH THE TAXMAN ABOUT POETRY	8
13 JUN 87	BACK TO BASICS	37
1 OCT 88	WORKERS PLAYTIME	17
12 MAY 90	THE INTERNATIONALE	34
28 SEP 91	DON'T TRY THIS AT HOME	8

•BLACK•

SINGLES

27 SEP 86	WONDERFUL LIFE	72
27 JUN 87	SWEETEST SMILE	8
22 AUG 87	WONDERFUL LIFE	8
16 JAN 88	PARADISE	38
24 SEP 88	THE BIG ONE	54
21 JAN 89	NOW YOU'RE GONE	66
4 MAY 91	FEEL LIKE CHANGE	56
15 JUN 91	HERE IT COMES AGAIN	70
5 MAR 94	WONDERFUL LIFE (RE-ISSUE)	42

ALBUMS

26 SEP 87	WONDERFUL LIFE	3
29 OCT 88	COMEDY	32
1 JUN 91	BLACK	42

• BLACK CROWES •

SINGLES

1 SEP 90	HARD TO HANDLE	45
12 JAN 91	TWICE AS HARD	47
22 JUN 91	JEALOUS AGAIN / SHE TALKS TO ANGELS	70
24 AUG 91	HARD TO HANDLE (RE-ISSUE)	39
26 OCT 91	SEEING THINGS	72
2 MAY 92	REMEDY	24
26 SEP 92	STING ME	42
28 NOV 92	HOTEL ILLNESS	47
11 FEB 95	HIGH HEAD BLUES / A CONSPIRACY	25
22 JUL 95	WISER TIME	34
27 JUL 96	ONE MIRROR TOO MANY	51
7 NOV 98	KICKIN MY HEART AROUND	55

ALBUMS

24 AUG 91	SHAKE YOUR MONEY MAKER	36
23 MAY 92	SOUTHERN HARMONY AND MUSICAL COMPANION	2
12 NOV 94	AMORICA	8

• BLACK SABBATH •

SINGLES

29 AUG 70	PARANOID	4
3 JUN 78	NEVER SAY DIE	21
14 OCT 78	HARD ROAD	33
5 JUL 80	NEON KNIGHTS	22
16 AUG 80	PARANOID (RE-ISSUE)	14
6 DEC 80	DIE YOUNG	41
7 NOV 81	MOB RULES	46
13 FEB 82	TURN UP THE NIGHT	37
15 APR 89	HEADLESS CROSS	62
13 JUN 92	TV CRIMES	33

ALBUMS

7 MAR 70	BLACK SABBATH	8
26 SEP 70	PARANOID	1
21 AUG 71	MASTER OF REALITY	5
30 SEP 72	BLACK SABBATH VOLUME 4	8
8 DEC 73	SABBATH BLOODY SABBATH	4
27 SEP 75	SABOTAGE	7
7 FEB 76	WE SOLD OUR SOUL FOR ROCK 'N' ROLL	35
6 NOV 76	TECHNICAL ECSTASY	13
14 OCT 78	NEVER SAY DIE	12
26 APR 80	HEAVEN AND HELL	9
5 JUL 80	BLACK SABBATH LIVE AT LAST	5
14 NOV 81	MOB RULES	12
22 JAN 83	LIVE EVIL	13
24 SEP 83	BORN AGAIN	4
1 MAR 86	SEVENTH STAR	27
28 NOV 87	THE ETERNAL IDOL	66
29 APR 89	HEADLESS CROSS	31
1 SEP 90	TYR	24
4 JUL 92	DEHUMANIZER	28
12 FEB 94	CROSS PURPOSES	41
17 JUN 95	FORBIDDEN	71

• BLONDIE •

SINGLES

18 FEB 78	DENIS	2
6 MAY 78	(I'M ALWAYS TOUCHED BY YOUR) PRESENCE DEAR	10
26 AUG 78	PICTURE THIS	12
11 NOV 78	HANGING ON THE TELEPHONE	5
27 JAN 79	HEART OF GLASS	1
19 MAY 79	SUNDAY GIRL	1
29 SEP 79	DREAMING	2
24 NOV 79	UNION CITY BLUE	13
23 FEB 80	ATOMIC	1
12 APR 80	CALL ME	1
8 NOV 80	THE TIDE IS HIGH	1
24 JAN 81	RAPTURE	5
8 MAY 82	ISLAND OF LOST SOULS	11
24 JUL 82	WAR CHILD	39
3 DEC 88	DENIS (RE-MIX)	50
11 FEB 89	CALL ME (RE-MIX)	61
10 SEP 94	ATOMIC (RE-MIX)	19
8 JUL 95	HEART OF GLASS (RE-MIX)	15
28 OCT 95	UNION CITY BLUE (RE-MIX)	31

ALBUMS

4 MAR 78	PLASTIC LETTERS	10
23 SEP 78	PARALLEL LINES	1
10 MAR 79	BLONDIE	75
13 OCT 79	EAT TO THE BEAT	1
29 NOV 80	AUTOAMERICAN	3
31 OCT 81	BEST OF BLONDIE	4
5 JUN 82	THE HUNTER	9
17 DEC 88	ONCE MORE INTO THE BLEACH	50
29 JUL 95	BEAUTIFUL - THE REMIX ALBUM	25

• BLUR •

SINGLES

27 OCT 90	SHE'S SO HIGH	48
27 APR 91	THERE'S NO OTHER WAY	8
10 AUG 91	BANG	24
11 APR 92	POPSCENE	32
1 MAY 93	FOR TOMORROW	28
10 JUL 93	CHEMICAL WORLD	28
16 OCT 93	SUNDAY SUNDAY	26
19 MAR 94	GIRLS AND BOYS	5
11 JUN 94	TO THE END	16
3 SEP 94	PARKLIFE	10
19 NOV 94	END OF A CENTURY	19
26 AUG 95	COUNTRY HOUSE	1
9 SEP 95	COUNTRY HOUSE	57
25 NOV 95	THE UNIVERSAL	5
24 FEB 96	STEREOTYPES	7
11 MAY 96	CHARMLESS MAN	5
1 FEB 97	BEETLEBUM	1
19 APR 97	SONG 2	2
26 APR 97	BEETLEBUM (RE-ENTRY)	59
28 JUN 97	ON YOUR OWN	5
27 SEP 97	MOR	15

ALBUMS

7 SEP 91	LEISURE	7
22 MAY 93	MODERN LIFE IS RUBBISH	15
7 MAY 94	PARKLIFE	1
23 SEP 95	THE GREAT ESCAPE	1

• BOB DYLAN •

SINGLES

25 MAR 65	TIMES THEY ARE A-CHANGIN'	9
29 APR 65	SUBTERRANEAN HOMESICK BLUES	9
17 JUN 65	MAGGIE'S FARM	22
19 AUG 65	LIKE A ROLLING STONE	4
28 OCT 65	POSITIVELY FOURTH STREET	8
27 JAN 66	CAN YOU PLEASE CRAWL OUT YOUR WINDOW	17
14 APR 66	ONE OF US MUST KNOW (SOONER OR LATER)	33
12 MAY 66	RAINY DAY WOMEN NOS. 12 & 35	7
21 JUL 66	I WANT YOU	16
14 MAY 69	I THREW IT ALL AWAY	30
13 SEP 69	LAY LADY LAY	5
10 JUL 71	WATCHING THE RIVER FLOW	24
6 OCT 73	KNOCKIN' ON HEAVENS DOOR	14
7 FEB 76	HURRICANE	43
29 JUL 78	BABY STOP CRYING	13
28 OCT 78	IS YOUR LOVE IN VAIN	56
20 MAY 95	DIGNITY	33
11 JUL 98	LOVE SICK	64

ALBUMS

23 MAY 64	THE FREEWHEELIN' BOB DYLAN	1
11 JUL 64	THE TIMES THEY ARE A-CHANGIN'	4
21 NOV 64	ANOTHER SIDE OF BOB DYLAN	8
8 MAY 65	BOB DYLAN	13
15 MAY 65	BRINGING IT ALL BACK HOME	1
9 OCT 65	HIGHWAY 61 REVISITED	4
20 AUG 66	BLONDE ON BLONDE	3
2 MAR 68	JOHN WESLEY HARDING	1
17 MAY 69	NASHVILLE SKYLINE	1
11 JUL 70	SELF PORTRAIT	1
28 NOV 70	NEW MORNING	1

•BOB DYLAN•

ALBUMS CONT...

29 SEP 73	PAT GARRETT AND BILLY THE KID (FILM SOUNDTRACK)	29
23 FEB 74	PLANET WAVES	7
13 JUL 74	BEFORE THE FLOOD	8
15 FEB 75	BLOOD ON THE TRACKS	4
26 JUL 75	THE BASEMENT TAPES	8
31 JAN 76	DESIRE	3
9 OCT 76	HARD RAIN	3
1 JUL 78	STREET LEGAL	2
26 MAY 79	BOB DYLAN AT BUDOKAN	4
8 SEP 79	SLOW TRAIN COMING	2
28 JUN 80	SAVED	3
29 AUG 81	SHOT OF LOVE	6
12 NOV 83	INFIDELS	9
15 DEC 84	REAL LIVE	54
22 JUN 85	EMPIRE BURLESQUE	11
2 AUG 86	KNOCKED OUT LOADED	35
25 JUN 88	DOWN IN THE GROOVE	32
18 FEB 89	DYLAN AND THE DEAD	38
14 OCT 89	OH MERCY	6
22 SEP 90	UNDER THE RED SKY	13
14 NOV 92	GOOD AS I BEEN TO YOU	18
20 NOV 93	WORLD GONE WRONG	35
29 APR 95	UNPLUGGED	10

• BON JOVI •

SINGLES

31 AUG 85	HARDEST PART IS THE NIGHT	68
9 AUG 86	YOU GIVE LOVE A BAD NAME	14
25 OCT 86	LIVIN' ON A PRAYER	4
11 APR 87	WANTED DEAD OR ALIVE	13
15 AUG 87	NEVER SAY GOODBYE	21
24 SEP 88	BAD MEDICINE	17
10 DEC 88	BORN TO BE MY BABY	22
29 APR 89	I'LL BE THERE FOR YOU	18
26 AUG 89	LAY YOUR HANDS ON ME	18
9 DEC 89	LIVING IN SIN	35
24 OCT 92	KEEP THE FAITH	5
23 JAN 93	BED OF ROSES	13
15 MAY 93	IN THESE ARMS	9
7 AUG 93	I'LL SLEEP WHEN I'M DEAD	17
2 OCT 93	I BELIEVE	11
26 MAR 94	DRY COUNTY	9
24 SEP 94	ALWAYS	2
17 DEC 94	PLEASE COME HOME FOR CHRISTMAS	7
25 FEB 95	SOMEDAY I'LL BE SATURDAY NIGHT	7
4 MAR 95	PLEASE COME HOME FOR CHRISTMAS (RE-ENTRY)	46
10 JUN 95	THIS AIN'T A LOVE SONG	6
30 SEP 95	SOMETHING FOR THE PAIN	8
25 NOV 95	LIE TO ME	10
9 MAR 96	THESE DAYS	7
6 JUL 96	HEY GOD	13
25 AUG 90	BLAZE OF GLORY / YOUNG GUNS II (FILM SOUNDTRACK)	2

ALBUMS

28 APR 84	BON JOVI	71
11 MAY 85	7800° FAHRENHEIT	28
20 SEP 86	SLIPPERY WHEN WET	6
1 OCT 88	NEW JERSEY	1
14 NOV 92	KEEP THE FAITH	1
1 JUL 95	THESE DAYS	1

• BOOMTOWN RATS •

SINGLES

27 AUG 77	LOOKING AFTER NO. 1	11
19 NOV 77	MARY OF THE 4TH FORM	15
15 APR 78	SHE'S SO MODERN	12
17 JUN 78	LIKE CLOCKWORK	6
14 OCT 78	RAT TRAP	1
21 JUL 79	I DON'T LIKE MONDAYS	1
17 NOV 79	DIAMOND SMILES	13
26 JAN 80	SOMEONE'S LOOKING AT YOU	4
22 NOV 80	BANANA REPUBLIC	3
31 JAN 81	THE ELEPHANT'S GRAVEYARD (GUILTY)	26
12 DEC 81	NEVER IN A MILLION YEARS	62
20 MAR 82	HOUSE ON FIRE	24
18 FEB 84	TONIGHT	73
19 MAY 84	DRAG ME DOWN	50
2 JUL 94	I DON'T LIKE MONDAYS (RE-ISSUE)	38

ALBUMS

17 SEP 77	BOOMTOWN RATS	18
8 JUL 78	TONIC FOR THE TROOPS	8
3 NOV 79	THE FINE ART OF SURFACING	7
24 JAN 81	MONDO BONGO	6
3 APR 82	V DEEP	64

• BREAD •

SINGLES

1 AUG 70	MAKE IT WITH YOU	5
15 JAN 72	BABY I'M A WANT YOU	14
29 APR 72	EVERYTHING I OWN	32
30 SEP 72	THE GUITAR MAN	16
25 DEC 76	LOST WITHOUT YOUR LOVE	27

ALBUMS

26 SEP 70	ON THE WATERS	34
18 MAR 72	BABY I'M A WANT-YOU	9
29 JAN 77	LOST WITHOUT YOUR LOVE	17
5 NOV 77	THE SOUND OF BREAD	1

SINGLES

Date	Title	Position
22 NOV 80	HUNGRY HEART	44
13 JUN 81	THE RIVER	35
26 MAY 84	DANCING IN THE DARK	28
6 OCT 84	COVER ME	38
12 JAN 85	DANCING IN THE DARK (RE-ENTRY)	4
23 MAR 85	COVER ME (RE-ENTRY)	16
15 JUN 85	I'M ON FIRE / BORN IN THE USA	5
3 AUG 85	GLORY DAYS	17
14 DEC 85	SANTA CLAUS IS COMIN' TO TOWN / MY HOMETOWN	9
29 NOV 86	WAR	18
7 FEB 87	FIRE	54
23 MAY 87	BORN TO RUN	16
3 OCT 87	BRILLIANT DISGUISE	20
12 DEC 87	TUNNEL OF LOVE	45
18 JUN 88	TOUGHER THAN THE REST	13
24 SEP 88	SPARE PARTS	32
21 MAR 92	HUMAN TOUCH	11
23 MAY 92	BETTER DAYS	34
25 JUL 92	57 CHANNELS (AND NOTHIN' ON)	32
24 OCT 92	LEAP OF FAITH	46
10 APR 93	LUCKY TOWN (LIVE)	48
19 MAR 94	STREETS OF PHILADELPHIA	2
22 APR 95	SECRET GARDEN	44
11 NOV 95	HUNGRYHEART (RE-ISSUE)	28
4 MAY 96	THE GHOST OF TOM JOAD	26
19 APR 97	SECRET GARDEN (RE-ISSUE)	17

ALBUMS

Date	Album	
1 NOV 75	BORN TO RUN	17
17 JUN 78	DARKNESS ON THE EDGE OF TOWN	16
25 OCT 80	THE RIVER	2
2 OCT 82	NEBRASKA	3
16 JUN 84	BORN IN THE USA	1
15 JUN 85	THE WILD THE INNOCENT AND THE E STREET SHUFFLE	33
15 JUN 85	GREETINGS FROM ASBURY PARK, N.J	41
17 OCT 87	TUNNEL OF LOVE	1
4 APR 92	HUMAN TOUCH	1
4 APR 92	LUCKY TOWN	2
24 APR 93	IN CONCERT - MTV PLUGGED	4
25 NOV 95	THE GHOST OF TOM JOAD	16

•BRYAN ADAMS•

SINGLES

12 JAN 85	RUN TO YOU	11
16 MAR 85	SOMEBODY	35
25 MAY 85	HEAVEN	38
10 AUG 85	SUMMER OF '69	42
2 NOV 85	IT'S ONLY LOVE	29
21 DEC 85	CHRISTMAS TIME	55
22 FEB 86	THIS TIME	41
12 JUL 86	STRAIGHT FROM THE HEART	51
28 MAR 87	HEAT OF THE NIGHT	50
20 JUN 87	HEARTS ON FIRE	57
17 OCT 87	VICTIM OF LOVE	68
29 JUN 91	(EVERYTHING I DO) I DO IT FOR YOU	1
14 SEP 91	CAN'T STOP THIS THING WE STARTED	12
23 NOV 91	THERE WILL NEVER BE ANOTHER TONIGHT	32
28 DEC 91	(EVERYTHING I DO) I DO IT FOR YOU (RE-ENTRY)	73
22 FEB 92	THOUGHT I'D DIED AND GONE TO HEAVEN	8
18 JUL 92	ALL I WANT IS YOU	22
26 SEP 92	DO I HAVE TO SAY THE WORDS	30
30 OCT 93	PLEASE FORGIVE ME	2
15 JAN 94	ALL FOR LOVE	2
22 APR 95	HAVE YOU EVER REALLY LOVED A WOMAN	4
11 NOV 95	ROCK STEADY	50
1 JUN 96	THE ONLY THING THAT LOOKS GOOD ON ME IS YOU	6
24 AUG 96	LET'S MAKE A NIGHT TO REMEMBER	10

•BRYAN ADAMS•

SINGLES CONT...

23 NOV 96	STAR	13
8 FEB 97	I FINALLY FOUND SOMEONE	10
19 APR 97	18 TIL I DIE	22
20 DEC 97	BACK TO YOU	18
21 MAR 98	I'M READY	20
10 OCT 98	ON A DAY LIKE TODAY	13
12 DEC 98	WHEN YOU'RE GONE	3

ALBUMS

2 MAR 85	RECKLESS	7
24 AUG 85	YOU WANT IT, YOU GOT IT	78
15 MAR 86	CUTS LIKE A KNIFE	21
11 APR 87	INTO THE FIRE	10
5 OCT 91	WAKING UP THE NEIGHBOURS	1
20 NOV 93	SO FAR SO GOOD	1
6 AUG 94	LIVE! LIVE! LIVE!	17

•BRYAN FERRY•

SINGLES

29 SEP 73	A HARD RAIN'S GONNA FALL	10
25 MAY 74	THE IN CROWD	13
31 AUG 74	SMOKE GETS IN YOUR EYES	17
5 JUL 75	YOU GO TO MY HEAD	33
12 JUN 76	LET'S STICK TOGETHER (LET'S WORK TOGETHER)	4
7 AUG 76	EXTENDED PLAY EP	7
5 FEB 77	THIS IS TOMORROW	9
14 MAY 77	TOKYO JOE	15
13 MAY 78	WHAT GOES ON	67
5 AUG 78	SIGN OF THE TIMES	37
11 MAY 85	SLAVE TO LOVE	10
31 AUG 85	DON'T STOP THE DANCE	21
7 DEC 85	WINDSWEPT	46
29 MAR 86	IS YOUR LOVE STRONG ENOUGH?	22
10 OCT 87	THE RIGHT STUFF	37
13 FEB 88	KISS AND TELL	41
29 OCT 88	LET'S STICK TOGETHER (RE-MIX)	12
11 FEB 89	THE PRICE OF LOVE (RE-MIX)	49
22 APR 89	HE'LL HAVE TO GO	63
6 MAR 93	I PUT A SPELL ON YOU	18
29 MAY 93	WILL YOU LOVE ME TOMORROW	23
4 SEP 93	GIRL OF MY BEST FRIEND	57
29 OCT 94	YOUR PAINTED SMILE	52
11 FEB 95	MAMOUNA	57

ALBUMS

3 NOV 73	THESE FOOLISH THINGS	5
20 JUL 74	ANOTHER TIME, ANOTHER PLACE	4
2 OCT 76	LET'S STICK TOGETHER	19
5 MAR 77	IN YUR MIND	5
30 SEP 78	THE BRIDE STRIPPED BARE	13
15 JUN 85	BOYS AND GIRLS	1
14 NOV 87	BETE NOIRE	9
3 APR 93	TAXI	2
17 SEP 94	MAMOUNA	11

• BUDDY HOLLY •

SINGLES

6 DEC 57	PEGGY SUE	6
14 MAR 58	LISTEN TO ME	16
20 JUN 58	RAVE ON	5
29 AUG 58	EARLY IN THE MORNING	17
16 JAN 59	HEARTBEAT	30
27 FEB 59	IT DOESN'T MATTER ANYMORE	1
31 JUL 59	MIDNIGHT SHIFT	26
11 SEP 59	PEGGY SUE GOT MARRIED	13
28 APR 60	HEARTBEAT (RE-ISSUE)	30
26 MAY 60	TRUE LOVE WAYS	25
20 OCT 60	LEARNIN' THE GAME	36
26 JAN 61	WHAT TO DO	34
6 JUL 61	BABY I DON'T CARE / VALLEY OF TEARS	12
15 MAR 62	LISTEN TO ME (RE-ISSUE)	48
13 SEP 62	REMINISCING	17
14 MAR 63	BROWN-EYED HANDSOME MAN	3
6 JUN 63	BO DIDDLEY	4
5 SEP 63	WISHING	10
19 DEC 63	WHAT TO DO	27
14 MAY 64	YOU'VE GOT LOVE	40
10 SEP 64	LOVE'S MADE A FOOL OF YOU	39
3 APR 68	PEGGY SUE / RAVE ON (RE-ISSUE)	32
10 DEC 88	TRUE LOVE WAYS (RE-ISSUE)	65

ALBUMS

2 MAY 59	BUDDY HOLLY STORY	2
15 OCT 60	BUDDY HOLLY STORY VOLUME 2	7
21 OCT 61	THAT'LL BE THE DAY	5
6 APR 63	REMINISCING	2
13 JUN 64	BUDDY HOLLY SHOWCASE	3
26 JUN 65	HOLLY IN THE HILLS	13
12 APR 69	GIANT	13

•CARL PERKINS•

SINGLES

18 MAY 56	BLUE SUEDE SHOES	10

ALBUMS

15 APR 78	OL' BLUE SUEDES IS BACK	38

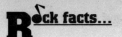

•CARS•

SINGLES

11 NOV 78	MY BEST FRIEND'S GIRL	3
17 FEB 79	JUST WHAT I NEEDED	17
28 JUL 79	LET'S GO	51
5 JUN 82	SINCE YOU'RE GONE	37
29 SEP 84	DRIVE	5
3 AUG 85	DRIVE (RE-ENTRY)	4

ALBUMS

2 DEC 78	CARS	29
7 JUL 79	CANDY-O	30
6 OCT 84	HEARTBEAT CITY	25
5 SEP 87	DOOR TO DOOR	72

•CAT STEVENS•

SINGLES

20 OCT 66	I LOVE MY DOG	28
12 JAN 67	MATTHEW AND SON	2
30 MAR 67	I'M GONNA GET ME A GUN	6
2 AUG 67	A BAD NIGHT	20
20 DEC 67	KITTY	47
27 JUN 70	LADY D'ARBANVILLE	8
28 AUG 71	MOON SHADOW	22
1 JAN 72	MORNING HAS BROKEN	9
9 DEC 72	CAN'T KEEP IT IN	13
24 AUG 74	ANOTHER SATURDAY NIGHT	19
2 JUL 77	(REMEMBER THE DAYS OF THE) OLD SCHOOL YARD	44

ALBUMS

25 MAR 67	MATTHEW AND SON	7
11 JUL 70	MONA BONE JAKON	63
28 NOV 70	TEA FOR THE TILLERMAN	20
2 OCT 71	TEASER AND THE FIRECAT	3
7 OCT 72	CATCH BULL AT FOUR	2
21 JUL 73	FOREIGNER	3
6 APR 74	BUDDAH AND THE CHOCOLATE BOX	3
14 MAY 77	IZITSO	18

•CHER•

SINGLES

19 AUG 65	ALL I REALLY WANT TO DO	9
31 MAR 66	BANG BANG (MY BABY SHOT ME DOWN)	3
4 AUG 66	I FEEL SOMETHING IN THE AIR	43
22 SEP 66	SUNNY	32
6 NOV 71	GYPSIES TRAMPS AND THIEVES	4
16 FEB 74	DARK LADY	36
16 MAR 74	DARK LADY (RE-ENTRY)	45
19 DEC 87	I FOUND SOMEONE	5
2 APR 88	WE ALL SLEEP ALONE	47
2 SEP 89	IF I COULD TURN BACK TIME	6
13 JAN 90	JUST LIKE JESSE JAMES	11
7 APR 90	HEART OF STONE	43
11 AUG 90	YOU WOULDN'T KNOW LOVE	55
13 APR 91	THE SHOOP SHOOP SONG (IT'S IN HIS KISS)	1
13 JUL 91	LOVE AND UNDERSTANDING	10
12 OCT 91	SAVE UP ALL YOUR TEARS	37
7 DEC 91	LOVE HURTS	43
18 APR 92	COULD'VE BEEN YOU	31
14 NOV 92	OH NO NOT MY BABY	33
16 JAN 93	MANY RIVERS TO CROSS	37
6 MAR 93	WHENEVER YOU'RE NEAR	72
15 JAN 94	I GOT YOU BABE	35
18 MAR 95	LOVE CAN BUILD A BRIDGE	1
28 OCT 95	WALKING IN MEMPHIS	11
20 JAN 96	ONE BY ONE	7
27 APR 96	NOT ENOUGH LOVE IN THE WORLD	31
17 AUG 96	THE SUN AIN'T GONNA SHINE ANYMORE	26
31 OCT 98	BELIEVE	1

• CHER •

ALBUMS

2 OCT 65	ALL I REALLY WANT TO DO	7
7 MAY 66	SONNY SIDE OF CHER	11
16 JAN 88	CHER	26
22 JUL 89	HEART OF STONE	7
29 JUN 91	LOVE HURTS	1
18 NOV 95	IT'S A MAN'S WORLD	28

•CHRIS REA•

SINGLES

7 OCT 78	FOOL (IF YOU THINK IT'S OVER)	30
21 APR 79	DIAMONDS	44
27 MAR 82	LOVING YOU	65
1 OCT 83	I CAN HEAR YOUR HEARTBEAT	60
17 MAR 84	I DON'T KNOW WHAT IT IS BUT I LOVE IT	65
30 MAR 85	STAINSBY GIRLS	26
29 JUN 85	JOSEPHINE	67
29 MAR 86	IT'S ALL GONE	69
31 MAY 86	ON THE BEACH	57
28 JUN 86	ON THE BEACH (RE-ENTRY)	75
12 JUL 86	ON THE BEACH (2ND RE-ENTRY)	66
6 JUN 87	LET'S DANCE	12
29 AUG 87	LOVING YOU AGAIN	47
5 DEC 87	JOYS OF CHRISTMAS	67
13 FEB 88	QUE SERA	73
13 AUG 88	ON THE BEACH SUMMER '88	12
22 OCT 88	I CAN HEAR YOUR HEARTBEAT	74
17 DEC 88	DRIVING HOME FOR CHRISTMAS EP	53
18 FEB 89	WORKING ON IT	53
14 OCT 89	THE ROAD TO HELL (PART 2)	10
10 FEB 90	TELL ME THERE'S A HEAVEN	24
5 MAY 90	TEXAS	69
16 FEB 91	AUBERGE	16
6 APR 91	HEAVEN	57
29 JUN 91	LOOKING FOR THE SUMMER	49
9 NOV 91	WINTER SONG	27
24 OCT 92	NOTHING TO FEAR	16

•CHRIS REA•

SINGLES CONT...

28 NOV 92	GOD'S GREAT BANANA SKIN	31
30 JAN 93	SOFT TOP HARD SHOULDER	53
23 OCT 93	JULIA	18
12 NOV 94	YOU CAN GO YOUR OWN WAY	28
24 DEC 94	TELL ME THERE'S A HEAVEN (RE-ISSUE)	70
16 NOV 96	'DISCO' LA PASSIONE	41
24 MAY 97	LETS DANCE	44

ALBUMS

28 APR 79	DELTICS	54
12 APR 80	TENNIS	60
3 APR 82	CHRIS REA	52
18 JUN 83	WATER SIGN	64
21 APR 84	WIRED TO THE MOON	35
25 MAY 85	SHAMROCK DIARIES	15
26 APR 86	ON THE BEACH	11
26 SEP 87	DANCING WITH STRANGERS	2
29 OCT 88	NEW LIGHT THROUGH OLD WINDOWS	5
11 NOV 89	THE ROAD TO HELL	1
9 MAR 91	AUBERGE	1
14 NOV 92	GOD'S GREAT BANANA SKIN	4
13 NOV 93	ESPRESSO LOGIC	8

• CHUCK BERRY •

SINGLES

21 JUN 57	SCHOOL DAY	24
12 JUL 57	SCHOOL DAY (RE-ENTRY)	24
25 APR 58	SWEET LITTLE SIXTEEN	16
11 JUL 63	GO GO GO	38
10 OCT 63	LET IT ROCK / MEMPHIS TENNESSEE	6
19 DEC 63	RUN RUDOLPH RUN	36
13 FEB 64	NADINE (IS IT YOU)	27
2 APR 64	NADINE (IS IT YOU) (RE-ENTRY)	43
7 MAY 64	NO PARTICULAR PLACE TO GO	3
20 AUG 64	YOU NEVER CAN TELL	23
14 JAN 65	PROMISED LAND	26
28 OCT 72	MY DING-A-LING	1
3 FEB 73	REELIN' AND ROCKIN'	18

ALBUMS

25 MAY 63	CHUCK BERRY	12
5 OCT 63	CHUCK BERRY ON STAGE	6
7 DEC 63	MORE CHUCK BERRY	9
30 MAY 64	HIS LATEST AND GREATEST	8
3 OCT 64	YOU NEVER CAN TELL	18
12 FEB 77	MOTORVATIN'	7

• CLIFF RICHARD •

SINGLES

12 SEP 58	MOVE IT	2
21 NOV 58	HIGH CLASS BABY	7
30 JAN 59	LIVIN' LOVIN' DOLL	20
8 MAY 59	MEAN STREAK	10
15 MAY 59	NEVER MIND	21
10 JUL 59	LIVING DOLL	1
9 OCT 59	TRAVELLIN' LIGHT	1
9 OCT 59	DYNAMITE	16
30 OCT 59	DYNAMITE (RE-ENTRY)	21
11 DEC 59	LIVING DOLL (RE-ENTRY)	26
1 JAN 60	LIVING DOLL (2ND RE-ENTRY)	28
15 JAN 60	EXPRESSO BONGO EP	14
22 JAN 60	VOICE IN THE WILDERNESS	2
24 MAR 60	FALL IN LOVE WITH YOU	2
5 MAY 60	VOICE IN THE WILDERNESS (RE-ENTRY)	36
30 JUN 60	PLEASE DON'T TEASE	1
22 SEP 60	NINE TIMES OUT OF TEN	3
1 DEC 60	I LOVE YOU	1
2 MAR 61	THEME FOR A DREAM	3
30 MAR 61	GEE WHIZ IT'S YOU	4
22 JUN 61	A GIRL LIKE YOU	3
19 OCT 61	WHEN THE GIRL IN YOUR ARMS IS THE GIRL IN YOUR HEART	3
11 JAN 62	THE YOUNG ONES	1
10 MAY 62	I'M LOOKING OUT THE WINDOW / DO YOU WANNA DANCE	2
6 SEP 62	IT'LL BE ME	2
6 DEC 62	THE NEXT TIME / BACHELOR BOY	1
21 FEB 63	SUMMER HOLIDAY	1
9 MAY 63	LUCKY LIPS	4

• CLIFF RICHARD •

SINGLES CONT...

22 AUG 63	IT'S ALL IN THE GAME	2
7 NOV 63	DON'T TALK TO HIM	2
6 FEB 64	I'M THE LONELY ONE	8
13 FEB 64	DON'T TALK TO HIM (RE-ENTRY)	50
30 APR 64	CONSTANTLY	4
2 JUL 64	ON THE BEACH	7
8 OCT 64	THE TWELFTH OF NEVER	8
10 DEC 64	I COULD EASILY FALL	9
11 MAR 65	THE MINUTE YOU'RE GONE	1
10 JUN 65	ON MY WORD	12
19 AUG 65	THE TIME IN BETWEEN	22
4 NOV 65	WIND ME UP (LET ME GO)	2
24 MAR 66	BLUE TURNS TO GREY	15
21 JUL 66	VISIONS	7
13 OCT 66	TIME DRAGS BY	10
15 DEC 66	IN THE COUNTRY	6
16 MAR 67	IT'S ALL OVER	9
8 JUN 67	I'LL COME RUNNING	26
16 AUG 67	THE DAY I MET MARIE	10
15 NOV 67	ALL MY LOVE	6
20 MAR 68	CONGRATULATIONS	1
26 JUN 68	I'LL LOVE YOU FOREVER TODAY	27
25 SEP 68	MARIANNE	22
27 NOV 68	DON'T FORGET TO CATCH ME	21
26 FEB 69	GOOD TIMES (BETTER TIMES)	12
28 MAY 69	BIG SHIP	8
13 SEP 69	THROW DOWN A LINE	7
6 DEC 69	WITH THE EYES OF A CHILD	20
21 FEB 70	JOY OF LIVING	25

•CLIFF RICHARD•

SINGLES CONT...

6 JUN 70	GOODBYE SAM, HELLO SAMANTHA	6
5 SEP 70l	AIN'T GOT TIME ANYMORE	21
23 JAN 71	SUNNY HONEY GIRL	19
10 APR 71	SILVERY RAIN	27
17 JUL 71	FLYING MACHINE	37
13 NOV 71	SING A SONG OF FREEDOM	13
11 MAR 72	JESUS	35
26 AUG 72	LIVING IN HARMONY	12
17 MAR 73	POWER TO ALL OUR FRIENDS	4
12 MAY 73	HELP IT ALONG / TOMORROW RISING	29
1 DEC 73	TAKE ME HIGH	27
18 MAY 74	(YOU KEEP ME) HANGIN' ON	13
7 FEB 76	MISS YOU NIGHTS	15
8 MAY 76	DEVIL WOMAN	9
21 AUG 76	I CAN'T ASK FOR ANYMORE THAN YOU	17
4 DEC 76	HEY MR. DREAM MAKER	31
5 MAR 77	MY KINDA LIFE	15
16 JUL 77	WHEN TWO WORLDS DRIFT APART	46
31 MAR 79	GREEN LIGHT	57
21 JUL 79	WE DON'T TALK ANYMORE	1
3 NOV 79	HOT SHOT	46
2 FEB 80	CARRIE	4
16 AUG 80	DREAMIN'	8
25 OCT 80	SUDDENLY	15
24 JAN 81	A LITTLE IN LOVE	15
29 AUG 81	WIRED FOR SOUND	4
21 NOV 81	DADDY'S HOME	2
17 JUL 82	THE ONLY WAY OUT	10
25 SEP 82	WHERE DO WE GO FROM HERE	60
4 DEC 82	LITTLE TOWN	11

• CLIFF RICHARD •

SINGLES CONT...

19 FEB 83	SHE MEANS NOTHING TO ME	9
16 APR 83	TRUE LOVE WAYS	8
4 JUN 83	DRIFTING	64
3 SEP 83	NEVER SAY DIE (GIVE A LITTLE BIT MORE)	15
26 NOV 83	PLEASE DON'T FALL IN LOVE	7
31 MAR 84	BABY YOU'RE DYNAMITE / OCEAN DEEP	27
19 MAY 84	OCEAN DEEP / BABY YOU'RE DYNAMITE (RE-ENTRY)	72
3 NOV 84	SHOOTING FROM THE HEART	51
9 FEB 85	HEART USER	46
14 SEP 85	SHE'S SO BEAUTIFUL	17
7 DEC 85	IT'S IN EVERY ONE OF US	45
22 MAR 86	LIVING DOLL	1
4 OCT 86	ALL I ASK OF YOU	3
29 NOV 86	SLOW RIVERS	44
20 JUN 87	MY PRETTY ONE	6
29 AUG 87	SOME PEOPLE	3
31 OCT 87	REMEMBER ME	35
13 FEB 88	TWO HEARTS	34
3 DEC 88	MISTLETOE AND WINE	1
10 JUN 89	THE BEST OF ME	2
26 AUG 89	I JUST DON'T HAVE THE HEART	3
14 OCT 89	LEAN ON YOU	17
9 DEC 89	WHENEVER GOD SHINES HIS LIGHT	20
24 FEB 90	STRONGER THAN THAT	14
25 AUG 90	SILHOUETTES	10
13 OCT 90	FROM A DISTANCE	11
8 DEC 90	SAVIOUR'S DAY	1
14 SEP 91	MORE TO LIFE	23
7 DEC 91	WE SHOULD BE TOGETHER	10

• CLIFF RICHARD •

SINGLES CONT...

11 JAN 92	THIS NEW YEAR	30
5 DEC 92	I STILL BELIEVE IN YOU	7
27 MAR 93	PEACE IN OUR TIME	8
12 JUN 93	HUMAN WORK OF ART	24
2 OCT 93	NEVER LET GO	32
18 DEC 93	HEALING LOVE	19
10 DEC 94	ALL I HAVE TO DO IS DREAM / MISS YOU NIGHTS (RE-ISSUE)	14
25 FEB 95	ALL I HAVE TO DO IS DREAM / MISS YOU NIGHTS (RE-ENTRY OF RE-ISSUE)	58
2 OCT 95	MISUNDERSTOOD MAN	19
9 DEC 95	HAD TO BE	22
30 MAR 96	THE WEDDING	40
25 JAN 97	BE WITH ME ALWAYS	52
24 OCT 98	CAN'T KEEP THIS FEELING IN	10

ALBUMS

18 APR 59	CLIFF	4
14 NOV 59	CLIFF SINGS	2
15 OCT 60	ME AND MY SHADOWS	2
22 APR 61	LISTEN TO CLIFF	2
21 OCT 61	21 TODAY	1
23 DEC 61	THE YOUNG ONES (FILM SOUNDTRACK)	1
29 SEP 62	32 MINUTES AND 17 SECONDS	3
26 JAN 63	SUMMER HOLIDAY (FILM SOUNDTRACK)	1
28 SEP 63	WHEN IN SPAIN	8
11 JUL 64	WONDERFUL LIFE (FILM SOUNDTRACK)	2
9 JAN 65	ALADDIN (PANTOMIME)	13
17 APR 65	CLIFF RICHARD	9
8 JAN 66	LOVE IS FOREVER	19
21 MAY 66	KINDA LATIN	9

•CLIFF RICHARD•

ALBUMS CONT...

17 DEC 66	FINDERS KEEPERS (FILM SOUNDTRACK)	6
7 JAN 67	CINDERELLA (PANTOMIME)	30
15 APR 67	DON'T STOP ME NOW...	23
11 NOV 67	GOOD NEWS	37
1 JUN 68	CLIFF IN JAPAN	29
16 NOV 68	ESTABLISHED 1958	30
27 SEP 69	SINCERELY	24
12 DEC 70	TRACKS 'N' GROOVES	37
19 JAN 74	TAKE ME HIGH (FILM SOUNDTRACK)	41
29 MAY 76	I'M NEARLY FAMOUS	5
26 MAR 77	EVERY FACE TELLS A STORY	8
4 MAR 78	SMALL CORNERS	33
21 OCT 78	GREEN LIGHT	25
17 FEB 79	THANK YOU VERY MUCH - REUNION	
	CONCERT AT THE LONDON PALLADIUM	5
15 SEP 79	ROCK 'N' ROLL JUVENILE	3
13 SEP 80	I'M NO HERO	4
4 JUL 81	LOVE SONGS	1
26 SEP 81	WIRED FOR SOUND	4
4 SEP 82	NOW YOU SEE ME, NOW YOU DON'T	4
21 MAY 83	DRESSED FOR THE OCCASION	7
15 OCT 83	SILVER	7
1 DEC 84	THE ROCK CONNECTION	43
26 SEP 87	ALWAYS GUARANTEED	5
19 NOV 88	PRIVATE COLLECTION	1
11 NOV 89	STRONGER	7
17 NOV 90	FROM A DISTANCE...THE EVENT	3
30 NOV 91	TOGETHER WITH CLIFF	10
1 MAY 93	THE ALBUM	1
11 NOV 95	SONGS FROM HEATHCLIFF	15

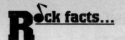

•CREAM•

SINGLES

20 OCT 66	WRAPPING PAPER	34
15 DEC 66	I FEEL FREE	11
8 JUN 67	STRANGE BREW	17
5 JUN 68	ANYONE FOR TENNIS (THE SAVAGE SEVEN THEME)	40
9 OCT 68	SUNSHINE OF YOUR LOVE	25
15 JAN 69	WHITE ROOM	28
9 APR 69	BADGE	18
28 OCT 72	BADGE (RE-ISSUE)	42

ALBUMS

24 DEC 66	FRESH CREAM	6
18 NOV 67	DISRAELI GEARS	5
17 AUG 68	WHEELS OF FIRE (DOUBLE)	3
17 AUG 68	WHEELS OF FIRE (SINGLE)	7
15 MAR 69	GOODBYE	1
4 JUL 70	LIVE CREAM	4
24 JUN 72	LIVE CREAM VOLUME 2	15
26 SEP 87	THE CREAM OF ERIC CLAPTON	3

• CREEDENCE CLEARWATER REVIVAL •

SINGLES

28 MAY 69	PROUD MARY	8
16 AUG 69	BAD MOON RISING	1
15 NOV 69	GREEN RIVER	19
14 FEB 70	DOWN ON THE CORNER	31
4 APR 70	TRAVELLIN' BAND	8
20 JUN 70	UP AROUND THE BEND	3
4 JUL 70	TRAVELLIN' BAND (RE-ENTRY)	46
5 SEP 70	LONG AS I CAN SEE THE LIGHT	20
20 MAR 71	HAVE YOU EVER SEEN THE RAIN	36
24 JUL 71	SWEET HITCH-HIKER	36
2 MAY 92	BAD MOON RISING (RE-ISSUE)	71

ALBUMS

24 JAN 70	GREEN RIVER	20
28 MAR 70	WILLY AND THE POOR BOYS	10
2 MAY 70	BAYOU COUNTRY	62
12 SEP 70	COSMO'S FACTORY	1
23 JAN 71	PENDULUM	23

• CROSBY STILLS NASH AND YOUNG •

SINGLES

| 16 AUG 69 | MARRAKESH EXPRESS | 17 |
| 21 JAN 89 | AMERICAN DREAM | 55 |

ALBUMS

23 AUG 69	CROSBY, STILLS AND NASH	25
30 MAY 70	DÈJA VU	5
22 MAY 71	FOUR-WAY STREET	5
21 MAY 74	SO FAR	25
9 JUL 77	CSN	23

• CROWDED HOUSE •

SINGLES

6 JUN 87	DON'T DREAM IT'S OVER	27
22 JUN 91	CHOCOLATE CAKE	69
2 NOV 91	FALL AT YOUR FEET	17
29 FEB 92	WEATHER WITH YOU	7
20 JUN 92	FOUR SEASONS IN ONE DAY	26
26 SEP 92	IT'S ONLY NATURAL	24
2 OCT 93	DISTANT SUN	19
20 NOV 93	NAILS IN MY FEET	22
19 FEB 94	LOCKED OUT	12
11 JUN 94	FINGERS OF LOVE	25
24 SEP 94	PINEAPPLE HEAD	27
22 JUN 96	INSTINCT	12
17 AUG 96	NOT THE GIRL YOU THINK YOU ARE	20
9 NOV 96	DON'T DREAM IT'S OVER (RE-ISSUE)	25

ALBUMS

13 JUL 91	WOODFACE	6
23 OCT 93	TOGETHER ALONE	4

•DAVID BOWIE•

SINGLES

6 SEP 69	SPACE ODDITY	48
20 SEP 69	SPACE ODDITY (RE-ENTRY)	5
24 JUN 72	STARMAN	10
16 SEP 72	JOHN I'M ONLY DANCING	12
9 DEC 72	THE JEAN GENIE	2
14 APR 73	DRIVE-IN SATURDAY	3
30 JUN 73	LIFE ON MARS	3
15 SEP 73	THE LAUGHING GNOME	6
20 OCT 73	SORROW	3
23 FEB 74	REBEL REBEL	5
20 APR 74	ROCK 'N' ROLL SUICIDE	22
22 JUN 74	DIAMOND DOGS	21
28 SEP 74	KNOCK ON WOOD	10
1 MAR 75	YOUNG AMERICANS	18
2 AUG 75	FAME	17
11 OCT 75	SPACE ODDITY (RE-ISSUE)	1
29 NOV 75	GOLDEN YEARS	8
22 MAY 76	TVC15	33
19 FEB 77	SOUND AND VISION	3
15 OCT 77	HEROES	24
21 JAN 78	BEAUTY AND THE BEAST	39
2 DEC 78	BREAKING GLASS (EP)	54
5 MAY 79	BOYS KEEP SWINGING	7
21 JUL 79	D.J.	29
15 DEC 79	JOHN I'M ONLY DANCING (AGAIN) (1975) / JOHN I'M ONLY DANCING (1972)	12
1 MAR 80	ALABAMA SONG	23
16 AUG 80	ASHES TO ASHES	1
1 NOV 80	FASHION	5
10 JAN 81	SCARY MONSTERS (AND SUPER CREEPS)	20
28 MAR 81	UP THE HILL BACKWARDS	32
14 NOV 81	UNDER PRESSURE	1

•DAVID BOWIE•

SINGLES CONT...

28 NOV 81	WILD IS THE WIND	24
6 MAR 82	BAAL'S HYMN (EP)	29
10 APR 82	CAT PEOPLE (PUTING OUT FIRE)	26
27 NOV 82	PEACE ON EARTH - LITTLE DRUMMER BOY	3
26 MAR 83	LET'S DANCE	1
11 JUN 83	CHINA GIRL	2
24 SEP 83	MODERN LOVE	2
5 NOV 83	WHITE LIGHT, WHITE HEAT	46
22 SEP 84	BLUE JEAN	6
8 DEC 84	TONIGHT	53
9 FEB 85	THIS IS NOT AMERICA (THE THEME FROM 'THE FALCON AND THE SNOWMAN')	14
8 JUN 85	LOVING THE ALIEN	19
27 JUL 85	LOVING THE ALIEN (RE-ENTRY)	67
7 SEP 85	DANCING IN THE STREET	1
15 MAR 86	ABSOLUTE BEGINNERS	2
21 JUN 86	UNDERGROUND	21
8 NOV 86	WHEN THE WIND BLOWS	44
4 APR 87	DAY-IN DAY-OUT	17
27 JUN 87	TIME WILL CRAWL	33
29 AUG 87	NEVER LET ME DOWN	34
7 APR 90	FAME (RE-MIX)	28
22 AUG 92	REAL COOL WORLD	53
27 MAR 93	JUMP THEY SAY	9
12 JUN 93	BLACK TIE WHITE NOISE	36
23 OCT 93	MIRACLE GOODNIGHT	40
4 DEC 93	BUDDHA OF SUBURBIA	35
23 SEP 95	THE HEART'S FILTHY LESSON	35
2 DEC 95	STRANGERS WHEN WE MEET / THE MAN WHO SOLD THE WORLD (LIVE)	39
2 MAR 96	HALLO SPACEBOY	12
8 FEB 97	LITTLE WONDER	14

• DAVID BOWIE •

SINGLES CONT...

26 APR 97	DEAD MAN WALKING	32
30 AUG 97	SEVEN YEARS IN TIBET	61
21 FEB 98	I CAN'T READ	73

ALBUMS

1 JUL 72	THE RISE AND FALL OF ZIGGY STARDUST AND THE SPIDERS FROM MARS	5
23 SEP 72	HUNKY DORY	3
25 NOV 72	SPACE ODDITY	17
25 NOV 72	THE MAN WHO SOLD THE WORLD	26
5 MAY 73	ALADDIN SANE	1
3 NOV 73	PIN-UPS	1
8 JUN 74	DIAMOND DOGS	1
16 NOV 74	DAVID LIVE	2
5 APR 75	YOUNG AMERICANS	2
7 FEB 76	STATION TO STATION	5
12 JUN 76	CHANGESONEBOWIE	2
29 JAN 77	LOW	2
29 OCT 77	HEROES	3
14 OCT 78	STAGE	5
9 JUN 79	LODGER	4
27 SEP 80	SCARY MONSTERS AND SUPER CREEPS	1
28 NOV 81	CHANGESTWOBOWIE	24
14 JAN 83	RARE	34
23 APR 83	LETS DANCE	1
20 AUG 83	GOLDEN YEARS	33
5 NOV 83	ZIGGY STARDUST - THE MOTION PICTURE	17
19 MAY 84	LOVE YOU TILL TUESDAY	53
6 OCT 84	TONIGHT	1
2 MAY 87	NEVER LET ME DOWN	6
24 MAR 90	CHANGESBOWIE	1
17 APR 93	BLACK TIE WHITE NOISE	1
7 MAY 94	SANTA MONICA '72	74
7 OCT 95	OUTSIDE	8

• DEEP PURPLE •

SINGLES

15 AUG 70	BLACK NIGHT	2
27 FEB 71	STRANGE KIND OF WOMAN	8
13 NOV 71	FIREBALL	15
1 APR 72	NEVER BEFORE	35
16 APR 77	SMOKE ON THE WATER	21
15 OCT 77	NEW LIVE AND RARE (EP)	31
7 OCT 78	NEW LIVE AND RARE II (EP)	45
2 AUG 80	BLACK NIGHT (RE-ISSUE)	43
1 NOV 80	NEW LIVE AND RARE VOLUME 3 (EP)	48
26 JAN 85	PERFECT STRANGERS	48
15 JUN 85	KNOCKING AT YOUR BACK DOOR / PERFECT STRANGERS	68
18 JUN 88	HUSH	62
20 OCT 90	KING OF DREAMS	70
2 MAR 91	LOVE CONQUERS ALL	57
24 JUN 95	BLACK NIGHT (RE-MIX)	66

•DEEP PURPLE•

ALBUMS

24 JAN 70	CONCERTO FOR GROUP AND ORCHESTRA	26
20 JUN 70	DEEP PURPLE IN ROCK	4
18 SEP 71	FIREBALL	1
15 APR 72	MACHINE HEAD	1
6 JAN 73	MADE IN JAPAN	16
17 FEB 73	WHO DO WE THINK WE ARE	4
2 MAR 74	BURN	3
23 NOV 74	STORM BRINGER	6
5 JUL 75	24 CARAT PURPLE	14
22 NOV 75	COME TASTE THE BAND	19
27 NOV 76	DEEP PURPLE LIVE	12
19 JUL 80	DEEPEST PURPLE	1
13 DEC 80	IN CONCERT	30
4 SEP 82	DEEP PURPLE LIVE IN LONDON	23
10 NOV 84	PERFECT STRANGERS	5
29 JUN 85	THE ANTHOLOGY	50
24 JAN 87	THE HOUSE OF BLUE LIGHT	10
16 JUL 88	NOBODY'S PERFECT	38
2 NOV 90	SLAVES AND MASTERS	45
7 AUG 93	THE BATTLE RAGES ON...	21

• DEF LEPPARD •

SINGLES

17 NOV 79	WASTED	61
23 FEB 80	HELLO AMERICA	45
5 FEB 83	PHOTOGRAPH	66
27 AUG 83	ROCK OF AGES	41
1 AUG 87	ANIMAL	6
19 SEP 87	POUR SOME SUGAR ON ME	18
28 NOV 87	HYSTERIA	26
9 JAN 88	HYSTERIA (RE-ENTRY)	74
9 APR 88	ARMAGEDDON IT	20
16 JUL 88	LOVE BITES	11
11 FEB 89	ROCKET	15
28 MAR 92	LET'S GET ROCKED	2
27 JUN 92	MAKE LOVE LIKE A MAN	12
12 SEP 92	HAVE YOU EVER NEEDED SOMEONE SO BAD	16
30 JAN 93	HEAVEN IS	13
1 MAY 93	TONIGHT	34
18 SEP 93	TWO STEPS BEHIND	32
15 JAN 94	ACTION	14
14 OCT 95	WHEN LOVE AND HATE COLLIDE	2
4 MAY 96	SLANG	17
13 JUL 96	WORK IT OUT	22
28 SEP 96	ALL I WANT IS EVERYTHING	38
30 NOV 96	BREATHE A SIGH	43

ALBUMS

22 MAR 80	ON THROUGH THE NIGHT	15
25 JUL 81	HIGH 'N' DRY	26
12 MAR 83	PYROMANIA	18
29 AUG 87	HYSTERIA	1
11 APR 92	ADRENALIZE	1
16 OCT 93	RETRO ACTIVE	6

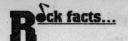

•DION•

SINGLES

26 JUN 59	A TEENAGER IN LOVE	28
19 JAN 61	LONELY TEENAGER	47
2 NOV 61	RUNAROUND SUE	11
15 FEB 62	THE WANDERER	10
22 MAY 76	THE WANDERER (RE-ISSUE)	16
19 AUG 89	KING OF NEW YORK STREET	74

•DIRE STRAITS•

SINGLES

10 MAR 79	SULTANS OF SWING	8
28 JUL 79	LADY WRITER	51
17 JAN 81	ROMEO AND JULIET	8
4 APR 81	SKATEAWAY	37
10 OCT 81	TUNNEL OF LOVE	54
4 SEP 82	PRIVATE INVESTIGATIONS	2
22 JAN 83	TWISTING BY THE POOL	14
18 FEB 84	LOVE OVER GOLD (LIVE) / SOLID ROCK (LIVE)	50
20 APR 85	SO FAR AWAY	20
6 JUL 85	MONEY FOR NOTHING	4
26 OCT 85	BROTHERS IN ARMS	16
11 JAN 86	WALK OF LIFE	2
3 MAY 86	YOUR LATEST TRICK	26
5 NOV 88	SULTANS OF SWING (RE-ISSUE)	62
31 AUG 91	CALLING ELVIS	21
2 NOV 91	HEAVY FUEL	55
29 FEB 92	ON EVERY STREET	42
27 JUN 92	THE BUG	67
22 MAY 93	ENCORES EP	31

ALBUMS

22 JUL 78	DIRE STRAITS	5
23 JUN 79	COMMUNIQUE	5
25 OCT 80	MAKIN' MOVIES	4
2 OCT 82	LOVE OVER GOLD	1
24 MAR 84	ALCHEMY - DIRE SRAITS LIVE	3
25 MAY 85	BROTHERS IN ARMS	1
29 OCT 88	MONEY FOR NOTHING	1
21 SEP 91	ON EVERY STREET	1
22 MAY 93	ON THE NIGHT	4
8 JUL 95	LIVE AT THE BBC	71

•DONOVAN•

SINGLES

25 MAR 65	CATCH THE WIND	4
3 JUN 65	COLOURS	4
11 NOV 65	TURQUOISE	30
8 DEC 66	SUNSHINE SUPERMAN	2
9 FEB 67	MELLOW YELLOW	8
25 OCT 67	THERE IS A MOUNTAIN	8
21 FEB 68	JENNIFER JUNIPER	5
29 MAY 68	HURDY GURDY MAN	4
4 DEC 68	ATLANTIS	23
9 JUL 69	GOO GOO BARABAJAGAL (LOVE IS HOT)	12
1 DEC 90	JENNIFER JUNIPER	68

ALBUMS

5 JUN 65	WHAT'S BIN DID AND WHAT'S BIN HID	3
6 NOV 65	FAIRY TALE	20
8 JUL 67	SUNSHINE SUPERMAN	25
14 OCT 67	UNIVERSAL SOLDIER	5
11 MAY 68	A GIFT FROM A FLOWER TO A GARDEN	13
12 SEP 70	OPEN ROAD	30
24 MAR 73	COSMIC WHEELS	15

• E.L.O. •

SINGLES

29 JUL 72	10538 OVERTURE	9
27 JAN 73	ROLL OVER BEETHOVEN	6
6 OCT 73	SHOWDOWN	12
9 MAR 74	MA-MA-MA-BELLE	22
10 JAN 76	EVIL WOMAN	10
3 JUL 76	STRANGE MAGIC	38
13 NOV 76	LIVIN' THING	4
19 FEB 77	ROCKARIA!	9
21 MAY 77	TELEPHONE LINE	8
29 OCT 77	TURN TO STONE	18
28 JAN 78	MR. BLUE SKY	6
10 JUN 78	WILD WEST HERO	6
7 OCT 78	SWEET TALKIN' WOMAN	6
9 DEC 78	ELO EP	34
19 MAY 79	SHINE A LITTLE LOVE	6
21 JUL 79	THE DIARY OF HORACE WIMP	8
1 SEP 79	DON'T BRING ME DOWN	3
17 NOV 79	CONFUSION / LAST TRAIN TO LONDON	8
24 MAY 80	I'M ALIVE	20
21 JUN 80	XANADU	1
2 AUG 80	ALL OVER THE WORLD	11
22 NOV 80	DON'T WALK AWAY	21
1 AUG 81	HOLD ON TIGHT	4
24 OCT 81	TWILIGHT	30
9 JAN 82	TICKET TO THE MOON / HERE IS THE NEWS	24
18 JUN 83	ROCK 'N' ROLL IS KING	13
3 SEP 83	SECRET MESSAGES	48
1 MAR 86	CALLING AMERICA	28
11 MAY 91	HONEST MEN	60

•E.L.O.•

ALBUMS

12 AUG 72	ELECTRIC LIGHT ORCHESTRA	32
31 MAR 73	ELO 2	35
11 DEC 76	A NEW WORLD RECORD	6
12 NOV 77	OUT OF THE BLUE	4
6 JAN 79	THREE LIGHT YEARS	38
16 JUN 79	DISCOVERY	1
8 AUG 81	TIME	1
2 JUL 83	SECRET MESSAGES	4
15 MAR 86	BALANCE OF POWER	9

•EDDIE COCHRAN•

SINGLES

7 NOV 58	SUMMERTIME BLUES	18
13 MAR 59	C'MON EVERYBODY	6
16 OCT 59	SOMETHIN' ELSE	22
22 JAN 60	HALLELUJAH I LOVE HER SO	28
5 FEB 60	HALLELUJAH I LOVE HER SO (RE-ENTRY)	22
12 MAY 60	THREE STEPS TO HEAVEN	1
6 OCT 60	SWEETIE PIE	38
3 NOV 60	LONELY	41
15 JUN 61	WEEKEND	15
30 NOV 61	JEANNIE, JEANNIE, JEANNIE	31
25 APR 63	MY WAY	23
24 APR 68	SUMMERTIME BLUES (RE-ISSUE)	34
13 FEB 88	C'MON EVERYBODY (RE-ISSUE)	14

ALBUMS

30 JUL 60	SINGING TO MY BABY	19
1 OCT 60	EDDIE COCHRAN MEMORIAL ALBUM	9

•ELTON JOHN•

SINGLES

23 JAN 71	YOUR SONG	7
22 APR 72	ROCKET MAN (I THINK IT'S GOING TO BE A LONG LONG TIME)	2
9 SEP 72	HONKY CAT	31
4 NOV 72	CROCODILE ROCK	5
20 JAN 73	DANIEL	4
7 JUL 73	SATURDAY NIGHT'S ALRIGHT FOR FIGHTING	7
29 SEP 73	GOODBYE YELLOW BRICK ROAD	6
8 DEC 73	STEP INTO CHRISTMAS	24
2 MAR 74	CANDLE IN THE WIND	11
1 JUN 74	DON'T LET THE SUN GO DOWN ON ME	16
14 SEP 74	THE BITCH IS BACK	15
23 NOV 74	LUCY IN THE SKY WITH DIAMONDS	10
8 MAR 75	PHILADELPHIA FREEDOM	12
28 JUN 75	SOMEONE SAVED MY LIFE TONIGHT	22
4 OCT 75	ISLAND GIRL	14
20 MAR 76	PINBALL WIZARD	7
3 JUL 76	DON'T GO BREAKING MY HEART	1
25 SEP 76	BENNIE AND THE JETS	37
13 NOV 76	SORRY SEEMS TO BE THE HARDEST WORD	11
26 FEB 77	CRAZY WATER	27
11 JUN 77	BITE YOUR LIP (GET UP AND DANCE)	28
15 APR 78	EGO	34
21 OCT 78	PART TIME LOVE	15
16 DEC 78	SONG FOR GUY	4
12 MAY 79	ARE YOU READY FOR LOVE	42
24 MAY 80	LITTLE JEANNIE	33
23 AUG 80	SARTORIAL ELOQUENCE	44
21 MAR 81	I SAW HER STANDING THERE	40
23 MAY 81	NOBODY WINS	42
27 MAR 82	BLUE EYES	8

•ELTON JOHN•

SINGLES CONT...

12 JUN 82	EMPTY GARDEN	51
30 APR 83	I GUESS THAT'S WHY THEY CALL IT THE BLUES	5
30 JUL 83	I'M STILL STANDING	4
15 OCT 83	KISS THE BRIDE	20
10 DEC 83	COLD AS CHRISTMAS	33
26 MAY 84	SAD SONGS (SAY SO MUCH)	7
11 AUG 84	PASSENGERS	5
20 OCT 84	WHO WEARS THESE SHOES	50
2 MAR 85	BREAKING HEARTS (AIN'T WHAT IT USED TO BE)	59
15 JUN 85	ACT OF WAR	32
12 OCT 85	NIKITA	3
9 NOV 85	THAT'S WHAT FRIENDS ARE FOR	16
7 DEC 85	WRAP HER UP	12
1 MAR 86	CRY TO HEAVEN	47
4 OCT 86	HEARTACHE ALL OVER THE WORLD	45
29 NOV 86	SLOW RIVERS	44
20 JUN 87	FLAMES OF PARADISE	59
16 JAN 88	CANDLE IN THE WIND	5
4 JUN 88	I DON'T WANNA GO ON WITH YOU LIKE THAT	30
3 SEP 88	TOWN OF PLENTY	74
6 MAY 89	THROUGH THE STORM	41
26 AUG 89	HEALING HANDS	45
4 NOV 89	SACRIFICE	55
9 JUN 90	SACRIFICE / HEALING HANDS (RE-ISSUE)	1
18 AUG 90	CLUB AT THE END OF THE STREET / WHISPERS	47
20 OCT 90	YOU GOTTA LOVE SOMEONE	33
15 DEC 90	EASIER TO WALK AWAY	67
29 DEC 90	EASIER TO WALK AWAY (RE-ENTRY)	63

• ELTON JOHN •

SINGLES CONT...

7 DEC 91	DON'T LET THE SUN GO DOWN ON ME	1
6 JUN 92	THE ONE	10
1 AUG 92	RUNAWAY TRAIN	31
7 NOV 92	THE LAST SONG	21
22 MAY 93	SIMPLE LIFE	44
20 NOV 93	TRUE LOVE	2
26 FEB 94	DON'T GO BREAKING MY HEART	7
14 MAY 94	AIN'T NOTHING LIKE THE REAL THING	24
9 JUL 94	CAN YOU FEEL THE LOVE TONIGHT	14
8 OCT 94	CIRCLE OF LIFE	11
4 MAR 95	BELIEVE	15
20 MAY 95	MADE IN ENGLAND	18
3 FEB 96	PLEASE	33
14 DEC 96	LIVE LIKE HORSES	9
20 SEP 97	CANDLE IN THE WIND 1997 / SOMETHING IN THE WAY…	1
14 FEB 98	RECOVER YOUR SOUL	16
13 JUN 98	IF THE RIVER CAN BEND	32

ALBUMS

23 MAY 70	ELTON JOHN	11
16 JAN 71	TUMBLEWEED CONNECTION	6
1 MAY 71	THE ELTON JOHN LIVE ALBUM 17-11-70	20
20 MAY 72	MADMAN ACROSS THE WATER	41
3 JUN 72	HONKY CHATEAU	2
10 FEB 73	DON'T SHOOT ME I'M ONLY THE PIANO PLAYER	1
3 NOV 73	GOODBYE YELLOW BRICK ROAD	1
13 JUL 74	CARIBOU	1
7 JUN 75	CAPTAIN FANTASTIC AND THE BROWN DIRT COWBOY	2
8 NOV 75	ROCK OF THE WESTIES	5

•ELTON JOHN•

ALBUMS CONT...

15 MAY 76	HERE AND THERE	6
6 NOV 76	BLUE MOVIES	3
4 NOV 78	A SINGLE MAN	8
20 OCT 79	VICTIM OF LOVE	41
8 MAR 80	LADY SAMANTHA	56
31 MAY 80	21 AT 33	12
30 MAY 81	THE FOX	12
17 APR 82	JUMP UP	13
6 NOV 82	LOVE SONGS	39
11 JUN 83	TOO LOW FOR ZERO	7
30 JUN 84	BREAKING HEARTS	2
16 NOV 85	ICE ON FIRE	3
15 NOV 86	LEATHER JACKETS	24
12 SEP 87	LIVE IN AUSTRALIA	43
16 JUL 88	REG STRIKES BACK	18
23 SEP 89	SLEEPING WITH THE PAST	1
27 JUN 92	THE ONE	2
4 DEC 93	DUETS	5
1 APR 95	MADE IN ENGLAND	3
18 NOV 95	LOVE SONGS	4

• ELVIS COSTELLO •

SINGLES

5 NOV 77	WATCHING THE DETECTIVES	15
11 MAR 78	(I DON'T WANNA GO TO) CHELSEA	16
13 MAY 78	PUMP IT UP	24
28 OCT 78	RADIO RADIO	29
10 FEB 79	OLIVER'S ARMY	2
12 MAY 79	ACCIDENTS WILL HAPPEN	28
16 FEB 80	I CAN'T STAND UP FOR FALLING DOWN	4
12 APR 80	HI FIDELITY	30
7 JUN 80	NEW AMSTERDAM	36
20 DEC 80	CLUBLAND	60
3 OCT 81	A GOOD YEAR FOR THE ROSES	6
12 DEC 81	SWEET DREAMS	42
10 APR 82	I'M YOUR TOY	51
19 JUN 82	YOU LITTLE FOOL	52
31 JUL 82	MAN OUT OF TIME	58
25 SEP 82	FROM HEAD TO TOE	43
11 DEC 82	PARTY PARTY	48
11 JUN 83	PILLS AND SOAP	16
9 JUL 83	EVERYDAY I WRITE THE BOOK	28
17 SEP 83	LET THEM ALL TALK	59
28 APR 84	PEACE IN OUR TIME	48
16 JUN 84	I WANNA BE LOVED / TURNING THE TOWN RED	25
25 AUG 84	THE ONLY FLAME IN TOWN	71
4 MAY 85	GREEN SHIRT	71
18 MAY 85	GREEN SHIRT (RE-ENTRY)	68
1 FEB 86	DON'T LET ME BE MISUNDERSTOOD	33

•ELVIS COSTELLO•

SINGLES CONT...

30 AUG 86	TOKYO STORM WARNING	73
4 MAR 89	VERONICA	31
20 MAY 89	BABY PLAYS AROUND (EP)	65
4 MAY 91	THE OTHER SIDE OF SUMMER	43
5 MAR 94	SULKY GIRL	22
30 APR 94	13 STEPS LEAD DOWN	59
26 NOV 94	LONDON'S BRILLIANT PARADE	48
11 MAY 96	IT'S TIME	58

ALBUMS

6 AUG 77	MY AIM IS TRUE	14
1 APR 78	THIS YEARS MODEL	4
20 JAN 79	ARMED FORCES	2
23 FEB 80	GET HAPPY	2
31 JAN 81	TRUST	9
31 OCT 81	ALMOST BLUE	7
10 JUL 82	IMPERIAL BEDROOM	6
6 AUG 83	PUNCH THE CLOCK	3
7 JUL 84	GOODBYE CRUEL WORLD	10
1 MAR 86	KING OF AMERICA	11
27 SEP 86	BLOOD AND CHOCOLATE	16
18 FEB 89	SPIKE	5
28 OCT 89	GIRLS GIRLS GIRLS	67
25 MAY 91	MIGHTY LIKE A ROSE	5
30 JAN 93	THE JULIET LETTERS	18
19 MAR 94	BRUTAL YOUTH	2
27 MAY 95	KOJAK VARIETY	21

•ELVIS PRESLEY•

SINGLES

11 MAY 56	HEARTBREAK HOTEL	2
25 MAY 56	BLUE SUEDE SHOES	9
13 JUL 56	I WANT YOU I NEED YOU I LOVE YOU	25
3 AUG 56	I WANT YOU I NEED YOU I LOVE YOU (RE-ENTRY)	14
17 AUG 56	BLUE SUEDE SHOES (RE-ENTRY)	26
21 SEP 56	HOUND DOG	2
26 OCT 56	HEARTBREAK HOTEL (RE-ENTRY)	23
16 NOV 56	BLUE MOON	9
23 NOV 56	I DON'T CARE IF THE SUN DON'T SHINE	29
7 DEC 56	LOVE ME TENDER	11
21 DEC 56	I DON'T CARE IF THE SUN DON'T SHINE (RE-ENTRY)	23
15 FEB 57	MYSTERY TRAIN	25
8 MAR 57	RIP IT UP	27
10 MAY 57	TOO MUCH	6
14 JUN 57	ALL SHOOK UP	24
28 JUN 57	ALL SHOOK UP (RE-ENTRY)	1
12 JUL 57	TEDDY BEAR	3
12 JUL 57	TOO MUCH (RE-ENTRY)	26
30 AUG 57	PARALYSED	8
4 OCT 57	PARTY	2
18 OCT 57	GOT A LOT O' LIVIN' TO DO	17
1 NOV 57	LOVING YOU	24
1 NOV 57	TRYING TO GET TO YOU	16
8 NOV 57	LAWDY MISS CLAWDY	15
15 NOV 57	SANTA BRING MY BABY BACK TO ME	7
17 JAN 58	I'M LEFT YOU'RE RIGHT SHE'S GONE	21
24 JAN 58	JAILHOUSE ROCK	1
31 JAN 58	JAILHOUSE ROCK EP	18
7 FEB 58	I'M LEFT YOU'RE RIGHT SHE'S GONE (RE-ENTRY)	29
28 FEB 58	DON'T	2

• ELVIS PRESLEY •

SINGLES CONT...

2 MAY 58	WEAR MY RING AROUND YOUR NECK	3
25 JUL 58	HARD HEADED WOMAN	2
3 OCT 58	KING CREOLE	2
23 JAN 59	ONE NIGHT/I GOT STUNG	1
24 APR 59	A FOOL SUCH AS I / I NEED YOUR LOVE TONIGHT	1
24 JUL 59	A BIG HUNK O' LOVE	4
12 FEB 60	STRICTLY ELVIS EP	26
7 APR 60	STUCK ON YOU	3
28 JUL 60	A MESS OF BLUES	2
3 NOV 60	IT'S NOW OR NEVER	1
19 JAN 61	ARE YOU LONESOME TONIGHT	1
9 MAR 61	WOODEN HEART	1
25 MAY 61	SURRENDER	1
7 SEP 61	WILD IN THE COUNTRY / I FEEL SO BAD	4
2 NOV 61	HIS LATEST FLAME / LITTLE SISTER	1
1 FEB 62	ROCK A HULA BABY / CAN'T HELP FALLING IN LOVE	1
10 MAY 62	GOOD LUCK CHARM	1
21 JUN 62	FOLLOW THAT DREAM EP	34
30 AUG 62	SHE'S NOT YOU	1
29 NOV 62	RETURN TO SENDER	1
28 FEB 63	ONE BROKEN HEART FOR SALE	12
4 JUL 63	DEVIL IN DISGUISE	1
24 OCT 63	BOSSA NOVA BABY	13
19 DEC 63	KISS ME QUICK	14
12 MAR 64	VIVA LAS VEGAS	17
25 JUN 64	KISSIN' COUSINS	10
20 AUG 64	SUCH A NIGHT	13
29 OCT 64	AIN'T THAT LOVIN' YOU BABY	15
3 DEC 64	BLUE CHRISTMAS	11
11 MAR 65	DO THE CLAM	19
27 MAY 65	CRYING IN THE CHAPEL	1

• ELVIS PRESLEY •

SINGLES CONT...

11 NOV 65	TELL ME WHY	15
24 FEB 66	BLUE RIVER	22
7 APR 66	FRANKIE AND JOHNNY	21
7 JUL 66	LOVE LETTERS	6
13 OCT 66	ALL THAT I AM	18
1 DEC 66	IF EVERY DAY WAS LIKE CHRISTMAS	9
9 FEB 67	INDESCRIBABLY BLUE	21
11 MAY 67	YOU GOTTA STOP / LOVE MACHINE	38
16 AUG 67	LONG LEGGED GIRL	49
21 FEB 68	GUITAR MAN	19
15 MAY 68	U.S. MALE	15
17 JUL 68	YOUR TIME HASN'T COME YET BABY	22
16 OCT 68	YOU'LL NEVER WALK ALONE	44
26 FEB 69	IF I CAN DREAM	11
11 JUN 69	IN THE GHETTO	2
6 SEP 69	CLEAN UP YOUR OWN BACK YARD	21
18 OCT 69	IN THE GHETTO (RE-ENTRY)	50
29 NOV 69	SUSPICIOUS MINDS	2
28 FEB 70	DON'T CRY DADDY	8
16 MAY 70	KENTUCKY RAIN	21
11 JUL 70	THE WONDER OF YOU	1
8 AUG 70	KENTUCKY RAIN (RE-ENTRY)	46
14 NOV 70	I'VE LOST YOU	9
9 JAN 71	YOU DON'T HAVE TO SAY YOU LOVE ME	9
23 JAN 71	THE WONDER OF YOU (RE-ENTRY)	47
6 MAR 71	YOU DON'T HAVE TO SAY YOU LOVE ME (RE-ENTRY)	35
20 MAR 71	THERE GOES MY EVERYTHING	6
15 MAY 71	RAGS TO RICHES	9
17 JUL 71	HEARTBREAK HOTEL / HOUND DOG (RE-ISSUE)	10
2 OCT 71	I'M LEAVIN'	23
4 DEC 71	I JUST CAN'T HELP BELIEVING	6

• ELVIS PRESLEY •

SINGLES CONT...

11 DEC 71	JAILHOUSE ROCK (RE-ISSUE)	42
1 APR 72	UNTIL IT'S TIME FOR YOU TO GO	5
17 JUN 72	AMERICAN TRILOGY	8
30 SEP 72	BURNING LOVE	7
16 DEC 72	ALWAYS ON MY MIND	9
26 MAY 73	POLK SALAD ANNIE	23
11 AUG 73	FOOL	15
24 NOV 73	RAISED ON ROCK	36
16 MAR 74	I'VE GOT A THING ABOUT YOU BABY	33
13 JUL 74	IF YOU TALK IN YOUR SLEEP	40
16 NOV 74	MY BOY	5
18 JAN 75	PROMISED LAND	9
24 MAY 75	T.R.O.U.B.L.E.	31
29 NOV 75	GREEN GREEN GRASS OF HOME	29
1 MAY 76	HURT	37
4 SEP 76	GIRL OF MY BEST FRIEND	9
25 DEC 76	SUSPICION	9
5 MAR 77	MOODY BLUE	6
13 AUG 77	WAY DOWN	1
3 SEP 77	ALL SHOOK UP (RE-ISSUE)	41
3 SEP 77	ARE YOU LONESOME TONIGHT (RE-ISSUE)	46
3 SEP 77	CRYING IN THE CHAPEL (RE-ISSUE)	43
3 SEP 77	IT'S NOW OR NEVER (RE-ISSUE)	39
3 SEP 77	JAILHOUSE ROCK (2ND RE-ISSUE)	44
3 SEP 77	RETURN TO SENDER (RE-ISSUE)	42
3 SEP 77	THE WONDER OF YOU (RE-ISSUE)	48
3 SEP 77	WOODEN HEART (RE-ISSUE)	49
10 DEC 77	MY WAY	9
24 JUN 78	DON'T BE CRUEL	24
15 DEC 79	IT WON'T SEEM LIKE CHRISTMAS (WITHOUT YOU)	13
30 AUG 80	IT'S ONLY LOVE / BEYOND THE REEF	3

•ELVIS PRESLEY•

SINGLES CONT...

6 DEC 80	SANTA CLAUS IS BACK IN TOWN	41
14 FEB 81	GUITAR MAN	43
18 APR 81	LOVING ARMS	47
13 MAR 82	ARE YOU LONESOME TONIGHT	25
26 JUN 82	THE SOUND OF YOUR CRY	59
5 FEB 83	JAILHOUSE ROCK (RE-ENTRY)	27
7 MAY 83	BABY I DON'T CARE	61
3 DEC 83	I CAN HELP	30
10 NOV 84	THE LAST FAREWELL	48
19 JAN 85	THE ELVIS MEDLEY	51
10 AUG 85	ALWAYS ON MY MIND	59
11 APR 87	AIN'T THAT LOVIN' YOU BABY / BOSSA NOVA BABY	47
22 AUG 87	L0VE ME TENDER / IF I CAN DREAM (RE-ISSUE)	56
16 JAN 88	STUCK ON YOU (RE-ISSUE)	58
17 AUG 91	ARE YOU LONESOME TONIGHT (LIVE) (RE-ISSUE)	68
29 AUG 92	DON'T BE CRUEL (RE-ISSUE)	42
11 NOV 95	THE TWELFTH OF NEVER	21
18 MAY 96	HEARTBREAK HOTEL/ I WAS THE ONE (2ND RE-ISSUE)	45
24 MAY 97	ALWAYS ON MY MIND (RE-ISSUE)	13

ALBUMS

8 NOV 58	KING CREOLE (FILM SOUNDTRACK)	4
4 APR 59	ELVIS (ROCK 'N' ROLL NO 1)	4
8 AUG 59	A DATE WITH ELVIS	4
18 JUN 60	ELVIS IS BACK	1
10 DEC 60	G.I. BLUES (FILM SOUNDTRACK)	1
20 MAY 61	HIS HAND IN MINE	3
4 NOV 61	SOMETHING FOR EVERYBODY	2
9 DEC 61	BLUE HAWAII (FILM SOUNDTRACK)	1
7 JUL 62	POT LUCK	1
26 JAN 63	GIRLS! GIRLS! GIRLS! (FILM SOUNDTRACK)	2

•ELVIS PRESLEY•

ALBUMS CONT...

11 MAY 63	IT HAPPENED AT THE WORLD'S FAIR (FILM SOUNDTRACK)	4
28 DEC 63	FUN IN ACAPULCO (FILM SOUNDTRACK)	9
4 JUL 64	KISSIN' COUSINS (FILM SOUNDTRACK)	5
9 JAN 65	ROUSTABOUT (FILM SOUNDTRACK)	12
1 MAY 65	GIRL HAPPY (FILM SOUNDTRACK)	8
25 SEP 65	FLAMING STAR AND SUMMER KISSES	11
4 DEC 65	ELVIS FOR EVERYBODY	8
15 JAN 66	HAREM HOLIDAY (FILM SOUNDTRACK)	11
30 APR 66	FRANKIE AND JOHNNY (FILM SOUNDTRACK)	11
6 AUG 66	PARADISE HAWAIIAN STYLE (FILM SOUNDTRACK)	7
26 NOV 66	CALIFORNIA HOLIDAY (FILM SOUNDTRACK)	17
8 APR 67	HOW GREAT THOU ART	11
2 SEP 67	DOUBLE TROUBLE (FILM SOUNDTRACK)	34
20 APR 68	CLAMBAKE (FILM SOUNDTRACK)	39
3 MAY 69	ELVIS - NBC TV SPECIAL	2
5 JUL 69	FLAMING STAR	2
23 AUG 69	FROM ELVIS IN MEMPHIS	1
28 FEB 70	PORTRAIT IN MUSIC (IMPORT)	36
14 MAR 70	FROM MEMPHIS TO VEGAS - FROM VEGAS TO MEMPHIS	3
1 AUG 70	ON STAGE	2
30 JAN 71	THAT'S THE WAY IT IS	12
10 APR 71	ELVIS COUNTRY	6
24 JUL 71	LOVE LETTERS FROM ELVIS	7
7 AUG 71	C'MON EVERYBODY	5
7 AUG 71	YOU'LL NEVER WALK ALONE	20
25 SEP 71	ALMOST IN LOVE	38
4 DEC 71	ELVIS' CHRISTMAS ALBUM	7
18 DEC 71	I GOT LUCKY	26
27 MAY 72	ELVIS NOW	12

• ELVIS PRESLEY •

ALBUMS CONT...

3 JUN 72	ELVIS FOR EVERYONE	48
15 JUL 72	ELVIS AT MADISON SQUARE GARDEN	3
12 AUG 72	HE TOUCHED ME	38
24 FEB 73	ALOHA FROM HAWAII VIA SATELLITE	11
15 SEP 73	ELVIS	16
25 MAY 74	GOOD TIMES	42
7 SEP 74	ELVIS PRESLEY LIVE ON STAGE IN MEMPHIS	44
22 FEB 75	PROMISED LAND	21
14 JUN 75	TODAY	48
19 JUN 76	FROM ELVIS PRESLEY BOULEVARD, MEMPHIS, TENNESSEE	29
19 FEB 77	ELVIS IN DEMAND	12
27 AUG 77	MOODY BLUE	3
3 SEP 77	WELCOME TO MY WORLD	7
10 SEP 77	PICTURES OF ELVIS	52
15 OCT 77	LOVING YOU	24
19 NOV 77	ELVIS IN CONCERT	13
22 APR 78	HE WALKS BESIDE ME	37
2 SEP 78	TV SPECIAL	50
21 JUN 80	ELVIS PRESLEY SINGS LIEBER AND STOLLER	32
14 MAR 81	GUITAR MAN	33
13 FEB 82	THE SOUND OF YOUR CRY	31
21 AUG 82	ROMANTIC ELVIS / ROCKIN' ELVIS	62
18 DEC 82	IT WON'T SEEM LIKE CHRISTMAS WITHOUT YOU	80
30 APR 83	JAILHOUSE ROCK / LOVE IN LAS VEGAS	40
20 AUG 83	I WAS THE ONE	83
7 APR 84	I CAN HELP	71
25 MAY 85	RECONSIDER BABY	92
12 OCT 85	BALLADS	23

•EMERSON LAKE AND PALMER•

SINGLES

| 4 JUN 77 | FANFARE FOR THE COMMON MAN | 2 |

ALBUMS

5 DEC 70	EMERSON, LAKE AND PALMER	4
19 JUN 71	TARKUS	1
4 DEC 71	PICTURES AT AN EXHIBITION	3
8 JUL 72	TRILOGY	2
22 DEC 73	BRAIN SALAD SURGERY	2
24 AUG 74	WELCOME BACK MY FRIENDS TO THE SHOW THAT NEVER ENDS - LADIES AND GENTLEMEN: EMERSON, LAKE AND PALMER	5

• ERIC CLAPTON •

SINGLES

20 DEC 69	COMIN' HOME	16
12 AUG 72	LAYLA	7
27 JUL 74	I SHOT THE SHERIFF	9
10 MAY 75	SWING LOW SWEET CHARIOT	19
16 AUG 75	KNOCKIN' ON HEAVEN'S DOOR	38
24 DEC 77	LAY DOWN SALLY	39
21 OCT 78	PROMISES	37
6 MAR 82	LAYLA (RE-ISSUE)	4
5 JUN 82	I SHOT THE SHERIFF (RE-ISSUE)	64
23 APR 83	THE SHAPE YOU'RE IN	75
16 MAR 85	FOREVER MAN	51
4 JAN 86	EDGE OF DARKNESS	65
17 JAN 87	BEHIND THE MASK	15
20 JUN 87	TEARING US APART	56
27 JAN 90	BAD LOVE	25
14 APR 90	NO ALIBIS	53
16 NOV 91	WONDERFUL TONIGHT (LIVE)	30
8 FEB 92	TEARS IN HEAVEN	50
7 MAR 92	TEARS IN HEAVEN (RE-ENTRY)	5
1 AUG 92	RUNAWAY TRAIN	31
29 AUG 92	IT'S PROBABLY ME	30
3 OCT 92	LAYLA (ACOUSTIC)	45
15 OCT 94	MOTHERLESS CHILD	63
18 MAR 95	LOVE CAN BUILD A BRIDGE	1
20 JUL 96	CHANGE THE WORLD	18
4 APR 98	MY FATHER'S EYES	33
4 JUL 98	CIRCUS	39

• ERIC CLAPTON •

ALBUMS

30 JUL 66	BLUES BREAKERS	6
5 SEP 70	ERIC CLAPTON	17
26 AUG 72	HISTORY OF ERIC CLAPTON	20
24 MAR 73	IN CONCERT	36
24 AUG 74	461 OCEAN BOULEVARD	3
12 APR 75	THERE'S ONE IN EVERY CROWD	15
13 SEP 75	E.C. WAS HERE	14
11 SEP 76	NO REASON TO CRY	8
26 NOV 77	SLOWHAND	23
9 DEC 78	BACKLESS	18
10 MAY 80	JUST ONE NIGHT	3
7 MAR 81	ANOTHER TICKET	18
19 FEB 83	MONEY & CIGARETTES	13
23 MAR 85	BEHIND THE SUN	8
6 DEC 86	AUGUST	3
18 NOV 89	JOURNEYMAN	2
26 OCT 91	24 NIGHTS	17
12 SEP 92	UNPLUGGED	2
24 SEP 94	FROM THE CRADLE	1

• EURYTHMICS •

SINGLES

4 JUL 81	NEVER GONNA CRY AGAIN	63
20 NOV 82	LOVE IS A STRANGER	54
12 FEB 83	SWEET DREAMS (ARE MADE OF THIS)	2
9 APR 83	LOVE IS A STRANGER (RE-ENTRY)	6
9 JUL 83	WHO'S THAT GIRL?	3
5 NOV 83	RIGHT BY YOUR SIDE	10
21 JAN 84	HERE COMES THE RAIN AGAIN	8
3 NOV 84	SEXCRIME (NINETEEN EIGHTY FOUR)	4
19 JAN 85	JULIA	44
20 APR 85	WOULD I LIE TO YOU?	17
6 JUL 85	THERE MUST BE AN ANGEL (PLAYING WITH MY HEART)	1
2 NOV 85	SISTERS ARE DOIN' IT FOR THEMSELVES	9
11 JAN 86	IT'S ALRIGHT (BABY'S COMING BACK)	12
14 JUN 86	WHEN TOMORROW COMES	30
6 SEP 86	THORN IN MY SIDE	5
29 NOV 86	THE MIRACLE OF LOVE	23
28 FEB 87	MISSIONARY MAN	31
24 OCT 87	BEETHOVEN (I LOVE TO LISTEN TO)	25
26 DEC 87	SHAME	41
9 APR 88	I NEED A MAN	26
11 JUN 88	YOU HAVE PLACED A CHILL IN MY HEART	16
26 AUG 89	REVIVAL	26
4 NOV 89	DON'T ASK ME WHY	25
3 FEB 90	THE KING AND QUEEN OF AMERICA	29
12 MAY 90	ANGEL	23
9 MAR 91	LOVE IS A STRANGER (RE-ISSUE)	46
16 NOV 91	SWEET DREAMS (ARE MADE OF THIS) (RE-MIX)	48

• EURYTHMICS •

ALBUMS

12 FEB 83	SWEET DREAMS (ARE MADE OF THIS)	3
26 NOV 83	TOUCH	1
9 JUN 84	TOUCH DANCE	31
24 NOV 84	1984 (FOR THE LOVE OF BIG BROTHER)	23
11 MAY 85	BE YOURSELF TONIGHT	3
12 JUL 86	REVENGE	3
21 NOV 87	SAVAGE	7
23 SEP 89	WE TOO ARE ONE	1
27 NOV 93	EURYTHMICS LIVE 1983-1989	22

• EXTREME •

SINGLES

8 JUN 91	GET THE FUNK OUT	19
27 JUL 91	MORE THAN WORDS	2
12 OCT 91	DECADENCE DANCE	36
23 NOV 91	HOLE HEARTED	12
2 MAY 92	SONG FOR LOVE	12
5 SEP 92	REST IN PEACE	13
14 NOV 92	STOP THE WORLD	22
6 FEB 93	TRAGIC COMIC	15
11 MAR 95	HIP TODAY	44

ALBUMS

1 JUN 91	EXTREME II PORNOGRAFFITI	12
26 SEP 92	III SIDES TO EVERY STORY	2
11 FEB 95	WAITING FOR THE PUNCHLINE	10

• FATS DOMINO •

SINGLES

27 JUL 56	I'M IN LOVE AGAIN	28
17 AUG 56	I'M IN LOVE AGAIN (RE-ENTRY)	12
30 NOV 56	BLUEBERRY HILL	26
21 DEC 56	BLUEBERRY HILL (RE-ENTRY)	6
25 JAN 57	AIN'T THAT A SHAME	23
1 FEB 57	HONEY CHILE	29
29 MAR 57	BLUE MONDAY	23
19 APR 57	BLUE MONDAY (RE-ENTRY)	30
19 APR 57	I'M WALKIN'	19
19 JUL 57	VALLEY OF TEARS	25
28 MAR 58	THE BIG BEAT	20
4 JUL 58	SICK AND TIRED	26
22 MAY 59	MARGIE	18
16 OCT 59	I WANT TO WALK YOU HOME	14
18 DEC 59	BE MY GUEST	11
19 FEB 60	BE MY GUEST (RE-ENTRY)	19
17 MAR 60	COUNTRY BOY	19
21 JUL 60	WALKING TO NEW ORLEANS	19
10 NOV 60	THREE NIGHTS A WEEK	45
5 JAN 61	MY GIRL JOSEPHINE	32
27 JUL 61	IT KEEPS RAININ'	49
30 NOV 61	WHAT A PARTY	43
29 MAR 62	JAMBALAYA	41
31 OCT 63	RED SAILS IN THE SUNSET	34
24 APR 76	BLUEBERRY HILL (RE-ISSUE)	41

ALBUMS

16 MAY 70	VERY BEST OF FATS DOMINO	56

• FLEETWOOD MAC •

SINGLES

10 APR 68	BLACK MAGIC WOMAN	37
17 JUL 68	NEED YOUR LOVE SO BAD	31
4 DEC 68	ALBATROSS	1
16 APR 69	MAN OF THE WORLD	2
23 JUL 69	NEED YOUR LOVE SO BAD (RE-ISSUE)	32
13 SEP 69	NEED YOUR LOVE SO BAD (RE-ENTRY OF RE-ISSUE)	42
4 OCT 69	OH WELL	2
23 MAY 70	THE GREEN MANALISHI (WITH THE TWO- PRONG CROWN)	10
12 MAY 73	ALBATROSS (RE-ISSUE)	2
13 NOV 76	SAY YOU LOVE ME	40
19 FEB 77	GO YOUR OWN WAY	38
30 APR 77	DON'T STOP	32
9 JUL 77	DREAMS	24
22 OCT 77	YOU MAKE LOVING FUN	45
11 MAR 78	RHIANNON	46
6 OCT 79	TUSK	6
22 DEC 79	SARA	37
25 SEP 82	GYPSY	46
18 DEC 82	OH DIANE	9
4 APR 87	BIG LOVE	9
11 JUL 87	SEVEN WONDERS	56
26 SEP 87	LITTLE LIES	5
26 DEC 87	FAMILY MAN	54
2 APR 88	EVERYWHERE	4
18 JUN 88	ISN'T IT MIDNIGHT	60
17 DEC 88	AS LONG AS YOU FOLLOW	66
5 MAY 90	SAVE ME	53
25 AUG 90	IN THE BACK OF MY MIND	58

• FLEETWOOD MAC •

ALBUMS

2 MAR 68	FLEETWOOD MAC	4
7 SEP 68	MR. WONDERFUL	10
30 AUG 69	PIOUS BIRD OF GOOD OMEN	18
4 OCT 69	THEN PLAY ON	6
10 OCT 70	KILN HOUSE	39
6 NOV 76	FLEETWOOD MAC	23
26 FEB 77	RUMOURS	1
27 OCT 79	TUSK	1
13 DEC 80	FLEETWOOD MAC LIVE	31
10 JUL 82	MIRAGE	5
25 APR 87	TANGO IN THE NIGHT	1
21 APR 90	BEHIND THE MASK	1
23 SEP 95	LIVE AT THE BBC	48
21 OCT 95	TIME	47

•FOREIGNER•

SINGLES

6 MAY 78	FEELS LIKE THE FIRST TIME	39
15 JUL 78	COLD AS ICE	24
28 OCT 78	HOT BLOODED	42
24 FEB 79	BLUE MORNING BLUE DAY	45
29 AUG 81	URGENT	54
10 OCT 81	JUKE BOX HERO	48
12 DEC 81	WAITING FOR A GIRL LIKE YOU	8
8 MAY 82	URGENT (RE-ISSUE)	45
8 DEC 84	I WANT TO KNOW WHAT LOVE IS	1
6 APR 85	THAT WAS YESTERDAY	28
22 JUN 85	COLD AS ICE (RE-MIX)	64
19 DEC 87	SAY YOU WILL	71
22 OCT 94	WHITE LIE	58

ALBUMS

26 AUG 78	DOUBLE VISION	32
25 JUL 81	4	5
18 DEC 82	RECORDS	58
22 DEC 84	AGENT PROVOCATEUR	1
19 DEC 87	INSIDE INFORMATION	64
6 JUL 91	UNUSUAL HEAT	56
12 NOV 94	MR. MOONLIGHT	59

• FREE •

SINGLES

6 JUN 70	ALL RIGHT NOW	2
1 MAY 71	MY BROTHER JAKE	4
27 MAY 72	LITTLE BIT OF LOVE	13
13 JAN 73	WISHING WELL	7
21 JUL 73	ALL RIGHT NOW (RE-ENTRY)	15
18 FEB 78	FREE EP	11
23 OCT 82	FREE EP (RE-ENTRY)	57
9 FEB 91	ALL RIGHT NOW (RE-MIX)	8

ALBUMS

11 JUL 70	FIRE AND WATER	2
23 JAN 71	HIGHWAY	41
26 JUN 71	FREE LIVE!	4
17 JUN 72	FREE AT LAST	9
3 FEB 73	HEARTBREAKER	9

•FRANK ZAPPA•

ALBUMS

28 FEB 70	HOT RATS	9
19 DEC 70	CHUNGA'S REVENGE	43
6 MAY 78	ZAPPA IN NEW YORK	55
10 MAR 79	SHEIK YERBOUTI	32
13 OCT 79	JOE'S GARAGE ACT 1	62
19 JAN 80	JOE'S GARAGE ACTS 2 & 3	75
16 MAY 81	TINSEL TOWN REBELLION	55
24 OCT 81	YOU ARE WHAT YOU IS	51
19 JUN 82	SHIP ARRIVING TOO LATE TO SAVE A DROWNING WITCH	61
18 JUN 83	THE MAN FROM UTOPIA	87
27 OCT 84	THEM OR US	53
30 APR 88	GUITAR	82

• GARY NUMAN •

SINGLES

19 MAY 79	ARE 'FRIENDS' ELECTRIC	1
1 SEP 79	CARS	1
24 NOV 79	COMPLEX	6
24 MAY 80	WE ARE GLASS	5
30 AUG 80	I DIE, YOU DIE	6
20 DEC 80	THIS WRECKAGE	20
29 AUG 81	SHE'S GOT CLAWS	6
5 DEC 81	LOVE NEEDS NO DISGUISE	33
6 MAR 82	MUSIC FOR CHAMELEONS	19
19 JUN 82	WE TAKE MYSTERY (TO BED)	9
28 AUG 82	WHITE BOYS AND HEROES	20
3 SEP 83	WARRIORS	20
22 OCT 83	SISTER SURPRISE	32
3 NOV 84	BERSERKER	32
22 DEC 84	MY DYING MACHINE	66
9 FEB 85	CHANGE YOUR MIND	17
25 MAY 85	THE LIVE EP	27
10 AUG 85	YOUR FASCINATION	46
21 SEP 85	CALL OUT THE DOGS	49
16 NOV 85	MIRACLES	49
19 APR 86	THIS IS LOVE	28
28 JUN 86	I CAN'T STOP	27
4 OCT 86	NEW THING FROM LONDON TOWN	52
6 DEC 86	I STILL REMEMBER	74
28 MAR 87	RADIO HEART	35
13 JUN 87	LONDON TIMES	48
19 SEP 87	CARS (E REG MODEL) / ARE 'FRIENDS' ELECTRIC (RE-MIX)	16
30 JAN 88	NO MORE LIES	34
1 OCT 88	NEW ANGER	46

• GARY NUMAN •

SINGLES CONT...

3 DEC 88	AMERICA	49
3 JUN 89	I'M ON AUTOMATIC	44
16 MAR 91	HEART	43
21 MAR 92	THE SKIN GAME	68
1 AUG 92	MACHINE + SOUL	72
4 SEP 93	CARS (2ND RE-MIX)	53
16 MAR 96	CARS (RE-ISSUE OF RE-MIX)	17

ALBUMS

9 JUN 79	REPLICAS	1
25 AUG 79	TUBEWAY ARMY	14
22 SEP 79	THE PLEASURE PRINCIPLE	1
13 SEP 80	TELEKON	1
2 MAY 81	LIVING ORNAMENTS 1979-1980	2
2 MAY 81	LIVING ORNAMENTS 1979	47
2 MAY 81	LIVING ORNAMENTS 1980	39
12 SEP 81	DANCE	3
18 SEP 82	I' ASSASSIN	8
24 SEP 83	WARRIORS	12
6 OCT 84	THE PLAN	29
24 NOV 84	BERSERKER	45
13 APR 85	WHITE NOISE - LIVE	29
28 SEP 85	THE FURY	24
8 NOV 86	STRANGE CHARM	59
3 OCT 87	EXHIBITION	43
8 OCT 88	METAL RHYTHM	48
8 JUL 89	AUTOMATIC	59
28 OCT 89	SKIN MECHANIC	55
30 MAR 91	OUTLAND	39
22 AUG 92	MACHINE AND SOUL	42

•GENESIS•

SINGLES

6 APR 74	I KNOW WHAT I LIKE (IN YOUR WARDROBE)	21
26 FEB 77	YOUR OWN SPECIAL WAY	43
28 MAY 77	SPOT THE PIGEON (EP)	14
11 MAR 78	FOLLOW YOU FOLLOW ME	7
8 JUL 78	MANY TOO MANY	43
15 MAR 80	TURN IT ON AGAIN	8
17 MAY 80	DUCHESS	46
13 SEP 80	MISUNDERSTANDING	42
22 AUG 81	ABACAB	9
31 OCT 81	KEEP IT DARK	33
13 MAR 82	MAN ON THE CORNER	41
22 MAY 82	3 X 3 EP	10
3 SEP 83	MAMA	4
12 NOV 83	THAT'S ALL	16
11 FEB 84	ILLEGAL ALIEN	46
10 MAR 84	ILLEGAL ALIEN (RE-ENTRY)	70
31 MAY 86	INVISIBLE TOUCH	15
30 AUG 86	IN TOO DEEP	19
22 NOV 86	LAND OF CONFUSION	14
14 MAR 87	TONIGHT TONIGHT TONIGHT	18
20 JUN 87	THROWING IT ALL AWAY	22
2 NOV 91	NO SON OF MINE	6
4 JAN 92	NO SON OF MINE (RE-ENTRY)	70
11 JAN 92	I CAN'T DANCE	7
18 APR 92	HOLD ON MY HEART	16
25 JUL 92	JESUS HE KNOWS ME	20
21 NOV 92	INVISIBLE TOUCH (LIVE)	7
20 FEB 93	TELL ME WHY	40
27 SEP 97	CONGO	29
13 DEC 97	SHIPWRECKED	54
7 MAR 98	NOT ABOUT US	66

•GENESIS•

ALBUMS

14 OCT 72	FOXTROT	12
11 AUG 73	GENESIS LIVE	9
20 OCT 73	SELLING ENGLAND BY THE POUND	3
11 MAY 74	NURSERY CRYME	39
7 DEC 74	THE LAMB LIES DOWN ON BROADWAY	10
28 FEB 76	A TRICK OF THE TAIL	3
15 JAN 77	WIND AND WUTHERING	7
29 OCT 77	SECONDS OUT	4
15 APR 78	AND THEN THERE WERE THREE	3
5 APR 80	DUKE	1
26 SEP 81	ABACAB	1
12 JUN 82	3 SIDES LIVE	2
15 OCT 83	GENESIS	1
21 APR 84	TRESPASS	98
21 JUN 86	INVISIBLE TOUCH1	
23 NOV 91	WE CAN'T DANCE	1
28 NOV 92	LIVE - THE WAY WE WALK VOLUME 1: THE SHORTS	3
23 JAN 93	LIVE - THE WAY WE WALK VOLUME 2: THE LONGS	1

• GEORGE HARRISON •

SINGLES

23 JAN 71	MY SWEET LORD	1
14 AUG 71	BANGLA DESH	10
2 JUN 73	GIVE ME LOVE (GIVE ME PEACE ON EARTH)	8
21 DEC 74	DING DONG	38
11 OCT 75	YOU	38
10 MAR 79	BLOW AWAY	51
23 MAY 81	ALL THOSE YEARS AGO	13
24 OCT 87	GOT MY MIND SET ON YOU	2
6 FEB 88	WHEN WE WAS FAB	25
25 JUN 88	THIS IS LOVE	55

ALBUMS

26 DEC 70	ALL THINGS MUST PASS	4
7 JUL 73	LIVING IN THE MATERIAL WORLD	2
18 OCT 75	EXTRA TEXTURE (READ ALL ABOUT IT)	16
18 DEC 76	THIRTY THREE AND A THIRD	35
17 MAR 79	GEORGE HARRISON	39
13 JUN 81	SOMEWHERE IN ENGLAND	13
14 NOV 87	CLOUD NINE	10

•GUNS 'N' ROSES•

SINGLES

3 OCT 87	WELCOME TO THE JUNGLE	67
20 AUG 88	SWEET CHILD O' MINE	24
29 OCT 88	WELCOME TO THE JUNGLE / NIGHTRAIN (RE-ISSUE)	24
18 MAR 89	PARADISE CITY	6
3 JUN 89	SWEET CHILD O' MINE (RE-MIX)	6
1 JUL 89	PATIENCE	10
2 SEP 89	NIGHTRAIN (RE-ISSUE)	17
13 JUL 91	YOU COULD BE MINE	3
21 SEP 91	DON'T CRY	8
21 DEC 91	LIVE AND LET DIE	5
7 MAR 92	NOVEMBER RAIN	4
23 MAY 92	KNOCKIN' ON HEAVEN'S DOOR	2
21 NOV 92	YESTERDAYS / NOVEMBER RAIN (RE-ISSUE)	8
29 MAY 93	THE CIVIL WAR EP	11
20 NOV 93	AIN'T IT FUN	9
4 JUN 94	SINCE I DON'T HAVE YOU	10
14 JAN 95	SYMPATHY FOR THE DEVIL	9

ALBUMS

1 AUG 87	APPETITE FOR DESTRUCTION	5
17 DEC 88	G N' R LIES	22
28 SEP 91	USE YOUR ILLUSION I	2
28 SEP 91	USE YOUR ILLUSION II	1
4 DEC 93	THE SPAGHETTI INCIDENT?	2

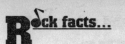

• HEART •

SINGLES

29 MAR 86	THESE DREAMS	62
13 JUN 87	ALONE	3
19 SEP 87	WHO WILL YOU RUN TO	30
12 DEC 87	THERE'S THE GIRL	34
5 MAR 88	NEVER / THESE DREAMS (RE-ISSUE)	8
14 MAY 88	WHAT ABOUT LOVE	14
22 OCT 88	NOTHIN' AT ALL	38
24 MAR 90	ALL I WANNA DO IS MAKE LOVE TO YOU	8
28 JUL 90	I DIDN'T WANT TO NEED YOU	47
17 NOV 90	STRANDED	60
14 SEP 91	YOU'RE THE VOICE	56
20 NOV 93	WILL YOU BE THERE (IN THE MORNING)	19

ALBUMS

22 JAN 77	DREAMBOAT ANNIE	36
23 JUL 77	LITTLE QUEEN	34
19 JUN 82	PRIVATE AUDITION	77
26 OCT 85	HEART	19
6 JUN 87	BAD ANIMALS	7
14 APR 90	BRIGADE	3
28 SEP 91	ROCK THE HOUSE 'LIVE'	45
11 DEC 93	DESIRE WALKS ON	32

• HOT CHOCOLATE •

SINGLES

15 AUG 70	LOVE IS LIFE	6
6 MAR 71	YOU COULD HAVE BEEN A LADY	22
28 AUG 71	I BELIEVE (IN LOVE)	8
28 OCT 72	YOU'LL ALWAYS BE A FRIEND	23
14 APR 73	BROTHER LOUIE	7
18 AUG 73	RUMOURS	44
16 MAR 74	EMMA	3
30 NOV 74	CHERI BABE	31
24 MAY 75	DISCO QUEEN	11
9 AUG 75	A CHILD'S PRAYER	7
8 NOV 75	YOU SEXY THING	2
20 MAR 76	DON'T STOP IT NOW	11
26 JUN 76	MAN TO MAN	14
21 AUG 76	HEAVEN IS THE BACK SEAT OF MY CADILLAC	25
18 JUN 77	SO YOU WIN AGAIN	1
26 NOV 77	PUT YOUR LOVE IN ME	10
4 MAR 78	EVERY 1'S A WINNER	12
2 DEC 78	I'LL PUT YOU TOGETHER AGAIN	13
19 MAY 79	MINDLESS BOOGIE	46
28 JUL 79	GOING THROUGH THE MOTIONS	53
3 MAY 80	NO DOUBT ABOUT IT	2
19 JUL 80	ARE YOU GETTING ENOUGH OF WHAT MAKES YOU HAPPY	17
13 DEC 80	LOVE ME TO SLEEP	50
30 MAY 81	YOU'LL NEVER BE SO WRONG	52
17 APR 82	GIRL CRAZY	7
10 JUL 82	IT STARTED WITH A KISS	5

• HOT CHOCOLATE •

SINGLES CONT...

25 SEP 82	CHANCES	32
7 MAY 83	WHAT KINDA BOY YOU LOOKING FOR (GIRL)	10
17 SEP 83	TEARS ON THE TELEPHONE	37
4 FEB 84	I GAVE YOU MY HEART (DIDN'T I)	13
17 JAN 87	YOU SEXY THING (RE-MIX)	10
4 APR 87	EVERY 1'S A WINNER (RE-MIX)	69
6 MAR 93	IT STARTED WITH A KISS (RE-ISSUE)	31
22 NOV 97	YOU SEXY THING (RE-ISSUE)	6
14 FEB 98	IT STARTED WITH A KISS (2ND RE-ISSUE)	18

ALBUMS

15 NOV 75	HOT CHOCOLATE	34
7 AUG 76	MAN TO MAN	32
8 APR 78	EVERY 1'S A WINNER	30
25 SEP 82	MYSTERY	24

•IGGY POP•

SINGLES

13 DEC 86	REAL WILD CHILD (WILD ONE)	10
10 FEB 90	LIVIN' ON THE EDGE OF THE NIGHT	51
13 OCT 90	CANDY	67
5 JAN 91	WELL DID YOU EVAH!	42
4 SEP 93	THE WILD AMERICA (EP)	63
21 MAY 94	BESIDE YOU	47
23 NOV 96	LUST FOR LIFE	26
7 MAR 98	THE PASSENGER	22

ALBUMS

9 APR 77	THE IDIOT	30
4 JUN 77	RAW POWER	44
1 OCT 77	LUST FOR LIFE	19
19 MAY 79	NEW VALUES	60
16 FEB 80	SOLDIER	62
11 OCT 86	BLAH-BLAH-BLAH	43
2 JUL 88	INSTINCT	61
21 JUL 90	BRICK BY BRICK	50
25 SEP 93	AMERICAN CAESAR	43
2 NOV 90	CURE FOR SANITY	33
19 SEP 92	THE LOOKS OR THE LIFESTYLE	15
6 MAR 93	WEIRD'S BAR AND GRILL	44
6 NOV 93	16 DIFFERENT FLAVOURS OF HELL	73
1 OCT 94	DOS DEDOS MIS AMIGOS	11
18 MAR 95	TWO FINGERS MY FRIENDS	25

• INXS •

SINGLES

19 APR 86	WHAT YOU NEED	51
28 JUN 86	LISTEN LIKE THIEVES	46
30 AUG 86	KISS THE DIRT (FALLING DOWN THE MOUNTAIN)	54
24 OCT 87	NEED YOU TONIGHT	58
9 JAN 88	NEW SENSATION	25
12 MAR 88	DEVIL INSIDE	47
25 JUN 88	NEVER TEAR US APART	24
12 NOV 88	NEED YOU TONIGHT (RE-ISSUE)	2
8 APR 89	MYSTIFY	14
15 SEP 90	SUICIDE BLONDE	11
8 DEC 90	DISAPPEAR	21
26 JAN 91	GOOD TIMES	18
30 MAR 91	BY MY SIDE	42
13 JUL 91	BITTER TEARS	30
2 NOV 91	SHINING STAR (EP)	27
18 JUL 92	HEAVEN SENT	31
5 SEP 92	BABY DON'T CRY	20
14 NOV 92	TASTE IT	21
13 FEB 93	BEAUTIFUL GIRL	23
23 OCT 93	THE GIFT	11
11 DEC 93	PLEASE (YOU GOT THAT...)	50
22 OCT 94	THE STRANGEST PARTY (THESE ARE THE TIMES)	15
22 MAR 97	ELEGANTLY WASTED	20
7 JUN 97	EVERYTHING	71

ALBUMS

8 FEB 86	LISTEN LIKE THIEVES	48
28 NOV 87	KICK	9
6 OCT 90	X	2
16 NOV 91	LIVE BABY LIVE	8
15 AUG 92	WELCOME TO WHEREVER YOU ARE	1
13 NOV 93	FULL MOON, DIRTY HEARTS	3

• IRON MAIDEN •

SINGLES

23 FEB 80	RUNNING FREE	34
7 JUN 80	SANCTUARY	29
8 NOV 80	WOMEN IN UNIFORM	35
14 MAR 81	TWILIGHT ZONE / WRATH CHILD	31
27 JUN 81	PURGATORY	52
26 SEP 81	MAIDEN JAPAN	43
20 FEB 82	RUN TO THE HILLS	7
15 MAY 82	THE NUMBER OF THE BEAST	18
23 APR 83	FLIGHT OF ICARUS	11
2 JUL 83	THE TROOPER	12
18 AUG 84	2 MINUTES TO MIDNIGHT	11
3 NOV 84	ACES HIGH	20
5 OCT 85	RUNNING FREE (LIVE)	19
14 DEC 85	RUN TO THE HILLS (LIVE)	26
6 SEP 86	WASTED YEARS	18
22 NOV 86	STRANGER IN A STRANGE LAND	22
27 DEC 86	STRANGER IN A STRANGE LAND (RE-ENTRY)	71
26 MAR 88	CAN I PLAY WITH MADNESS	3
13 AUG 88	THE EVIL THAT MEN DO	5
19 NOV 88	THE CLAIRVOYANT	6
18 NOV 89	INFINITE DREAMS	6
30 DEC 89	INFINITE DREAMS (RE-ENTRY)	74
22 SEP 90	HOLY SMOKE	3
5 JAN 91	BRING YOUR DAUGHTER... TO THE SLAUGHTER	1
25 APR 92	BE QUICK OR BE DEAD	2
11 JUL 92	FROM HERE TO ETERNITY	21
13 MAR 93	FEAR OF THE DARK (LIVE)	8
16 OCT 93	HALLOWED BE THY NAME (LIVE)	9
7 OCT 95	MAN ON THE EDGE	10
21 SEP 96	VIRUS	16
21 MAR 98	THE ANGEL AND THE GAMBLER	18

•IRON MAIDEN•

ALBUMS

26 APR 80	IRON MAIDEN	4
28 FEB 81	KILLERS	12
10 APR 82	THE NUMBER OF THE BEAST	1
28 MAY 83	PIECE OF MIND	3
15 SEP 84	POWERSLAVE	2
26 OCT 85	LIVE AFTER DEATH	2
11 OCT 86	SOMEWHERE IN TIME	3
23 APR 88	SEVENTH SON OF A SEVENTH SON	1
24 FEB 90	RUNNING FREE / SANCTUARY	10
3 MAR 90	WOMEN IN UNIFORM / TWILIGHT ZONE	10
10 MAR 90	PURGATORY / MAIDEN JAPAN	5
17 MAR 90	RUN TO THE HILLS / THE NUMBER OF THE BEAST	3
24 MAR 90	FLIGHT OF ICARUS / THE TROOPER	7
31 MAR 90	2 MINUTES TO MIDNIGHT / ACES HIGH	11
7 APR 90	RUNNING FREE (LIVE) / RUN TO THE HILLS (LIVE)	9
14 APR 90	WASTED YEARS / STRANGER IN A STRANGE LAND	9
21 APR 90	CAN I PLAY WITH MADNESS / THE EVIL THAT MEN DO	10
28 APR 90	THE CLAIRVOYANT / INFINITE DREAMS (LIVE)	11
13 OCT 90	NO PRAYER FOR THE DYING	2
23 MAY 92	FEAR OF THE DARK	1
3 APR 93	A REAL LIVE ONE	3
30 OCT 93	A REAL DEAD ONE	12
20 NOV 93	LIVE AT DONNINGTON	23
14 OCT 95	THE X FACTOR	8

• JAMES •

SINGLES

12 MAY 90	HOW WAS IT FOR YOU	32
7 JUL 90	COME HOME	32
8 DEC 90	LOSE CONTROL	38
30 MAR 91	SIT DOWN	2
30 NOV 91	SOUND	9
1 FEB 92	BORN OF FRUSTRATION	13
4 APR 92	RING THE BELLS	37
18 JUL 92	SEVEN EP	46
11 SEP 93	SOMETIMES	18
13 NOV 93	LAID	25
2 APR 94	JAM J / SAY SOMETHING	24
22 FEB 97	SHE'S A STAR	9
3 MAY 97	TOMORROW	12
5 JUL 97	WALTZING ALONG	23
21 MAR 98	DESTINY CALLING	17
6 JUN 98	RUNAGROUND	29
21 NOV 98	SIT DOWN (RE-MIX)	7

ALBUMS

2 AUG 86	STUTTER	68
8 OCT 88	STRIP MINE	90
16 JUN 90	GOLD MOTHER	2
29 FEB 92	SEVEN	2
9 OCT 93	LAID	3
24 SEP 94	WAH WAH	11

• JAMES BROWN •

SINGLES

23 SEP 65	PAPA'S GOT A BRAND NEW BAG	25
24 FEB 66	I GOT YOU	29
16 JUN 66	IT'S A MAN'S MAN'S MAN'S WORLD	13
10 OCT 70	GET UP I FEEL LIKE BEING A SEX MACHINE	32
27 NOV 71	HEY AMERICA	47
18 SEP 76	GET UP OFFA THAT THING	22
29 JAN 77	BODY HEAT	36
10 JAN 81	RAPP PAYBACK (WHERE IZ MOSES?)	39
2 JUL 83	BRING IT ON...BRING IT ON	45
1 SEP 84	UNITY (PART 1 - THE THIRD COMING)	49
27 APR 85	FROGGY MIX	50
1 JUN 85	GET UP I FEEL LIKE BEING A SEX MACHINE (RE-ISSUE)	47
25 JAN 86	LIVING IN AMERICA	5
1 MAR 86	GET UP I FEEL LIKE BEING A SEX MACHINE (RE-ENTRY OF RE-ISSUE)	46
18 OCT 86	GRAVITY	65
30 JAN 88	SHE'S THE ONE	45
23 APR 88	THE PAYBACK MIX	12
4 JUN 88	I'M REAL	31
23 JUL 88	I GOT YOU (I FEEL GOOD) (RE-ISSUE)	52
16 NOV 91	GET UP (I FEEL LIKE BEING A) SEX MACHINE (2ND RE-ISSUE)	69
24 OCT 92	I GOT YOU (I FEEL GOOD) (RE-MIX)	72
17 APR 93	CAN'T GET ANY HARDER	59

ALBUMS

18 OCT 86	GRAVITY	85
25 JUN 88	I'M REAL	27

• JANET JACKSON •

SINGLES

22 MAR 86	WHAT HAVE YOU DONE FOR ME LATELY	3
31 MAY 86	NASTY	19
9 AUG 86	WHEN I THINK OF YOU	10
1 NOV 86	CONTROL	42
21 MAR 87	LET'S WAIT AWHILE	3
13 JUN 87	PLEASURE PRINCIPLE	24
14 NOV 87	FUNNY HOW TIME FLIES (WHEN YOU'RE HAVING FUN)	59
2 SEP 89	MISS YOU MUCH	22
4 NOV 89	RHYTHM NATION	23
27 JAN 90	COME BACK TO ME	20
31 MAR 90	ESCAPADE	17
7 JUL 90	ALRIGHT	20
8 SEP 90	BLACK CAT	15
27 OCT 90	LOVE WILL NEVER DO (WITHOUT YOU)	34
15 AUG 92	THE BEST THINGS IN LIFE ARE FREE	2
8 MAY 93	THAT'S THE WAY LOVE GOES	2
31 JUL 93	IF	14
20 NOV 93	AGAIN	6
12 MAR 94	BECAUSE OF LOVE	19
18 JUN 94	ANY TIME ANY PLACE	13
26 NOV 94	YOU WANT THIS	14
18 MAR 95	WHOOPS NOW / WHAT'LL I DO	9
10 JUN 95	SCREAM	3
24 JUN 95	SCREAM (RE-MIX)	43
23 SEP 95	RUNAWAY	6
2 DEC 95	SCREAM (RE-ENTRY)	72

• JANET JACKSON •

SINGLES CONT...

16 DEC 95	THE BEST THINGS IN LIFE ARE FREE (RE-MIX)	7
6 APR 96	TWENTY FOREPLAY	22
4 OCT 97	GOT 'TIL IT'S GONE	6
13 DEC 97	TOGETHER AGAIN	4
4 APR 98	I GET LONELY	5
27 JUN 98	GO DEEP	13
19 DEC 98	EVERY TIME	46

ALBUMS

5 APR 86	CONTROL	8
14 NOV 87	CONTROL - THE RE-MIXES	20
30 SEP 89	RHYTHM NATION 1814	4
29 MAY 93	JANET / JANET REMIXED	1

• JANIS JOPLIN •

ALBUMS

17 APR 71	PEARL	50
22 JUL 72	JANIS JOPLIN IN CONCERT	30

• JEFFERSON AIRPLANE •

ALBUMS

28 JUN 69	BLESS ITS POINTED LITTLE HEAD	38
7 MAR 70	VOLUNTEERS	34
2 OCT 71	BARK	42
2 SEP 72	LONG JOHN SILVER	30
31 JUL 76	SPITFIRE	30
9 FEB 80	FREEDOM AT POINT ZERO	22
18 JUL 87	NO PROTECTION	26

• JERRY LEE LEWIS •

SINGLES

27 SEP 57	WHOLE LOTTA SHAKIN' GOIN' ON	8
20 DEC 57	GREAT BALLS OF FIRE	1
27 DEC 57	WHOLE LOTTA SHAKIN' GOIN' ON (RE-ENTRY)	26
11 APR 58	BREATHLESS	8
23 JAN 59	HIGH SCHOOL CONFIDENTIAL	12
1 MAY 59	LOVIN' UP A STORM	28
9 JUN 60	BABY BABY BYE BYE	47
4 MAY 61	WHAT'D I SAY	10
3 AUG 61	WHAT'D I SAY (RE-ENTRY)	49
6 SEP 62	SWEET LITTLE SIXTEEN	38
14 MAR 63	GOOD GOLLY MISS MOLLY	31
6 MAY 72	CHANTILLY LACE	33

ALBUMS

2 JUN 62	JERRY LEE LEWIS VOLUME 2	14

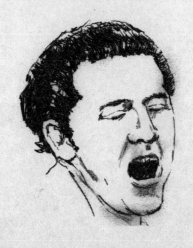

•JETHRO TULL•

SINGLES

1 JAN 69	LOVE STORY	29
14 MAY 69	LIVING IN THE PAST	3
1 NOV 69	SWEET DREAM	7
24 JAN 70	TEACHER / THE WITCH'S PROMISE	4
18 SEP 71	LIFE IS A LONG SONG / UP THE POOL	11
11 DEC 76	RING OUT SOLSTICE BELLS EP	28
15 SEP 84	LAP OF LUXURY	70
16 JAN 88	SAID SHE WAS A DANCER	55
21 MAR 92	ROCKS ON THE ROAD	47
22 MAY 93	LIVING IN THE (SLIGHTLY MORE RECENT) PAST	32

• JETHRO TULL •

ALBUMS

2 NOV 68	THIS WAS	10
9 AUG 69	STAND UP	1
9 MAY 70	BENEFIT	3
3 APR 71	AQUALUNG	4
18 MAR 72	THICK AS A BRICK	5
15 JUL 72	LIVING IN THE PAST	8
28 JUL 73	A PASSION PLAY	13
2 NOV 74	WAR CHILD	14
27 SEP 75	MINSTREL IN THE GALLERY	20
15 MAY 76	TOO OLD TO ROCK 'N' ROLL TOO YOUNG TO DIE	25
19 FEB 77	SONGS FROM THE WOOD	13
29 APR 78	HEAVY HORSES	20
14 OCT 78	LIVE BURSTING OUT	17
6 OCT 79	STORM WATCH	27
6 SEP 80	A	25
17 APR 82	BROADSWORD AND THE BEAST	27
15 SEP 84	UNDER WRAPS	18
2 NOV 85	ORIGINAL MASTERS	63
19 SEP 87	CREST OF A KNAVE	19
2 SEP 89	ROCK ISLAND	18
14 SEP 91	CATFISH RISING	27
26 SEP 92	A LITTLE LIGHT MUSIC	34
16 SEP 95	ROOTS TO BRANCHES	20

•JIMI HENDRIX•

SINGLES

5 JAN 67	HEY JOE	6
23 MAR 67	PURPLE HAZE	3
11 MAY 67	THE WIND CRIES MARY	6
30 AUG 67	BURNING OF THE MIDNIGHT LAMP	18
23 OCT 68	ALL ALONG THE WATCHTOWER	5
16 APR 69	CROSSTOWN TRAFFIC	37
7 NOV 70	VOODOO CHILE	1
30 OCT 71	GYPSY EYES / REMEMBER	35
12 FEB 72	JOHNNY B. GOODE	35
21 APR 90	CROSSTOWN TRAFFIC (RE-ISSUE)	61
20 OCT 90	ALL ALONG THE WATCHTOWER (EP)	52

ALBUMS

27 MAY 67	ARE YOU EXPEIENCED	2
16 DEC 67	AXIS: BOLD AS LOVE	5
27 APR 68	SMASH HITS	4
18 MAY 68	GET THAT FEELING	39
16 NOV 68	ELECTRIC LADYLAND	6
4 JUL 70	BAND OF GYPSIES	6
3 APR 71	CRY OF LOVE	2
28 AUG 71	EXPERIENCE	9
20 NOV 71	JIMI HENDRIX AT THE ISLE OF WIGHT	17
4 DEC 71	RAINBOW BRIDGE	16
5 FEB 72	HENDRIX IN THE WEST	7
11 NOV 72	WAR HEROES	23
21 JUL 73	SOUNDTRACK RECORDINGS FROM THE FILM 'JIMI HENDRIX'	37
29 MAR 75	JIMI HENDRIX	35
30 AUG 75	CRASH LANDING	35
29 NOV 75	MIDNIGHT LIGHTNING	46
14 AUG 82	THE JIMI HENDRIX CONCERTS	16
11 MAR 89	RADIO ONE	30
30 APR 94	BLUES	10

• JOAN ARMATRADING •

SINGLES

16 OCT 76	LOVE AND AFFECTION	10
23 FEB 80	ROSIE	49
14 JUN 80	ME MYSELF I	21
6 SEP 80	ALL THE WAY FROM AMERICA	54
12 SEP 81	I'M LUCKY	46
16 JAN 82	NO LOVE	50
19 FEB 83	DROP THE PILOT	11
16 MAR 85	TEMPTATION	65
26 MAY 90	MORE THAN ONE KIND OF LOVE	75
23 MAY 92	WRAPPED AROUND HER	56

ALBUMS

4 SEP 76	JOAN ARMATRADING	12
1 OCT 77	SHOW SOME EMOTION	6
14 OCT 78	TO THE LIMIT	13
24 MAY 80	ME MYSELF I	5
12 SEP 81	WALK UNDER LADDERS	6
12 MAR 83	THE KEY	10
26 NOV 83	TRACK RECORD	18
16 FEB 85	SECRET SECRETS	14
24 MAY 86	SLEIGHT OF HAND	34
16 JUL 88	THE SHOUTING STAGE	28
16 JUN 90	HEARTS AND FLOWERS	29
20 JUN 92	SQUARE THE CIRCLE	34
10 JUN 95	WHAT'S INSIDE	48

• JOE COCKER •

SINGLES

22 MAY 68	MARJORINE	48
2 OCT 68	WITH A LITTLE HELP FROM MY FRIENDS	1
27 SEP 69	DELTA LADY	10
4 JUL 70	THE LETTER	39
26 SEP 81	I'M SO GLAD I'M STANDING HERE TODAY	61
15 JAN 83	UP WHERE WE BELONG	7
14 NOV 87	UNCHAIN MY HEART	46
13 JAN 90	WHEN THE NIGHT COMES	65
7 MAR 92	(ALL I KNOW) FEELS LIKE FOREVER	25
9 MAY 92	NOW THAT THE MAGIC HAS GONE	28
4 JUL 92	UNCHAIN MY HEART (RE-ISSUE)	17
21 NOV 92	WHEN THE NIGHT COMES (RE-ISSUE)	61
13 AUG 94	THE SIMPLE THINGS	17
22 OCT 94	TAKE ME HOME	41
17 DEC 94	LET THE HEALING BEGIN	32
23 SEP 95	HAVE A LITTLE FAITH	67
12 OCT 96	DON'T LET ME BE MISUNDERSTOOD	53

ALBUMS

26 SEP 70	MAD DOGS AND ENGLISHMEN	16
6 MAY 72	JOE COCKER / WITH A LITTLE HELP FROM MY FRIENDS	29
30 JUN 84	A CIVILISED MAN	100
11 APR 92	NIGHT CALLS	25
17 SEP 94	HAVE A LITTLE FAITH	9

• JOHN LENNON •

SINGLES

9 JUL 69	GIVE PEACE A CHANCE	2
1 NOV 69	COLD TURKEY	14
21 FEB 70	INSTANT KARMA	5
20 MAR 71	POWER TO THE PEOPLE	7
9 DEC 72	HAPPY XMAS (WAR IS OVER)	4
24 NOV 73	MIND GAMES	26
19 OCT 74	WHATEVER GETS YOU THROUGH THE NIGHT	36
4 JAN 75	HAPPY XMAS (WAR IS OVER) (RE-ENTRY)	48
8 FEB 75	NUMBER 9 DREAM	23
3 MAY 75	STAND BY ME	30
1 NOV 75	IMAGINE	6
8 NOV 80	(JUST LIKE) STARTING OVER	1
20 DEC 80	HAPPY XMAS (WAR IS OVER) (2ND RE-ENTRY)	2
27 DEC 80	IMAGINE (RE-ENTRY)	1
24 JAN 81	WOMAN	1
24 JAN 81	GIVE PEACE A CHANCE (RE-ENTRY)	33
21 MAR 81	I SAW HER STANDING THERE	40
4 APR 81	WATCHING THE WHEELS	30
19 DEC 81	HAPPY XMAS (WAR IS OVER) (3RD RE-ENTRY)	28
20 NOV 82	LOVE	41
25 DEC 82	HAPPY XMAS (WAR IS OVER) (4TH RE-ENTRY)	56
21 JAN 84	NOBODY TOLD ME	6
17 MAR 84	BORROWED TIME	32
30 NOV 85	JEALOUS GUY	65
10 DEC 88	IMAGINE / JEALOUS GUY / HAPPY XMAS (WAR IS OVER) (RE-ISSUE)	45

•JOHN LENNON•

ALBUMS

16 JAN 71	JOHN LENNON AND THE PLASTIC ONO BAND	11
30 OCT 71	IMAGINE	1
14 OCT 72	SOMETIME IN NEW YORK CITY	11
8 DEC 73	MIND GAMES	13
19 OCT 74	WALLS AND BRIDGES	6
8 MAR 75	ROCK 'N' ROLL	6
8 NOV 75	SHAVED FISH	8
22 NOV 80	DOUBLE FANTASY	1
4 FEB 84	MILK AND HONEY	3
8 MAR 86	LIVE IN NEW YORK CITY	55
22 OCT 88	IMAGINE (FILM SOUNDTRACK)	64

• KATE BUSH •

SINGLES

11 FEB 78	WUTHERING HEIGHTS	1
13 MAY 78	WUTHERING HEIGHTS (RE-ENTRY)	75
10 JUN 78	MAN WITH THE CHILD IN HIS EYES	6
11 NOV 78	HAMMER HORROR	44
17 MAR 79	WOW	14
15 SEP 79	KATE BUSH ON STAGE (EP)	10
26 APR 80	BREATHING	16
5 JUL 80	BABOOSHKA	5
4 OCT 80	ARMY DREAMERS	16
6 DEC 80	DECEMBER WILL BE MAGIC AGAIN	29
11 JUL 81	SAT IN YOUR LAP	11
7 AUG 82	THE DREAMING	48
17 AUG 85	RUNNING UP THAT HILL	3
26 OCT 85	CLOUDBUSTING	20
1 MAR 86	HOUNDS OF LOVE	18
10 MAY 86	THE BIG SKY	37
1 NOV 86	DON'T GIVE UP	9
8 NOV 86	EXPERIMENT IV	23
30 SEP 89	THE SENSUAL WORLD	12
2 DEC 89	THIS WOMAN'S WORK	25
10 MAR 90	LOVE AND ANGER	38
7 DEC 91	ROCKET MAN (I THINK IT'S GOING TO BE A LONG LONG TIME)	12
18 SEP 93	RUBBERBAND GIRL	12
27 NOV 93	MOMENTS OF PLEASURE	26
16 APR 94	THE RED SHOES	21
30 JUL 94	THE MAN I LOVE	27
19 NOV 94	AND SO IS LOVE	26

•KATE BUSH•

ALBUMS

11 MAR 78	THE KICK INSIDE	3
25 NOV 78	LIONHEART	6
20 SEP 80	NEVER FOR EVER	1
25 SEP 82	THE DREAMING	3
28 SEP 85	HOUNDS OF LOVE	1
22 NOV 86	THE WHOLE STORY	1
28 OCT 89	THE SENSUAL WORLD	2
13 NOV 93	THE RED SHOES	2

•KENNY ROGERS•

SINGLES

18 OCT 69	RUBY DON'T TAKE YOUR LOVE TO TOWN	2
7 FEB 70	SOMETHING'S BURNING	8
30 APR 77	LUCILLE	1
17 SEP 77	DAYTIME FRIENDS	39
2 JUN 79	SHE BELIEVES IN ME	42
26 JAN 80	COWARD OF THE COUNTY	1
15 NOV 80	LADY	12
12 FEB 83	WE'VE GOT TONIGHT	28
22 OCT 83	EYES THAT SEE IN THE DARK	61
12 NOV 83	ISLANDS IN THE STREAM	7

ALBUMS

18 JUN 77	KENNY ROGERS	14
9 FEB 80	KENNY	7
31 JAN 81	LADY	40
1 OCT 83	EYES THAT SEE IN THE DARK	53
27 OCT 84	WHAT ABOUT ME?	97
27 JUL 85	THE KENNY ROGERS STORY	4

• KISS •

SINGLES

30 JUN 79	I WAS MADE FOR LOVIN' YOU	50
20 FEB 82	A WORLD WITHOUT HEROES	55
30 APR 83	CREATURES OF THE NIGHT	34
29 OCT 83	LICK IT UP	31
8 SEP 84	HEAVEN'S ON FIRE	43
9 NOV 85	TEARS ARE FALLING	57
3 OCT 87	CRAZY CRAZY NIGHTS	4
5 DEC 87	REASON TO LIVE	33
10 SEP 88	TURN ON THE NIGHT	41
18 NOV 89	HIDE YOUR HEART	59
31 MAR 90	FOREVER	65
11 JAN 92	GOD GAVE ROCK AND ROLL TO YOU II	4
9 MAY 92	UNHOLY	26

ALBUMS

29 MAY 76	DESTROYER	22
25 JUN 76	ALIVE!	49
17 DEC 77	ALIVE	60
7 JUL 79	DYNASTY	50
28 JUN 80	UNMASKED	48
5 DEC 81	THE ELDER	51
26 JUN 82	KILLERS	42
6 NOV 82	CREATURES OF THE NIGHT	22
8 OCT 83	LICK IT UP	7
6 OCT 84	ANIMALISE	11
5 OCT 85	ASYLUM	12
7 NOV 87	CRAZY NIGHTS	4
10 DEC 88	SMASHES, THRASHES AND HITS	62
4 NOV 89	HOT IN THE SHADE	35
23 MAY 92	REVENGE	10
29 MAY 93	ALIVE III	24

•LED ZEPPELIN•

SINGLES

| 13 SEP 97 | WHOLE LOTTA LOVE | 21 |

ALBUMS

12 APR 69	LED ZEPPELIN	6
8 NOV 69	LED ZEPPELIN 2	1
7 NOV 70	LED ZEPPELIN 3	1
27 NOV 71	FOUR SYMBOLS	1
14 APR 73	HOUSES OF THE HOLY	1
15 MAR 75	PHYSICAL GRAFFITI	1
24 APR 76	PRESENCE	1
6 NOV 76	THE SONG REMAINS THE SAME	1
8 SEP 79	IN THROUGH THE OUT DOOR	1
4 DEC 82	CODA	4
27 OCT 90	REMASTERS	10
10 NOV 90	LED ZEPPELIN	48

•LIONEL RICHIE•

SINGLES

12 SEP 81	ENDLESS LOVE	7
20 NOV 82	TRULY	6
29 JAN 83	YOU ARE	43
7 MAY 83	MY LOVE	70
1 OCT 83	ALL NIGHT LONG (ALL NIGHT)	2
3 DEC 83	RUNNING WITH THE NIGHT	9
10 MAR 84	HELLO	1
23 JUN 84	STUCK ON YOU	12
20 OCT 84	PENNY LOVER	18
16 NOV 85	SAY YOU, SAY ME	8
26 JUL 86	DANCING ON THE CEILING	7
11 OCT 86	LOVE WILL CONQUER ALL	45
20 DEC 86	BALLERINA GIRL / DEEP RIVER WOMAN	17
28 MAR 87	SELA	43
9 MAY 92	DO IT TO ME	33
22 AUG 92	MY DESTINY	7
28 NOV 92	LOVE OH LOVE	52
26 DEC 92	LOVE OH LOVE (RE-ENTRY)	73
6 APR 96	DON'T WANNA LOSE YOU	17
23 NOV 96	STILL IN LOVE	66
27 JUN 98	CLOSEST THING TO HEAVEN	26

ALBUMS

27 NOV 82	LIONEL RICHIE	9
29 OCT 83	CAN'T SLOW DOWN	1
23 AUG 86	DANCING ON THE CEILING	2
6 JUN 92	BACK TO FRONT	1

•LITTLE RICHARD•

SINGLES

14 DEC 56	RIP IT UP	30
8 FEB 57	LONG TALL SALLY	3
22 FEB 57	TUTTI FRUTTI	29
8 MAR 57	SHE'S GOT IT	15
15 MAR 57	THE GIRL CAN'T HELP IT	9
24 MAY 57	SHE'S GOT IT (RE-ENTRY)	28
28 JUN 57	LUCILLE	10
13 SEP 57	JENNY JENNY	11
29 NOV 57	KEEP A KNOCKIN'	21
28 FEB 58	GOOD GOLLY MISS MOLLY	8
11 JUL 58	OOH MY SOUL	30
25 JUL 58	OOH MY SOUL (RE-ENTRY)	22
2 JAN 59	BABY FACE	2
3 APR 59	BY THE LIGHT OF THE SILVERY MOON	17
5 JUN 59	KANSAS CITY	26
11 OCT 62	HE GOT WHAT HE WANTED	38
4 JUN 64	BAMA LAMA BAMA LOO	20
2 JUL 77	GOOD GOLLY MISS MOLLY / RIP IT UP	37
14 JUN 86	GREAT GOSH A'MIGHTY (IT'S A MATTER OF TIME)	62
25 OCT 86	OPERATOR	67

• LULU •

SINGLES

14 MAY 64	SHOUT	7
12 NOV 64	HERE COMES THE NIGHT	50
17 JUN 65	LEAVE A LITTLE LOVE	8
2 SEP 65	TRY TO UNDERSTAND	25
13 APR 67	THE BOAT THAT I ROW	6
29 JUN 67	LET'S PRETEND	11
8 NOV 67	LOVE LOVES TO LOVE LOVE	32
28 FEB 68	ME THE PEACEFUL HEART	9
5 JUN 68	BOY	15
6 NOV 68	I'M A TIGER	9
12 MAR 69	BOOM BANG-A-BANG	2
22 NOV 69	OH ME OH MY (I'M A FOOL FOR YOU BABY)	47
26 JAN 74	THE MAN WHO SOLD THE WORLD	3
19 APR 75	TAKE YOUR MAMA FOR A RIDE	37
12 DEC 81	I COULD NEVER MISS YOU (MORE THAN I DO)	62
16 JAN 82	I COULD NEVER MISS YOU (MORE THAN I DO) (RE-ENTRY)	63
19 JUL 86	SHOUT	8
30 JAN 93	INDEPENDENCE	11
3 APR 93	I'M BACK FOR MORE	27
4 SEP 93	LET ME WAKE UP IN YOUR ARMS	51
9 OCT 93	RELIGHT MY FIRE	1
27 NOV 93	HOW 'BOUT US	46
27 AUG 94	GOODBYE BABY AND AMEN	40
26 NOV 94	EVERY WOMAN KNOWS	44

ALBUMS

25 SEP 71	THE MOST OF LULU	15
6 MAR 93	INDEPENDENCE	67

• MADNESS •

SINGLES

1 SEP 79	THE PRINCE	16
10 NOV 79	ONE STEP BEYOND	7
5 JAN 80	MY GIRL	3
5 APR 80	WORK REST AND PLAY EP	6
13 SEP 80	BAGGY TROUSERS	3
22 NOV 80	EMBARRASSMENT	4
24 JAN 81	THE RETURN OF THE LOS PALMAS SEVEN	7
25 APR 81	GREY DAY	4
26 SEP 81	SHUT UP	7
5 DEC 81	IT MUST BE LOVE	4
20 FEB 82	CARDIAC ARREST	14
22 MAY 82	HOUSE OF FUN	1
24 JUL 82	DRIVING IN MY CAR	4
27 NOV 82	OUR HOUSE	5
19 FEB 83	TOMORROW'S (JUST ANOTHER DAY) / MADNESS (IS ALL IN THE MIND)	8
20 AUG 83	WINGS OF A DOVE	2
5 NOV 83	THE SUN AND THE RAIN	5
11 FEB 84	MICHAEL CAINE	11
2 JUN 84	ONE BETTER DAY	17
31 AUG 85	YESTERDAY'S MEN	18
26 OCT 85	UNCLE SAM	21
1 FEB 86	SWEETEST GIRL	35
8 NOV 86	(WAITING FOR) THE GHOST TRAIN	18
3 JAN 87	(WAITING FOR) THE GHOST TRAIN (RE-ENTRY)	74
19 MAR 88	I PRONOUNCE YOU	44
15 FEB 92	IT MUST BE LOVE (RE-ISSUE)	6
25 APR 92	HOUSE OF FUN (RE-ISSUE)	40
8 AUG 92	MY GIRL (RE-ISSUE)	27
28 NOV 92	THE HARDER THEY COME	44
27 FEB 93	NIGHT BOAT TO CAIRO	56

•MADNESS•

ALBUMS

3 NOV 79	ONE STEP BEYOND	2
4 OCT 80	ABSOLUTELY	2
10 OCT 81	MADNESS 7	5
1 MAY 82	COMPLETE MADNESS	1
13 NOV 82	THE RISE AND FALL	10
3 MAR 84	KEEP MOVING	6
12 OCT 85	MAD NOT MAD	16
6 DEC 86	UTTER MADNESS	29
7 MAY 88	THE MADNESS	65
7 MAR 92	DIVINE MADNESS	1
14 NOV 92	MADSTOCK	22

•MADONNA•

SINGLES

14 JAN 84	HOLIDAY	6
17 MAR 84	LUCKY STAR	14
2 JUN 84	BORDERLINE	56
17 NOV 84	LIKE A VIRGIN	3
2 MAR 85	MATERIAL GIRL	3
8 JUN 85	CRAZY FOR YOU	2
27 JUL 85	INTO THE GROOVE	1
3 AUG 85	HOLIDAY (RE-ENTRY)	2
21 SEP 85	ANGEL	5
12 OCT 85	GAMBLER	4
7 DEC 85	DRESS YOU UP	5
4 JAN 86	GAMBLER (RE-ENTRY)	61
25 JAN 86	BORDERLINE (RE-ENTRY)	2
26 APR 86	LIVE TO TELL	2
28 JUN 86	PAPA DON'T PREACH	1
4 OCT 86	TRUE BLUE	1
13 DEC 86	OPEN YOUR HEART	4
4 APR 87	LA ISLA BONITA	1
18 JUL 87	WHO'S THAT GIRL	1
19 SEP 87	CAUSING A COMMOTION	4
12 DEC 87	THE LOOK OF LOVE	9
18 MAR 89	LIKE A PRAYER	1
3 JUN 89	EXPRESS YOURSELF	5
16 SEP 89	CHERISH	3
16 DEC 89	DEAR JESSIE	5
7 APR 90	VOGUE	1
21 JUL 90	HANKY PANKY	2
8 DEC 90	JUSTIFY MY LOVE	2
2 MAR 91	CRAZY FOR YOU (RE-MIX)	2
13 APR 91	RESCUE ME	3
8 JUN 91	HOLIDAY (RE-ISSUE)	5
25 JUL 92	THIS USED TO BE MY PLAYGROUND	3

•MADONNA•

SINGLES CONT...

17 OCT 92	EROTICA	3
12 DEC 92	DEEPER AND DEEPER	6
9 JAN 93	EROTICA (RE-ENTRY)	65
6 MAR 93	BAD GIRL	10
3 APR 93	FEVER	6
31 JUL 93	RAIN	7
2 APR 94	I'LL REMEMBER	7
8 OCT 94	SECRET	5
17 DEC 94	TAKE A BOW	16
25 FEB 95	BEDTIME STORY	4
6 MAY 95	BEDTIME STORY (RE-ENTRY)	66
26 AUG 95	HUMAN NATURE	8
4 NOV 95	YOU'LL SEE	5
6 JAN 96	OH FATHER	16
23 MAR 96	ONE MORE CHANCE	11
2 NOV 96	YOU MUST LOVE ME	10
28 DEC 96	DON'T CRY FOR ME ARGENTINA	3
18 JAN 97	YOU MUST LOVE ME (RE-ENTRY)	71
29 MAR 97	ANOTHER SUITCASE IN ANOTHER HALL	7
7 MAR 98	FROZEN	1
9 MAY 98	RAY OF LIGHT	2
5 SEP 98	DROWNED WORLD (SUBSTITUTE FOR LOVE)	10
5 DEC 98	THE POWER OF GOODBYE / LITTLE STAR	6

ALBUMS

11 FEB 84	MADONNA / THE FIRST ALBUM	6
24 NOV 84	LIKE A VIRGIN	1
12 JUL 86	TRUE BLUE	1
28 NOV 87	YOU CAN DANCE	5
1 APR 89	LIKE A PRAYER	1
2 JUN 90	I'M BREATHLESS	2
24 OCT 92	EROTICA	2
5 NOV 94	BEDTIME STORIES	2
18 NOV 95	SOMETHING TO REMEMBER	3

•MANIC STREET PREACHERS•

SINGLES

25 MAY 91	YOU LOVE US	62
10 AUG 91	STAY BEAUTIFUL	40
9 NOV 91	LOVE'S SWEET EXILE / REPEAT	26
1 FEB 92	YOU LOVE US (RE-ISSUE)	16
28 MAR 92	SLASH 'N' BURN	20
13 JUN 92	MOTORCYCLE EMPTINESS	17
19 SEP 92	THEME FROM M.A.S.H. (SUICIDE IS PAINLESS)	7
21 NOV 92	LITTLE BABY NOTHING	29
12 JUN 93	FROM DESPAIR TO WHERE	25
31 JUL 93	LA TRISTESSE DURERA (SCREAM TO A SIGH)	22
2 OCT 93	ROSES IN HOSPITAL	15
12 FEB 94	LIFE BECOMING A LANDSLIDE	36
11 JUN 94	FASTER / PCP	16
13 AUG 94	REVOL	22
15 OCT 94	SHE IS SUFFERING	25
27 APR 96	A DESIGN FOR LIFE	2
27 JUL 96	A DESIGN FOR LIFE (RE-ENTRY)	71
3 AUG 96	EVERYTHING MUST GO	5
12 OCT 96	KEVIN CARTER	9
14 DEC 96	AUSTRALIA	7
13 SEP 97	MOTORCYCLE EMPTINESS (RE-ISSUE)	41
13 SEP 97	LITTLE BABY NOTHING (RE-ISSUE)	50
13 SEP 97	YOU LOVE US (2ND RE-ISSUE)	?
13 SEP 97	STAY BEAUTIFUL (RE-ISSUE)	52
13 SEP 97	SLASH 'N' BURN (RE-ISSUE)	54

•MANIC STREET PREACHERS•

13 SEP 97	LOVE'S SWEET EXILE (RE-ISSUE)	55
5 SEP 98	IF YOU TOLERATE THIS YOUR CHILDREN WILL BE NEXT	1
12 DEC 98	THE EVERLASTING	11

ALBUMS

22 FEB 92	GENERATION TERRORISTS	13
3 JUL 93	GOLD AGAINST THE SOUL	8
10 SEP 94	THE HOLY BIBLE	6

• MARILLION •

SINGLES

20 NOV 82	MARKET SQUARE HEROES	60
12 FEB 83	HE KNOWS YOU KNOW	35
16 APR 83	MARKET SQUARE HEROES (RE-ENTRY)	53
18 JUN 83	GARDEN PARTY	16
11 FEB 84	PUNCH AND JUDY	29
12 MAY 84	ASSASSING	22
18 MAY 85	KAYLEIGH	2
7 SEP 85	LAVENDER	5
30 NOV 85	HEART OF LOTHIAN	29
23 MAY 87	INCOMMUNICADO	6
25 JUL 87	SUGAR MICE	22
7 NOV 87	WARM WET CIRCLES	22
26 NOV 88	FREAKS (LIVE)	24
9 SEP 89	HOOKS IN YOU	30
9 DEC 89	UNINVITED GUEST	53
14 APR 90	EASTER	34
8 JUN 91	COVER MY EYES (PAIN AND HEAVEN)	34
3 AUG 91	NO ONE CAN	33
5 OCT 91	DRY LAND	34
23 MAY 92	SYMPATHY	17
1 AUG 92	NO ONE CAN (RE-ISSUE)	26
26 MAR 94	THE HOLLOW MAN	30
7 MAY 94	ALONE AGAIN IN THE LAP OF LUXURY	53
10 JUN 95	BEAUTIFUL	29

ALBUMS

26 MAR 83	SCRIPT FOR A JESTER'S TEAR	7
24 MAR 84	FUGAZI	5
17 NOV 84	REAL TO REEL	8
29 JUN 85	MISPLACED CHILDHOOD	1
4 JUL 87	CLUTCHING AT STRAWS	2
10 DEC 88	THE THIEVING MAGPIE	25
7 OCT 89	SEASON'S END	7
6 JUL 91	HOLIDAYS IN EDEN	7
19 FEB 94	BRAVE	10
8 JUL 95	AFRAID OF SUNLIGHT	16

•MEAT LOAF•

SINGLES

20 MAY 78	YOU TOOK THE WORDS RIGHT OUT OF MY MOUTH	33
19 AUG 78	TWO OUT OF THREE AIN'T BAD	32
10 FEB 79	BAT OUT OF HELL	15
26 SEP 81	I'M GONNA LOVE HER FOR BOTH OF US	62
28 NOV 81	DEAD RINGER FOR LOVE	5
28 MAY 83	IF YOU REALLY WANT TO	59
24 SEP 83	MIDNIGHT AT THE LOST AND FOUND	17
14 JAN 84	RAZOR'S EDGE	41
6 OCT 84	MODERN GIRL	17
22 DEC 84	NOWHERE FAST	67
23 MAR 85	PIECE OF THE ACTION	47
30 AUG 86	ROCK 'N' ROLL MERCENARIES	31
22 JUN 91	DEAD RINGER FOR LOVE (RE-ISSUE)	53
27 JUN 92	TWO OUT OF THREE AIN'T BAD (RE-ISSUE)	69
9 OCT 93	I'D DO ANYTHING FOR LOVE (BUT I WON'T DO THAT)	1
18 DEC 93	BAT OUT OF HELL (RE-ISSUE)	8
19 FEB 94	ROCK AND ROLL DREAMS COME THROUGH	11
7 MAY 94	OBJECTS IN THE REAR VIEW MIRROR MAY APPEAR CLOSER THAN THEY ARE	26
28 OCT 95	I'D LIE FOR YOU (AND THAT'S THE TRUTH)	2
27 JAN 96	NOT A DRY EYE IN THE HOUSE	7
27 APR 96	RUNNIN' FOR THE RED LIGHT (I GOTTA LIFE)	21

•MEAT LOAF•

ALBUMS

11 MAR 78	BAT OUT OF HELL	9
12 SEP 81	DEAD RINGER	1
7 MAY 83	MIDNIGHT AT THE LOST AND FOUND	7
10 NOV 84	BAD ATTITUDE	8
26 JAN 85	HITS OUT OF HELL	2
11 OCT 86	BLIND BEFORE I STOP	28
7 NOV 87	LIVE AT WEMBLEY	60
18 SEP 93	BAT OUT OF HELL II - BACK INTO HELL	1
22 OCT 94	ALIVE IN HELL	33
11 NOV 95	WELCOME TO THE NEIGHBOURHOOD	3

• MICHAEL JACKSON •

SINGLES

12 FEB 72	GOT TO BE THERE	5
20 MAY 72	ROCKIN' ROBIN	3
19 AUG 72	AIN'T NO SUNSHINE	8
25 NOV 72	BEN	7
18 NOV 78	EASE ON DOWN THE ROAD	45
15 SEP 79	DON'T STOP TILL YOU GET ENOUGH	3
24 NOV 79	OFF THE WALL	7
9 FEB 80	ROCK WITH YOU	7
3 MAY 80	SHE'S OUT OF MY LIFE	3
26 JUL 80	GIRLFRIEND	41
23 MAY 81	ONE DAY IN YOUR LIFE	1
1 AUG 81	WE'RE ALMOST THERE	46
6 NOV 82	THE GIRL IS MINE	8
15 JAN 83	THE GIRL IS MINE (RE-ENTRY)	75
29 JAN 83	BILLIE JEAN	1
9 APR 83	BEAT IT	3
11 JUN 83	WANNA BE STARTIN' SOMETHING	8
23 JUL 83	HAPPY (LOVE THEME FROM ('LADY SINGS THE BLUES')	52
15 OCT 83	SAY SAY SAY	2
19 NOV 83	THRILLER	10
31 MAR 84	P.Y.T. (PRETTY YOUNG THING)	11
2 JUN 84	FAREWELL MY SUMMER LOVE	7
11 AUG 84	GIRL YOU'RE SO TOGETHER	33
8 AUG 87	I JUST CAN'T STOP LOVING YOU	1
26 SEP 87	BAD	3
5 DEC 87	THE WAY YOU MAKE ME FEEL	3
20 FEB 88	MAN IN THE MIRROR	21
28 MAY 88	GET IT	37

• MICHAEL JACKSON •

SINGLES CONT...

16 JUL 88	DIRTY DIANA	4
10 SEP 88	ANOTHER PART OF ME	15
26 NOV 88	SMOOTH CRIMINAL	8
25 FEB 89	LEAVE ME ALONE	2
15 JUL 89	LIBERIAN GIRL	13
23 NOV 91	BLACK OR WHITE	1
18 JAN 92	BLACK OR WHITE (RE-MIX)	14
15 FEB 92	REMEMBER THE TIME / COME TOGETHER	3
2 MAY 92	IN THE CLOSET	8
25 JUL 92	WHO IS IT	10
12 SEP 92	JAM	13
5 DEC 92	HEAL THE WORLD	2
27 FEB 93	GIVE IN TO ME	2
10 JUL 93	WILL YOU BE THERE	9
18 DEC 93	GONE TOO SOON	33
10 JUN 95	SCREAM	3
24 JUN 95	SCREAM (RE-MIX)	43
1 SEP 95	SCREAM (RE-ENTRY)	72
2 DEC 95	YOU ARE NOT ALONE	1
9 DEC 95	EARTH SONG	1
20 APR 96	THEY DON'T CARE ABOUT US	4
3 AUG 96	THEY DON'T CARE ABOUT US (RE-ENTRY)	66
17 AUG 96	THEY DON'T CARE ABOUT US (2ND RE-ENTRY)	66
24 AUG 96	WHY	2
16 NOV 96	STRANGER IN MOSCOW	4
3 MAY 97	BLOOD ON THE DANCEFLOOR	1
19 JUL 97	HISTORY / GHOSTS	5

•MICHAEL JACKSON•

ALBUMS

3 JUN 72	GOT TO BE THERE	37
13 JAN 73	BEN	17
29 SEP 79	OFF THE WALL	5
18 JUL 81	ONE DAY IN YOUR LIFE	29
11 DEC 82	THRILLER	1
12 FEB 83	E.T. THE EXTRA TERRESTRIAL	82
9 JUN 84	FAREWELL MY SUMMER LOVE	9
12 SEP 87	BAD	1
31 OCT 87	LOVE SONGS	12
26 DEC 87	THE MICHAEL JACKSON MIX	27
30 NOV 91	DANGEROUS	1
24 JUN 95	HISTORY - PAST PRESENT AND FUTURE BOOK 1	1

• MOTLEY CRUE •

SINGLES

24 AUG 85	SMOKIN' IN THE BOYS ROOM	71
8 FEB 86	HOME SWEET HOME / SMOKIN' IN THE BOYS ROOM (RE-ISSUE)	51
1 AUG 87	GIRLS GIRLS GIRLS	26
16 JAN 88	YOU'RE ALL I NEED / WILD SIDE	23
4 NOV 89	DR. FEELGOOD	50
12 MAY 90	WITHOUT YOU	39
7 SEP 91	PRIMAL SCREAM	32
11 JAN 92	HOME SWEET HOME (RE-MIX)	37
5 MAR 94	HOOLIGAN'S HOLIDAY	36
19 JUL 97	AFRAID	58

ALBUMS

13 JUL 85	THEATRE OF PAIN	36
30 MAY 87	GIRLS GIRLS GIRLS	14
16 SEP 89	DR. FEELGOOD	4
19 OCT 91	DECADE OF DECADENCE	20
26 MAR 94	MOTLEY CRUE	17

•MOTORHEAD•

SINGLES

16 SEP 78	LOUIE LOUIE	75
30 SEP 78	LOUIE LOUIE (RE-ENTRY)	68
10 MAR 79	OVERKILL	39
14 APR 79	OVERKILL (RE-ENTRY)	57
30 JUN 79	NO CLASS	61
1 DEC 79	BOMBER	34
3 MAY 80	THE GOLDEN YEARS EP	8
1 NOV 80	ACE OF SPADES	15
22 NOV 80	BEER DRINKERS AND HELL RAISERS	43
21 FEB 81	ST. VALENTINES DAY MASSACRE EP	5
11 JUL 81	MOTORHEAD LIVE	6
3 APR 82	IRON FIST	29
21 MAY 83	I GOT MINE	46
30 JUL 83	SHINE	59
1 SEP 84	KILLED BY DEATH	51
5 JUL 86	DEAF FOREVER	67
5 JAN 91	THE ONE TO SING THE BLUES	45
14 NOV 92	'92 TOUR EP	63
11 SEP 93	ACE OF SPADES	23
10 DEC 94	BORN TO RAISE HELL	47

• MOTORHEAD •

ALBUMS

24 SEP 77	MOTORHEAD	43
24 MAR 79	OVERKILL	24
27 OCT 79	BOMBER	12
8 DEC 79	ON PARADE	65
8 NOV 80	ACE OF SPADES	4
27 JUN 81	NO SLEEP TILL HAMMERSMITH	1
17 APR 82	IRONFIST	6
26 FEB 83	WHAT'S WORD WORTH	71
4 JUN 83	ANOTHER PERFECT DAY	20
15 SEP 84	NO REMORSE	14
9 AUG 86	ORGASMATRON	21
5 SEP 87	ROCK 'N' ROLL	34
15 OCT 88	NO SLEEP AT ALL	79
2 FEB 91	1916	24
8 AUG 92	MARCH OR DIE	60

• NEIL YOUNG •

SINGLES

11 MAR 72	HEART OF GOLD	10
6 JAN 79	FOUR STRONG WINDS	57
27 FEB 93	HARVEST MOON	36
17 JUL 93	THE NEEDLE AND THE DAMAGE DONE	75
30 OCT 93	LONG MAY YOU RUN (LIVE)	71
9 APR 94	PHILADELPHIA	62

•NEIL YOUNG•

ALBUMS

31 OCT 70	AFTER THE GOLD RUSH	7
4 MAR 72	HARVEST	1
27 OCT 73	TIME FADES AWAY	20
10 AUG 74	ON THE BEACH	42
5 JUL 75	TONIGHT'S THE NIGHT	48
27 DEC 75	ZUMA	44
9 OCT 76	LONG MAY YOU RUN	12
9 JUL 77	AMERICAN STARS 'N' BARS	17
17 DEC 77	DECADE	46
28 OCT 78	COMES A TIME	42
14 JUL 79	RUST NEVER SLEEPS	13
1 DEC 79	LIVE RUST	55
15 NOV 80	HAWKS AND DOVES	34
14 NOV 81	RE-AC-TOR	69
5 FEB 83	TRANS	29
3 SEP 83	EVERYBODY'S ROCKIN'	50
14 SEP 85	OLD WAYS	39
2 AUG 86	LANDING ON WATER	52
4 JUL 87	LIFE	71
30 APR 88	THIS NOTES FOR YOU	56
21 OCT 89	FREEDOM	17
22 SEP 90	RAGGED GLORY	15
2 NOV 91	WELD	20
14 NOV 92	HARVEST MOON	9
23 JAN 93	LUCKY THIRTEEN	69
26 JUN 93	UNPLUGGED	4
27 AUG 94	SLEEPS WITH ANGELS	2

•NEW ORDER•

SINGLES

Date	Title	
14 MAR 81	CEREMONY	34
3 OCT 81	PROCESSION / EVERYTHING'S GONE GREEN	38
22 MAY 82	TEMPTATION	29
19 MAR 83	BLUE MONDAY	12
13 AUG 83	BLUE MONDAY (RE-ENTRY)	9
3 SEP 83	CONFUSION	12
7 JAN 84	BLUE MONDAY (2ND RE-ENTRY)	52
28 APR 84	THIEVES LIKE US	18
25 MAY 85	THE PERFECT KISS	46
9 NOV 85	SUB-CULTURE	63
29 MAR 86	SHELLSHOCK	28
27 SEP 86	STATE OF THE NATION	30
27 SEP 86	THE PEEL SESSIONS (1ST JUNE 1982)	54
15 NOV 86	BIZARRE LOVE TRIANGLE	56
1 AUG 87	TRUE FAITH	4
19 DEC 87	TOUCHED BY THE HAND OF GOD	20
7 MAY 88	BLUE MONDAY (RE-MIX)	3
10 DEC 88	FINE TIME	11
11 MAR 89	ROUND AND ROUND	21
9 SEP 89	RUN 2	49
2 JUN 90	WORLD IN MOTION	1
17 APR 93	REGRET	4
3 JUL 93	RUINED IN A DAY	22
4 SEP 93	WORLD (THE PRICE OF LOVE)	13
18 DEC 93	SPOOKY	22
19 NOV 94	TRUE FAITH (RE-MIX)	9
21 JAN 95	NINETEEN63	21
5 AUG 95	BLUE MONDAY (2ND RE-MIX)	17

•NEW ORDER•

ALBUMS

28 NOV 81	MOVEMENT	30
14 MAY 83	POWER, CORRUPTION AND LIES	4
25 MAY 85	LOW-LIFE	7
11 OCT 86	BROTHERHOOD	9
29 AUG 87	SUBSTANCE	3
11 FEB 89	TECHNIQUE	1
22 FEB 92	BBC RADIO 1 LIVE IN CONCERT	33
15 MAY 93	REPUBLIC	1

•NICK CAVE AND THE BAD SEEDS•

SINGLES

11 APR 92	STRAIGHT TO YOU / JACK THE RIPPER	68
12 DEC 92	WHAT A WONDERFUL WORLD	72
9 APR 94	DO YOU LOVE ME	68
14 OCT 95	WHERE THE WILD ROSES GROW	11
9 MAR 96	HENRY LEE	36
22 FEB 97	INTO MY ARMS	53
31 MAY 97	(ARE YOU) THE ONE THAT I'VE BEEN...	67

ALBUMS

2 JUN 84	FROM HER TO ETERNITY	40
15 JUN 85	THE FIRST BORN IS DEAD	53
30 AUG 86	KICKING AGAINST THE PRICKS	89
1 OCT 88	TENDER PREY	67
28 APR 90	THE GOOD SON	47
9 MAY 92	HENRY'S DREAM	29
18 SEP 93	LIVE SEEDS	67
30 APR 94	LET LOVE IN	12

•NIRVANA•

SINGLES

30 NOV 91	SMELLS LIKE TEEN SPIRIT	7
14 MAR 92	COME AS YOU ARE	9
25 JUL 92	LITHIUM	11
12 DEC 92	IN BLOOM	28
6 MAR 93	OH THE GUILT	12
11 SEP 93	HEART-SHAPED BOX	5
18 DEC 93	ALL APOLOGIES / RAPE ME	32

ALBUMS

5 OCT 91	NEVERMIND	7
7 MAR 92	BLEACH	33
26 DEC 92	INCESTICIDE	14
25 SEP 93	IN UTERO	1
12 NOV 94	UNPLUGGED IN NEW YORK	1

•OASIS•

SINGLES

23 APR 94	SUPERSONIC	31
2 JUL 94	SHAKERMAKER	11
20 AUG 94	LIVE FOREVER	10
22 OCT 94	CIGARETTES AND ALCOHOL	7
31 DEC 94	WHATEVER	3
31 DEC 94	CIGARETTES AND ALCOHOL (RE-ENTRY)	69
6 MAY 95	SOME MIGHT SAY	1
13 MAY 95	SOME MIGHT SAY (RE-ENTRY)	71
24 JUN 95	SUPERSONIC (RE-ENTRY)	44
24 JUN 95	WHATEVER (RE-ENTRY)	48
24 JUN 95	LIVE FOREVER (RE-ENTRY)	50
24 JUN 95	SHAKERMAKER (RE-ENTRY)	52
24 JUN 95	CIGARETTES AND ALCOHOL (2ND RE-ENTRY)	53
26 AUG 95	ROLL WITH IT	2
26 AUG 95	SOME MIGHT SAY (RE-ENTRY)	73
11 NOV 95	WONDERWALL	2
25 NOV 95	WIBBLING RIVALRY (INTERVIEWS WITH NOEL AND LIAM GALLAGHER)	52
9 DEC 95	WHATEVER (2ND RE-ENTRY)	75
30 DEC 95	CIGARETTES AND ALCOHOL (3RD RE-ENTRY)	58
30 DEC 95	WHATEVER (3RD RE-ENTRY)	55
30 DEC 95	SUPERSONIC (2ND RE-ENTRY)	54
6 JAN 96	SHAKERMAKER (2ND RE-ENTRY)	61
6 JAN 96	LIVE FOREVER (2ND RE-ENTRY)	64
6 JAN 96	SOME MIGHT SAY (2ND RE-ENTRY)	59
6 JAN 96	ROLL WITH IT (RE-ENTRY)	65
20 JAN 96	LIVE FOREVER (3RD RE-ENTRY)	71
27 JAN 96	WHATEVER (4TH RE-ENTRY)	61
24 FEB 96	WHATEVER (5TH RE-ENTRY)	55
2 MAR 96	DON'T LOOK BACK IN ANGER	1
2 MAR 96	CIGARETTES AND ALCOHOL (4TH RE-ENTRY)	62

• OASIS •

SINGLES CONT...

2 MAR 96	SUPERSONIC (3RD RE-ENTRY)	71
2 MAR 96	SHAKERMAKER (3RD RE-ENTRY)	74
2 MAR 96	LIVE FOREVER (4TH RE-ENTRY)	74
16 MAR 96	SOME MIGHT SAY (3RD RE-ENTRY)	75
13 APR 96	CIGARETTES AND ALCOHOL (5TH RE-ENTRY)	74
11 MAY 96	CIGARETTES AND ALCOHOL (6TH RE-ENTRY)	72
17 AUG 96	WHATEVER (6TH RE-ENTRY)	62
24 AUG 96	WONDERWALL (RE-ENTRY)	60
24 AUG 96	SOME MIGHT SAY (4TH RE-ENTRY)	70
24 AUG 96	CIGARETTES AND ALCOHOL (7TH RE-ENTRY)	72
21 SEP 96	WHATEVER (7TH RE-ENTRY)	66
16 NOV 96	WHATEVER (8TH RE-ENTRY)	34
16 NOV 96	WONDERWALL (2ND RE-ENTRY)	36
16 NOV 96	CIGARETTES AND ALCOHOL (8TH RE-ENTRY)	38
16 NOV 96	SOME MIGHT SAY (5TH RE-ENTRY)	40
16 NOV 96	LIVE FOREVER (5TH RE-ENTRY)	42
16 NOV 96	SUPERSONIC (4TH RE-ENTRY)	47
16 NOV 96	SHAKERMAKER (3RD RE-ENTRY)	48
16 NOV 96	DON'T LOOK BACK IN ANGER (RE-ENTRY)	53
16 NOV 96	ROLL WITH IT (2ND RE-ENTRY)	55
28 DEC 96	DON'T LOOK BACK IN ANGER (2ND RE-ENTRY)	67
28 DEC 96	CIGARETTES AND ALCOHOL (9TH RE-ENTRY)	71
28 DEC 96	SOME MIGHT SAY (6TH RE-ENTRY)	73
28 DEC 96	LIVE FOREVER (6TH RE-ENTRY)	75
26 JUL 97	D'YOU KNOW WHAT I MEAN?	1
4 OCT 97	STAND BY ME	2
24 JAN 98	ALL AROUND THE WORLD	1

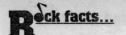
•OASIS•

ALBUMS

10 SEP 94	DEFINITELY MAYBE	1
14 OCT 95	(WHAT'S THE STORY) MORNING GLORY	1

•PAUL McCARTNEY•

SINGLES

22 FEB 71	ANOTHER DAY	2
28 AUG 71	BACK SEAT OF MY CAR	39
26 FEB 72	GIVE IRELAND BACK TO THE IRISH	16
27 MAY 72	MARY HAD A LITTLE LAMB	9
9 DEC 72	HI HI HI / C MOON	5
7 APR 73	MY LOVE	9
9 JUN 73	LIVE AND LET DIE	9
15 SEP 73	LIVE AND LET DIE (RE-ENTRY)	49
3 NOV 73	HELEN WHEELS	12
2 MAR 74	JET	7
6 JUL 74	BAND ON THE RUN	3
9 NOV 74	JUNIOR'S FARM	16
31 MAY 75	LISTEN TO WHAT THE MAN SAID	6
18 OCT 75	LETTING GO	41
15 MAY 76	SILLY LOVE SONGS	2
7 AUG 76	LET 'EM IN	2
19 FEB 77	MAYBE I'M AMAZED	28
19 NOV 77	MULL OF KINTYRE / GIRLS' SCHOOL	1
1 APR 78	WITH A LITTLE LUCK	5
1 JUL 78	I'VE HAD ENOUGH	42
9 SEP 78	LONDON TOWN	60
7 APR 79	GOODNIGHT TONIGHT	5
16 JUN 79	OLD SIAM SIR	35
1 SEP 79	GETTING CLOSER / BABY'S REQUEST	60
1 DEC 79	WONDERFUL CHRISTMASTIME	6
19 APR 80	COMING UP	2
21 JUN 80	WATERFALLS	9

• PAUL McCARTNEY •

SINGLES CONT...

10 APR 82	EBONY AND IVORY	1
3 JUL 82	TAKE IT AWAY	15
9 OCT 82	TUG OF WAR	53
6 NOV 82	THE GIRL IS MINE	8
15 JAN 83	THE GIRL IS MINE (RE-ENTRY)	75
15 OCT 83	SAY SAY SAY	2
17 DEC 83	PIPES OF PEACE	1
6 OCT 84	NO MORE LONELY NIGHTS (BALLAD)	2
24 NOV 84	WE ALL STAND TOGETHER	3
30 NOV 85	SPIES LIKE US	13
21 DEC 85	WE ALL STAND TOGETHER (RE-ENTRY)	32
26 JUL 86	PRESS	25
13 DEC 86	ONLY LOVE REMAINS	34
28 NOV 87	ONCE UPON A LONG AGO	10
20 MAY 89	FERRY 'CROSS THE MERSEY	1
20 MAY 89	MY BRAVE FACE	18
29 JUL 89	THIS ONE	18
25 NOV 89	FIGURE OF EIGHT	42
17 FEB 90	PUT IT THERE	32
20 OCT 90	BIRTHDAY	29
8 DEC 90	ALL MY TRIALS	35
5 FEB 93	HOPE OF DELIVERANCE	18
6 MAR 93	C'MON PEOPLE	41
10 MAY 97	YOUNG BOYS	19
26 JUL 97	THE WORLD TONIGHT	23
27 DEC 97	BEAUTIFUL TONIGHT	25

• PAUL McCARTNEY •

ALBUMS

2 MAY 70	McCARTNEY	2
5 JUN 71	RAM	1
18 DEC 71	WILD LIFE	11
19 MAY 73	RED ROSE SPEEDWAY	5
15 DEC 73	BAND ON THE RUN	1
21 JUN 75	VENUS AND MARS	1
17 APR 76	WINGS AT THE SPEED OF SOUND	2
15 JAN 77	WINGS OVER AMERICA	8
15 APR 78	LONDON TOWN	4
16 DEC 78	WINGS GREATEST HITS	5
23 JUN 79	BACK TO THE EGG	6
31 MAY 80	McCARTNEY II	1
7 MAR 81	McCARTNEY INTERVIEW	34
8 MAY 82	TUG OF WAR	1
12 NOV 83	PIPES OF PEACE	4
3 NOV 84	GIVE MY REGARDS TO BROAD STREET	1
13 SEP 86	PRESS TO PLAY	8
14 NOV 87	ALL THE BEST!	2
17 JUN 89	FLOWERS IN THE DIRT	1
17 NOV 89	FLOWERS IN THE DIRT	1
17 NOV 90	TRIPPING THE LIVE FANTASTIC	17
1 JUN 91	UNPLUGGED - THE OFFICIAL BOOTLEG	7
12 OCT 91	CHOBA B CCCP (THE RUSSIAN ALBUM)	63
13 FEB 93	OFF THE GROUND	5
20 NOV 93	PAUL IS LIVE	34

• PAUL WELLER •

SINGLES

18 MAY 91	INTO TOMORROW	36
15 AUG 92	UH HUH OH YEH	18
10 OCT 92	ABOVE THE CLOUDS	47
17 JUL 93	SUNFLOWER	16
4 SEP 93	WILD WOOD	14
13 NOV 93	THE WEAVER EP	18
9 APR 94	HUNG UP	11
5 NOV 94	OUT OF THE SINKING	20
6 MAY 95	THE CHANGINGMAN	7
22 JUL 95	YOU DO SOMETHING TO ME	9
30 SEP 95	BROKEN STONES	20
9 MAR 96	OUT OF THE SINKING	16
17 AUG 96	PEACOCK SUIT	5
9 AUG 97	BRUSHED	14
11 OCT 97	FRIDAY STREET	21
6 DEC 97	MERMAIDS	30
14 NOV 98	BRAND NEW START	16

ALBUMS

12 SEP 92	PAUL WELLER	8
18 SEP 93	WILD WOOD	2
24 SEP 94	LIVE WOOD	13
27 MAY 95	STANLEY ROAD	1

•PEARL JAM•

SINGLES

15 FEB 92	ALIVE	16
18 APR 92	EVEN FLOW	27
26 SEP 92	JEREMY	15
1 JAN 94	DAUGHTER	18
28 MAY 94	DISSIDENT	14
26 NOV 94	SPIN THE BLACK CIRCLE	10
25 FEB 95	NOT FOR YOU	34
16 DEC 95	I GOT ID	25
17 AUG 96	WHO ARE YOU	18
31 JAN 98	GIVEN TO FLY	12
23 MAY 98	WISHLIST	30

ALBUMS

7 MAR 92	TEN	18
23 OCT 93	VS	2
3 DEC 94	VITALOGY	4

•PINK FLOYD•

SINGLES

30 MAR 67	ARNOLD LAYNE	20
22 JUN 67	SEE EMILY PLAY	6
1 DEC 79	ANOTHER BRICK IN THE WALL (PART 2)	1
7 AUG 82	WHEN THE TIGERS BROKE FREE	39
7 MAY 83	NOT NOW JOHN	30
19 DEC 87	ON THE TURNING AWAY	55
25 JUN 88	ONE SLIP	50
4 JUN 94	TAKE IT BACK	23
29 OCT 94	HIGH HOPES / KEEP TALKING	26

ALBUMS

19 AUG 67	PIPER AT THE GATES OF DAWN	6
13 JUL 68	SAUCERFUL OF SECRETS	9
28 JUN 69	MORE (FILM SOUNDTRACK)	9
15 NOV 69	UMMAGUMMA	5
24 OCT 70	ATOM HEART MOTHER	1
7 AUG 71	RELICS	32
20 NOV 71	MEDDLE	3
17 JUN 72	OBSCURED BY CLOUDS (FILM SOUNDTRACK)	6
31 MAR 73	THE DARK SIDE OF THE MOON	2
27 SEP 75	WISH YOU WERE HERE	1
19 FEB 77	ANIMALS	2
8 DEC 79	THE WALL	3
5 DEC 81	A COLLECTION OF GREAT DANCE SONGS	37
2 APR 83	THE FINAL CUT	1
19 SEP 87	A MOMENTARY LAPSE OF REASON	3
3 DEC 88	DELICATE SOUND OF THUNDER	11
9 APR 94	THE DIVISION BELL	1
10 JUN 95	PULSE	1

• PRINCE •

SINGLES

19 JAN 80	I WANNA BE YOUR LOVER	41
29 JAN 83	1999	25
30 APR 83	LITTLE RED CORVETTE	54
26 NOV 83	LITTLE RED CORVETTE (RE-ISSUE)	66
30 JUN 84	WHEN DOVES CRY	4
22 SEP 84	PURPLE RAIN	8
8 DEC 84	I WOULD DIE 4 U	58
19 JAN 85	1999 / LITTLE RED CORVETTE (RE-ISSUE)	2
23 FEB 85	LET'S GO CRAZY / TAKE ME WITH U	7
25 MAY 85	PAISLEY PARK	18
27 JUL 85	RASPBERRY BERET	25
26 OCT 85	POP LIFE	60
8 MAR 86	KISS	6
14 JUN 86	MOUNTAINS	45
16 AUG 86	GIRLS AND BOYS	11
1 NOV 86	ANOTHERLOVERHOLENYOHEAD	36
14 MAR 87	SIGN 'O' THE TIMES	10
20 JUN 87	IF I WAS YOUR GIRLFRIEND	20
15 AUG 87	U GOT THE LOOK	11
28 NOV 87	I COULD NEVER TAKE THE PLACE OF YOUR MAN	29
7 MAY 88	ALPHABET STREET	9
23 JUL 88	GLAM SLAM	29
5 NOV 88	I WISH U HEAVEN	24
24 JUN 89	BATDANCE	2
9 SEP 89	PARTYMAN	14
18 NOV 89	THE ARMS OF ORION	27
4 AUG 90	THIEVES IN THE TEMPLE	7
10 NOV 90	NEW POWER GENERATION	26
31 AUG 91	GETT OFF	4
21 SEP 91	CREAM	15
7 DEC 91	DIAMONDS AND PEARLS	25

• PRINCE •

SINGLES CONT...

28 MAR 92	MONEY DON'T MATTER 2 NIGHT	19
27 JUN 92	THUNDER	28
18 JUL 92	SEXY MF / STROLLIN'	4
10 OCT 92	MY NAME IS PRINCE	7
14 NOV 92	MY NAME IS PRINCE (RE-MIX)	51
5 DEC 92	7	27
13 MAR 93	THE MORNING PAPERS	52
16 OCT 93	CONTROVERSY	5
9 APR 94	THE MOST BEAUTIFUL GIRL IN THE WORLD	1
4 JUN 94	THE BEAUTIFUL EXPERIENCE (RE-MIX)	18
10 SEP 94	LETITGO	30
18 MAR 95	PURPLE MEDLEY	33
23 SEP 95	EYE HATE U	20
9 DEC 95	GOLD	10
3 AUG 96	DINNER WITH DELORES	36
14 DEC 96	BETCHA BY GOLLY WOW	11
8 MAR 97	THE HOLY RIVER	19

ALBUMS

21 JUL 84	PURPLE RAIN (FILM SOUNDTRACK)	7
8 SEP 84	1999	30
4 MAY 85	AROUND THE WORLD IN A DAY	5
12 APR 86	PARADE - MUSIC FROM 'UNDER THE CHERRY MOON' (FILM SOUNDTRACK)	4
11 APR 87	SIGN 'O' THE TIMES	4
21 MAY 88	LOVESEXY	1
1 JUL 89	BATMAN (FILM SOUNDTRACK)	1
1 SEP 90	GRAFFITI BRIDGE	1
24 AUG 91	GETT OFF (IMPORT)	33
12 OCT 91	DIAMONDS AND PEARLS	2
17 OCT 92	SYMBOL	1
27 AUG 94	COME	1
3 DEC 94	THE BLACK ALBUM	36
7 OCT 95	THE GOLD EXPERIENCE	4

•PRODIGY•

SINGLES

24 AUG 91	CHARLY	3
4 JAN 92	EVERYBODY IN THE PLACE EP	2
26 SEP 92	FIRE / JERICHO	11
21 NOV 92	OUT OF SPACE / RUFF IN THE JUNGLE BIZNESS	5
17 APR 93	WIND IT UP (REWOUND)	11
16 OCT 93	ONE LOVE	8
28 MAY 94	NO GOOD (START THE DANCE)	4
24 SEP 94	VOODOO PEOPLE	13
18 MAR 95	POISON	15
30 MAR 96	FIRESTARTER	1
20 APR 96	OUT OF SPACE / RUFF IN THE JUNGLE BIZNESS (RE-ENTRY)	52
20 APR 96	NO GOOD (START THE DANCE) (RE-ENTRY)	57
20 APR 96	POISON (RE-ENTRY)	62
20 APR 96	FIRE / JERICHO (RE-ENTRY)	63
20 APR 96	CHARLY (RE-ENTRY)	66
20 APR 96	WIND IT UP (REWOUND) (RE-ENTRY)	71
20 APR 96	VOODOO PEOPLE (RE-ENTRY)	75
27 APR 96	EVERYBODY IN THE PLACE EP (RE-ENTRY)	69
23 NOV 96	BREATHE	1
14 DEC 96	FIRESTARTER (RE-ENTRY)	70
25 JAN 97	FIRESTARTER (RE-ENTRY)	53
5 APR 97	BREATHE (RE-ENTRY)	71
29 NOV 97	SMACK MY BITCH UP	8

ALBUMS

10 OCT 92	EXPERIENCE	12
16 JUL 94	MUSIC FOR THE JILTED GENERATION	1

• PUBLIC IMAGE LTD •

SINGLES

21 OCT 78	PUBLIC IMAGE	9
7 JUL 79	DEATH DISCO	20
20 OCT 79	MEMORIES	60
4 APR 81	FLOWERS OF ROMANCE	24
17 SEP 83	THIS IS NOT A LOVE SONG	5
19 MAY 84	BAD LIFE	71
1 FEB 86	RISE	11
3 MAY 86	HOME	75
22 AUG 87	SEATTLE	47
6 MAY 89	DISAPPOINTED	38
20 OCT 90	DON'T ASK ME	22
22 FEB 92	CRUEL	49

ALBUMS

23 DEC 78	PUBLIC IMAGE	22
8 DEC 79	METAL BOX	18
8 MAR 80	SECOND EDITION OF PIL	46
22 NOV 80	PARIS IN THE SPRING	61
18 APR 81	FLOWERS OF ROMANCE	11
8 OCT 83	LIVE IN TOKYO	28
21 JUL 84	THIS IS WHAT YOU WANT... THIS IS WHAT YOU GET	56
15 FEB 86	ALBUM / CASSETTE	14
26 SEP 87	HAPPY?	40
10 JUN 89	9	36
7 MAR 92	THAT WHAT IS NOT	46

•PULP•

SINGLES

27 NOV 93	LIP GLOSS	50
2 APR 94	DO YOU REMEMBER THE FIRST TIME	33
4 JUN 94	THE SISTERS EP	19
3 JUN 95	COMMON PEOPLE	2
7 OCT 95	MIS-SHAPES / SORTED FOR E'S AND WIZZ	2
9 DEC 95	DISCO 2000	7
30 DEC 95	MIS-SHAPES / SORTED FOR E'S AND WIZZ (RE-ENTRY)	62
6 APR 96	SOMETHING CHANGED	10
8 JUN 96	SOMETHING CHANGED (RE-ENTRY)	62
22 JUN 96	SOMETHING CHANGED (2ND RE-ENTRY)	61
7 SEP 96	DO YOU REMEMBER THE FIRST TIME (RE-ENTRY)	73
22 NOV 97	HELP THE AGED	8
24 JAN 98	HELP THE AGED (RE-ENTRY)	74
28 MAR 98	THIS IS HARDCORE	12
20 JUN 98	A LITTLE SOUL	22
19 SEP 98	PARTY HARD	29

ALBUMS

30 APR 94	HIS 'N' HERS	9
11 NOV 95	DIFFERENT CLASS	1

•QUEEN•

SINGLES

Date	Title	Position
9 MAR 74	SEVEN SEAS OF RHYE	10
26 OCT 74	KILLER QUEEN	2
25 JAN 75	NOW I'M HERE	11
8 NOV 75	BOHEMIAN RHAPSODY	1
3 JUL 76	YOU'RE MY BEST FRIEND	7
27 NOV 76	SOMEBODY TO LOVE	2
19 MAR 77	TIE YOUR MOTHER DOWN	31
4 JUN 77	QUEEN'S FIRST EP	17
22 OCT 77	WE ARE THE CHAMPIONS	2
25 FEB 78	SPREAD YOUR WINGS	34
28 OCT 78	BICYCLE RACE / FAT BOTTOMED GIRLS	11
10 FEB 79	DON'T STOP ME NOW	9
14 JUL 79	LOVE OF MY LIFE	11
20 OCT 79	CRAZY LITTLE THING CALLED LOVE	2
2 FEB 80	SAVE ME	11
14 JUN 80	PLAY THE GAME	14
6 SEP 80	ANOTHER ONE BITES THE DUST	7
6 DEC 80	FLASH	10
14 NOV 81	UNDER PRESSURE	1
1 MAY 82	BODY LANGUAGE	25
12 JUN 82	LAS PALABRAS DE AMOR	17
21 AUG 82	BACKCHAT	40
4 FEB 84	RADIO GAGA	2
14 APR 84	I WANT TO BREAK FREE	3
28 JUL 84	IT'S A HARD LIFE	6
22 SEP 84	HAMMER TO FALL	13
8 DEC 84	THANK GOD IT'S CHRISTMAS	21

•QUEEN•

SINGLES CONT...

16 NOV 85	ONE VISION	7
29 MAR 86	A KIND OF MAGIC	3
21 JUN 86	FRIENDS WILL BE FRIENDS	14
27 SEP 86	WHO WANTS TO LIVE FOREVER	24
13 MAY 89	I WANT IT ALL	3
1 JUL 89	BREAKTHRU'	7
19 AUG 89	THE INVISIBLE MAN	12
21 OCT 89	SCANDAL	25
9 DEC 89	THE MIRACLE	21
26 JAN 91	INNUENDO	1
25 MAY 91	I'M GOING SLIGHTLY MAD	22
25 MAY 91	HEADLONG	14
26 OCT 91	THE SHOW MUST GO ON	16
7 DEC 91	THE SHOW MUST GO ON (RE-ENTRY)	27
21 DEC 91	BOHEMIAN RHAPSODY (RE-ISSUE) / THESE ARE THE DAYS OF OUR LIVES	1
1 MAY 93	FIVE LIVE EP	1
24 JUL 93	FIVE LIVE EP (RE-ENTRY)	74
4 NOV 95	HEAVEN FOR EVERYONE	2
23 DEC 95	A WINTER'S TALE	6
9 MAR 96	TOO MUCH LOVE WILL KILL YOU	15
29 JUN 96	LET ME LIVE	9
30 NOV 96	YOU DON'T FOOL ME	17
17 JAN 98	NO-ONE BUT YOU / TIE YOUR MOTHER DOWN	13
14 NOV 98	ANOTHER ONE BITES THE DUST	5

•QUEEN•

ALBUMS

23 MAR 74	QUEEN 2	5
30 MAR 74	QUEEN	24
23 NOV 74	SHEER HEART ATTACK	2
13 DEC 75	A NIGHT AT THE OPERA	1
25 DEC 76	A DAY AT THE RACES	1
12 NOV 77	NEWS OF THE WORLD	4
25 NOV 78	JAZZ	2
7 JUL 79	LIVE KILLERS	3
12 JUL 80	THE GAME	1
20 DEC 80	FLASH GORDON (FILM SOUNDTRACK)	10
15 MAY 82	HOT SPACE	4
10 MAR 84	THE WORKS	2
14 JUN 86	A KIND OF MAGIC	1
13 DEC 86	LIVE MAGIC	3
3 JUN 89	THE MIRACLE	1
16 DEC 89	QUEEN AT THE BEEB	67
16 FEB 91	INNUENDO	1
6 JUN 92	LIVE AT WEMBLEY '86	2
18 NOV 95	MADE IN HEAVEN	1

•R.E.M•

SINGLES

28 NOV 87	THE ONE I LOVE	51
30 APR 88	FINEST WORKSONG	50
4 FEB 89	STAND	51
3 JUN 89	ORANGE CRUSH	28
12 AUG 89	STAND (RE-ISSUE)	48
9 MAR 91	LOSING MY RELIGION	19
18 MAY 91	SHINY HAPPY PEOPLE	6
17 AUG 91	NEAR WILD HEAVEN	27
21 SEP 91	THE ONE I LOVE (RE-ISSUE)	16
16 NOV 91	RADIO SONG	28
14 DEC 91	IT'S THE END OF THE WORLD AS WE KNOW IT	39
3 OCT 92	DRIVE	11
28 NOV 92	MAN ON THE MOON	18
20 FEB 93	THE SINDWINDER SLEEPS TONITE	17
17 APR 93	EVERYBODY HURTS	7
24 JUL 93	NIGHTSWIMMING	27
11 DEC 93	FIND THE RIVER	54
17 SEP 94	WHAT'S THE FREQUENCY, KENNETH	9
12 NOV 94	BANG AND BLAME	15
4 FEB 95	CRUSH WITH EYELINER	23
15 APR 95	STRANGE CURRENCIES	9
29 JUL 95	TONGUE	13
31 AUG 96	E-BOW THE LETTER	4
2 NOV 96	BITTERSWEET ME	19
14 DEC 96	ELECTROLITE	29
24 OCT 98	DAYSLEEPER	6
19 DEC 98	LOTUS	26

•R.E.M•

ALBUMS

28 APR 84	RECKONING	91
29 JUN 85	FABLES OF THE RECONSTRUCTION	35
6 SEP 86	LIFE'S RICH PAGEANT	43
16 MAY 87	DEAD LETTER OFFICE	60
26 SEP 87	DOCUMENT	28
29 OCT 88	EPONYMOUS	69
19 NOV 88	GREEN	27
23 MAR 91	OUT OF TIME	1
10 OCT 92	AUTOMATIC FOR THE PEOPLE	1
8 OCT 94	MONSTER	1

• RADIOHEAD •

SINGLES

13 FEB 93	ANYONE CAN PLAY GUITAR	32
22 MAY 93	POP IS DEAD	42
18 SEP 93	CREEP	7
8 OCT 94	MY IRON LUNG	24
11 MAR 95	HIGH AND DRY / PLANET TELEX	17
27 MAY 95	FAKE PLASTIC TREES	20
2 SEP 95	JUST	19
3 FEB 96	STREET SPIRIT (FADE OUT)	5
7 JUN 97	PARANOID ANDROID	3
6 SEP 97	KARMA POLICE	8
24 JAN 98	NO SURPRISES	4

ALBUMS

| 6 MAR 93 | PABLO HONEY | 25 |
| 25 MAR 95 | THE BENDS | 6 |

•RAINBOW•

SINGLES

17 SEP 77	KILL THE KING	44
8 APR 78	LONG LIVE ROCK 'N' ROLL	33
30 SEP 78	L.A. CONNECTION	40
15 SEP 79	SINCE YOU'VE BEEN GONE	6
16 FEB 80	ALL NIGHT LONG	5
31 JAN 81	I SURRENDER	3
20 JUN 81	CAN'T HAPPEN HERE	20
11 JUL 81	KILL THE KING (RE-ISSUE)	41
3 APR 82	STONE COLD	34
27 AUG 83	STREET OF DREAMS	52
5 NOV 83	CAN'T LET GO	43

ALBUMS

13 SEP 75	RITCHIE BLACKMORE'S RAINBOW	11
5 JUN 76	RAINBOW RISING	11
30 JUL 77	ON STAGE	7
6 MAY 78	LONG LIVE ROCK 'N' ROLL	7
18 AUG 79	DOWN TO EARTH	6
21 FEB 81	DIFFICULT TO CURE	3
24 APR 82	STRAIGHT BETWEEN THE EYES	5
17 SEP 83	BENT OUT OF SHAPE	11
8 MAR 86	FINYL VINYL	31

• RED HOT CHILI PEPPERS •

SINGLES

10 FEB 90	HIGHER GROUND	55
23 JUN 90	TASTE THE PAIN	29
8 SEP 90	HIGHER GROUND (RE-ISSUE)	54
14 MAR 92	UNDER THE BRIDGE	26
15 AUG 92	BREAKING THE GIRL	41
5 FEB 94	GIVE IT AWAY	9
30 APR 94	UNDER THE BRIDGE (RE-ISSUE)	13
2 SEP 95	WARPED	31
21 OCT 95	MY FRIENDS	29
17 FEB 96	AEROPLANE	11
14 JUN 97	LOVE ROLLERCOASTER	7

ALBUMS

12 OCT 91	BLOOD SUGAR SEX MAGIK	25
17 OCT 92	WHAT HITS!?	23
19 NOV 94	OUT IN L.A.	61
23 SEP 95	ONE HOT MINUTE	2

•ROBERT PALMER•

SINGLES

20 MAY 78	EVERY KINDA PEOPLE	53
7 JUL 79	BAD CASE OF LOVIN' YOU (DOCTOR DOCTOR)	61
6 SEP 80	JOHNNY AND MARY	44
22 NOV 80	LOOKING FOR CLUES	33
13 FEB 82	SOME GUYS HAVE ALL THE LUCK	16
2 APR 83	YOU ARE IN MY SYSTEM	53
18 JUN 83	YOU CAN HAVE IT (TAKE MY HEART)	66
10 MAY 86	ADDICTED TO LOVE	5
19 JUL 86	I DIDN'T MEAN TO TURN YOU ON	9
1 NOV 86	DISCIPLINE OF LOVE	68
26 MAR 88	SWEET LIES	58
11 JUN 88	SIMPLY IRRESISTABLE	44
15 OCT 88	SHE MAKES MY DAY	6
13 MAY 89	CHANGE HIS WAYS	28
26 AUG 89	IT COULD HAPPEN TO YOU	71
3 NOV 90	I'LL BE YOUR BABY TONIGHT	6
5 JAN 91	MERCY MERCY ME - I WANT YOU	9
15 JUN 91	DREAMS TO REMEMBER	68
7 MAR 92	EVERY KINDA PEOPLE (RE-ISSUE)	43
17 OCT 92	WITCHCRAFT	50
9 JUL 94	GIRL U WANT	57
3 SEP 94	KNOW BY NOW	25
24 DEC 94	YOU BLOW ME AWAY	38
14 OCT 95	RESPECT YOURSELF	45

• ROBBIE WILLIAMS •

SINGLES

29 JUL 96	FREEDOM	2
14 APR 97	OLD BEFORE I DIE	2
14 JUL 97	LAZY DAYS	8
15 SEP 97	SOUTH OF THE BORDER	14
1 DEC 97	ANGELS	4
16 MAR 98	LET ME ENTERTAIN YOU	3
7 SEP 98	MILLENNIUM	1
30 NOV 98	NO REGRETS	4
15 MAR 99	STRONG	4
8 NOV 99	SHE'S THE ONE / ITS ONLY US	1

ALBUMS

29 SEP 97	LIFE THRU A LENS	1
26 OCT 98	I'VE BEEN EXPECTING YOU	1

•ROBERT PLANT•

SINGLES

9 OCT 82	BURNING DOWN ONE SIDE	73
16 JUL 83	BIG LOG	11
30 JAN 88	HEAVEN KNOWS	33
28 APR 90	HURTING KIND (I'VE GOT MY EYES ON YOU)	45
8 MAY 93	29 PALMS	21
3 JUL 93	I BELIEVE	64
25 DEC 93	IF I WERE A CARPENTER	63
17 DEC 94	GALLOWS POLE	35
11 APR 98	MOST HIGH	26

ALBUMS

10 JUL 82	PICTURES AT ELEVEN	2
23 JUL 83	THE PRINCIPLES OF MOMENTS	7
1 JUN 85	SHAKEN 'N' STIRRED	19
12 FEB 88	NOW AND ZEN	10
31 MAR 90	MANIC NIRVANA	15
5 JUN 93	FATE OF NATIONS	6
19 NOV 94	NO QUARTER	7

• ROBERT PALMER •

ALBUMS

6 NOV 76	SOME PEOPLE CAN DO WHAT THEY LIKE	46
14 JUL 79	SECRETS	54
6 SEP 80	CLUES	31
3 APR 82	MAYBE IT'S LIVE	32
23 APR 83	PRIDE	37
16 NOV 85	RIPTIDE	5
9 JUL 88	HEAVY NOVA	17
11 NOV 89	ADDICTIONS VOLUME 1	7
17 NOV 90	DON'T EXPLAIN	9
4 APR 92	ADDICTIONS VOLUME 2	12
31 OCT 92	RIDIN' HIGH	32
24 SEP 94	HONEY	25

• ROD STEWART •

SINGLES

Date	Title	Position
4 SEP 71	REASON TO BELIEVE	19
18 SEP 71	MAGGIE MAY	1
12 AUG 72	YOU WEAR IT WELL	1
18 NOV 72	ANGEL / WHAT MADE MILWAUKEE FAMOUS (HAS MADE A LOSER OUT OF ME)	4
5 MAY 73	I'VE BEEN DRINKING	27
8 SEP 73	OH NO NOT MY BABY	6
5 OCT 74	FAREWELL - BRING IT ON HOME TO ME / YOU SEND ME	7
16 AUG 75	SAILING	1
15 NOV 75	THIS OLD HEART OF MINE	4
5 JUN 76	TONIGHT'S THE NIGHT	5
21 AUG 76	THE KILLING OF GEORGIE	2
4 SEP 76	SAILING (RE-ENTRY)	3
20 NOV 76	GET BACK	11
4 DEC 76	MAGGIE MAY (RE-ENTRY)	31
23 APR 77	I DON'T WANT TO TALK ABOUT IT / FIRST CUT IS THE DEEPEST	1
15 OCT 77	YOU'RE IN MY HEART	3
28 JAN 78	HOTLEGS / I WAS ONLY JOKING	5
27 MAY 78	OLE OLA (MULHER BRASILEIRA)	4
18 NOV 78	DA YA THINK I'M SEXY?	1
3 FEB 79	AIN'T LOVE A BITCH	11
5 MAY 79	BLONDES (HAVE MORE FUN)	63
31 MAY 80	IF LOVING YOU IS WRONG (I DON'T WANT TO BE RIGHT)	23
8 NOV 80	PASSION	17
20 DEC 80	MY GIRL	32
17 OCT 81	TONIGHT I'M YOURS (DON'T HURT ME)	8
12 DEC 81	YOUNG TURKS	11
27 FEB 82	HOW LONG	41

• ROD STEWART •

SINGLES CONT...

4 JUN 83	BABY JANE	1
27 AUG 83	WHAT AM I GONNA DO (I'M SO IN LOVE WITH YOU)	3
10 DEC 83	SWEET SURRENDER	23
26 MAY 84	INFATUATION	27
28 JUL 84	SOME GUYS HAVE ALL THE LUCK	15
24 MAY 86	LOVE TOUCH	27
5 JUL 86	LOVE TOUCH (RE-ENTRY)	69
12 JUL 86	EVERY BEAT OF MY HEART	2
20 SEP 86	ANOTHER HEARTACHE	54
28 MAR 87	SAILING (2ND RE-ENTRY)	41
28 MAY 88	LOST IN YOU	21
13 AUG 88	FOREVER YOUNG	57
6 MAY 89	MY HEART CAN'T TELL YOU NO	49
11 NOV 89	THIS OLD HEART OF MINE	51
13 JAN 90	DOWNTOWN TRAIN	10
24 NOV 90	IT TAKES TWO	5
16 MAR 91	RHYTHM OF MY HEART	3
15 JUN 91	THE MOTOWN SONG	10
7 SEP 91	BROKEN ARROW	54
7 MAR 92	PEOPLE GET READY	49
18 APR 92	YOUR SONG / BROKEN ARROW (RE-ISSUE)	41
5 DEC 92	TOM TRAUBERT'S BLUES (WALTZING MATILDA)	6
20 FEB 93	RUBY TUESDAY	11
17 APR 93	SHOTGUN WEDDING	21
26 JUN 93	HAVE I TOLD YOU LATELY	5
21 AUG 93	REASON TO BELIEVE	51
18 DEC 93	PEOPLE GET READY	45

•ROD STEWART•

SINGLES CONT...

15 JAN 94	ALL FOR LOVE	2
20 MAY 95	YOU'RE THE STAR	19
19 AUG 95	LADY LUCK	56
15 JUN 96	PURPLE HEATHER	16
14 DEC 96	IF WE FALL IN LOVE TONIGHT	58
1 NOV 97	DA YA THINK I'M SEXY	7
30 MAY 98	OOH LA LA	16
5 SEP 98	ROCKS	55

ALBUMS

3 OCT 70	GASOLINE ALLEY	62
24 JUL 71	EVERY PICTURE TELLS A STORY	1
5 AUG 72	NEVER A DULL MOMENT	1
25 AUG 73	SING IT AGAIN ROD	1
19 OCT 74	SMILER	1
30 AUG 75	ATLANTIC CROSSING	1
3 JUL 76	A NIGHT ON THE TOWN	1
19 NOV 77	FOOT LOOSE AND FANCY FREE	3
9 DEC 78	BLONDES HAVE MORE FUN	3
22 NOV 80	FOOLISH BEHAVIOUR	4
14 NOV 81	TONIGHT I'M YOURS	8
13 NOV 82	ABSOLUTELY LIVE	35
18 JUN 83	BODY WISHES	5
23 JUN 84	CAMOUFLAGE	8
5 JUL 86	EVERY BEAT OF MY HEART	5
4 JUN 88	OUT OF ORDER	11
6 APR 91	VAGABOND HEART	2
6 MAR 93	ROD STEWART, LEAD VOCALIST	3
5 JUN 93	UNPLUGGED...AND SEATED	2
10 JUN 95	A SPANNER IN THE WORKS	4

• ROY ORBISON •

SINGLES

28 JUL 60	ONLY THE LONELY	36
11 AUG 60	ONLY THE LONELY (RE-ENTRY)	1
27 OCT 60	BLUE ANGEL	11
25 MAY 61	RUNNING SCARED	9
21 SEP 61	CRYIN'	25
8 MAR 62	DREAM BABY	2
28 JUN 62	THE CROWD	40
8 NOV 62	WORKIN' FOR THE MAN	50
28 FEB 63	IN DREAMS	6
30 MAY 63	FALLING	9
19 SEP 63	BLUE BAYOU / MEAN WOMAN BLUES	3
20 FEB 64	BORNE ON THE WIND	15
30 APR 64	IT'S OVER	1
10 SEP 64	OH PRETTY WOMAN	1
19 NOV 64	PRETTY PAPER	6
11 FEB 65	GOODNIGHT	14
22 JUL 65	(SAY) YOU'RE MY GIRL	23
9 SEP 65	RIDE AWAY	34
4 NOV 65	CRAWLIN' BACK	19
27 JAN 66	BREAKIN' UP IS BREAKIN' MY HEART	22
7 APR 66	TWINKLE TOES	29
16 JUN 66	LANA	15
18 AUG 66	TOO SOON TO KNOW	3
1 DEC 66	THERE WONT BE MANY COMING HOME	12
23 FEB 67	SO GOOD	32
24 JUL 68	WALK ON	39
25 SEP 68	HEARTACHE	44
30 APR 69	MY FRIEND	35
13 SEP 69	PENNY ARCADE	40
11 OCT 69	PENNY ARCADE (RE-ENTRY)	27

•ROY ORBISON•

SINGLES CONT...

14 JAN 89	YOU GOT IT	3
1 APR 89	SHE'S A MYSTERY TO ME	27
4 JUL 92	I DROVE ALL NIGHT	7
22 AUG 92	CRYING	13
7 NOV 92	HEARTBREAK RADIO	36
13 NOV 93	I DROVE ALL NIGHT (RE-ISSUE)	47

ALBUMS

8 JUN 63	LONELY AND BLUE	15
29 JUN 63	CRYING	17
30 NOV 63	IN DREAMS	6
25 JUL 64	EXCITING SOUNDS OF ROY ORBISON	17
5 DEC 64	OH PRETTY WOMAN	4
25 SEP 65	THERE IS ONLY ONE ROY ORBISON	10
26 FEB 66	THE ORBISON WAY	11
22 JUL 67	ORBISONGS	40
11 FEB 89	MYSTERY GIRL	2
25 NOV 89	A BLACK AND WHITE NIGHT	51
2 NOV 90	BALLADS	38
28 NOV 92	KING OF HEARTS	23

• SANTANA •

SINGLES

28 SEP 74	SAMBA PA TI	27
15 OCT 77	SHE'S NOT THERE	11
25 NOV 78	WELL ALL RIGHT	53
22 MAR 80	ALL I EVER WANTED	57

ALBUMS

2 MAY 70	SANTANA	26
28 NOV 70	ABRAXAS	7
13 NOV 71	SANTANA 3	6
26 AUG 72	CARLOS SANTANA AND BUDDY MILES LIVE	29
25 NOV 72	CARAVANSERAI	6
28 JUL 73	LOVE DEVOTION SURRENDER	7
8 DEC 73	WELCOME	8
2 NOV 74	ILLUMINATIONS	40
30 NOV 74	BARBOLETTA	18
10 APR 76	AMIGOS	21
8 JAN 77	FESTIVAL	27
5 NOV 77	MOONFLOWER	7
11 NOV 78	INNER SECRETS	17
24 MAR 79	ONENESS - SILVER DREAMS GOLDEN REALITY	55
27 OCT 79	MARATHON	28
20 SEP 80	THE SWING OF DELIGHT	65
18 APR 81	ZE BOP	33
14 AUG 82	SHANGO	35
30 APR 83	HAVANA MOON	84
23 MAR 85	BEYOND APPEARANCES	58
14 JUL 90	SPIRITS DANCING IN THE FLESH	68

• SEX PISTOLS •

SINGLES

18 DEC 76	ANARCHY IN THE UK	38
4 JUN 77	GOD SAVE THE QUEEN	2
9 JUL 77	PRETTY VACANT	6
22 OCT 77	HOLIDAYS IN THE SUN	8
8 JUL 78	NO ONE IS INNOCENT / MY WAY	7
3 MAR 79	SOMETHING ELSE / FRIGGIN' IN THE RIGGIN'	3
7 APR 79	SILLY THING	6
30 JUN 79	C'MON EVERYBODY	3
13 OCT 79	THE GREAT ROCK 'N' ROLL SWINDLE	21
14 JUN 80	(I'M NOT YOUR) STEPPING STONE	21
3 OCT 92	ANARCHY IN THE UK (RE-ISSUE)	33
5 DEC 92	PRETTY VACANT (RE-ISSUE)	56
27 JUL 96	PRETTY VACANT (LIVE)	18

ALBUMS

12 NOV 77	NEVER MIND THE BOLLOCKS HERE'S THE SEX PISTOLS	1
10 MAR 79	THE GREAT ROCK 'N' ROLL SWINDLE (FILM SOUNDTRACK)	7
11 AUG 79	SOME PRODUCT - CARRI ON SEX PISTOLS	6
16 FEB 80	FLOGGING A DEAD HORSE	23
17 OCT 92	KISS THIS	10

•SIMON AND GARFUNKEL•

SINGLES

24 MAR 66	HOMEWARD BOUND	9
16 JUN 66	I AM A ROCK	17
10 JUL 68	MRS ROBINSON	4
8 JAN 69	MRS ROBINSON (EP)	9
30 APR 69	THE BOXER	6
21 FEB 70	BRIDGE OVER TROUBLED WATER	1
15 AUG 70	BRIDGE OVER TROUBLED WATER (RE-ENTRY)	45
7 OCT 72	AMERICA	25
7 DEC 91	A HAZY SHADE OF WINTER / SILENT NIGHT - SEVEN O'CLOCK NEWS	30
15 FEB 92	THE BOXER (RE-ISSUE)	75

ALBUMS

16 APR 66	SOUNDS OF SILENCE	13
3 AUG 68	BOOKENDS	1
31 AUG 68	PARSLEY, SAGE, ROSEMARY AND THYME	13
26 OCT 68	THE GRADUATE (FILM SOUNDTRACK)	3
9 NOV 68	WEDNESDAY MORNING 3 A.M.	24
21 FEB 70	BRIDGE OVER TROUBLED WATER	1
20 MAR 82	THE CONCERT IN CENTRAL PARK	6

•SIMPLE MINDS•

SINGLES

12 MAY 79	LIFE IN A DAY	62
23 MAY 81	THE AMERICAN	59
15 AUG 81	LOVE SONG	47
7 NOV 81	SWEAT IN BULLET	52
10 APR 82	PROMISED YOU A MIRACLE	13
28 AUG 82	GLITTERING PRIZE	16
13 NOV 82	SOMEONE SOMEWHERE (IN SUMMERTIME)	36
26 NOV 83	WATERFRONT	13
28 JAN 84	SPEED YOUR LOVE TO ME	20
24 MAR 84	UP ON THE CATWALK	27
20 APR 85	DON'T YOU (FORGET ABOUT ME)	7
17 AUG 85	DON'T YOU (FORGET ABOUT ME) (RE-ENTRY)	61
12 OCT 85	ALIVE AND KICKING	7
28 DEC 85	DON'T YOU (FORGET ABOUT ME) (2ND RE-ENTRY)	74
4 JAN 86	ALIVE AND KICKING (RE-ENTRY)	60
1 FEB 86	SANCTIFY YOURSELF	10
15 FEB 86	DON'T YOU (FORGET ABOUT ME) (3RD RE-ENTRY)	62
15 MAR 86	DON'T YOU (FORGET ABOUT ME) (4TH RE-ENTRY)	68
12 APR 86	ALL THE THINGS SHE SAID	9
14 JUN 86	ALL THE THINGS SHE SAID (RE-ENTRY)	73
15 NOV 86	GHOSTDANCING	13
3 JAN 87	GHOSTDANCING (RE-ENTRY)	68
20 JUN 87	PROMISED YOU A MIRACLE	19
18 FEB 89	BELFAST CHILD	1
22 APR 89	THIS IS YOUR LAND	13

•SIMPLE MINDS•

SINGLES CONT...

29 JUL 89	KICK IT IN	15
9 DEC 89	THE AMSTERDAM EP	18
23 MAR 91	LET THERE BE LOVE	6
25 MAY 91	SEE THE LIGHTS	20
31 AUG 91	STAND BY LOVE	13
26 OCT 91	REAL LIFE	34
10 OCT 92	LOVE SONG / ALIVE AND KICKING (RE-ISSUE)	6
28 JAN 95	SHE'S A RIVER	9
8 APR 95	HYPNOTISED	18
14 MAR 98	GLITTERBALL	18
30 MAY 98	WAR BABIES	43

ALBUMS

5 MAY 79	A LIFE IN THE DAY	30
27 SEP 80	EMPIRES AND DANCE	41
12 SEP 81	SONS AND FASCINATIONS / SISTERS FEELINGS CALL	11
27 FEB 82	CELEBRATION	45
25 SEP 82	NEW GOLD DREAM (81, 82, 83, 84)	3
18 FEB 84	SPARKLE IN THE RAIN	1
2 NOV 85	ONCE UPON A TIME	1
6 JUN 87	LIVE IN THE CITY OF LIGHT	1
13 MAY 89	STREET FIGHTING YEARS	1
20 APR 91	REAL LIFE	2
11 FEB 95	GOOD NEWS FROM THE NEXT WORLD	2

• SISTERS OF MERCY •

SINGLES

16 JUN 84	BODY AND SOUL / TRAIN	46
20 OCT 84	WALK AWAY	45
9 MAR 85	NO TIME TO CRY	63
3 OCT 87	THIS CORROSION	7
27 FEB 88	LUCRETIA MY REFLECTION	20
13 OCT 90	MORE	14
22 DEC 90	DOCTOR JEEP	37
2 MAY 92	TEMPLE OF LOVE	3
28 AUG 93	UNDER THE GUN	19

ALBUMS

23 MAR 85	FIRST AND LAST AND ALWAYS	14
28 NOV 87	FLOODLAND	9
2 NOV 90	VISION THING	11
9 MAY 92	SOME GIRLS WANDER BY MISTAKE	5

•SLADE•

SINGLES

Date	Title	Pos
19 JUN 71	GET DOWN AND GET WITH IT	16
30 OCT 71	COZ I LUV YOU	1
5 FEB 72	LOOK WOT YOU DUN	4
3 JUN 72	TAKE ME BAK 'OME	1
2 SEP 72	MAMA WEER ALL CRAZEE NOW	1
25 NOV 72	GUDBUY T' JANE	2
3 MAR 73	CUM ON FEEL THE NOIZE	1
30 JUN 73	SKWEEZE ME PLEEZE ME	1
6 OCT 73	MY FREND STAN	2
15 DEC 73	MERRY XMAS EVERYBODY	1
6 APR 74	EVERYDAY	3
6 JUL 74	BANGIN' MAN	3
19 OCT 74	FAR FAR AWAY	2
15 FEB 75	HOW DOES IT FEEL	15
17 MAY 75	THANKS FOR THE MEMORY (WHAM BAM THANK YOU MAM)	7
22 NOV 75	IN FOR A PENNY	11
7 FEB 76	LET'S CALL IT QUITS	11
5 FEB 77	GYPSY ROAD HOG	48
29 OCT 77	MY BABY LEFT ME - THAT'S ALL RIGHT	32
18 OCT 80	SLADE ALIVE AT READING '80 EP	44
27 DEC 80	MERRY XMAS EVERYBODY (RE-ENTRY)	70
31 JAN 81	WE'LL BRING THE HOUSE DOWN	10
4 APR 81	WHEELS AIN'T COMING DOWN	60
19 SEP 81	LOCK UP YOUR DAUGHTERS	29
19 DEC 81	MERRY XMAS EVERYBODY (RE-ENTRY)	32
27 MAR 82	RUBY RED	51
27 NOV 82	(AND NOW - THE WALTZ) C'EST LA VIE	50
25 DEC 82	MERRY XMAS EVERYBODY (2ND RE-ENTRY)	67

• SLADE •

SINGLES

19 NOV 83	MY OH MY	2
10 DEC 83	MERRY XMAS EVERYBODY (3RD RE-ENTRY)	20
4 FEB 84	RUN RUN AWAY	7
17 NOV 84	ALL JOIN HANDS	15
15 DEC 84	MERRY XMAS EVERYBODY (4TH RE-ENTRY)	47
26 JAN 85	7 YEAR BITCH	60
23 MAR 85	MYZSTERIOUS MIZTER JONES	50
30 NOV 85	DO YOU BELIEVE IN MIRACLES	54
21 DEC 85	MERRY XMAS EVERYBODY (RE-ISSUE)	48
27 DEC 86	MERRY XMAS EVERYBODY (RE-ENTRY OF RE-ISSUE)	71
21 FEB 87	STILL THE SAME	73
19 OCT 91	RADIO WALL OF SOUND	21
26 DEC 98	MERRY XMAS EVERYBODY '98 (RE-MIX)	30

ALBUMS

8 APR 72	SLADE ALIVE	2
9 DEC 72	SLAYED?	1
6 OCT 73	SLADEST	1
23 FEB 74	OLD NEW BORROWED AND BLUE	1
14 DEC 74	SLADE IN FLAME	6
27 MAR 76	NOBODY'S FOOL	14
21 MAR 81	WE'LL BRING THE HOUSE DOWN	25
28 NOV 81	TILL DEAF US DO PART	68
18 DEC 82	SLADE ON STAGE	58
24 DEC 83	THE AMAZING KAMIKAZE SYNDROME	49
6 APR 85	ROGUES GALLERY	60
30 NOV 85	CRACKERS - THE SLADE CHRISTMAS PARTY ALBUM	34
9 MAY 87	YOU BOYZ MAKE BIG NOIZE	98

SMASHING PUMPKINS

SINGLES

5 SEP 92	I AM ONE	73
3 JUL 93	CHERUB ROCK	31
25 SEP 93	TODAY	44
5 MAR 94	DISARM	11
28 OCT 95	BULLET WITH BUTTERFLY WINGS	20
10 FEB 96	1979	16
18 MAY 96	TONIGHT TONIGHT	7
23 NOV 96	THIRTY THREE	21
14 JUN 97	THE END IS THE BEGINNING IS THE END	10
23 AUG 97	THE END IS THE BEGINNING IS THE END	72
30 MAY 98	AVA ADORE	11
19 SEP 98	PERFECT	24

ALBUMS

31 JUL 93	SIAMESE DREAM	4
4 NOV 95	MELLON COLLIE AND THE INFINITE SADNESS	4

•SONIC YOUTH•

SINGLES

11 JUL 92	100%	28
7 NOV 92	YOUTH AGAINST FASCISM	52
3 APR 93	SUGAR KANE	26
7 MAY 94	BULL IN THE HEATHER	24
10 SEP 94	SUPERSTAR	45
11 JUL 98	SUNDAY	72

ALBUMS

29 OCT 88	DAYDREAM NATION	99
4 FEB 89	THE WHITEY ALBUM	63
7 JUL 90	GOO	32
4 MAY 91	DIRTY BOOTS - PLUS 5 LIVE TRACKS	69
1 AUG 92	DIRTY	6
21 MAY 94	EXPERIMENTAL JET SET TRASH AND NO STAR	10
14 OCT 95	WASHING MACHINE	39

•SQUEEZE•

SINGLES

8 APR 78	TAKE ME I'M YOURS	19
10 JUN 78	BANG BANG	49
18 NOV 78	GOODBYE GIRL	63
24 MAR 79	COOL FOR CATS	2
2 JUN 79	UP THE JUNCTION	2
8 SEP 79	SLAP AND TICKLE	24
1 MAR 80	ANOTHER NAIL IN MY HEART	17
10 MAY 80	PULLING MUSSELS (FROM THE SHELL)	44
16 MAY 81	IS THAT LOVE	35
25 JUL 81	TEMPTED	41
10 OCT 81	LABELLED WITH LOVE	4
24 APR 82	BLACK COFFEE IN BED	51
23 OCT 82	ANNIE GET YOUR GUN	43
15 JUN 85	LAST TIME FOREVER	45
8 AUG 87	HOURGLASS	16
17 OCT 87	TRUST ME TO OPEN MY MOUTH	72
25 APR 92	COOL FOR CATS (RE-ISSUE)	62
24 JUL 93	THIRD RAIL	39
11 SEP 93	SOME FANTASTIC PLACE	73
9 SEP 95	THIS SUMMER	36
18 NOV 95	ELECTRIC TRAINS	44
15 JUN 96	HEAVEN KNOWS	27
24 AUG 96	THIS SUMMER (RE-MIX)	32

ALBUMS

28 APR 79	COOL FOR CATS	45
16 FEB 80	ARGY BARGY	32
23 MAY 81	EAST SIDE STORY	19
15 MAY 82	SWEETS FROM A STRANGER	20
7 SEP 85	COSI FAN TUTTI FRUTTI	31
19 SEP 87	BABYLON AND ON	14
23 SEP 89	FRANK	58
7 APR 90	A ROUND AND A BOUT	50
7 SEP 91	PLAY	41
25 SEP 93	SOME FANTASTIC PLACE	26
25 NOV 95	RIDICULOUS	50

•STATUS QUO•

SINGLES

24 JAN 68	PICTURES OF MATCHSTICK MEN	7
21 AUG 68	ICE IN THE SUN	8
28 MAY 69	ARE YOU GROWING TIRED OF MY LOVE	46
18 JUN 69	ARE YOU GROWING TIRED OF MY LOVE (RE-ENTRY)	50
2 MAY 70	DOWN THE DUSTPIPE	12
7 NOV 70	IN MY CHAIR	21
13 JAN 73	PAPER PLANE	8
14 APR 73	MEAN GIRL	20
8 SEP 73	CAROLINE	5
4 MAY 74	BREAK THE BLUES	8
7 DEC 74	DOWN DOWN	1
17 MAY 75	ROLL OVER LAY DOWN	9
14 FEB 76	RAIN	7
10 JUL 76	MYSTERY SONG	11
11 DEC 76	WILD SIDE OF LIFE	9
8 OCT 77	ROCKIN' ALL OVER THE WORLD	3
2 SEP 78	AGAIN AND AGAIN	13
25 NOV 78	ACCIDENT PRONE	36
22 SEP 79	WHATEVER YOU WANT	4
24 NOV 79	LIVING ON AN ISLAND	16
11 OCT 80	WHAT YOU'RE PROPOSING	2
6 DEC 80	LIES / DON'T DRIVE MY CAR	11
28 FEB 81	SOMETHING 'BOUT YOU BABY I LIKE	9
28 NOV 81	ROCK 'N' ROLL	8
27 MAR 82	DEAR JOHN	10
12 JUN 82	SHE DON'T FOOL ME	36
30 OCT 82	CAROLINE (LIVE AT THE N.E.C)	13
10 SEP 83	OL' RAG BLUES	9
5 NOV 83	A MESS OF THE BLUES	15
10 DEC 83	MARGUERITA TIME	3
19 MAY 84	GOING DOWN TOWN TONIGHT	20

•STATUS QUO•

SINGLES CONT...

27 OCT 84	THE WANDERER	7
17 MAY 86	ROLLIN' HOME	9
26 JUL 86	RED SKY	19
4 OCT 86	IN THE ARMY NOW	2
6 DEC 86	DREAMIN'	15
26 MAR 88	AIN'T COMPLAINING	19
21 MAY 88	WHO GETS THE LOVE	34
20 AUG 88	RUNNING ALL OVER THE WORLD	17
3 DEC 88	BURNING BRIDGES (ON AND OFF AND ON AGAIN)	5
28 OCT 89	NOT AT ALL	50
29 SEP 90	THE ANNIVERSARY WALTZ - PART 1	2
15 DEC 90	THE ANNIVERSARY WALTZ - PART 2	16
7 SEP 91	CAN'T GIVE YOU MORE	37
18 JAN 92	ROCK 'TIL YOU DROP	38
10 OCT 92	ROADHOUSE MEDLEY (ANNIVERSARY WALTZ PART 25)	21
6 AUG 94	I DIDN'T MEAN IT	21
22 OCT 94	SHERRI DON'T FAIL ME NOW	38
3 DEC 94	RESTLESS	39
4 NOV 95	WHEN YOU WALK IN THE ROOM	34
2 MAR 96	FUN FUN FUN	24
13 APR 96	DON'T STOP	35
9 NOV 96	ALL AROUND MY HAT	47

ALBUMS

20 JAN 73	PILEDRIVER	5
6 OCT 73	HELLO	1
18 MAY 74	QUO	2
1 MAR 75	ON THE LEVEL	1
8 MAR 75	DOWN THE DUSTPIPE	20
20 MAR 76	BLUE FOR YOU	1
12 MAR 77	LIVE	3

•STATUS QUO•

ALBUMS CONT...

26 NOV 77	ROCKIN' ALL OVER THE WORLD	5
11 NOV 78	IF YOU CAN'T STAND THE HEAT	3
20 OCT 79	WHATEVER YOU WANT	3
22 MAR 80	12 GOLD BARS	3
25 OCT 80	JUST SUPPOSIN'	4
28 MAR 81	NEVER TOO LATE	2
10 OCT 81	FRESH QUOTA	74
24 APR 82	1982	1
13 NOV 82	FRFOM THE MAKERS OF...	4
3 DEC 83	BACK TO BACK	9
4 AUG 84	STATUS QUO LIVE AT THE NEC	83
1 DEC 84	12 GOLD BARS VOLUME 2 (AND 1)	12
6 SEP 86	IN THE ARMY NOW	7
18 JUN 88	AIN'T COMPLAINING	12
2 DEC 89	PERFECT REMEDY	49
5 OCT 91	ROCK TIL' YOU DROP	10
14 NOV 92	LIVE ALIVE QUO	37
3 SEP 94	THIRSTY WORK	13

• STEREOPHONICS •

SINGLES

29 MAR 97	LOCAL BOY IN THE PHOTOGRAPH	51
31 MAY 97	MORE LIFE IN A TRAMP'S VEST	33
23 AUG 97	A THOUSAND TREES	22
8 NOV 97	TRAFFIC	20
21 FEB 98	LOCAL BOY IN THE PHOTOGRAPH (RE-ISSUE)	14
21 NOV 98	THE BARTENDER AND THE THIEF	3

•SUEDE•

SINGLES

23 MAY 92	THE DROWNERS / TO THE BIRDS	49
26 SEP 92	METAL MICKEY	17
6 MAR 93	ANIMAL NITRATE	7
29 MAY 93	SO YOUNG	22
26 FEB 94	STAY TOGETHER	3
24 SEP 94	WE ARE THE PIGS	18
19 NOV 94	THE WILD ONES	18
11 FEB 95	NEW GENERATION	21
11 MAR 95	NEW GENERATION (RE-ENTRY)	75
10 AUG 96	TRASH	3
26 OCT 96	BEAUTIFUL ONES	8
25 JAN 97	SATURDAY NIGHT	6
19 APR 97	LAZY	9
23 AUG 97	FILMSTAR	9

ALBUMS

10 APR 93	SUEDE	1
22 OCT 94	DOG MAN STAR	3

• SUPER FURRY
ANIMALS •

SINGLES

9 MAR 96	HOMETOWN UNICORN	47
11 MAY 96	GOD! SHOW ME MAGIC	33
13 JUL 96	SOMETHING 4 THE WEEKEND	18
12 OCT 96	IF YOU DON'T WANT ME TO DESTROY YOU	18
14 DEC 96	THE MAN DON'T GIVE A FUCK	22
24 MAY 97	HERMANN LOVES PAULINE	26
26 JUL 97	THE INTERNATIONAL LANGUAGE OF SCREAMING	24
4 OCT 97	PLAY IT COOL	27
6 DEC 97	DEMONS	27
6 JUN 98	ICE HOCKEY HAIR	12

• SUPERGRASS •

SINGLES

29 OCT 94	CAUGHT BY THE FUZZ	43
18 FEB 95	MANSIZE ROOSTER	20
25 MAR 95	LOSE IT	75
13 MAY 95	LENNY	10
15 JUL 95	ALRIGHT / TIME	2
9 MAR 96	GOING OUT	5
12 APR 97	RICHARD III	2
21 JUN 97	SUN HITS THE SKY	10
18 OCT 97	LATE IN THE DAY	18

ALBUMS

| 27 MAY 95 | I SHOULD COCO | 1 |

• SUPERTRAMP •

SINGLES

15 FEB 75	DREAMER	13
25 JUN 77	GIVE A LITTLE BIT	29
31 MAR 79	THE LOGICAL SONG	7
30 JUN 79	BREAKFAST IN AMERICA	9
27 OCT 79	GOODBYE STRANGER	57
30 OCT 82	IT'S RAINING AGAIN	26

ALBUMS

23 NOV 74	CRIME OF THE CENTURY	4
6 DEC 75	CRISIS? WHAT CRISIS?	20
23 APR 77	EVEN IN THE QUIETEST MOMENTS	12
31 MAR 79	BREAKFAST IN AMERICA	3
4 OCT 80	PARIS	7
6 NOV 82	FAMOUS LAST WORDS	6
25 MAY 85	BROTHER WHERE YOU BOUND	20
31 OCT 87	FREE AS A BIRD	93

• SWEET •

SINGLES

13 MAR 71	FUNNY FUNNY	13
12 JUN 71	CO-CO	2
16 OCT 71	ALEXANDER GRAHAM BELL	33
5 FEB 72	POPPA JOE	11
10 JUN 72	LITTLE WILLY	4
9 SEP 72	WIG-WAM BAM	4
13 JAN 73	BLOCKBUSTER	1
5 MAY 73	HELL RAISER	2
22 SEP 73	BALLROOM BLITZ	2
19 JAN 74	TEENAGE RAMPAGE	2
13 JUL 74	THE SIX TEENS	9
9 NOV 74	TURN IT DOWN	41
15 MAR 75	FOX ON THE RUN	2
12 JUL 75	ACTION	15
24 JAN 76	LIES IN YOUR EYES	35
28 JAN 78	LOVE IS LIKE OXYGEN	9
26 JAN 85	IT'S IT'S THE SWEET MIX	45

ALBUMS

| 18 MAY 74 | SWEET FANNY ADAMS | 27 |

•T'PAU•

SINGLES

8 AUG 87	HEART AND SOUL	4
24 OCT 87	CHINA IN YOUR HAND	1
30 JAN 88	VALENTINE	9
2 APR 88	SEX TALK (LIVE)	23
25 JUN 88	I WILL BE WITH YOU	14
1 OCT 88	SECRET GARDEN	18
3 DEC 88	ROAD TO OUR DREAM	42
25 MAR 89	ONLY THE LONELY	28
18 MAY 91	WHENEVER YOU NEED ME	16
27 JUL 91	WALK ON AIR	62
20 FEB 93	VALENTINE (RE-ISSUE)	53

ALBUMS

26 SEP 87	BRIDGE OF SPIES	1
5 NOV 88	RAGE	4
22 JUN 91	THE PROMISE	10

• T. REX •

SINGLES

8 MAY 68	DEBORA	34
4 SEP 68	ONE INCH ROCK	28
9 AUG 69	KING OF THE RUMBLING SPIRES	44
24 OCT 70	RIDE A WHITE SWAN	2
27 FEB 71	HOT LOVE	1
10 JUL 71	GET IT ON	1
13 NOV 71	JEEPSTER	2
29 JAN 72	TELEGRAM SAM	1
1 APR 72	DEBORA / ONE INCH ROCK (RE-ISSUE)	7
13 MAY 72	METAL GURU	1
16 SEP 72	CHILDREN OF THE REVOLUTION	2
9 DEC 72	SOLID GOLD EASY ACTION	2
10 MAR 73	20TH CENTURY BOY	3
16 JUN 73	THE GROOVER	4
24 NOV 73	TRUCK ON (TYKE)	12
9 FEB 74	TEENAGE DREAM	13
13 JUL 74	LIGHT OF LOVE	22
16 NOV 74	ZIP GUN BOOGIE	41
12 JUL 75	NEW YORK CITY	15
11 OCT 75	DREAM LADY	30
6 MAR 76	LONDON BOYS	40
19 JUN 76	I LOVE TO BOOGIE	13
2 OCT 76	LASER LOVE	41
2 APR 77	THE SOUL OF MY SUIT	42
9 MAY 81	RETURN TO THE ELECTRIC WARRIOR EP	50
19 SEP 81	YOU SCARE ME TO DEATH	51
27 MAR 82	TELEGRAM SAM (RE-ENTRY)	69
18 MAY 85	MEGAREX	72
9 MAY 87	GET IT ON (RE-MIX)	54
24 AUG 91	20TH CENTURY BOY (RE-ISSUE)	13

•T.REX•

ALBUMS

13 JUL 68	MY PEOPLE WERE FAIR AND HAD SKY IN THEIR HAIR BUT NOW THEY'RE CONTENT TO WEAR STARS ON THEIR BROWS	15
7 JUN 69	UNICORN	12
14 MAR 70	A BEARD OF STARS	21
16 JAN 71	T. REX	13
9 OCT 71	ELECTRIC WARRIOR	1
29 MAR 72	PROPHETS, SEERS AND SAGES THE ANGELS OF THE AGES / MY PEOPLE WERE FAIR...	1
20 MAY 72	BOLAN BOOGIE	1
5 AUG 72	THE SLIDER	4
31 MAR 73	TANX	4
16 MAR 74	ZINC ALLOY AND THE HIDDEN RIDERS OF TOMORROW	12
21 FEB 76	FUTURISTIC DRAGON	50
9 APR 77	DANDY IN THE UNDERWORLD	26
30 JUN 79	SOLID GOLD	51
12 SEP 81	T. REX IN CONCERT	35
7 NOV 81	YOU SCARE ME TO DEATH	88
24 SEP 83	DANCE IN THE MIDNIGHT	83
4 MAY 85	BEST OF THE 20TH CENTURY BOY	5

Rock facts... ...and quiz book

•TALKING HEADS•

SINGLES

7 FEB 81	ONCE IN A LIFETIME	14
9 MAY 81	HOUSES IN MOTION	50
21 JAN 84	THIS MUST BE THE PLACE	51
3 NOV 84	SLIPPERY PEOPLE	68
12 OCT 85	ROAD TO NOWHERE	6
8 FEB 86	AND SHE WAS	17
6 SEP 86	WILD WILD LIFE	43
16 MAY 87	RADIO HEAD	52
13 AUG 88	BLIND	59
10 OCT 92	LIFETIME PILING UP	50

ALBUMS

25 FEB 78	TALKING HEADS '77	60
29 JUL 78	MORE SONGS ABOUT BUILDINGS AND FOOD	21
15 SEP 79	FEAR OF MUSIC	33
1 NOV 80	REMAIN IN LIGHT	21
10 APR 82	THE NAME OF THIS BAND IS TALKING HEADS	22
18 JUN 83	SPEAKING IN TONGUES	21
27 OCT 84	STOP MAKING SENSE	37
29 JUN 85	LITTLE CREATURES	10
27 SEP 86	TRUE STORIES	7
26 MAR 88	NAKED	3
24 OCT 92	ONCE IN A LIFETIME / SAND IN THE VASELINE	7

•TEXAS•

SINGLES

4 FEB 89	I DON'T WANT A LOVER	8
6 MAY 89	THRILL HAS GONE	60
5 AUG 89	EVERYDAY NOW	44
2 DEC 89	PRAYER FOR YOU	73
7 SEP 91	WHY BELIEVE IN YOU	66
26 OCT 91	IN MY HEART	74
8 FEB 92	ALONE WITH YOU	32
25 APR 92	TIRED OF BEING ALONE	19
11 SEP 93	SO CALLED FRIEND	30
30 OCT 93	YOU OWE IT ALL TO ME	39
18 JAN 97	SAY WHAT YOU WANT	3
12 FEB 94	SO IN LOVE WITH YOU	28
9 AUG 97	BLACK EYED BOY	5
15 NOV 97	PUT YOUR ARMS AROUND ME	10
3 JAN 98	PUT YOUR ARMS AROUND ME (RE-ENTRY)	75
17 JAN 98	PUT YOUR ARMS AROUND ME (2ND RE-ENTRY)	64
21 MAR 98	SAY WHAT YOU WANT / INSANE	4

ALBUMS

25 MAR 89	THE NEW ORDER	81
5 OCT 91	MOTHER'S HEAVEN	32
13 NOV 93	RICK'S ROAD	18

• THE ANIMALS •

SINGLES

16 APR 64	BABY LET ME TAKE YOU HOME	21
25 JUN 64	HOUSE OF THE RISING SUN	1
17 SEP 64	I'M CRYING	8
4 FEB 65	DON'T LET ME BE MISUNDERSTOOD	3
8 APR 65	BRING IT ON HOME TO ME	7
15 JUL 65	WE GOTTA GET OUT OF THIS PLACE	2
28 OCT 65	IT'S MY LIFE	7
17 FEB 66	INSIDE-LOOKING OUT	12
2 JUN 66	DON'T BRING ME DOWN	6
27 OCT 66	HELP ME GIRL	14
15 JUN 67	WHEN I WAS YOUNG	45
6 SEP 67	GOOD TIMES	20
18 OCT 67	SAN FRANCISCAN NIGHTS	7
14 FEB 68	SKY PILOT	40
15 JAN 69	RING OF FIRE	35
7 OCT 72	HOUSE OF THE RISING SUN (RE-ISSUE)	25
18 SEP 82	HOUSE OF THE RISING SUN (RE-ENTRY OF RE-ISSUE)	11

ALBUMS

14 NOV 64	THE ANIMALS	6
22 MAY 65	ANIMAL TRACKS	6
28 MAY 66	ANIMALISMS	4

• THE BEACH BOYS •

SINGLES

1 AUG 63	SURFIN' USA	34
9 JUL 64	I GET AROUND	7
29 OCT 64	WHEN I GROW UP (TO BE A MAN)	44
19 NOV 64	WHEN I GROW UP (TO BE A MAN) (RE-ENTRY)	27
21 JAN 65	DANCE DANCE DANCE	24
3 JUN 65	HELP ME RHONDA	27
2 SEP 65	CALIFORNIA GIRLS	26
17 FEB 66	BARBARA ANN	3
21 APR 66	SLOOP JOHN B	2
28 JUL 66	GOD ONLY KNOWS	2
3 NOV 66	GOOD VIBRATIONS	1
4 MAY 67	THEN I KISSED HER	4
23 AUG 67	HEROES AND VILLAINS	8
22 NOV 67	WILD HONEY	29
17 JAN 68	DARLIN'	11
8 MAY 68	FRIENDS	25
24 JUL 68	DO IT AGAIN	1
25 DEC 68	BLUEBIRDS OVER THE MOUNTAIN	33
26 FEB 69	I CAN HEAR MUSIC	10
11 JUN 69	BREAK AWAY	6
16 MAY 70	COTTONFIELDS	5
3 MAR 73	CALIFORNIA SAGA-CALIFORNIA	37
3 JUL 76	GOOD VIBRATIONS (RE-ISSUE)	18
10 JUL 76	ROCK AND ROLL MUSIC	36
31 MAR 79	HERE COMES THE NIGHT	37
16 JUN 79	LADY LYNDA	6
29 SEP 79	SUMAHAMA	45

•THE BEACH BOYS•

SINGLES CONT...

29 AUG 81	BEACH BOYS MEDLEY	47
22 AUG 87	WIPEOUT	2
19 NOV 88	KOKOMO	25
2 JUN 90	WOULDN'T IT BE NICE	58
29 JUN 91	DO IT AGAIN (RE-ISSUE)	61
2 MAR 96	FUN FUN FUN	24

ALBUMS

25 SEP 65	SURFIN' USA	17
19 FEB 66	BEACH BOYS PARTY	3
16 APR 66	BEACH BOYS TODAY	6
9 JUL 66	PET SOUNDS	2
16 JUL 66	SUMMER DAYS	4
11 MAR 67	SURFER GIRL	13
18 NOV 67	SMILEY SMILE	9
16 MAR 68	WILD HONEY	7
21 SEP 68	FRIENDS	13
29 MAR 69	20 / 20	3
5 DEC 70	SUNFLOWER	29
27 NOV 71	SURF'S UP	15
24 JUN 72	CARL AND THE PASSIONS / SO TOUGH	25
17 FEB 73	HOLLAND	20
24 JUL 76	15 BIG ONES	31
7 MAY 77	THE BEACH BOYS LOVE YOU	28
21 APR 79	LA (LIGHT ALBUM)	32
12 APR 80	KEEPING THE SUMMER ALIVE	54
23 JUN 90	SUMMER DREAMS	2

•THE BEATLES•

SINGLES

11 OCT 62	LOVE ME DO	17
17 JAN 63	PLEASE PLEASE ME	2
18 APR 63	FROM ME TO YOU	1
6 JUN 63	MY BONNIE	48
29 AUG 63	SHE LOVES YOU	1
5 DEC 63	I WANT TO HOLD YOUR HAND	1
26 MAR 64	CAN'T BUY ME LOVE	1
9 APR 64	SHE LOVES YOU (RE-ENTRY)	42
14 MAY 64	I WANT TO HOLD YOUR HAND (RE-ENTRY)	48
11 JUN 64	AIN'T SHE SWEET	29
9 JUL 64	CAN'T BUY ME LOVE (RE-ENTRY)	47
16 JUL 64	A HARD DAY'S NIGHT	1
3 DEC 64	I FEEL FINE	1
15 APR 65	TICKET TO RIDE	1
29 JUL 65	HELP!	1
9 DEC 65	DAY TRIPPER / WE CAN WORK IT OUT	1
16 JUN 66	PAPERBACK WRITER	1
11 AUG 66	YELLOW SUBMARINE / ELEANOR RIGBY	1
23 FEB 67	PENNY LANE / STRAWBERRY FIELDS FOREVER	2
12 JUL 67	ALL YOU NEED IS LOVE	1
29 NOV 67	HELLO GOODBYE	1
13 DEC 67	MAGICAL MYSTERY TOUR (DOUBLE EP)	2
20 MAR 68	LADY MADONNA	1
4 SEP 68	HEY JUDE	1
23 APR 69	GET BACK	1
4 JUN 69	BALLAD OF JOHN AND YOKO	1
8 NOV 69	SOMETHING / COME TOGETHER	4
14 MAR 70	LET IT BE	2
24 OCT 70	LET IT BE (RE-ENTRY)	43
13 MAR 76	YESTERDAY	8
27 MAR 76	HEY JUDE (RE-ENTRY)	12

• THE BEATLES •

SINGLES CONT...

Date	Title	Pos
27 MAR 76	PAPERBACK WRITER (RE-ENTRY)	23
3 APR 76	GET BACK (RE-ENTRY)	28
3 APR 76	STRAWBERRY FIELDS FOREVER (RE-ENTRY)	32
10 APR 76	HELP! (RE-ENTRY)	37
10 JUL 76	BACK IN THE U.S.S.R	19
7 OCT 78	SGT. PEPPERS LONELY HEARTS CLUB BAND - WITH A LITTLE HELP FROM MY FRIENDS	63
5 JUN 82	BEATLES MOVIE MEDLEY	10
16 OCT 82	LOVE ME DO (RE-ENTRY)	4
22 JAN 83	PLEASE PLEASE ME (RE-ENTRY)	29
23 APR 83	FROM ME TO YOU (RE-ENTRY)	40
3 SEP 83	SHE LOVE YOU (2ND RE-ENTRY)	45
26 NOV 83	I WANT TO HOLD YOUR HAND (2ND RE-ENTRY)	62
31 MAR 84	CAN'T BUY ME LOVE (2ND RE-ENTRY)	53
21 JUL 84	A HARD DAY'S NIGHT (RE-ENTRY)	52
8 DEC 84	I FEEL FINE (RE-ENTRY)	65
20 APR 85	TICKET TO RIDE (RE-ENTRY)	70
30 AUG 86	ELEANOR RIGBY / YELLOW SUBMARINE (RE-ENTRY)	63
28 FEB 87	PENNY LANE / STRAWBERRY FIELDS FOREVER (2ND RE-ENTRY)	65
18 JUL 87	ALL YOU NEED IS LOVE (RE-ENTRY)	47
5 DEC 87	HELLO GOODBYE (RE-ENTRY)	63
26 MAR 88	LADY MADONNA (RE-ENTRY)	67
10 SEP 88	HEY JUDE (2ND RE-ENTRY)	52
22 APR 89	GET BACK (2ND RE-ENTRY)	74
17 OCT 92	LOVE ME DO (2ND RE-ENTRY)	53
1 APR 95	BABY IT'S YOU	7
8 JUL 95	BABY IT'S YOU (RE-ENTRY)	71
16 DEC 95	FREE AS A BIRD	2
16 MAR 96	REAL LOVE	4

•THE BEATLES•

ALBUMS

6 APR 63	PLEASE PLEASE ME	1
30 NOV 63	WITH THE BEATLES	1
18 JUL 64	A HARD DAY'S NIGHT	1
12 DEC 64	BEATLES FOR SALE	1
14 AUG 65	HELP	1
11 DEC 65	RUBBER SOUL	1
13 AUG 66	REVOLVER	1
3 JUN 67	SERGEANT PEPPER'S LONELY HEARTS CLUB BAND	1
13 JAN 68	MAGICAL MYSTERY TOUR (IMPORT)	31
7 DEC 68	THE BEATLES	1
1 FEB 69	YELLOW SUBMARINE	3
4 OCT 69	ABBEY ROAD	1
23 MAY 70	LET IT BE	1
26 JUN 76	ROCK 'N' ROLL MUSIC	11
21 AUG 76	THE BEATLES TAPES	45
21 MAY 77	THE BEATLES AT THE HOLLYWOOD BOWL	1
17 DEC 77	LOVE SONGS	7
3 NOV 79	RARITIES	71
15 NOV 80	BEATLES BALLADS	17
10 DEC 94	LIVE AT THE BBC	1

• THE BYRDS •

SINGLES

17 JUN 65	MR. TAMBOURINE MAN	1
12 AUG 65	ALL I REALLY WANT TO DO	4
11 NOV 65	TURN! TURN! TURN!	26
5 MAY 66	EIGHT MILES HIGH	24
5 JUN 68	YOU AIN'T GOIN' NOWHERE	45
13 FEB 71	CHESTNUT MARE	19

ALBUMS

28 AUG 65	MR. TAMBOURINE MAN	7
9 APR 66	TURN, TURN, TURN	11
1 OCT 66	5TH DIMENSION	27
22 APR 67	YOUNGER THAN YESTERDAY	37
4 MAY 68	THE NOTORIOUS BYRD BROTHERS	12
24 MAY 69	DR. BYRDS AND MR. HYDE	15
14 FEB 70	BALLAD OF EASY RIDER	41
28 NOV 70	UNTITLED	11
14 APR 73	BYRDS	31

• THE CLASH •

SINGLES

2 APR 77	WHITE RIOT	38
8 OCT 77	COMPLETE CONTROL	28
4 MAR 78	CLASH CITY ROCKERS	35
24 JUN 78	(WHITE MAN) IN HAMMERSMITH PALAIS	32
2 DEC 78	TOMMY GUN	19
3 MAR 79	ENGLISH CIVIL WAR (JOHNNY COMES MARCHING HOME)	25
19 MAY 79	THE COST OF LIVING EP	22
15 DEC 79	LONDON CALLING	11
9 AUG 80	BANKROBBER	12
6 DEC 80	THE CALL UP	40
24 JAN 81	HITSVILLE UK	56
25 APR 81	THE MAGNIFICENT SEVEN	34
28 NOV 81	THIS IS RADIO CLASH	47
1 MAY 82	KNOW YOUR RIGHTS	43
26 JUN 82	ROCK THE CASBAH	30
25 SEP 82	SHOULD I STAY OR SHOULD I GO / STRAIGHT TO HELL	17
12 OCT 85	THIS IS ENGLAND	24
12 MAR 88	I FOUGHT THE LAW	29
7 MAY 88	LONDON CALLING (RE-ISSUE)	46
21 JUL 90	RETURN TO BRIXTON	57
2 MAR 91	SHOULD I STAY OR SHOULD I GO (RE-ISSUE)	1
13 APR 91	ROCK THE CASBAH (RE-ISSUE)	15
8 JUN 91	LONDON CALLING (RE-ISSUE)	64

ALBUMS

30 APR 77	CLASH	12
25 NOV 78	GIVE 'EM ENOUGH ROPE	2
22 DEC 79	LONDON CALLING	9
20 DEC 80	SANDINISTA	19
22 MAY 82	COMBAT ROCK	2
16 NOV 85	CUT THE CRAP	16
2 APR 88	THE STORY OF THE CLASH	7

•THE CULT•

SINGLES

22 DEC 84	RESURRECTION JOE	74
25 MAY 85	SHE SELLS SANCTUARY	15
28 SEP 85	SHE SELLS SANCTUARY (RE-ENTRY)	61
5 OCT 85	RAIN	17
30 NOV 85	REVOLUTION	30
28 FEB 87	LOVE REMOVAL MACHINE	18
2 MAY 87	LIL' DEVIL	11
22 AUG 87	WILD FLOWER (DOUBLE SINGLE)	24
29 AUG 87	WILD FLOWER	30
1 APR 89	FIRE WOMAN	15
8 JUL 89	EDIE (CIAO BABY)	32
18 NOV 89	SUN KING / EDIE (CIAO BABY) (RE-ISSUE)	39
10 MAR 90	SWEET SOUL SISTER	42
14 SEP 91	WILD HEARTED SON	40
29 FEB 92	HEART OF SOUL	51
30 JAN 93	SHE SELLS SANCTUARY (RE-MIX)	15
8 OCT 94	COMING DOWN	50
7 JAN 95	STAR	65

ALBUMS

18 JUN 83	SOUTHERN DEATH CULT	43
8 SEP 84	DREAMTIME	21
26 OCT 85	LOVE	4
18 APR 87	ELECTRIC	4
22 APR 89	SONIC TEMPLE	3
5 OCT 91	CEREMONY	9
13 FEB 93	PURE CULT	1
22 OCT 94	CULT	21

• THE DAMNED •

SINGLES

5 MAY 79	LOVE SONG	20
20 OCT 79	SMASH IT UP	35
1 DEC 79	I JUST CAN'T BE HAPPY TODAY	46
4 OCT 80	HISTORY OF THE WORLD (PART 1)	51
28 NOV 81	FRIDAY 13TH (EP)	50
10 JUL 82	LOVELY MONEY	42
9 JUN 84	THANKS FOR THE NIGHT	43
30 MAR 85	GRIMLY FIENDISH	21
22 JUN 85	THE SHADOW OF LOVE	25
21 SEP 85	IS IT A DREAM	34
8 FEB 86	ELOISE	3
19 APR 86	ELOISE (RE-ENTRY)	72
22 NOV 86	ANYTHING	32
7 FEB 87	GIGOLO	29
25 APR 87	ALONE AGAIN OR	27
28 NOV 87	IN DULCE DECORUM	72

ALBUMS

12 MAR 77	DAMNED DAMNED DAMNED	36
17 NOV 79	MACHINE GUN ETIQUETTE	31
29 NOV 80	THE BLACK ALBUM	29
23 OCT 82	STRAWBERRIES	15
27 JUL 85	PHANTASMAGORIA	11
13 DEC 86	ANYTHING	40
12 DEC 87	LIGHT AT THE END OF THE TUNNEL	87

THE DAVE CLARK FIVE

SINGLES

3 OCT 63	DO YOU LOVE ME	30
21 NOV 63	GLAD ALL OVER	1
20 FEB 64	BITS AND PIECES	2
28 MAY 64	CAN'T YOU SEE THAT SHE'S MINE	10
13 AUG 64	THINKING OF YOU BABY	26
22 OCT 64	ANYWAY YOU WANT IT	25
14 JAN 65	EVERYBODY KNOWS	37
11 MAR 65	REELIN' AND ROCKIN'	24
27 MAY 65	COME HOME	16
15 JUL 65	CATCH US IF YOU CAN	5
11 NOV 65	OVER AND OVER	45
19 MAY 66	LOOK BEFORE YOU LEAP	50
16 MAR 67	YOU GOT WHAT IT TAKES	28
1 NOV 67	EVERYBODY KNOWS	2
28 FEB 68	NO ONE CAN BREAK A HEART LIKE YOU	28
18 SEP 68	RED BALLOON	7
27 NOV 68	LIVE IN THE SKY	39
25 OCT 69	PUT A LITTLE LOVE IN YOUR HEART	31
6 DEC 69	GOOD OLD ROCK 'N' ROLL	7
7 MAR 70	EVERYBODY GET TOGETHER	8
4 JUL 70	HERE COMES SUMMER	44
7 NOV 70	MORE GOOD OLD ROCK 'N' ROLL	34
1 MAY 93	GLAD ALL OVER (RE-ISSUE)	37

ALBUMS

18 APR 64	A SESSION WITH DAVE CLARK FIVE	3
14 AUG 65	CATCH US IF YOU CAN	8

• THE DOORS •

SINGLES

16 AUG 67	LIGHT MY FIRE	49
28 AUG 68	HELLO I LOVE YOU	15
16 OCT 71	RIDERS ON THE STORM	50
30 OCT 71	RIDERS ON THE STORM (RE-ENTRY)	22
20 MAR 76	RIDERS ON THE STORM (RE-ISSUE)	33
3 FEB 79	HELLO I LOVE YOU (RE-ISSUE)	71
27 APR 91	BREAK ON THROUGH	64
1 JUN 91	LIGHT MY FIRE (RE-ISSUE)	7
10 AUG 91	RIDERS ON THE STORM (RE-ISSUE)	68

ALBUMS

28 SEP 68	WAITING FOR THE SUN	16
11 APR 70	MORRISON HOTEL	12
26 SEP 70	ABSOLUTELY LIVE	69
31 JUL 71	L.A. WOMAN	28
1 APR 72	WEIRD SCENES INSIDE THE GOLD MINE	50
29 OCT 83	ALIVE, SHE CRIED	36
4 JUL 87	LIVE AT THE HOLLYWOOD BOWL	51
6 APR 91	THE DOORS (FILM SOUNDTRACK)	11

•THE EAGLES•

SINGLES

9 AUG 75	ONE OF THESE NIGHTS	23
1 NOV 75	LYIN' EYES	23
6 MAR 76	TAKE IT TO THE LIMIT	12
15 JAN 77	NEW KID IN TOWN	20
16 APR 77	HOTEL CALIFORNIA	8
16 DEC 78	PLEASE COME HOME FOR CHRISTMAS	30
13 OCT 79	HEARTACHE TONIGHT	40
1 DEC 79	THE LONG RUN	66
13 JUL 96	LOVE WILL KEEP US ALIVE	52

ALBUMS

27 APR 74	ON THE BORDER	28
12 JUL 75	ONE OF THESE NIGHTS	8
12 JUL 75	DESPERADO	39
25 DEC 76	HOTEL CALIFORNIA	2
13 OCT 79	THE LONG RUN	4
22 NOV 80	LIVE	24
19 NOV 94	HELL FREEZES OVER	28

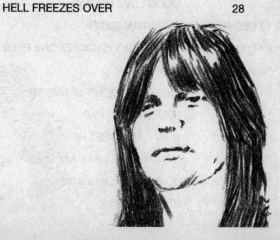

•THE EVERLY BROTHERS•

SINGLES

12 JUL 57	BYE BYE LOVE	6
8 NOV 57	WAKE UP LITTLE SUSIE	2
23 MAY 58	ALL I HAVE TO DO IS DREAM / CLAUDETTE	1
12 SEP 58	BIRD DOG	2
23 JAN 59	PROBLEMS	6
22 MAY 59	TAKE A MESSAGE TO MARY	29
29 MAY 59	POOR JENNY	14
19 JUN 59	TAKE A MESSAGE TO MARY (RE-ENTRY)	27
3 JUL 59	TAKE A MESSAGE TO MARY (2ND RE-ENTRY)	20
11 SEP 59	('TIL) I KISSED YOU	2
12 FEB 60	LET IT BE ME	13
31 MAR 60	LET IT BE ME (RE-ENTRY)	26
14 APR 60	CATHY'S CLOWN	1
14 JUL 60	WHEN WILL I BE LOVED	4
22 SEP 60	LUCILLE / SO SAD (TO WATCH GOOD LOVE GO BAD)	4
15 DEC 60	LIKE STRANGERS	11
9 FEB 61	WALK RIGHT BACK / EBONY EYES	1
15 JUN 61	TEMPTATION	1
5 OCT 61	MUSKRAT / DON'T BLAME ME	20
18 JAN 62	CRYIN' IN THE RAIN	6
17 MAY 62	HOW CAN I MEET HER	12
25 OCT 62	NO ONE CAN MAKE MY SUNSHINE SMILE	11
21 MAR 63	SO IT WILL ALWAYS BE	23
13 JUN 63	IT'S BEEN NICE	26

•THE EVERLY BROTHERS•

SINGLES CONT...

17 OCT 63	THE GIRL SANG THE BLUES	25
16 JUL 64	FERRIS WHEEL	22
3 DEC 64	GONE GONE GONE	36
6 MAY 65	THAT'LL BE THE DAY	30
20 MAY 65	THE PRICE OF LOVE	2
26 AUG 65	I'LL NEVER GET OVER YOU	35
21 OCT 65	LOVE IS STRANGE	11
8 MAY 68	IT'S MY TIME	39
22 SEP 84	ON THE WINGS OF A NIGHTINGALE	41

ALBUMS

2 JUL 60	IT'S EVERLY TIME	2
15 OCT 60	FABULOUS STYLE OF THE EVERLY BROTHERS	4
4 MAR 61	A DATE WITH THE EVERLY BROTHERS	3
21 JUL 62	INSTANT PARTY	20
7 JAN 84	EVERLY BROTHERS REUNION CONCERT	47
3 NOV 84	THE EVERLY BROTHERS	36

• THE FOUR SEASONS •

SINGLES

4 OCT 62	SHERRY	8
17 JAN 63	BIG GIRLS DON'T CRY	13
28 MAR 63	WALK LIKE A MAN	12
27 JUN 63	AIN'T THAT A SHAME	38
27 AUG 64	RAG DOLL	2
18 NOV 65	LET'S HANG ON	4
31 MAR 66	WORKIN' MY WAY BACK TO YOU	50
2 JUN 66	OPUS 17 (DON'T YOU WORRY 'BOUT ME)	20
29 SEP 66	I'VE GOT YOU UNDER MY SKIN	12
12 JAN 67	TELL IT TO THE RAIN	37
19 APR 75	NIGHT	7
20 SEP 75	WHO LOVES YOU	6
31 JAN 76	DECEMBER '63 (OH WHAT A NIGHT)	1
24 APR 76	SILVER STAR	3
27 NOV 76	WE CAN WORK IT OUT	34
18 JUN 77	RHAPSODY	37
20 AUG 77	DOWN THE HALL	34
29 OCT 88	DECEMBER '63 (OH WHAT A NIGHT) (RE-MIX)	49

ALBUMS

6 JUL 63	SHERRY	20
10 APR 71	EDIZIONE D'ORO	11
20 NOV 71	THE BIG ONES	37
6 MAR 76	WHO LOVES YOU	12

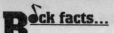

•THE GRATEFUL DEAD•

ALBUMS

19 SEP 70	WORKINGMAN'S DEAD	69
3 AUG 74	GRATEFUL DEAD FROM THE MARS HOTEL	47
1 NOV 75	BLUES FOR ALLAH	45
4 SEP 76	STEAL YOUR FACE	42
20 AUG 77	TERRAPIN STATION	30
19 SEP 87	IN THE DARK	57
18 FEB 89	DYLAN AND THE DEAD	38

• THE JAM •

SINGLES

7 MAY 77	IN THE CITY	40
23 JUL 77	ALL AROUND THE WORLD	13
5 NOV 77	THE MODERN WORLD	36
11 MAR 78	NEWS OF THE WORLD	27
26 AUG 78	DAVID WATTS / 'A' BOMB IN WARDOUR STREET	25
21 OCT 78	DOWN IN THE TUBE STATION AT MIDNIGHT	15
17 MAR 79	STRANGE TOWN	15
25 AUG 79	WHEN YOU'RE YOUNG	17
3 NOV 79	THE ETON RIFLES	3
22 MAR 80	GOING UNDERGROUND / DREAMS OF CHILDREN	1
26 APR 80	ALL AROUND THE WORLD (RE-ENTRY)	43
26 APR 80	DAVID WATTS / 'A' BOMB IN WARDOUR STREET (RE-ENTRY)	54
26 APR 80	IN THE CITY (RE-ENTRY)	40
26 APR 80	NEWS OF THE WORLD (RE-ENTRY)	53
26 APR 80	STRANGE TOWN (RE-ENTRY)	44
26 APR 80	THE MODERN WORLD (RE-ENTRY)	52
23 AUG 80	START	1
7 FEB 81	THAT'S ENTERTAINMENT (IMPORT)	21
6 JUN 81	FUNERAL PYRE	4
24 OCT 81	ABSOLUTE BEGINNERS	4
13 FEB 82	TOWN CALLED MALICE / PRECIOUS	1
3 JUL 82	JUST WHO IS THE FIVE O'CLOCK HERO	8
18 SEP 82	THE BITTEREST PILL (I EVER HAD TO SWALLOW)	2
4 DEC 82	BEAT SURRENDER	1
22 JAN 83	ALL AROUND THE WORLD (2ND RE-ENTRY)	38

• THE JAM •

SINGLES CONT...

22 JAN 83	DAVID WATTS / 'A' BOMB IN WARDOUR STREET (2ND RE-ENTRY)	50
22 JAN 83	DOWN IN THE TUBE STATION AT MIDNIGHT (RE-ENTRY)	30
22 JAN 83	GOING UNDERGROUND / DREAMS OF CHILDREN (RE-ENTRY)	21
22 JAN 83	IN THE CITY (2ND RE-ENTRY)	47
22 JAN 83	NEWS OF THE WORLD (2ND RE-ENTRY)	39
22 JAN 83	STRANGE TOWN (2ND RE-ENTRY)	42
22 JAN 83	THE MODERN WORLD (2ND RE-ENTRY)	51
22 JAN 83	WHEN YOU'RE YOUNG (RE-ENTRY)	53
29 JAN 83	THAT'S ENTERTAINMENT (RE-ISSUE)	60
5 FEB 83	START (RE-ENTRY)	62
5 FEB 83	THE ETON RIFLES (RE-ENTRY)	54
5 FEB 83	TOWN CALLED MALICE / PRECIOUS (RE-ENTRY)	73
29 JUN 91	THAT'S ENTERTAINMENT (2ND RE-ISSUE)	57
11 OCT 97	THE BITTEREST PILL (I EVER HAD TO SWALLOW) (RE-ISSUE)	30

ALBUMS

28 MAY 77	IN THE CITY	20
26 NOV 77	THIS IS THE MODERN WORLD	22
11 NOV 78	ALL MOD CONS	6
24 NOV 79	SETTING SONS	4
6 DEC 80	SOUND AFFECTS	2
20 MAR 82	THE GIFT	1
18 DEC 82	DIG THE NEW BREED	2
22 OCT 83	SNAP	2
18 APR 92	EXTRAS	15
6 NOV 93	LIVE JAM	28

• THE KINKS •

SINGLES

13 AUG 64	YOU REALLY GOT ME	1
29 OCT 64	ALL DAY AND ALL OF THE NIGHT	2
21 JAN 65	TIRED OF WAITING FOR YOU	1
25 MAR 65	EVERYBODY'S GONNA BE HAPPY	17
27 MAY 65	SET ME FREE	9
5 AUG 65	SEE MY FRIEND	10
2 DEC 65	TILL THE END OF THE DAY	8
3 MAR 66	DEDICATED FOLLOWER OF FASHION	4
9 JUN 66	SUNNY AFTERNOON	1
24 NOV 66	DEAD END STREET	5
11 MAY 67	WATERLOO SUNSET	2
18 OCT 67	AUTUMN ALMANAC	3
17 APR 68	WONDERBOY	36
17 JUL 68	DAYS	12
16 APR 69	PLASTIC MAN	31
10 JAN 70	VICTORIA	33
4 JUL 70	LOLA	2
12 DEC 70	APEMAN	5
27 MAY 72	SUPERSONIC ROCKET SHIP	16
27 JUN 81	BETTER THINGS	46
6 AUG 83	COME DANCING	12
15 OCT 83	DON'T FORGET TO DANCE	58
15 OCT 83	YOU REALLY GOT ME (RE-ISSUE)	47
18 JAN 97	THE DAYS EP	35

ALBUMS

17 OCT 64	KINKS	3
13 MAR 65	KINDA KINKS	3
4 DEC 65	KINKS KONTROVERSY	9
11 SEP 66	WELL RESPECTED KINKS	5
5 NOV 66	FACE TO FACE	12
14 OCT 67	SOMETHING ELSE	35
2 DEC 67	SUNNY AFTERNOON	9
23 OCT 71	GOLDEN HOUR OF THE KINKS	21

•THE MONKEYS•

SINGLES

5 JAN 67	I'M A BELIEVER	1
26 JAN 67	LAST TRAIN TO CLARKSVILLE	23
6 APR 67	A LITTLE BIT ME A LITTLE BIT YOU	3
22 JUN 67	ALTERNATE TITLE	2
16 AUG 67	PLEASANT VALLEY SUNDAY	11
15 NOV 67	DAYDREAM BELIEVER	5
27 MAR 68	VALLERI	12
26 JUN 68	D.W. WASHBURN	17
26 MAR 69	TEARDROP CITY	46
25 JUN 69	SOMEDAY MAN	47
15 MAR 80	THE MONKEES EP	33
18 OCT 86	THAT WAS THEN, THIS IS NOW	68

ALBUMS

28 JAN 67	THE MONKEES	1
15 APR 67	MORE OF THE MONKEES	1
8 JUL 67	HEADQUARTERS	2
13 JAN 68	PISCES, AQUARIUS, CAPRICORN & JONES LTD.	5
28 NOV 81	THE MONKEES	99

SINGLES

10 DEC 64	GO NOW	1
4 MAR 65	I DON'T WANT TO GO ON WITHOUT YOU	33
10 JUN 65	FROM THE BOTTOM OF MY HEART	22
18 NOV 65	EVERYDAY	44
27 DEC 67	NIGHTS IN WHITE SATIN	19
7 AUG 68	VOICES IN THE SKY	27
4 DEC 68	RIDE MY SEE-SAW	42
2 MAY 70	QUESTION	2
6 MAY 72	ISN'T LIFE STRANGE	13
2 DEC 72	NIGHTS IN WHITE SATIN (RE-ENTRY)	9
10 FEB 73	I'M JUST A SINGER (IN A ROCK AND ROLL BAND)	36
10 NOV 79	NIGHTS IN WHITE SATIN (2ND RE-ENTRY)	14
20 AUG 83	BLUE WORLD	35
25 JUN 88	I KNOW YOU'RE OUT THERE SOMEWHERE	52

ALBUMS

27 JAN 68	DAYS OF FUTURE PASSED	27
3 AUG 68	IN SEARCH OF THE LOST CHORD	5
3 MAY69	ON THE THRESHOLD OF A DREAM	1
6 DEC 69	TO OUR CHILDREN'S CHILDREN'S CHILDREN	2
15 AUG 70	A QUESTION OF BALANCE	1
7 AUG 71	EVERY GOOD BOY DESERVES FAVOUR	1
2 DEC 72	SEVENTH SOJOURN	5
16 NOV 74	THIS IS THE MOODY BLUES	14
24 JUN 78	OCTAVE	6
10 JUN 79	OUT OF THIS WORLD	15
23 MAY 81	LONG DISTANCE VOYAGER	7
10 SEP 83	THE PRESENT	15
10 MAY 86	THE OTHER SIDE OF LIFE	24
25 JUN 88	SUR LA MER	21
13 JUL 91	KEYS OF THE KINGDOM	54

•THE MOVE•

SINGLES

5 JAN 67	NIGHT OF FEAR	2
6 APR 67	I CAN HEAR THE GRASS GROW	5
6 SEP 67	FLOWERS IN THE RAIN	2
7 SEP 68	FIRE BRIGADE	3
25 DEC 68	BLACKBERRY WAY	1
23 JUL 69	CURLY	12
25 APR 70	BRONTOSAURUS	7
3 JUL 71	TONIGHT	11
23 OCT 71	CHINATOWN	23
13 MAY 72	CALIFORNIA MAN	7

ALBUMS

13 APR 68	MOVE	15

• THE POLICE •

SINGLES

7 OCT 78	CAN'T STAND LOSING YOU	42
28 APR 79	ROXANNE	12
7 JUL 79	CAN'T STAND LOSING YOU (RE-ENTRY)	2
22 SEP 79	MESSAGE IN A BOTTLE	1
17 NOV 79	FALL OUT	47
1 DEC 79	WALKING ON THE MOON	1
16 FEB 80	SO LONELY	6
14 JUN 80	SIX PACK	17
27 SEP 80	DON'T STAND SO CLOSE TO ME	1
13 DEC 80	DE DO DO DO, DE DA DA DA	5
26 SEP 81	INVISIBLE SUN	2
24 OCT 81	EVERY LITTLE THING SHE DOES IS MAGIC	1
12 DEC 81	SPIRITS IN THE MATERIAL WORLD	12
28 MAY 83	EVERY BREATH YOU TAKE	1
23 JUL 83	WRAPPED AROUND YOUR FINGER	7
5 NOV 83	SYNCHRONICITY II	17
14 JAN 84	KING OF PAIN	17
11 OCT 86	DON'T STAND SO CLOSE TO ME '86 (RE-MIX)	24
13 MAY 95	CAN'T STAND LOSING YOU (LIVE)	27
20 DEC 97	ROXANNE '97 (RE-MIX)	17

ALBUMS

21 APR 79	OUTLANDOS D'AMOUR	6
13 OCT 79	REGGATTA DE BLANC	1
11 OCT 80	ZENYATTA MONDATTA	1
10 OCT 81	GHOST IN THE MACHINE	1
25 JUN 83	SYNCHRONICITY	1
10 JUN 95	LIVE	25

• THE PRETENDERS •

SINGLES

10 FEB 79	STOP YOUR SOBBING	34
14 JUL 79	KID	33
17 NOV 79	BRASS IN POCKET	1
5 APR 80	TALK OF THE TOWN	8
14 FEB 81	MESSAGE OF LOVE	11
12 SEP 81	DAY AFTER DAY	45
14 NOV 81	I GO TO SLEEP	7
2 OCT 82	BACK ON THE CHAIN GANG	17
26 NOV 83	2000 MILES	15
9 JUN 84	THIN LINE BETWEEN LOVE AND HATE	49
3 AUG 85	I GOT YOU BABE	1
11 OCT 86	DON'T GET ME WRONG	10
13 DEC 86	HYMN TO HER	8
15 AUG 87	IF THERE WAS A MAN	49
18 JUN 88	BREAKFAST IN BED	6
12 OCT 91	SPIRITUAL HIGH (STATE OF INDEPENDENCE)	66
23 APR 94	I'LL STAND BY YOU	10
2 JUL 94	NIGHT IN MY VEINS	25
15 OCT 94	977	66
18 MAR 95	LOVE CAN BUILD A BRIDGE	1
14 OCT 95	KID	73
10 MAY 97	FEVERPITCH THE EP	65

ALBUMS

19 JAN 80	PRETENDERS	1
15 AUG 81	PRETENDERS II	7
21 JAN 84	LEARNING TO CRAWL	11
1 NOV 86	GET CLOSE	6
26 MAY 90	PACKED!	19
21 MAY 94	LAST OF THE INDEPENDENTS	8
28 OCT 95	THE ISLE OF VIEW	23

•THE RAMONES•

SINGLES

21 MAY 77	SHEENA IS A PUNK ROCKER	22
6 AUG 77	SWALLOW MY PRIDE	36
30 SEP 78	DON'T COME CLOSE	39
8 SEP 79	ROCK 'N' ROLL HIGH SCHOOL	67
26 JAN 80	BABY I LOVE YOU	8
19 APR 80	DO YOU REMEMBER ROCK 'N' ROLL RADIO	54
10 MAY 86	SOMEBODY PUT SOMETHING IN MY DRINK / SOMETHING TO BELIEVE IN	69
19 DEC 92	POISON HEART	69

ALBUMS

23 APR 77	LEAVE HOME	45
24 DEC 77	ROCKET TO RUSSIA	60
7 OCT 78	ROAD TO RUIN	32
16 JUN 79	IT'S ALIVE	27
19 JAN 80	END OF THE CENTURY	14
26 JAN 85	TOO TOUGH TO DIE	63
31 MAY 86	ANIMAL BOY	38
10 OCT 87	HALFWAY TO SANITY	78
19 AUG 89	BRAIN DRAIN	75
8 JUL 95	¡ADIOS AMIGOS!	62

•THE ROLLING
STONES•

SINGLES

25 JUL 63	COME ON	21
14 NOV 63	I WANNA BE YOUR MAN	12
27 FEB 64	NOT FADE WAY	3
2 JUL 64	IT'S ALL OVER NOW	1
19 NOV 64	LITTLE RED ROOSTER	1
4 MAR 65	THE LAST TIME	1
26 AUG 65	(I CAN'T GET NO) SATISFACTION	1
28 OCT 65	GET OFF MY CLOUD	1
10 FEB 66	NINETEENTH NERVOUS BREAKDOWN	2
19 MAY 66	PAINT IT, BLACK	1
29 SEP 66	HAVE YOU SEEN YOUR MOTHER BABY STANDING IN THE SHADOW	5
19 JAN 67	LET'S SPEND THE NIGHT TOGETHER / RUBY TUESDAY	3
23 AUG 67	WE LOVE YOU / DANDELION	8
29 MAY 68	JUMPING JACK FLASH	1
9 JUL 69	HONKY TONK WOMEN	1
24 APR 71	BROWN SUGAR / BITCH / LET IT ROCK	2
3 JUL 71	STREET FIGHTING MAN	21
29 APR 72	TUMBLING DICE	5
1 SEP 73	ANGIE	5
3 AUG 74	IT'S ONLY ROCK AND ROLL	10
20 SEP 75	OUT OF TIME	45
1 MAY 76	FOOL TO CRY	6
3 JUN 78	MISS YOU / FAR AWAY EYES	3
30 SEP 78	RESPECTABLE	23
5 JUL 80	EMOTIONAL RESCUE	9
4 OCT 80	SHE'S SO COLD	33

•THE ROLLING STONES•

SINGLES CONT...

29 AUG 81	START ME UP	7
12 DEC 81	WAITING ON A FRIEND	50
12 JUN 82	GOING TO A GO GO	26
2 OCT 82	TIME IS ON MY SIDE	62
12 NOV 83	UNDERCOVER OF THE NIGHT	11
11 FEB 84	SHE WAS HOT	42
21 JUL 84	BROWN SUGAR (RE-ISSUE)	58
15 MAR 86	HARLEM SHUFFLE	13
2 SEP 89	MIXED EMOTIONS	36
2 DEC 89	ROCK AND A HARD PLACE	63
23 JUN 90	PAINT IT, BLACK (RE-ISSUE)	61
30 JUN 90	ALMOST HEAR YOU SIGH	31
30 MAR 91	HIGHWIRE	29
1 JUN 91	RUBY TUESDAY (LIVE)	59
16 JUL 94	LOVE IS STRONG	14
8 OCT 94	YOU GOT ME ROCKING	23
10 DEC 94	OUT OF TEARS	36
15 JUL 95	I GO WILD	29
11 NOV 95	LIKE A ROLLING STONE	12

ALBUMS

25 APR 64	ROLLING STONES	1
23 JAN 65	ROLLING STONES NO. 2	1
2 OCT 65	OUT OF OUR HEADS	2
23 APR 66	AFTERMATH	1
12 NOV 66	BIG HITS (HIGH TIDE AND GREEN GRASS)	4
28 JAN 67	BETWEEN THE BUTTONS	3
23 DEC 67	THEIR SATANIC MAJESTIES REQUEST	3

•THE ROLLING STONES•

ALBUMS CONT...

21 DEC 68	BEGGARS BANQUET	3
20 DEC 69	LET IT BLEED	1
19 SEP 70	'GET YOUR YA-YA'S OUT!	1
3 APR 71	STONE AGE	4
8 MAY 71	STICKY FINGERS	1
18 SEP 71	GIMME SHELTER	19
11 MAR 72	MILESTONES	14
10 JUN 72	EXILE ON MAIN STREET	1
11 NOV 72	ROCK 'N' ROLLING STONES	41
22 SEP 73	GOAT'S HEAD SOUP	1
2 NOV 74	IT'S ONLY ROCK 'N' ROLL	2
28 JUN 75	MADE IN THE SHADE	14
28 JUN 75	METAMORPHOSIS	45
8 MAY 76	BLACK AND BLUE	2
8 OCT 77	LOVE YOU LIVE	3
5 NOV 77	GET STONED	8
24 JUN 78	SOME GIRLS	2
5 JUL 80	EMOTIONAL RESCUE	1
12 SEP 81	TATTOO YOU	2
12 JUN 82	STILL LIFE (AMERICAN CONCERTS 1981)	4
31 JUL 82	IN CONCERT (IMPORT)	94
19 NOV 83	UNDERCOVER	3
5 APR 86	DIRTY WORK	4
23 SEP 89	STEEL WHEELS	2
20 APR 91	FLASHPOINT	6
23 JUL 94	VOODOO LOUNGE	1
25 NOV 95	STRIPPED	9

Rock facts... ...and quiz book

• THE SMALL FACES •

SINGLES

2 SEP 65	WHATCHA GONNA DO ABOUT IT?	14
10 FEB 66	SHA LA LA LA LEE	3
12 MAY 66	HEY GIRL	10
11 AUG 66	ALL OR NOTHING	1
17 NOV 66	MY MIND'S EYE	4
9 MAR 67	I CAN'T MAKE IT	26
8 JUN 67	HERE COME THE NICE	12
9 AUG 67	ITCHYCOO PARK	3
6 DEC 67	TIN SOLDIER	9
17 APR 68	LAZY SUNDAY	2
10 JUL 68	UNIVERSAL	16
19 MAR 69	AFTERGLOW OF YOUR LOVE	36
13 DEC 75	ITCHYCOO PARK (RE-ISSUE)	9
20 MAR 76	LAZY SUNDAY (RE-ISSUE)	39

ALBUMS

14 MAY 66	SMALL FACES	3
17 JUN 67	FROM THE BEGINNING	17
1 JUL 67	SMALL FACES	12
15 JUN 68	OGDEN'S NUT GONE FLAKE	1

• THE SMITHS •

SINGLES

12 NOV 83	THIS CHARMING MAN	25
28 JAN 84	WHAT DIFFERENCE DOES IT MAKE	12
2 JUN 84	HEAVEN KNOWS I'M MISERABLE NOW	10
1 SEP 84	WILLIAM, IT WAS REALLY NOTHING	17
9 FEB 85	HOW SOON IS NOW?	24
30 MAR 85	SHAKESPEARE'S SISTER	26
13 JUL 85	THAT JOKE ISN'T FUNNY ANYMORE	49
5 OCT 85	THE BOY WITH THE THORN IN HIS SIDE	23
31 MAY 86	BIG MOUTH STRIKES AGAIN	26
2 AUG 86	PANIC	11
1 NOV 86	ASK	14
7 FEB 87	SHOPLIFTERS OF THE WORLD UNITE	12
25 APR 87	SHEILA TAKE A BOW	10
22 AUG 87	GIRLFRIEND IN A COMA	13
14 NOV 87	I STARTED SOMETHING I COULDN'T FINISH	23
19 DEC 87	LAST NIGHT I DREAMT THAT SOMEBODY LOVED ME	30
15 AUG 92	THIS CHARMING MAN (RE-ISSUE)	8
12 SEP 92	HOW SOON IS NOW (RE-ISSUE)	16
24 OCT 92	THERE IS A LIGHT THAT NEVER GOES OUT	25
18 FEB 95	ASK (RE-ISSUE)	62

ALBUMS

3 MAR 84	THE SMITHS	2
24 NOV 84	HATFUL OF HOLLOW	7
23 FEB 85	MEAT IS MURDER	1
28 JUN 86	THE QUEEN IS DEAD	2
7 MAR 87	THE WORLD WON'T LISTEN	2
30 MAY 87	LOUDER THAN BOMBS (IMPORT)	38
10 OCT 87	STRANGEWAYS HERE WE COME	2
17 SEP 88	RANK	2
29 AUG 92	BEST...1	1
14 NOV 92	BEST...II	29

Rock facts... ...and quiz book
• THE STONE ROSES •

SINGLES

29 JUL 89	SHE BANGS THE DRUMS	36
25 NOV 89	WHAT THE WORLD IS WAITING FOR / FOOL'S GOLD	8
6 JAN 90	SALLY CINNAMON	75
20 JAN 90	SALLY CINNAMON (RE-ENTRY)	46
3 MAR 90	ELEPHANT STONE	8
17 MAR 90	MADE OF STONE	20
31 MAR 90	SHE BANGS THE DRUMS (RE-ENTRY)	34
14 JUL 90	ONE LOVE	4
15 SEP 90	WHAT THE WORLD IS WAITING FOR / FOOL'S GOLD (RE-ENTRY)	22
14 SEP 91	I WANNA BE ADORED	20
11 JAN 92	WATERFALL	27
11 APR 92	I AM THE RESURRECTION	33
30 MAY 92	FOOL'S GOLD (RE-MIX)	73
3 DEC 94	LOVE SPREADS	2
11 MAR 95	TEN STOREY LOVE SONG	11
29 APR 95	FOOL'S GOLD (2ND RE-MIX)	25
11 NOV 95	BEGGING YOU	15

ALBUMS

13 MAY 89	THE STONE ROSES	19
1 AUG 92	TURNS INTO STONE	32
17 DEC 94	SECOND COMING	4
27 MAY 95	THE COMPLETE STONE ROSES	4

R♪ck facts... ...and quiz b♪♪k
• THE STRANGLERS •

SINGLES

19 FEB 77	(GET A) GRIP (ON YOURSELF)	44
21 MAY 77	PEACHES / GO BUDDY GO	8
30 JUL 77	SOMETHING BETTER CHANGE / STRAIGHTEN OUT	9
24 SEP 77	NO MORE HEROES	8
4 FEB 78	FIVE MINUTES	11
6 MAY 78	NICE 'N' SLEAZY	18
12 AUG 78	WALK ON BY	21
18 AUG 79	DUCHESS	14
20 OCT 79	NUCLEAR DEVICE (THE WIZARD OF AUS)	36
1 DEC 79	DON'T BRING HARRY EP	41
22 MAR 80	BEAR CAGE	36
7 JUN 80	WHO WANTS THE WORLD	39
31 JAN 81	THROWN AWAY	42
14 NOV 81	LET ME INTRODUCE YOU TO THE FAMILY	42
9 JAN 82	GOLDEN BROWN	2
24 APR 82	LA FOLIE	47
24 JUL 82	STRANGE LITTLE GIRL	7
8 JAN 83	EUROPEAN FEMALE	9
26 FEB 83	MIDNIGHT SUMMER DREAM	35
6 AUG 83	PARADISE	48
6 OCT 84	SKIN DEEP	15
1 DEC 84	NO MERCY	37
16 FEB 85	LET ME DOWN EASY	48
23 AUG 86	NICE IN NICE	30
18 OCT 86	ALWAYS THE SUN	30
13 DEC 86	BIG IN AMERICA	48
7 MAR 87	SHAKIN' LIKE A LEAF	58

• THE STRANGLERS •

SINGLES

9 JAN 88	ALL DAY AND ALL OF THE NIGHT	7
28 JAN 89	GRIP '89 (GET A) GRIP (ON YOURSELF) (RE-MIX)	33
17 FEB 90	96 TEARS	17
21 APR 90	SWEET SMELL OF SUCCESS	65
5 JAN 91	ALWAYS THE SUN (RE-MIX)	29
30 MAR 91	GOLDEN BROWN (RE-MIX)	68
22 AUG 92	HEAVEN OR HELL	46

ALBUMS

30 APR 77	STRANGLERS IV (RATTUS NORVEGICUS)	4
8 OCT 77	NO MORE HEROES	2
3 JUN 78	BLACK AND WHITE	2
10 MAR 79	LIVE (X CERT)	7
6 OCT 79	THE RAVEN	4
21 FEB 81	THEMENINBLACK	8
21 NOV 81	LA FOLIE	11
22 JAN 83	FELINE	4
17 NOV 84	AURAL SCULPTURE	14
20 SEP 86	OFF THE BEATEN TRACK	80
8 NOV 86	DREAMTIME	16
20 FEB 88	ALL LIVE AND ALL OF THE NIGHT	12
17 MAR 90	10	15
19 SEP 92	STRANGLERS IN THE NIGHT	33
27 MAY 95	ABOUT TIME	31

•THE VELVET UNDERGROUND•

SINGLES

ALBUMS

•THE VERVE•

SINGLES

4 JUL 92	SHE'S A SUPERSTAR	66
22 MAY 93	BLUE	69
13 MAY 95	THIS IS MUSIC	35
24 JUN 95	ON YOUR OWN	28
30 SEP 95	HISTORY	24
28 JUN 97	BITTER SWEET SYMPHONY	2
13 SEP 97	THE DRUGS DON'T WORK	1
6 DEC 97	LUCKY MAN	7
3 JAN 98	THE DRUGS DON'T WORK (RE-ENTRY)	66
3 JAN 98	BITTER SWEET SYMPHONY (RE-ENTRY)	70
30 MAY 98	SONNET	74

ALBUMS

3 JUL 93	A STORM IN HEAVEN	27
15 JUL 95	A NORTHERN SOUL	13

•THE WHO•

SINGLES

18 FEB 65	I CAN'T EXPLAIN	8
27 MAY 65	ANYWAY ANYHOW ANYWHERE	10
4 NOV 65	MY GENERATION	2
10 MAR 66	SUBSTITUTE	5
24 MAR 66	A LEGAL MATTER	32
1 SEP 66	I'M A BOY	2
1 SEP 66	THE KIDS ARE ALRIGHT	41
22 SEP 66	THE KIDS ARE ALRIGHT (RE-ENTRY)	48
15 DEC 66	HAPPY JACK	3
27 APR 67	PICTURES OF LILY	4
26 JUL 67	THE LAST TIME / UNDER MY THUMB	44
18 OCT 67	I CAN SEE FOR MILES	10
19 JUN 68	DOGS	25
23 OCT 68	MAGIC BUS	26
19 MAR 69	PINBALL WIZARD	4
4 APR 70	THE SEEKER	19
8 AUG 70	SUMMERTIME BLUES	38
10 JUL 71	WON'T GET FOOLED AGAIN	9
23 OCT 71	LET'S SEE ACTION	16
24 JUN 72	JOIN TOGETHER	9
13 JAN 73	RELAY	21
13 OCT 73	5:15	20
24 JAN 76	SQUEEZE BOX	10
30 OCT 76	SUBSTITUTE (RE-ISSUE)	7
22 JUL 78	WHO ARE YOU	18
28 APR 79	LONG LIVE ROCK	48
7 MAR 81	YOU BETTER YOU BET	9
9 MAY 81	DON'T LET GO THE COAT	47
2 OCT 82	ATHENA	40
26 NOV 83	READY STEADY WHO EP	58
20 FEB 88	MY GENERATION (RE-ISSUE)	68
27 JUL 96	MY GENERATION (2ND RE-ISSUE)	31

• THE WHO •

ALBUMS

25 DEC 65	MY GENERATION	5
17 DEC 66	A QUICK ONE	4
13 JAN 68	THE WHO SELL-OUT	13
7 JUN 69	TOMMY	2
6 JUN 70	LIVE AT LEEDS	3
11 SEP 71	WHO'S NEXT	1
18 DEC 71	MEATY, BEATY, BIG AND BOUNCY	9
17 NOV 73	QUADROPHENIA	2
26 OCT 74	ODDS AND SODS	10
23 AUG 75	TOMMY (FILM SOUNDTRACK)	30
18 OCT 75	THE WHO BY NUMBERS	7
9 SEP 78	WHO ARE YOU	6
30 JUN 79	THE KIDS ARE ALRIGHT	26
28 MAR 81	FACE DANCES	2
11 SEP 82	IT'S HARD	11
17 NOV 84	WHO'S LAST	48
19 MAR 88	WHO'S BETTER WHO'S BEST	10

• THE YARDBIRDS •

SINGLES

12 NOV 64	GOOD MORNING LITTLE SCHOOLGIRL	44
18 MAR 65	FOR YOUR LOVE	3
17 JUN 65	HEART FULL OF SOUL	2
14 OCT 65	EVIL HEARTED YOU / STILL I'M SAD	3
3 MAR 66	SHAPES OF THINGS	3
2 JUN 66	OVER UNDER SIDEWAYS DOWN	10
27 OCT 66	HAPPENINGS TEN YEARS TIME AGO	43

ALBUMS

23 JUL 66	YARDBIRDS	20

• THIN LIZZY •

SINGLES

20 JAN 73	WHISKY IN THE JAR	6
29 MAY 76	THE BOYS ARE BACK IN TOWN	8
14 AUG 76	JAILBREAK	31
15 JAN 77	DON'T BELIEVE A WORD	12
13 AUG 77	DANCIN' IN THE MOONLIGHT (IT'S CAUGHT ME IN THE SPOTLIGHT)	14
13 MAY 78	ROSALIE - COWGIRLS' SONG (MEDLEY)	20
3 MAR 79	WAITING FOR AN ALIBI	9
16 JUN 79	DO ANYTHING YU WANT TO	14
20 OCT 79	SARAH	24
24 MAY 80	CHINATOWN	21
27 SEP 80	KILLER ON THE LOOSE	10
2 MAY 81	KILLERS LIVE EP	19
8 AUG 81	TROUBLE BOYS	53
6 MAR 82	HOLLYWOOD (DOWN ON YOUR LUCK)	53
12 FEB 83	COLD SWEAT	27
7 MAY 83	THUNDER AND LIGHTNING	39
6 AUG 83	THE SUN GOES DOWN	52
26 JAN 91	DEDICATION	35
23 MAR 91	THE BOYS ARE BACK IN TOWN (RE-ISSUE)	63

ALBUMS

27 SEP 75	FIGHTING	60
10 APR 76	JAILBREAK	10
6 NOV 76	JOHNNY THE FOX	11
1 OCT 77	BAD REPUTATION	4
17 JUN 78	LIVE AND DANGEROUS	2
5 MAY 79	BLACK ROSE (A ROCK LEGEND)	2
18 OCT 80	CHINA TOWN	7
11 APR 81	ADVENTURES OF THIN LIZZY	6
5 DEC 81	RENEGADE	38
12 MAR 83	THUNDER AND LIGHTNING	4
26 NOV 83	LIFE	29

• TINA TURNER •

SINGLES

19 NOV 83	LET'S STAY TOGETHER	6
25 FEB 84	HELP	40
16 JUN 84	WHAT'S LOVE GOT TO DO WITH IT	3
15 SEP 84	BETTER BE GOOD TO ME	45
17 NOV 84	PRIVATE DANCER	26
2 MAR 85	I CAN'T STAND THE RAIN	57
20 JUL 85	WE DON'T NEED ANOTHER HERO (THUNDERDOME)	3
12 OCT 85	ONE OF THE LIVING	55
2 NOV 85	IT'S ONLY LOVE	29
23 AUG 86	TYPICAL MALE	33
8 NOV 86	TWO PEOPLE	43
14 MAR 87	WHAT YOU GET IS WHAT YOU SEE	30
13 JUN 87	BREAK EVERY RULE	43
20 JUN 87	TEARING US APART	56
19 MAR 88	ADDICTED TO LOVE (LIVE)	71
2 SEP 89	THE BEST	5
18 NOV 89	I DON'T WANNA LOSE YOU	8
17 FEB 90	STEAMY WINDOWS	13
11 AUG 90	LOOK ME IN THE HEART	31
13 OCT 90	BE TENDER WITH ME BABY	28
24 NOV 90	IT TAKES TWO	5
21 SEP 91	NUTBUSH CITY LIMITS	23
23 NOV 91	WAY OF THE WORLD	13
15 FEB 92	LOVE THING	29
6 JUN 92	I WANT YOU NEAR ME	22
22 MAY 93	I DON'T WANNA FIGHT	7
28 AUG 93	DISCO INFERNO	12

• TINA TURNER •

SINGLES CONT...

30 OCT 93	WHY MUST WE WAIT UNTIL TONIGHT	16
18 NOV 95	GOLDENEYE	10
23 MAR 96	WHATEVER YOU WANT	23
8 JUN 96	ON SILENT WINGS	13
27 JUL 96	MISSING YOU	12
19 OCT 96	SOMETHING BEAUTIFUL REMAINS	27
21 DEC 96	IN YOUR WILDEST DREAMS	32

ALBUMS

30 JUN 84	PRIVATE DANCER	2
20 SEP 86	BREAK EVERY RULE	2
2 APR 88	LIVE IN EUROPE	8
30 SEP 89	FOREIGN AFFAIR	1
12 OCT 91	SIMPLY THE BEST	2
19 JUN 93	WHAT'S LOVE GOT TO DO WITH IT (FILM SOUNDTRACK)	1

•TORI AMOS•

SINGLES

ALBUMS

• TRAFFIC •

SINGLES

1 JUN 67	PAPER SUN	5
6 SEP 67	HOLE IN MY SHOE	2
29 NOV 67	HERE WE GO ROUND THE MULBERRY BUSH	8
6 MAR 68	NO FACE, NO NAME, NO NUMBER	40

ALBUMS

30 DEC 67	MR. FANTASY	8
26 OCT 68	TRAFFIC	9
8 AUG 70	JOHN BARLEYCORN MUST DIE	11
24 NOV 73	ON THE ROAD	40
28 SEP 74	WHEN THE EAGLE FLIES	31
21 MAY 94	FAR FROM HOME	29

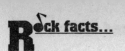

•U2•

SINGLES

8 AUG 81	FIRE	35
17 OCT 81	GLORIA	55
3 APR 82	A CELEBRATION	47
22 JAN 83	NEW YEARS DAY	10
2 APR 83	TWO HEARTS BEAT AS ONE	18
15 SEP 84	PRIDE (IN THE NAME OF LOVE)	3
4 MAY 85	THE UNFORGETTABLE FIRE	6
28 MAR 87	WITH OR WITHOUT YOU	4
6 JUN 87	I STILL HAVEN'T FOUND WHAT I'M LOOKING FOR	6
12 SEP 87	WHERE THE STREETS HAVE NO NAME	4
26 DEC 87	IN GOD'S CUNTRY (IMPORT)	48
1 OCT 88	DESIRE	1
17 DEC 88	ANGEL OF HARLEM	9
15 APR 89	WHEN LOVE COMES TO TOWN	6
24 JUN 89	ALL I WANT IS YOU	4
2 NOV 91	THE FLY	1
14 DEC 91	THE FLY (RE-ENTRY)	62
4 JAN 92	MYSTERIOUS WAYS	13
7 MAR 92	ONE	7
20 JUN 92	EVEN BETER THAN THE REAL THING	12
11 JUL 92	EVEN BETTER THAN THE REAL THING (RE-MIX)	8
5 DEC 92	WHO'S GONNA RIDE YOUR WILD HORSES	14
4 DEC 93	STAY (FARAWAY, SO CLOSE)	4
17 JUN 95	HOLD ME THRILL ME KISS ME KILL ME	2
15 FEB 97	DISCOTHEQUE	1
26 APR 97	STARING AT THE SUN	3
17 MAY 97	DISCOTHEQUE (RE-ENTRY)	72
2 AUG 97	LAST NIGHT ON EARTH	10
4 OCT 97	PLEASE	7
20 DEC 97	IF GOD WILL SEND HIS ANGELS	12
31 OCT 98	SWEETEST THING	3

•U2•

ALBUMS

29 AUG 81	BOY	52
24 OCT 81	OCTOBER	11
12 MAR 83	WAR	1
3 DEC 83	U2 LIVE: UNDER A BLOOD RED SKY	2
13 OCT 84	THE UNFORGETTABLE FIRE	1
27 JUL 85	WIDE AWAKE IN AMERICA (IMPORT)	11
21 MAR 87	THE JOSHUA TREE	1
22 OCT 88	RATTLE AND HUM	1
30 NOV 91	ACHTUNG BABY	2
17 JUL 93	ZOOROPA	1

•VAN HALEN•

SINGLES

28 JUN 80	RUNNIN' WITH THE DEVIL	52
4 FEB 84	JUMP	7
19 MAY 84	PANAMA	61
5 APR 86	WHY CAN'T THIS BE LOVE	8
12 JUL 86	DREAMS	62
6 AUG 88	WHEN IT'S LOVE	28
1 APR 89	FEELS SO GOOD	63
22 JUN 91	POUNDCAKE	74
19 OCT 91	TOP OF THE WORLD	63
27 MAR 93	JUMP (LIVE)	26
21 JAN 95	DON'T TELL ME	27
1 APR 95	CAN'T STOP LOVIN' YOU	33

ALBUMS

27 MAY 78	VAN HALEN	34
14 APR 79	VAN HALEN II	23
5 APR 80	WOMEN AND CHILDREN FIRST	15
23 MAY 81	FAIR WARNING	49
1 MAY 82	DIVER DOWN	36
4 FEB 84	1984	15
5 APR 86	5150	16
4 JUN 88	OU812	16
29 JUN 91	FOR UNLAWFUL CARNAL KNOWLEDGE	12
6 MAR 93	LIVE: RIGHT HERE RIGHT NOW	24
4 FEB 95	BALANCE	8

• WHITESNAKE •

SINGLES

24 JUN 78	SNAKE BITE EP	61
10 NOV 79	LONG WAY FROM HOME	55
26 APR 80	FOOL FOR YOUR LOVING	13
12 JUL 80	READY AN' WILLING (SWEET SATISFACTION)	43
22 NOV 80	AIN'T NO LOVE IN THE HEART OF THE CITY	51
11 APR 81	DON'T BREAK MY HEART AGAIN	17
6 JUN 81	WOULD I LIE TO YOU	37
6 NOV 82	HERE I GO AGAIN / BLOODY LUXURY	34
13 AUG 83	GUILTY OF LOVE	31
14 JAN 84	GIVE ME MORE TIME	29
28 APR 84	STANDING IN THE SHADOW	62
9 FEB 85	LOVE AIN'T NO STRANGER	44
28 MAR 87	STILL OF THE NIGHT	16
6 JUN 87	IS THIS LOVE	9
31 OCT 87	HERE I GO AGAIN (RE-MIX)	9
6 FEB 88	GIVE ME ALL YOUR LOVE	18
2 DEC 89	FOOL FOR YOUR LOVING	43
10 MAR 90	THE DEEPER THE LOVE	35
25 AUG 90	NOW YOU'RE GONE	31
6 AUG 94	IS THIS LOVE (RE-ISSUE) / SWEET LADY LUCK	25
7 JUN 97	TOO MANY TEARS	46

ALBUMS

18 NOV 78	TROUBLE	50
13 OCT 79	LOVE HUNTER	29
7 JUN 80	READY AND WILLING	6
8 NOV 80	LIVE IN THE HEART OF THE CITY	5
18 APR 81	COME AND GET IT	2
27 NOV 82	SAINTS 'N' SINNERS	9
11 FEB 84	SLIDE IT IN	9
11 APR 87	WHITESNAKE 1987	8
25 NOV 89	SLIP OF THE TONGUE	10

SINGLES

Date	Title	Position
16 NOV 85	SAVING ALL MY LOVE FOR YOU	1
25 JAN 86	HOW WILL I KNOW	5
25 JAN 86	HOLD ME	44
12 APR 86	GREATEST LOVE OF ALL	8
23 MAY 87	I WANNA DANCE WITH SOMEBODY (WHO LOVES ME)	1
22 AUG 87	DIDN'T WE ALMOST HAVE IT ALL	14
14 NOV 87	SO EMOTIONAL	5
12 MAR 88	WHERE DO BROKEN HEARTS GO	14
28 MAY 88	LOVE WILL SAVE THE DAY	10
24 SEP 88	ONE MOMENT IN TIME	1
9 SEP 89	IT ISN'T, IT WASN'T, IT AIN'T NEVER GONNA BE	29
20 OCT 90	I'M YOUR BABY TONIGHT	5
22 DEC 90	ALL THE MAN THAT I NEED	13
29 DEC 90	I'M YOUR BABY TONIGHT (RE-ENTRY)	69
6 JUL 91	MY NAME IS NOT SUSAN	29
28 SEP 91	I BELONG TO YOU	54
14 NOV 92	I WILL ALWAYS LOVE YOU	1
20 FEB 93	I'M EVERY WOMAN	4
24 APR 93	I HAVE NOTHING	3
31 JUL 93	RUN TO YOU	15
6 NOV 93	QUEEN OF THE NIGHT	14
18 DEC 93	I WILL ALWAYS LOVE YOU (RE-ENTRY)	25
22 JAN 94	SOMETHING IN COMMON	16
18 NOV 95	EXHALE (SHOOP SHOOP)	11
24 FEB 96	COUNT ON ME	12
21 DEC 96	STEP BY STEP	17
29 MAR 97	I BELIEVE IN YOU AND ME	16
19 DEC 98	WHEN YOU BELIEVE	4

ALBUMS

14 DEC 85	WHITNEY HOUSTON	2
13 JUN 87	WHITNEY	1
17 NOV 90	I'M YOUR BABY TONIGHT	4

• WIZZARD •

SINGLES

9 DEC 72	BALL PARK INCIDENT	6
21 APR 73	SEE MY BABY JIVE	1
1 SEP 73	ANGEL FINGERS	1
8 DEC 73	I WISH IT COULD BE CHRISTMAS EVERYDAY	4
27 APR 74	ROCK 'N' ROLL WINTER	6
10 AUG 74	THIS IS THE STORY OF MY LOVE (BABY)	34
21 DEC 74	ARE YOU READY TO ROCK	8
19 DEC 81	I WISH IT COULD BE CHRISTMAS EVERYDAY (RE-ISSUE)	41
15 DEC 84	I WISH IT COULD BE CHRISTMAS EVERYDAY (RE-ENTRY OF RE-ISSUE)	23

ALBUMS

19 MAY 73	WIZZARD BREW	29
17 AUG 74	INTRODUCING EDDY AND THE FALCONS	19

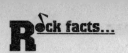

•XTC•

SINGLES

12 MAY 79	LIFE BEGINS AT THE HOP	54
22 SEP 79	MAKING PLANS FOR NIGEL	17
6 SEP 80	GENERALS AND MAJORS / DON'T LOSE YOUR TEMPER	32
18 OCT 80	TOWERS OF LONDON	31
24 JAN 81	SGT ROCK (IS GOING TO HELP ME)	16
23 JAN 82	SENSES WORKING OVERTIME	10
27 MAR 82	BALL AND CHAIN	58
15 OCT 83	LOVE ON A FARMBOY'S WAGES	50
29 SEP 84	ALL YOU PRETTY GIRLS	55
28 JAN 89	MAYOR OF SIMPLETON	46
4 APR 92	THE DISAPPOINTED	33
13 JUN 92	THE BALLAD OF PETER PUMPKINHEAD	71

ALBUMS

11 FEB 78	WHITE MUSIC	38
28 OCT 78	GO 2	21
1 SEP 79	DRUMS AND WIRES	34
20 SEP 80	BLACK SEA	16
20 FEB 82	ENGLISH SETTLEMENT	5
10 SEP 83	MUMMER	51
27 OCT 84	THE BIG EXPRESS	38
8 NOV 86	SKYLARKING	90
11 MAR 89	ORANGES AND LEMONS	28
9 MAY 92	NONSUCH	28

•YES•

SINGLES

17 SEP 77	WONDEROUS STORIES	7
26 NOV 77	GOING FOR THE ONE	24
9 SEP 78	DON'T KILL THE WHALE	36
12 NOV 83	OWNER OF A LONELY HEART	28
31 MAR 84	LEAVE IT	56
3 OCT 87	LOVE WILL FIND A WAY	73

ALBUMS

1 AUG 70	TIME AND A WORD	45
3 APR 71	THE YES ALBUM	7
4 DEC 71	FRAGILE	7
23 SEP 72	CLOSE TO THE EDGE	4
26 MAY 73	YESSONGS	7
22 DEC 73	TALES FROM TOPOGRAPHIC OCEANS	1
21 DEC 74	RELAYER	4
29 MAR 75	YESTERDAYS	27
30 JUL 77	GOING FOR THE ONE	1
7 OCT 78	TORMATO	8
30 AUG 80	DRAMA	2
10 JAN 81	YESSHOWS	22
26 NOV 83	90125	16
29 MAR 86	9012 LIVE: THE SOLOS	44
10 OCT 87	BIG GENERATOR	17
11 MAY 91	UNION	7
2 APR 94	TALK	20

• ZZ TOP •

SINGLES

3 SEP 83	GIMME ALL YOUR LOVIN'	61
26 NOV 83	SHARP DRESSED MAN	53
31 MAR 84	TV DINNERS	67
6 OCT 84	GIMME ALL YOUR LOVIN' (RE-ENTRY)	10
15 DEC 84	SHARP DRESSED MAN (RE-ENTRY)	22
23 FEB 85	LEGS	16
13 JUL 85	SUMMER HOLIDAY EP	51
19 OCT 85	SLEEPING BAG	27
15 FEB 86	STAGES	43
19 APR 86	ROUGH BOY	23
4 OCT 86	VELCRO FLY	54
21 JUL90	DOUBLEBACK	29
13 APR 91	MY HEAD'S IN MISSISSIPPI	37
11 APR 92	VIVA LAS VEGAS	10
20 JUN 92	ROUGH BOY (RE-ISSUE)	49
29 JAN 94	PINCUSHION	15
7 MAY 94	BREAKAWAY	60
29 JUN 96	WHAT'S UP WITH THAT	58

ALBUMS

12 JUL 75	FANDANGO	60
8 AUG 81	EL LOCO	88
30 APR 83	ELIMINATOR	3
9 NOV 85	AFTERBURNER	2
27 OCT 90	RECYCLER	8
5 FEB 94	ANTENNA	3

•HAPPY BIRTHDAY!•

JANUARY

Country Joe McDonald	1st January 1942
Grandmaster Flash	1st January 1958
George Martin (The Beatles' producer)	3rd January 1926
Van Dyke Parks	3rd January 1941
Steven Stills (Buffalo Springfield)	3rd January 1945
Barney Sumner (New Order)	4th January 1956
Michael Stipe (R.E.M)	4th January 1960
Chris Stein (Blondie)	5th January 1950
Syd Barrett (Pink Floyd)	6th January 1946
Kenny Loggins	7th January 1948
Elvis Presley	8th January 1935
Robbie Krieger (The Doors)	8th January 1946
David Bowie	8th January 1947
Les Paul	9th January 1915
Joan Baez	9th January 1941
Jimmy Page (Led Zeppelin)	9th January 1944
Johnny Ray	10th January 1927
Rod Stewart	10th January 1945
Pat Benatar	10th January 1953
Vicki Peterson (The Bangles)	11th January 1951
Long John Baldry	12th January 1941
Suggs (Madness)	13th January 1961
Captain Beefheart	15th January 1941
Peter Trewavas (Marillion)	15th January 1959

• HAPPY BIRTHDAY! •

Mick Taylor (The Rolling Stones)	17th January 1948
Paul Young	17th January 1956
Susanna Hoffs (The Bangles)	17th January 1957
David Ruffin (The Temptations)	18th January 1941
Phil Everly	19th January 1939
Janis Joplin	19th January 1943
Dolly Parton	19th January 1946
Robert Palmer	19th January 1949
Eric Stewart (10cc)	20th January 1945
Malcolm McLaren	20th January 1947
Paul Stanley (Kiss)	20th January 1950
Gary Barlow (Take That)	20th January 1971
Billy Ocean	21st January 1950
Wendy James (Transvision Vamp)	21st January 1966
Sam Cooke	22nd January 1931
Michael Hutchence	22nd January 1962
Andrew Roachford	22nd January 1965
Robin Zander (CheapTrick)	23rd January 1953
Neil Diamond	24th January 1941
Ray Stevens	24th January 1941
Jools Holland	24th January 1955
Gary Tibbs (Roxy Music)	25th January 1958
Eddie Van Halen	26th January 1957
Andrew Ridgeley	26th January 1963
Jazzie B. (Soul II Soul)	26th January 1963

•HAPPY BIRTHDAY!•

Elmore James	27th January 1914
Nick Mason (Pink Floyd)	27th January 1945
Mark Owen (Take That)	27th January 1974
Sacha Distel	28th January 1933
Roddy Fame (Aztec Camera)	29th January 1964
Marty Balin (Jefferson Airplane)	30th January 1942
Steve Marriott (Small Faces/Humble Pie)	30th January 1947
Phil Collins	31st January 1951
John Lydon (a.k.a Johnny Rotten, The Sex Pistols)	31st January 1956
Lloyd Cole	31st January 1961

FEBRUARY

Don Everly	1st February 1937
Ray Sawyer (Dr. Hook)	1st February 1937
Graham Nash (The Hollies)	2nd February 1941
Roberta Flack	2nd February 1937
Dave Davies (The Kinks)	3rd February 1947
Alice Cooper (a.k.a Vincent Furnier)	4th February 1948
Tim Booth (James)	4th February 1960
Bobby Brown	5th February 1969

•HAPPY BIRTHDAY!•

Axl Rose (Guns N'Roses)	6th February 1962
Bob Marley	6th February 1945
Dave Berry	6th February 1941
Mike Batt	6th February 1950
Rick Astley	6th February 1966
Carole King	9th February 1942
Gene Vincent	11th February 1935
Gerry Goffin	11th February 1939
Sheryl Crow	11th February 1962
Ray Manzarek	12th February 1935
Peter Hook (New Order)	13th February 1956
Peter Tork (The Monkees)	13th February 1944
Robbie Williams	13th February 1974
Steve Priest (Sweet)	23rd February 1950
Ali Campbell (UB40)	15th February 1959
Gene Pitney	17th February 1941
John Travolta	18th February 1954
Holly Johnson (Frankie Goes To Hollywood)	19th February 1960
Smokey Robinson	19th February 1940
Tony Iommi (Black Sabbath)	19th February 1948
Ian Brown (The Stone Roses)	20th February 1963
Kurt Cobain (Nirvana)	20th February 1967
David Sylvian (Japan)	23rd February 1958
Howard Jones	23rd February 1955
George Harrison (The Beatles)	24th February 1943

• HAPPY BIRTHDAY! •

Paul Jones (Manfred Mann)	24th February 1942
Elkie Brooks	25th February 1945
Mike Peters (The Alarm)	25th February 1959
Stuart "Woody" Wood (The Bay City Rollers)	25th February 1957
Fats Domino	26th February 1928
Michael Bolton	26th February 1953
Sandie Shaw	26th February 1947
Steve Harley	27th February 1951
Brian Jones (The Rolling Stones)	28th February 1942

MARCH

Nick Kershaw	1st March 1958
Roger Daltrey (The Who)	1st March 1944
Jay Osmond (The Osmonds)	2nd March 1955
Jon Bon Jovi	2nd March 1962
Karen Carpenter	2nd March 1950
Lou Reed (Velvet Underground)	2nd March 1943
Bobby Womack	4th March 1944
Chris Rea	4th March 1951
Chris Squire (Yes)	4th March 1948
Gloria Estefan	4th March 1953

•HAPPY BIRTHDAY!•

Shakin' Stevens	4th March 1948
Andy Gibb	5th March 1958
Eddie Grant	5th March 1948
Dave Gilmour (Pink Floyd)	6th March 1947
Kiki Dee	6th March 1947
Arthur Lee (Love)	7th March 1945
Gary Newman	8th March 1958
Mickey Dolenz (The Monkees)	8th March 1945
Martin Fry (ABC)	9th March 1958
Trevor Burton (The Move)	9th March 1949
Dean Torrence (Jan and Dean)	10th March 1940
James Taylor	12th March 1948
Paul Kantner (Jefferson Airplane)	12th March 1941
Steve Harris (Iron Maiden)	12th March 1957
Adam Clayton (U2)	13th March 1960
Neil Sedaka	13th March 1939
Quincy Jones	14th March 1938
Dee Snider (Twisted Sister)	15th March 1955
Mike Love (The Beach Boys)	15th March 1941
Ry Cooder	15th March 1947
Sly Stone	15th March 1944
Terence Trent D'Arby	15th March 1962
Clare Grogan (Altered Images)	17th March 1962
John Sebastian (The Lovin' Spoonful)	17th March 1944
Scott Gorham (Thin Lizzie)	17th March 1951

•HAPPY BIRTHDAY!•

Wilson Pickett	18th March 1941
Carl Palmer (Emerson, Lake and Palmer)	20th March 1947
Roger Hodgson (Supertramp)	21st March 1950
George Benson	22nd March 1943
Keith Relf (The Yardbirds)	22nd March 1943
Chaka Khan	23rd March 1953
Damon Albarn (Blur)	23rd March 1968
Marti Pellow	23rd March 1966
Ric Ocasek (The Cars)	23rd March 1949
Aretha Franklin	25th March 1942
Elton John	25th March 1947
Diana Ross	26th March 1944
Richard Tandy (ELO)	26th March 1948
Steven Tyler (Aerosmith)	26th March 1948
Mariah Carey	27th March 1970
Tony Banks (Genesis)	27th March 1950
John Evan (Jethro Tull)	28th March 1948
Vangelis	29th March 1943
Dave Ball (The Turtles)	30th March 1946
Eric Clapton	30th March 1945
Graham Edge (The Moody Blues)	30th March 1942
Lene Lovich	30th March 1954
Tracy Chapman	30th March 1964
Angus Young (AC/DC)	31st March 1959
Herb Alpert	31st March 1935

•HAPPY BIRTHDAY!•

APRIL

Ronnie Lane (The Faces)	1st April 1946
Rudolph Isley (The Isley Brothers)	1st April 1939
Karen Woodward (Bananarama)	2nd April 1961
Marvin Gaye	2nd April 1939
Jan Berry (Jan and Dean)	3rd April 1941
Dave Hill (Slade)	4th April 1952
Gary Moore	4th April 1952
Muddy Waters	4th April 1915
Agnetha Faltskog (ABBA)	5th April 1950
Alan Clarke (The Hollies)	5th April 1942
Michelle Phillips (The Mamas and Papas)	6th April 1944
Julian Lennon	8th April 1963
Steve Howe (Yes)	8th April 1947
Carl Perkins	9th April 1932
Brian Setzer (The Stray Cats)	10th April 1959
David Cassidy	12th April 1950
Herbie Hancock	12th April 1940
John Kay (Steppenwolf)	12th April 1944
Ritchie Blackmore (Deep Purple)	14th April 1945
Dave Edmunds	15th April 1944
Marty Wilde	15th April 1939
Bobby Vinton	16th April 1935
Dusty Springfield	16th April 1939
Jimmy Osmond	16th April 1963

•HAPPY BIRTHDAY!•

Alan Price (The Animals)	19th April 1941
Alexis Korner	19th April 1928
Luther Vandross	20th April 1951
Iggy Pop	21st April 1947
Robert Smith (The Cure)	21st April 1959
Ace Frehley (Kiss)	22nd April 1951
Charlie Mingus	22nd April 1922
Glen Campbell	22nd April 1936
Peter Frampton	22nd April 1950
Captain Sensible (The Damned)	23rd April 1955
Roy Orbison	23rd April 1936
Barbra Streisand	24th April 1942
Bjorn Ulvaeus (ABBA)	25th April 1945
Ella Fitzgerald	25th April 1918
Fish (aka Derek Dick, Marillion)	25th April 1958
Duane Eddy	26th April 1938
Howard Donald (Take That)	27th April 1970
Sheena Easton	27th April 1959
Francis Rossi (Status Quo)	29th April 1949
Lonnie Donegan	29th April 1931
Bobby Vee	30th April 1943

• HAPPY BIRTHDAY! •

MAY

Bernard Butler (Suede)	1st May 1970
Ray Parker Jr.	1st May 1954
Bing Crosby	2nd May 1904
Engelbert Hunperdinck	2nd May 1936
Frankie Valli (The Four Seasons)	3rd May 1937
James Brown	3rd May 1933
Dick Dale	4th May 1937
Tammy Wynette	4th May 1942
Ian McCulloch (Echo And The Bunnymen)	5th May 1959
Peggy Lee	6th May 1920
Alex Van Halen	8th May 1955
Gary Glitter (a.k.a Paul Gadd)	8th May 1940
Philip Bailey (Earth, Wind and Fire)	8th May 1951
Billy Joel	9th May 1949
Paul Heaton (Housemartins/Beautiful South)	9th May 1962
Bono (U2)	10th May 1960
Dave Mason (Traffic)	10th May 1945
Donovan (Leitch)	10th May 1946
Graham Gouldman (10cc)	10th May 1946
Sid Vicious (The Sex Pistols)	10th May 1957
Eric Burdon (The Animals)	11th May 1941
Burt Bacharach	12th May 1928
Ian Dury	12th May 1942
Steve Winwood	12th May 1948

• HAPPY BIRTHDAY! •

Peter Gabriel	13th May 1950
Ritchie Valens	13th May 1941
Stevie Wonder	13th May 1950
Bobby Darin	14th May 1936
David Byrne (Talking Heads)	14th May 1952
Ian Astbury (The Cult)	14th May 1962
Jack Bruce (Cream)	14th May 1943
Andrew Eldritch (Sisters Of Mercy)	15th May 1959
Brian Eno (Roxy Music)	15th May 1948
Mike Oldfield	15th May 1953
Janet Jackson	16th May 1966
Bill Bruford (Yes)	17th May 1950
Enya (Clannad)	17th May 1961
Perry Como	18th May 1912
Dusty Hill (ZZ Top)	19th May 1949
Grace Jones	19th May 1952
Pete Townsend (The Who)	19th May 1945
Cher	20th May 1946
Joe Cocker	20th May 1944
Nick Heyward	20th May 1961
Leo Sayer	21st May 1948
Bernie Taupin	22nd May 1950
Morrissey (The Smiths)	22nd May 1959
Bob Dylan	24th May 1941
Paul Weller (The Jam)	25th May 1958

• HAPPY BIRTHDAY! •

Lenny Kravitz	26th May 1964
Mick Ronson (Mott The Hoople)	26th May 1949
Stevie Nicks (Fleetwood Mac)	26th May 1948
Wayne Hussey (The Mission)	26th May 1958
Neil Finn (Crowded House)	27th May 1956
Siouxsie Sioux	27th May 1957
Kylie Minogue	28th May 1968
Roland Gift (Fine Young Cannibals)	28th May 1962
Noel Gallagher (Oasis)	29th May 1967
Tim Burgess (The Charlatans)	30th May 1968
John Bonham (Led Zeppelin)	31st May 1948

JUNE

Alanis Morissette	1st June 1974
Jason Donovan	1st June 1968
Pat Boone	1st June 1934
Ron Wood (The Faces/ The Rolling Stones)	1st June 1947
Charlie Watts (The Rolling Stones)	2nd June 1941
Michel Steele (The Bangles)	2nd June 1954
Tony Hadley (Spandau Ballet)	2nd June 1960
Ian Hunter (Mott The Hoople)	3rd June 1946

• HAPPY BIRTHDAY! •

John Paul Jones (Led Zeppelin)	3rd June 1946
Suzi Quatro	3rd June 1950
Roger Fraser (Tangerine Dream)	6th June 1944
Prince	7th June 1958
Tom Jones	7th June 1940
Bonnie Tyler	8th June 1953
Mick Hucknall	8th June 1960
Nancy Sinatra	8th June 1940
Jackie Wilson	9th June 1934
Jon Lord (Deep Purple)	9th June 1941
Frank Beard (ZZ Top)	11th June 1949
Reg Presley (The Troggs)	12th June 1943
Roy Harper	12th June 1941
Boy George	14th June 1961
Jimmy Lea (Slade)	14th June 1952
Harry Nilsson	15th June 1941
Noddy Holder (Slade)	15th June 1946
Barry Manilow	17th June 1946
Alison Moyet	18th June 1961
Paul McCartney (The Beatles)	18th June 1942
Ann Wilson (Heart)	19th June 1950
Brian Wilson (The Beach Boys)	20th June 1942
Cindy Lauper	20th June 1953
Lionel Richie	20th June 1949
Michael Anthony (Van Halen)	20th June 1955

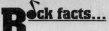

•HAPPY BIRTHDAY!•

Joey Kramer (Aerosmith)	21st June 1956
Ray Davies (The Kinks)	21st June 1944
Kris Kristofferson	22nd June 1936
Adam Faith	23rd June 1940
Arthur Brown (The Crazy World Of Arthur Brown)	24th June 1944
Jeff Beck	24th June 1944
Mick Fleetwood (Fleetwood Mac)	24th June 1942
Carly Simon	25th June 1945
George Michael	25th June 1963
Ian Paice (Deep Purple)	29th June 1948
Andy Scott (Sweet)	30th June 1951
Florence Ballard (The Supremes)	30th June 1943

JULY

Debbie Harry	1st July 1945
Vince Clarke	3rd July 1961
Louis Armstrong	4th July 1900
Huey Lewis	5th July 1950
Bill Haley	6th July 1925
Nanci Griffith	6th July 1953
Ringo Starr (The Beatles)	7th July 1940

• HAPPY BIRTHDAY! •

Andy Fletcher (Depeche Mode)	8th July 1961
Bon Scott (AC/DC)	9th July 1946
Jim Kerr (Simple Minds)	9th July 1959
Marc Almond	9th July 1959
Arlo Guthrie	10th July 1947
Jason Orange (Take That)	10th July 1970
Neil Tennant (Pet Shop Boys)	10th July 1954
Ronnie James Dio	10th July 1949
Richie Sambora (Bon Jovi)	11th July 1959
Eric Carr (Kiss)	12th July 1950
Jim McGuinn (The Byrds)	13th July 1942
Woody Guthrie	14th July 1912
Linda Ronstadt	15th July 1946
Trevor Horne	15th July 1949
Stewart Copeland (The Police)	16th July 1952
Geezer Butler (Black Sabbath)	17th July 1949
Mick Tucker (Sweet)	17th July 1949
Brian Auger	18th July 1939
Martha Reeves	18th July 1941
Bernie Leadon (The Eagles)	19th July 1947
Brian May (Queen)	19th July 1947
Keith Godchaux (The Grateful Dead)	19th July 1948
Carlos Santana	20th July 1947
Cat Stevens	21st July 1947
Don Henley (The Eagles)	22nd July 1947

• HAPPY BIRTHDAY! •

Richard Davies (Supertramp)	22nd July 1944
David Essex	23rd July 1947
Martin Gore (Depeche Mode)	23rd July 1961
Slash (Guns N'Roses)	23rd July 1965
Gary Cherone (Extreme)	24th July 1961
Mick Jagger (The Rolling Stones)	26th July 1943
Roger Taylor (Queen)	26th July 1949
Bobby Gentry	27th July 1944
Rick Wright (Pink Floyd)	28th July 1945
Steve Peregrine Took (Tyrannosaurus Rex)	28th July 1949
Kate Bush	30th July 1958
Paul Anka	30th July 1941

AUGUST

Jerry Garcia (The Grateful Dead)	1st August 1942
Joe Elliot (Def Leppard)	1st August 1959
Ian Broudie (The Lightning Seeds)	4th August 1958
Jimmy Webb	5th August 1946
Bruce Dickinson (Iron Maiden)	7th August 1958
Andy Fairweather-Low (Amen Corner)	8th August 1959

•HAPPY BIRTHDAY!•

The Edge (U2)	8th August 1961
Whitney Houston	9th August 1963
Bobby Hatfield (The Righteous Brothers)	10th August 1940
Ian Anderson (Jethro Tull)	10th August 1947
Ronnie Spector (The Ronettes)	10th August 1947
Mark Knopfler (Dire Straits)	12th August 1949
Ron Mael (Sparks)	12th August 1948
Suzanne Vega	12th August 1959
Tanita Tikaram	12th August 1969
Feargal Sharkey	13th August 1958
David Crosby (The Byrds)	14th August 1941
Matt Johnson (The The)	15th August 1961
Madonna	16th August 1958
Belinda Carlisle	17th August 1958
Kevin Rowland (Dexy's Midnight Runners)	17th August 1953
Carl Wayne (The Move)	18th August 1944
Billy J. Kramer	19th August 1943
Ginger Baker (Cream)	19th August 1939
Ian Gillan (Deep Purple)	19th August 1945
John Deacon (Queen)	19th August 1951
Phil Lynott (Thin Lizzy)	20th August 1951
Robert Plant (Led Zeppelin)	20th August 1948
Kenny Rogers	21st August 1938
Debbie Peterson (The Bangles)	22nd August 1961
Ian Mitchell (The Bay City Rollers)	22nd August 1958

• HAPPY BIRTHDAY! •

Tori Amos	22nd August 1963
Keith Moon (The Who)	23rd August 1947
Shaun Ryder (Happy Mondays)	23rd August 1962
Jean-Michel Jarre	24th August 1948
Elvis Costello	25th August 1954
Gene Simmons (Kiss)	25th August 1949
Glen Matlock (The Sex Pistols)	27th August 1956
Hugh Cornwell (The Stranglers)	28th August 1949
Eddi Reader (Fairground Attraction)	29th August 1959
Michael Jackson	29th August 1958
John Phillips (The Mamas and Papas)	30th August 1935
Van Morrison	31st August 1945

SEPTEMBER

Barry Gibb (The Bee Gees)	1st September 1947
Mik Kaminsky (ELO)	2nd September 1951
Al Jardine (The Beach Boys)	3rd September 1942
Martin Chambers (The Pretenders)	4th September 1951
Al Stewart	5th September 1945
Buddy Miles (Band of Gypsies)	5th September 1946

• HAPPY BIRTHDAY! •

Freddie Mercury (Queen)	5th September 1946
Roger Waters (Pink Floyd)	6th September 1944
Buddy Holly	7th September 1936
Chrissie Hynde	7th September 1951
Gloria Gaynor	7th September 1949
Patsy Cline	8th September 1932
Billy Preston	9th September 1946
Dave Stewart	9th September 1952
Otis Redding	9th September 1941
Carol Decker (T'Pau)	10th September 1957
Don Powell (Slade)	10th September 1950
Joe Perry (Aerosmith)	10th September 1950
Siobhan Fahey (Bananarama)	10th September 1957
Jon Moss (Culture Club)	11th September 1957
Mick Talbot (The Style Council)	11th September 1958
Barry White	12th September 1944
Zak Starkey	13th September 1965
Morten Harket (A-Ha)	14th September 1959
Paul Kossoff (Free)	14th September 1950
Lee Dorman (Iron Butterfly)	15th September 1942
Bernie Calvert (The Hollies)	16th September 1944
Kenny Jones (The Faces/The Who)	16th September 1948
Hank Williams	17th September 1923
Frankie Avalon	18th September 1939
Bill Medley (The Righteous Brothers)	19th September 1940

• HAPPY BIRTHDAY! •

Brian Epstein (The Beatles' manager)	19th September 1934
Cass Elliot (a.k.a Mama Cass, The Mamas and Papas)	19th September 1941
Lol Créme (10cc)	19th September 1947
Nile Rodgers (Chic)	19th September 1952
Alannah Currie (Thompson Twins)	20th September 1959
Nuno Bettencourt (Extreme)	20th September 1966
Leonard Cohen	21st September 1934
Liam Gallagher (Oasis)	21st September 1972
David Coverdale (Whitesnake)	22nd September 1949
Joan Jett	22nd September 1960
Bruce Springsteen	23rd September 1949
Julio Iglesias	23rd September 1943
Ray Charles	23rd September 1930
Anthony Newley	24th September 1931
Gerry Marsden (Gerry And The Pacemakers)	24th September 1942
Linda McCartney	24th September 1941
Bryan Ferry (Roxy Music)	26th September 1945
Georgie Fame	26th September 1943
Olivia Newton-John	26th September 1948
Tracey Thorn (Everything But The Girl)	26th September 1962
Alvin Stardust	27th September 1942
Brett Anderson (Suede)	27th September 1967
Meat Loaf	27th September 1951
Randy Bachman (Bachman-Turner Overdrive)	27th September 1943

•HAPPY BIRTHDAY!•

Ben E. King	28th September 1938
Jerry Lee Lewis	29th September 1935
Matt and Luke Goss (Bros)	29th September 1968
Frankie Lymon	30th September 1942
Marc Bolan (T.Rex)	30th September 1947

OCTOBER

Don McLean	2nd October 1945
Philip Oakey (Human League)	2nd October 1955
Sting	2nd October 1951
Chubby Checker	3rd October 1941
Eddie Cochran	3rd October 1938
Lindsey Buckingham (Fleetwood Mac)	3rd October 1947
Stevie Ray Vaughan	3rd October 1954
Chris Lowe (Pet Shop Boys)	4th October 1959
Patti Labelle	4th October 1944
Bob Geldof	5th October 1954
Brian Connolly (Sweet)	5th October 1949
Steve Miller	5th October 1943
Kevin Godley (10cc)	7th October 1945

• HAPPY BIRTHDAY! •

John Entwistle (The Who)	9th October 1944
John Lennon (The Beatles)	9th October 1940
David Lee Roth (Van Halen)	10th October 1955
Martin Kemp (Spandau Ballet)	10th October 1961
Midge Ure	10th October 1953
Neneh Cherry	10th October 1964
Rick Parfitt (Status Quo)	12th October 1948
Paul Simon	13th October 1941
Cliff Richard	14th October 1940
Justin Hayward (The Moody Blues)	14th October 1946
Chris De Burgh	15th October 1948
Richard Carpenter	15th October 1946
Gary Kemp (Spandau Ballet)	16th October 1959
Nico (The Velvet Underground)	16th October 1938
Chuck Berry	18th October 1926
Mark King (Level 42)	20th October 1958
Tom Petty	20th October 1952
Eric Falkner (The Bay City Rollers)	21st October 1955
Julian Cope	21st October 1957
Manfred Man (a.k.a Michael Lubowitz)	21st October 1940
Tony Mortimer (East 17)	21st October 1970
Bill Wyman (The Rolling Stones)	24th October 1936
Jon Anderson (Yes)	25th October 1944
Simon Le Bon	27th October 1958
Hank Marvin	28th October 1941

•HAPPY BIRTHDAY!•

Denny Laine (The Moody Blues/Wings)	29th October 1944
Peter Green (Fleetwood Mac)	29th October 1946
Grace Slick (Jefferson Airplane/Starship)	30th October 1939
Larry Mullen (U2)	31st October 1961

NOVEMBER

Eddie Macdonald (The Alarm)	1st November 1959
Rick Allen (Def Leppard)	1st November 1963
Brian Poole (The Tremeloes)	2nd November 1941
Bruce Welch (The Shadows)	2nd November 1941
Keith Emerson (Emerson, Lake and Palmer)	2nd November 1944
Adam Ant (aka Stuart Goddard)	3rd November 1954
John Barry	3rd November 1933
Lulu	3rd November 1948
Art Garfunkel	5th November 1941
Bryan Adams	5th November 1959
Ike Turner	5th November 1951
Peter Noone (Herman's Hermits)	5th November 1947
Glen Frey (The Eagles)	6th November 1948
P.J.Proby	6th November 1938

• HAPPY BIRTHDAY! •

Joni Mitchell	7th November 1943
Charleen Spiteri (Texas)	7th November 1967
Bonnie Raitt	8th November 1949
Roy Wood (The Move/ELO/Wizzard)	8th November 1947
Greg Lake (Emerson, Lake and Palmer)	10th November 1948
Screamin' Lord Sutch	10th November 1940
Andy Partridge (XTC)	11th November 1953
Chris Dreja (The Yardbirds)	11th November 1945
Errol Brown (Hot Chocolate)	12th November 1948
Leslie McKeown (The Bay City Rollers)	12th November 1955
Neil Young (Buffalo Springfield)	12th November 1945
Alexander O'Neal	14th November 1954
Petula Clarke	15th November 1932
Gene Clarke (The Byrds)	17th November 1944
Gordon Lightfoot	17th November 1938
Kim Wilde	18th November 1960
Duane Allman (The Allman Brothers Band)	20th November 1946
Joe Walsh (The Eagles)	20th November 1947
Norman Greenbaum	20th November 1942
Bjork	21st November 1965
Bruce Hornsby	23rd November 1954
Bev Bevan (The Move/ELO)	24th November 1946
Steve Rothery (Marillion)	25th November 1959
John McVie (Fleetwood Mac)	26th November 1945
Tina Turner	26th November 1939

• HAPPY BIRTHDAY! •

Jimi Hendrix	27th November 1942
Berry Gordy	28th November 1929
Denny Doherty (The Mamas and Papas)	29th November 1941
John Mayall	29th November 1933
Billy Idol	30th November 1955
Roger Glover (Deep Purple)	30th November 1945

DECEMBER

Gilbert O'Sullivan	1st December 1946
John Densmore (The Doors)	1st December 1944
Rick Savage (Def Leppard)	2nd December 1960
Ozzy Osbourne (Black Sabbath)	3rd December 1948
Chris Hillman (The Byrds)	4th December 1942
Dennis Wilson (The Beach Boys)	4th December 1944
John Cale (The Velvet Underground)	4th December 1940
Little Richard	5th December 1932
Jonathan King	6th December 1944
Tom Waits	7th December 1949
Gregg Allman (The Allman Brothers Band)	8th December 1947
Jim Morrison (The Doors)	8th December 1943